Wise Up

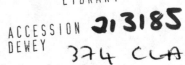

Wise Up

The Challenge of Lifelong Learning

GUY CLAXTON

BLOOMSBURY

Published by Bloomsbury Publishing, New York and London.
Distributed to the trade by St. Martin's Press

A CIP catalogue record for this book
is available from the Library of Congress

ISBN 1-58234-092-7

First published in the U.S. by
Bloomsbury Publishing in 1999

This paperback edition published 2000
10 9 8 7 6 5 4 3 2 1

Typeset by Hewer Text Ltd, Scotland
Printed in the United States of America by
R.R. Donnelly & Sons Company, Harrisonburg, Virginia

Contents

All our lives long, every day and every hour, we are engaged in the process of accommodating our changed and unchanged selves to changed and unchanged surroundings; living, in fact, is nothing else than this accommodation: when we fail in it a little we are stupid, when we fail flagrantly we are mad, when we suspend it temporarily we sleep, when we give up the attempt altogether we die.

Samuel Butler, *The Way of All Flesh*

For Angus, Mara, Claire and Moses, who will have to live it.

Acknowledgements

It is a pleasure to acknowledge the many people who, in a variety of ways, have educated and supported me during the gestation and the writing of this book.

I was lucky enough to have two beautiful 'retreats' in which to get away from the phone and write. Thanks to Stephen and Martine Batchelor, Maurice Ash and Roberta Newton for making it possible for me to stay at Sharpham House in Devon; and, again, to Malcolm and Margaret Carr for the use of their beach-house at Raglan, New Zealand, in which the book was started one February and finished the next. Retreating would not have been an option without the help of my friend and cat-sitter Tasha Mundy.

I would like to thank the following for stimulating conversations, provocative ideas and practical help in the areas of learning and education over the years: Miles Barker, Bill Barton, Chris Base, Beverley Bell, Susan Blackmore, Patricia Broadfoot, Jerome Bruner, Mark Cosgrove, Jo Diamond, Margaret Donaldson, Wendy Drewery, Jenny Edwards, Isabelle Gall, Susan Greenfield, Kathy Hall, Valery Hall, Karen Hinett, John Holt, Satish Kumar, Ruth Leitch, Ian Mitchell, Bernie Neville, Keith Oatley, Graham Powell, Sally Power, Lyn Schaverien, Jonathan Schooler, Rosamund Sutherland, Chris Watkins, Gordon Wells and Jim Wertsch. I am grateful to Hilary Dyer, Jenny Edwards, Mike Forret, Kathy Hall, Dave Smith and Mary van der Riet for letting me make use of their materials. Especial thanks to Margaret Carr for thrilling conversations, and for sharing her ideas and resources so willingly; and to

Peter Mountstephen and the marvellous staff at Christ Church Primary School, Bradford-on-Avon, for the enthusiasm and ingenuity with which they are helping me discover how these ideas work in practice.

For help in understanding and gathering materials on the world of work, I would like to thank Mark Brown, John Cleese, Charlene Collason, Ian Deamer, Shaun Deeney, Janine Edge, Gill Gregory, Sean Hardie, Maggie Tree, Michael West and most especially Natasha Owen.

Several people kindly read a very overweight draft, and their perceptive comments helped immeasurably to make the book better in a number of ways: more coherent, more accessible and mercifully shorter. They were Jim Flynn, Peter Mountstephen, Natasha Owen, my agent Liz Puttick, and Esther Jagger, Kate Morris and Alan Wherry of Bloomsbury. Alan's continual enthusiasm, and Peter's pencilled comments, by turn encouraging, witty and downright cheeky, played an important part in keeping me going during the rewriting, especially at the times when my own faith in the book was flagging.

I would also like to thank Trevor Habeshaw and Technical and Educational Services Ltd for permission to reproduce the table 'Reading Flexibly' from *53 Interesting Ways of Helping your Students to Study*, by Trevor Habeshaw, Graham Gibbs and Sue Habeshaw (© Technical and Educational Services Ltd, Bristol).

Introduction: Learning for Life

Ravi and Ben are twenty-one months old, born in the same week. They are in an unfamiliar room at the university, taking part, with their mothers, in an experiment on learning. Though the boys have not met before, Ravi is keen to make contact, approaching Ben, smiling at him and holding out a toy he has been playing with. Ben, however, shrinks away nervously and clings to his mother's leg. Ravi looks at his mother occasionally to make sure all is well, and continues to explore the room. A man dressed as a clown enters and talks to the children. Ben starts to whimper and hides his face in his mother's skirt. Ravi smiles at the clown and is soon chatting. When he reaches for a toy, the clown says something sternly. Ravi stops, looks first towards his mother, then intently at the clown. He reaches for the toy again, keeping an eye on the clown. Ben has burst into tears and is being comforted on his mother's lap. These responses are typical of the children.[1]

People in general, just like Ravi and Ben, differ enormously in how, and how well, they learn. And these differences in style and effectiveness start to develop early. Already Ravi is generally able to handle more strangeness than Ben. He is a more *resilient* learner: more willing to have a go. He is more able to detect, and more willing to trust, his mother's assessment of the situation. From her positive expression he borrows the courage to explore. The ability to 'read' learning situations correctly, to know when to explore and when to withdraw, and the willingness to tolerate the feelings that go along with learning, lay the foundations of this essential resilience.

But these early differences are not set in stone. Depending on what happens to them over the rest of their lives, Ben and Ravi will either consolidate their initial robust, or fragile, response to the feeling of learning, or they will change. In an uncertain world, resilience is a vital quality which needs to be fostered in children and adults alike. We now know what resilience is, what undermines it and how it can be developed: how to help Ben become better at hanging in with uncertainty. This book is about what it means to be a good learner, and how the growth of good learning can be fostered. The development of resilience in the face of uncertainty and difficulty is one of its major themes.

Emmi and Eliza are fourteen, both thought of as 'bright', both in the top group in their school for mathematics. They are working their way through a booklet of problems that includes, by mistake, a few questions that are too difficult for them to solve. On the early, manageable problems the girls work equally effectively and successfully, but on the hard ones Eliza quickly goes to pieces. She looks furtively across at Emmi to see how she is coping, and begins to fidget and look upset. She whispers to her friend: 'These sums are stupid!' Emmi, meanwhile, is giving it her best shot. She tries starting the problem from the end and working back. She says to herself: 'Well, suppose x is 1: what happens then?' She tries various guesses before she eventually calls the teacher over and confesses that she is stuck. The teacher quickly realizes the mistake and tells the class to ignore problems 7 to 10 and skip to number 11. Emmi does so, working with determination, trying out some of the strategies which she has discovered in the course of grappling with the hard problems, to see if they work on the easier ones. Eliza, however, is still upset. She looks at problem 11 and cannot think how to tackle it, even though number 6, which she solved successfully only a few minutes previously, was exactly the same type.[2]

Resilience is not just a concern of little kids, or of those who find learning generally hard. Both Emmi and Eliza are 'good students', but Eliza's confidence in her ability to solve her mathematical problems is brittle. Like Ben she has a low tolerance for frustration, and quickly gets upset when things are not going her way. Instead of focusing on trying to solve the problem, her priority becomes saving face. Emmi experiences her difficulty as a challenge; Eliza perceives her failure as a threat. Where Ben felt frightened, Eliza has learnt to feel ashamed of her difficulty. Another of the themes of this book is the relationship between learning and defending. How do we know when it is right to hang on in there, and when it is smart to quit? What happened to Eliza to make her see the world the way she does? And can we help her distinguish between challenges and threats more accurately?

When Emmi encounters difficulty, she is not only more resilient but a more *resourceful* learner than Eliza, ingeniously searching for new ways to beat the problem. She has several strings to her bow, and if her first approach is not successful she is not stumped. When she doesn't know exactly what to do, she has things she can try. She has more than one tool in her learning toolkit: a greater range and variety of learning and problem-solving strategies. Her resilience and her resourcefulness positively reinforce each other. Because she has greater learning capacity, she feels more confident. Because she feels more confident, she tries longer, harder and with more ingenuity than does Eliza – and is therefore more likely to discover a new way to crack the problem, a new learning tool. As she learns, so she is becoming a more powerful learner. Her 'learning to learn' is on an upward spiral, whereas Eliza's is becalmed. Another theme of this book is: how can we describe this learning toolkit; what are its main compartments? And how can we help people engage with learning challenges in such a way that their general *learning power* is progressively expanded?

Patrick and Polly are the managers of different departments at a large town hall. They are in a meeting to discuss the apportionment of next year's budget. Patrick tentatively questions the prevailing wisdom that each department which has spent its full quota in the current year gets the same again plus a small percentage increase; while departments that have underspent have their budget reduced. The logic, naturally, is that those who don't spend it don't need it. But Patrick points out that this often leads to departments rushing to use up their budgets before the end of the financial year, wasting money for fear of losing it next year. The meeting circles

round the issue without getting anywhere. Polly gets impatient and moves that they carry on as usual. Patrick suggests
they take a ten-minute break to clear their minds, and then
give it another five minutes. During the break, he muses over
different ways of encouraging people to save. When they
reconvene, he suggests that they try a different scheme whereby next year's departmental budgets are computed as 95 per
cent of the current year, plus 50 per cent of any savings
achieved. To maintain their current budget, a department
would effectively have to save 10 per cent. If they save 20
per cent their budget increases by 5 per cent; and so on. This
way frugality is rewarded, and both individual departments
and the central treasury are happy. The meeting thanks
Patrick for his innovative suggestion and agrees to try it the
following year. Polly is quietly envious of Patrick's ability to
reflect creatively.[3]

It may be that Patrick has learnt better than Polly how to use
this softer, more ruminative approach to learning. She may
not have realized yet that creative inspiration often strikes
when the mind is in a state of playful relaxation, or, if she has,
is not able to induce that state at will. Or it may equally be that
she possesses the tool, but it did not come to mind. The
difference between Patrick and Polly could be that he has
developed a more *reflective* attitude towards his own learning.
He is better able to stop and take stock of the situation, to ask
himself: 'Now what kind of learning approach would work
best here?' He has the same tools as Polly, but is able to
manage them better. Another theme of this book is the
development of this reflective ability to monitor one's own
learning and take a strategic overview. What does that kind of
self-awareness involve, and how does it grow?

At home, work and play, learning continues throughout
life. For Polly and Patrick, 'what to do about the budget?' is not
so very different, in essence, from Ben and Ravi's 'what to do
about the clown?', or Eliza and Emmi's 'what to do about
these (impossible) sums?' At root, the experience of staying
engaged with something that is not yet understood or mastered demands a similar attitude. Clearly, however, the problems are of different kinds, and they succumb to different
kinds of learning. For Ravi, the key lies in being willing to try

things out – to make small, judicious, practical experiments – and see what happens. He learns by cautiously immersing himself in the experience. For Emmi, the learning required is of a more deliberate, analytical kind. She is thinking hard. While for Patrick, it is a much more ruminative state of mind that does the trick. Not all learning, by any means, requires conscious deliberation. Learning is not a homogeneous activity: it comes in many different shapes and sizes. And these start to kick in at different stages of development. Another theme of this book is the idea that learning is a much wider, richer concept than is captured within current models of education and training. And learning to learn is likewise a much more interesting and pervasive possibility than a concern with study skills.

Debbie and Kelvin, a young married couple, both have difficulty reading. They have mastered a variety of tricks for concealing the fact: Debbie often claims to have left her spectacles at home; Kelvin challenges their bright eight-year-old daughter Helen to read things out loud that he thinks might be important. One day Debbie comes home and tells Kel that she and a friend have signed up for an adult literacy course at the local college. Kel's immediate reaction is to worry about the stigma when their friends find out. Debbie says: 'If Helen can do it, so can I. I'm not going to spend the rest of my life pretending to be blind.'

As we saw with Eliza, the art of good learning involves making sure the brakes are off, just as much as it does learning ways of accelerating learning. How people behave as learners is as much to do with what they believe as it is with the skills they have mastered. Kelvin is perfectly able to learn how to read. He has all the necessary equipment. But his learning is blocked by a lack of self-belief. To him the risks of failure loom large, and the risks of humiliation even larger. He fears he will not be able to do it. He assumes that the fact that he did not learn to read at the 'right' time reflects badly on his character, his intelligence or his self-worth. Debbie has jumped the shame barrier and is willing to risk being a learner. Kelvin stays stuck behind it. Another theme of the book is the extent to which it is people's often unconscious beliefs about themselves, and even about the nature of learning itself, that limit their learning power; not any intrinsic differences in ability or intelligence. The focus in Europe and the USA on intelligence as a – perhaps the – major determinant of people's learning has been an enormous hindrance to the development of a genuine learning culture. Too many people believe that, if they find something difficult, it means they are lacking in intelligence, rather than simply that they haven't yet developed, or retrieved, the right learning tool.

The main themes

I have used these vignettes, each of them based on research which will be discussed later, to introduce the broad scope and some of the main themes of this book – in particular what we might call the three Rs of learning power: resilience, resourcefulness and reflectiveness. Let me now stake out the territory rather more systematically, and offer a preview of the main conclusions.

Living is learning

To be alive is to be learning. Learning is not something we do sometimes, in special places or at certain periods of our lives. It is part of our nature. We are born learners. Indeed, it is arguably our most distinctive human characteristic. As the eleventh-century Sufi philosopher El-Ghazali put it: 'A camel is stronger than a man; an elephant is larger; a lion has greater valour; cattle can eat more; birds are more virile. Man was made for the purpose of learning.' And modern cognitive science concurs.

Everyone is born with a starter-kit of reflexes that tell them, innately, what to do when cold or hungry, or when an object suddenly looms up in front of them. You shiver; you cry; you duck. We come into the world with a rudimentary map, and a crude set of responses. But more than any other animal, we human beings arrive unfinished, waiting to attune ourselves to the peculiarities of the terrain into which we have emerged. Human beings serve the longest apprenticeship of any creature, because we come with the capacity – and the necessity –

to mould our own minds and habits to fit the contours of the world in which we find ourselves. How we do that is learning. Learning enables us to anticipate what goes with what, what happens next, what is likely to follow if we do this rather than that; and thus to intervene in the flow of events to our own advantage, in ever more sophisticated and confident ways.

On this view, learning is not primarily intellectual. What happens in schools and colleges, through the instruction of teachers, books or computer programs, is just one kind of learning – and a culturally local, historically recent, and generally rather odd kind at that. There is an abundance of evidence now to show that conscious understanding is not only unnecessary for many learning tasks, but may substantially interfere with learning. The brain, it turns out, is built to perform certain kinds of learning with a subtle brilliance that can be easily disturbed by thinking too much and trying too hard. The relationship between conscious knowledge and practical know-how is much more problematic than current attitudes admit. Of course intellect provides us with a set of very refined tools that have an important role in learning, but you do not throw away your spade just because you have bought a scalpel. Even brain surgeons still have to dig the garden from time to time. And a lot of lifelong learning is more like gardening than surgery.

We learn many different kinds of things

We do accumulate facts and information as we read a manual or watch the news, certainly. And we digest this *knowledge* into opinions. But we also continue throughout life to develop *know-how*: how to use new technology, how to ride a bike, how to make a soufflé, how to tell a good story, how to write, how to play the trumpet. We learn to make new *discriminations*: to tell a new friend's mood from their voice on the phone, to tell a bordeaux from a burgundy, to tell Brahms from Mendelssohn. We learn new *preferences*: our likes and dislikes change as we grow up and keep different company. A drink that at one time seemed peculiar or unpleasant becomes an acquired taste. We develop new *dispositions*: the tendency no longer to laugh at jokes that once were funny but now seem crude or cruel; to have more time for kinds of people with whom we were once impatient. We learn roles and new aspects of *character*. We discover what it means to be a girl, a grandparent, a professor, a football supporter, a migraine sufferer, and to act accordingly. We may broaden our *emotional range*, and learn when and how to express indignation or sympathy. Learning changes not just our knowing and our doing, but our being too.

Take me, for example. In the last year I have been learning to live with a degree of financial insecurity, after a working lifetime of the monthly pay cheque; learning to write in some new styles; learning to speak the language of the builders who have been working on my house ('purlins', 'torching'). I have learnt how to use the new 'octopus' smart cards to get around the Hong Kong subway; how much the Star Ferry costs; how Chinese students behave differently from English ones in large groups and in tutorials; what snake tastes like. I have finally learnt how to set my new video recorder. I plug away at watching the rise and fall of my breathing as I sit in meditation. I have learnt to drive a car with unfamiliar kinds of controls; to work a new e-mail system; to begin to move my hips in the strange, sinuous way demanded by marengue. I have got a slightly better grasp on post-modernism and begun to fit some of its insights into the way I think and talk about learning. I am beginning, rather late in life, to appreciate the shadowy aesthetics of new kinds of poetry and music. Anyone, I fancy, could construct their own, equivalent, list of learning projects and achievements. Lifelong learning is not, after all, a special new requirement; it is an age-old reality.

We can get better and worse at learning

The basic, automatic tuning of the brain in response to experience is just the start. It is the sine qua non of learning, its foundation, but not its be-all and end-all. The natural learning ability of the brain can be augmented, transformed – and diminished – in a whole host of ways. First through biological evolution, and then through the growth of culture, we have developed a range of learning capabilities, the extended toolkit of learning strategies, that have enabled us to create miracles like nuclear power and jumbo jets; Shakespeare sonnets and Beethoven symphonies; international politics and the Internet. From the sophisticated procedures that enable scientists to carry out arcane experiments to the mnemonic tricks that actors use to learn their lines, from meditation to brainstorming, the world is full of techniques, both general-purpose and highly specific, for developing our learning power.

Learning to learn is the lifelong shadow of learning itself. Whatever you are grappling with – a storyline, a sliced backhand, a complex negotiation, a family dispute – you are also grappling with learning. Each bout of learning is also an opportunity to strengthen and elaborate learning power. So learning happens in layers. On the surface, as you are introduced to the game of bridge, for example, you are learning what the game is about: you are acquiring specific, conscious knowledge. As you play, so you also develop the more intuitive know-how necessary to make and 'read' bids, how to score and to shuffle; and also to know *when* to use different skills: when to discard and when to finesse. But deeper down you are also practising learning skills and developing learning power. You learn to be very observant, noticing the cards people play, how they play them, even the expressions on their faces as they do so. You are learning to use such slight clues to make inferences about an opponent's hand and their strategy. You develop your powers of memory until it is second nature to retain who has played what cards, how many clubs are left and where they are.

Learning is learnable, but, as we have seen, learning power does not develop automatically. Not all of us, it appears, amplify our basic brain learning capacity to the maximum. Ben, Eliza, Polly and Kelvin are, in their different ways, less adventurous, less curious, less skilful, less aware as learners than Ravi, Emmi, Patrick and Debbie. Indeed, the development of learning can be neglected, or even undermined. Ben seems to treat the world as more dangerous than it actually is, and misses out on opportunities to have fun and find things out which Ravi is willing to take. Eliza gets rattled when her learning is blocked, and retreats from the fray, forfeiting the chance to develop her 'learning muscles' and her 'learning stamina' through making a more extended effort. Like Eliza, Polly is impatient. She quickly feels uncomfortable with confusion, and her frustration disables the learning and thinking abilities which she does possess. And Kelvin is as capable as Debbie of learning to read and write. It isn't that difficult. But his learning is paralysed by his beliefs about himself and what people will think: beliefs which generate a sense of shame, and which cause him to hide rather than engage.

Learning power *can* be developed, and blocks dissolved, under the right conditions. Learning to learn is a possibility for everyone: not just those who are doing well in school, or who are credited with high 'intelligence'. This book is about why some people come to be better learners than others, and how societies and organizations can help everyone develop their learning power. Recent developments in experimental psychology, cognitive science, artificial intelligence and neuroscience are leading us towards a new, practical understanding of learning: one which turns much of our conventional corporate and educational wisdom on its head. The book attempts to weave together the strands of this research into a coherent and sometimes surprising account of human learning, and to draw out its implications for the organization of learning, from parenting through school to the world of work.

Learning is multifarious

Learning happens in a whole host of different ways. Some learning we just seem to soak up through our pores: it requires little in the way of conscious planning or deliberation. Other kinds of learning are highly organized and structured. Some require a lot of thought; some none at all. Some seem to happen in an instant; some take years to mature. Some seem to proceed effortlessly; others are hard work. Some are relatively smooth and unruffled; others are accompanied by a great deal of emotion. Some seem to require books and teachers; others need solitude and an absence of external stimulation. Learning to do long division is not the same kind of thing as learning to swim. Learning to hear an irregular heart-beat through your new stethoscope does not rely on the same processes and skills as learning how to structure your day when you retire from your job.

There are four main compartments to the learning toolkit. First, there is direct *immersion* in experience and the practical tools of exploration, investigation and experimentation that go with it. Some of this kind of learning focuses on the physical world, but much of it is social, involving interaction and imitation, the principal media through which people pass on their practical skills to each other. Then there is *imagination*, and the skills of fantasy, visualization and story-telling that enable you to create and explore hypothetical worlds. Next come all the *intellectual* skills of language and reasoning, through which experience can be segmented, analysed and communicated. And finally there is *intuition*, a general name for the family of softer, more receptive processes whereby creative ideas are germinated and developed.

Let me be clear. Learning, in the way I am using the term, is what you do when you don't know what to do. Learning to learn, or the development of learning power, is getting better at knowing when, how and what to do when you don't know what to do. Getting used to new surroundings is learning. Solving a technical problem is learning. Ruminating on a difficult personal predicament is learning. Trying to stack up blocks is learning. A first date is learning. Preparing for an important interview is learning. Coming to terms with bereavement is learning. Going back to college in your fifties is learning. Creativity is learning. All this is included in what I am going to talk about here.

Learning to learn is developmental

The metaphor of the toolkit is useful, and I shall make good use of it; but it breaks down when we come to think about how these learning resources are themselves acquired. A toolkit is a collection of separate instruments which can be built up independently and in any sequence. They accumulate. But the array of learning capacities which people can develop are not picked up one by one in this way. They grow out of each other, as the branches of a tree grow out of the trunk. First comes the main stem of 'brain learning': picking up patterns through immersion in experience. Out of that grow in turn the shoots of imagination, intellect and intuition, and each shoot develops into a major branch of the tree of learning, growing its own collection of more specific tactical twigs.

The different learning modes of immersion, imagination, intellect and intuition do not supplant each other. Though they start to develop at different ages, each can continue to grow in power and sophistication throughout life. And they all remain useful. The young executive needs all her wits about her as she arranges her desk, is introduced to colleagues, and encounters unfamiliar rituals and jargon on her first day in a new job. The aspiring novelist needs all his powers of observation, imagination, organization and deduction as he plans a story and masters his new word-processing software. As we move up the ladder of lifelong learning, and through the different phases of education, we need to keep practising and honing the earlier learning modes at the same time as we are adding new ones.

Minds are organs, not machines, and can no more be assembled than a flower can. The growth of mind takes time, and that applies all the more to the growth of the mind's learning power. Cognition, despite its name, is not an assemblage of cogs. It cannot be put together like a car in a factory. Attempts to train people intensively on the 'next' skill they should logically be ready for are notoriously unsuccessful.

Learning involves the discovery of relevance

To be a good learner, you need not only to have developed all kinds of learning skills; you need a good working knowledge of their function. It's no use having the finest toolkit in the world if you don't know what a screwdriver and a paint brush are for. Part of learning to learn is learning the relevance of your strategies – their appropriate domain of application, you might say. Much learning involves the gradual discovery of when skills apply and what they are good for. Research shows that when we learn something it is initially tied to the particular situation in which it was originally learnt, and the purposes for which it was learnt. Relevance is not magically given; it has to be discovered, and is often only gradually realized as a result of further experience and reflection. Even this simple truth, as we shall see, seems contrary to educational 'common sense', which has often assumed that anything that has been learnt 'properly' should automatically pop up, like toast from a toaster, in the context of any problem that might call for it in the future.

Learning tools are in the world as well as in the mind

One of the most interesting developments in the science of learning is showing that the 'intelligent agent' is actually the person, with all their internalized knowledge and know-how, *plus* the social and material tools and resources that the world currently makes available to them. In all areas of life, people's accomplishments are a joint function of their inner and outer resources. The sound that the cellist produces is an inextricable function of both her skill *and* the cello, and as instrument-making technology changes, so new ranges and techniques become possible. A doctor's skill depends on his books, his stethoscope and his lab service, and on his intelligent use of these resources, as well as on his experience. In the same way, a vital part of being a good learner is being good at spotting the assets and possibilities that the situation affords, and making good use of them. One of the dictionary definitions of 'resourceful' is to be skilful at devising expedients, or possessing practical ingenuity, and good learners need to be resourceful in this sense, as well as having well-developed *internal* resources. Conventional wisdom, however, has tended to assume that learning power is 'all in the mind': that intelligence, however we define it, is an individual, psychological kind of thing, capable of being manifested in the absence of the customary external aids. But it makes no more sense to treat learning in this way than it does to take the cello away and say: '*Now* show me how good a cellist you are.'

Learning involves self-knowledge and self-awareness

Learning demands many kinds of awareness and reflection, and research tells us that these faculties, too, can be cultivated.

Lifelong learning demands, for example, the ability to think strategically about your own learning path, and this requires the self-awareness to know one's own goals, the resources that are needed to pursue them, and your current strengths and weaknesses in that regard. You have to assume the responsibility of being your own learning coach: watching your own learning out of the corner of your eye, and calling to mind, at the appropriate moment, useful maxims and information. You have to be able to *monitor* your progress; if necessary even to *measure* it; to *mull* over different options and courses of development; to be *mindful* of your own assumptions and habits, and able to stand back from them and appraise them when learning gets stuck; and in general to *manage* yourself as a learner – prioritizing, planning, reviewing progress, revising strategy and if necessary changing tack. Good learners need to assume the ability to evaluate their own progress: to tell for themselves when they have done 'good work'. In conventional forms of education and training, the extent to which people's awareness – especially their self-awareness – can be developed, and their contribution to learning power, has been largely ignored.

Learning is always a gamble

Engaging with something unknown always involves a risk – sometimes slight, sometimes grave. You bet that this current oddity is safe enough to investigate: that it is not going to blow up in your face. (That is why Ravi looks at his mother: he has learnt that her expression will signal whether the situation is safe enough for him to explore.) You bet that your resources are likely to be up to the job; that investing some effort in learning will deliver the required knowledge or know-how. (Emmi, as it turned out, was not able to solve the hard mathematics problems, but her efforts paid off later.) You bet that the understanding that accrues will be relevant to your own goals, interests and anxieties. (Debbie is betting that the gains of learning to read will outweigh the costs; for Kelvin, at the moment, the odds stack up differently.) When we choose to learn, we hope that the fruits of our exploration will be knowledge, mastery, resources and alliances that will help us further our life agendas (whatever they may be). And to gain those rewards it is necessary, temporarily, to sacrifice competence and control. Learning is a survival strategy that entails risks and promises returns. It demands the ability to tolerate frustration and confusion; to act without knowing what will happen; to be uncertain without becoming insecure.

Two things follow from this. First, learning is not always the best policy. Sometimes the situation really is too dangerous to explore, and then discretion is the better part of valour. Sometimes one is better off by trying to maintain the status quo, rather than going along with a change that might turn out to be in someone else's best interests, not one's own. Sometimes one needs to take stock and gather one's resources before engaging. Sometimes it simply doesn't matter enough, or there are other, more pressing claims on one's time and attention. Whether to engage with the unknown or to protect oneself from it is always an open decision. Yet to hear contemporary promoters of lifelong learning and the 'learning organization' talk, you would be forgiven for thinking that every learning opportunity should be embraced with open arms, and that every invitation declined is evidence of cowardice or recalcitrance. The interests and the survival of individuals and groups are not always best served by the attempt to engage and adapt. Sometimes the smart thing to do is hunker down. Defensiveness and resistance per se are not wrong; the question is only whether they are deployed appropriately or not.

Second, learning itself is an intrinsically emotional business. That is why resilience, the ability to tolerate these emotions, is so important. Even when learning is going smoothly, there is always the possibility of surprise, confusion, frustration, disappointment or apprehension – as well, of course, as fascination, absorption, exhilaration, awe or relief. If the first whiff of frustration makes you want to withdraw, your learning is going to be shallow and unadventurous. It is sometimes assumed that learning, when you get it right, should proceed smoothly and calmly. But nothing could be further from the truth. Learning is often hard and protracted, confusing and frustrating, and it is necessary to be able to stick with it and recover from setbacks. New understandings of the biological bases of emotion show that our feelings are absolutely integral to our learning. Emotion is not an occasional irritant or a signal that learning is going wrong. On the contrary, feelings are vital indicators of what kind of learning is needed, and how it is going, which we ignore or suppress at our peril.

Learning is not like assembling flat-pack furniture. There is no reason to suppose that, if the teacher provides all the pieces and clear instructions, anybody (or anybody with the requisite 'ability' who makes the necessary 'effort') ought to be able to put it together without too much difficulty. Comprehension is not a process of adding little pieces of information one-by-one to an expanding structure of knowledge, or assembling 'mastery' out of a regime of carefully defined and practised component skills. Much learning involves exhilarating spurts, frustrating plateaus and upsetting regressions. That's why resilience is so important.

Learning is not always fast and smooth

Good learners don't always learn fast. The ability to hang out in the fog, to tolerate confusion, to dare to wait in a state of incomprehension while the glimmerings of an idea take their time to form is another vital aspect of resilience and thus of learning power: slow is often smart. Good learners, those able to get to the bottom of things and come up with solutions that are truly effective rather than superficially convincing, are emphatically not fast answerers. The speed of one's processor and the size of one's database are no guarantees of a Nobel Prize. In some quarters there are those who do not seem to have realized this. The current computer-led obsession with increasing speed of information processing, instant analysis, tidy lists of bullet points and flat-pack comprehension, for example, betrays a woefully inadequate view of learning and the mind. In our impatient age it is widely assumed that faster is better, and that if we can accelerate learning we should. 'Quick' is widely used as a synonym for bright or clever, while 'slow', in education-speak, is a euphemism for stupid. But creativity cannot be rushed, and the deeper forms of learning often take time to mature.

Learning power develops through culture, not through instruction

If learning power cannot be deliberately assembled piece by piece, how can its development be facilitated? Under what conditions do the qualities, dispositions and capabilities of the good learner germinate and blossom? The short answer is that teaching for learning power is much more about the creation of a culture than about the design of a training programme. Recent research, from fields as far apart as early childhood education and organizational development, shows that every organization has a 'culture' that is either learning-positive or learning-negative. Whether we are aware of it or not, parents and managers, as well as schoolteachers and professors, are socializing their children, their teams and their students into a view of what learning is, how it proceeds, who creates knowledge, what kinds are most valuable, how it is assessed and by whom, and so on. Every corporate ritual, from family mealtimes to board meetings, is a medium that embodies messages about learning. It is through these cultures, for good or ill, that people develop their learning power.

The development of learning power is a matter of belief

Learning power is capable of being strengthened – if you believe it is. A culture that invites you to see your own learning mind as expandable encourages you to look for and value opportunities to expand it; and through the engagement and persistence which this attitude generates it may indeed expand. Being a good learner, and developing your learning power, are more to do with how you think about your own mind, and how you feel about yourself, than with the size of the mental motherboard they gave you at birth. Without these core attitudes and beliefs, neither scholarly nor practical learning proceeds very well or very far. Yet schools, colleges, training courses, even sometimes families, have based their ways of doing learning on a range of assumptions that are looking increasingly suspect and out-of-date. If we want to help people, young and old, to develop their learning muscles, these attitudes and beliefs need to be unearthed and, where necessary, replaced.

Learning matters now

Though learning is ubiquitous, its intensity today is much greater than it has been in traditional societies. In stable times, when a single homogeneous culture holds unquestioned sway, there are traditions and authorities to tell you who you are, what matters, who to love, what to worship, how to live. Personal learning is always needed to solve problems and add interest and enjoyment to life, but the big questions are not up for discussion. Religion, history and cosmology form a powerful, only partly articulated, framework which channels choice and constrains imagination.

But today's young people, and many of their parents, are a generation of choosers. As traditional sources of indigenous authority lose their power, and diverse cultures intermingle, so more and more people are confronted not with a narrow range of life options and adaptations but a vast array of choice. Shall we have a child? Shall we live in Kidderminster, Kansas or Khartoum? Shall we have your mother to live with us or put her in a home? What does it mean to be 'good'? How can I construct a satisfying life, a stable identity, out of the exis-tential supermarket in which I find myself? The pressure to be a learner not just on the surface, but deep down in the moral core of one's life, is intense. The opportunity and the respon-sibility to craft one's own existence is unprecedented, and thorough-going learning power is at a premium. Identifying the conditions that best grow good learners, in this funda-mental sense, is perhaps the most urgent priority of contem-porary societies.

'Lifelong learning' must mean more than grown-ups going to school to be taught how to use the Internet, or parenting skills, or team-building. It is about not panicking when your baby cries too long; not feeling hopeless and running away when your relationship gets stuck in an unhappy groove; not needing violent stimulation to entertain you because you have forgotten how to amuse yourself. It is about having the ability to engage intelligently with uncertainty, and to persist in the face of difficulty, when it matters. It is about making choices about which learning invitations to accept, and which to decline, based on an astute appraisal of your own goals and resources, and not on insecurity and self-doubt. It is about having a varied toolkit of learning approaches and the ability, the courage and the enthusiasm to deploy them effectively.

When people don't feel equipped to engage with complexity, the option is some kind of self-protection. The risk is that Kelvin's inability to engage with uncertainty – to put himself at risk of incomprehension, to be a learner – without feeling insecure or shameful makes him look for security in some kind of ready-made certainty. Lacking the ability, the courage and the weapons to embark on the learning journey, people may be forced to latch on to whatever shallow source of security comes along. It is perhaps not too fanciful to see the signs of 'illearnacy' in the rise of fundamentalism; in the complaints about culture being dumbed down; in the appeal of the worlds of soaps and tabloids; in the slacker culture and political apathy; in the substitution of gossip about the sex lives of celebrities for sustained, frustrating, demanding engagement with personal, political, moral and global complexity. The conjunction of moral complexity and individual responsibility with a widespread neglect of learning power as a vital and educable resource is socially dangerous. Not only can learning power be developed; it must be.

So to create a true learning society we need a new conception of the human mind and its powers of learning: one that has at its heart the learnability of learning itself. With such an image, the imagination of parents, schoolteachers, professors and managers can be freed to focus on the process of learning and on people's development as learners, rather than being mesmerized by 'performance indicators' and qualifications. That is what this book aims to offer: a liberating conception, soundly based in up-to-the-minute research, of the capacity of the human brain-mind to magnify its own learning potential, and of the climate that it needs to realize that potential. Nothing, in complex, confusing, fast-changing societies such as ours, in the midst of the age of uncertainty, could be more important.

ONE

Beliefs about Learning

The development of learning power starts not with the cultivation of its skills and qualities, but with the preparation of
the ground. For the possibilities that people see for learning,
and the ways in which they relate to themselves as learners,
depend on what they already believe learning to be. In the
Introduction, I mapped out some of the insights that have
emerged from the new science of learning. Some of these may
have seemed little more than common sense. But others pose
a significant challenge to the ways in which our society has
come to think about learning. If parents, teachers, managers
and politicians have at the back of their minds a set of
assumptions about learning which are out of date, then we
have to start by identifying what they are. New understandings are unlikely to take root and bear fruit if the mental
ground is already choked with misconceptions. In this chapter I shall first illustrate how different communities can hold
quite different views about learning, and then expose some of
the misapprehensions that are dissolved in what we take to be
'common sense'.

Cultural differences in learning

People who live in different environments and societies develop different aspects of their learning power. This may be for
any of a number of reasons. First, their world may regularly
present them with different kinds of tasks, so that different

'learning muscles' are continually being exercised. Just as a swimmer and a gymnast develop quite different physiques and skills, so do a poet and an engineer develop different compartments of their learning toolkit. Joining a group of meditators develops learning that is quiet and inward. Becoming a mechanic develops the ability to combine intuition and logical thinking in a way that generates, and then systematically eliminates, possible reasons for an engine fault.

But the way people develop and express themselves as learners is also influenced by the often unconscious beliefs and values that their culture holds. Some of the cultural assumptions that influence the way learning power develops reflect broad social values. Asian children's relative success on traditional school curricula, for example, is the outcome of a whole set of beliefs in the value of education, prosperity and family pride, and their interconnections. A child's performance at school brings credit or shame to the whole family, who therefore invest considerable time and effort in ensuring the child's success. The extraordinary level of achievement of Indochinese refugees in American schools, despite arriving with no English language, is testament to the power of these family attitudes.[1]

Some of these beliefs, though, are more specific to the process of learning itself. Asian students traditionally not only have a different attitude to schooling from that held by some other cultural groups; they have also come to value, and be good at, different kinds of learning. There is a widespread assumption that creativity and innovation can only grow properly out of a strong mastery of convention and technique. Children are therefore encouraged to learn in a way that involves much dutiful effort to remember verbatim what they have been told, and to emulate models of good practice, whether in art, language or physical skill. They develop the tools of memory and emulation, but only much later, if at all, do they begin to balance these with a more critical or creative perspective. Though things are changing now, as cultures meet and blend, it is only a few years since Professor John Biggs of Hong Kong University was able to cite evidence that 'Asian students typically take a low profile [in class], rarely asking questions or volunteering answers, let alone making public observations or criticism of course content. . . . [Specifically] Hong Kong students display almost unquestioning acceptance of the knowledge of the teacher . . . rather than an expression of opinion, independence [or] self-mastery.'[2]

In a progressive US elementary school, or a New Zealand kindergarten, on the other hand, the priorities may well be inverted. Creativity and independent initiative may be valued and praised highly by teachers, while a child's need to be told explicitly what to do, or their desire to copy rather than create, may be seen as undesirable traits to be changed. Indeed, within such a progressive belief system the very idea of rote learning is often treated as if it were an insult to the human spirit, and so the skills of literal memory or accurate imitation may not be developed at all. From within each culture, the attitudes and practices of the other look strange, risky or deviant.

Some examples of beliefs about learning

So what are the general assumptions about learning which Western culture tends to make? How does our culture act as if it believed about learning? And what does it say? What kinds of explanations does it offer for failure or deviance, for example? Are the attitudes and habits to which they give rise innocuous, or do they have practical effects on the ways in which we, as human societies, relate to our children, and on the ways in which we design our facilities for school, college and work-based education? It turns out that many of these assumptions are the exact opposite of what the new science of learning, the 'headlines' which I previewed in the Introduction, is telling us.

'Learning is the acquisition of knowledge'

When people think of 'learning', they tend to focus on the end product rather than the activity. If you ask European or American students, or their parents, what 'learning' is, they will mostly describe it in terms of its outcomes: of the knowledge (and, to a lesser extent, the know-how) to which it gives rise. Learning is what results in being able to 'do' more, and in 'knowledge' in the sense of acquiring and retaining information and facts. At root, then, Westerners find it easier to think of learning in terms of its product rather than its process, and, traditionally, in terms of the solution to a problem, or the retention of some material.[3] One of the predominant uses of the word 'learn' in everyday speech certainly refers to rote memory, as in, 'I can't come out. I've got to learn this poem / these French verbs / some chemical formulae.' This orientation towards the result of learning makes it more difficult to think about learning as an activity in its own right: one which people might be able to get better at.

'Knowledge is true'

Along with the focus on 'knowledge' may go the belief (or at least the hope) that such knowledge, if properly accredited, can be trusted. Only a slight caricature of this view would see 'knowledge' as discovered by experts (mostly from universities) like diamonds that are mined (by a difficult process called 'research'), polished and then put on display (in books and lectures) for other people to 'learn' and 'believe'. In school, once knowledge has made its way through the syllabus and text-book barriers it has been certified accurate and important.[4] Clearly such a view would lead to a more 'traditional' approach to teaching and learning, while a belief in knowledge as a provisional human creation would open up the possibility of a more active and critical stance on the part of learners.[5]

'Learning is for the young'

Who learns? Who is learning for? A general view would have it that learning is mainly an activity of, and for, the young. A 'Far Side' cartoon by Gary Larsen shows the nature, and the effect, of this belief. A circus dog is balanced on a tightrope, performing a complex manoeuvre that involves juggling with five balls whilst balancing a vase on his head, swirling a hula-hoop round his hips, and holding a reluctant cat in his mouth. The caption reads: 'High above the hushed crowd, Rex tried to remain focused. But still he could not rid himself of one nagging thought. He was an old dog – and this was a new trick.' Like all these beliefs, the assumption that old dogs can't learn new tricks may turn out to be self-fulfilling. The nagging thought may distract Rex enough for him to lose his balance – and thus to validate the belief. Social movements such as 'grey power' and the University of the Third Age are dedicated to combating the stultifying effect of this belief on the learning of older people. If lifelong learning is indeed a reality, this belief needs re-examination.

'Learning is simple'

It is sometimes assumed that, whatever learning is, it is a simple process which involves adding new bits of information, making connections and developing habits. Learning is felt to be like building a house brick by brick, or like training a dog to come when you whistle. Whatever the root metaphor, according to this model learning is all one kind of thing, and learners and learning vary on a single dimension from good to bad. Some modern Western versions of this concept, only slightly less crude, assume that there are a small number of learning styles with individuals being good at one style and less good at the others. It is the teacher's job to capitalize upon, and maximize, the 'best learning', and/or to create a mixture of activities so that everyone gets a chance to use their preferred style. But if we believed that lifelong learning could involve the continual development of learning power in a whole variety of forms, quite a different attitude might be possible.

'Learning involves teaching'

On one widespread view, learning involves special activities, usually intellectual and often hard work, that are quite separate from just being alive and doing things. There are places that specialize in 'learning' just as there are special places for swimming or dining out or shopping: schools and colleges, where you also find people who are experts at 'teaching', which is the main activity through which learning happens. Teachers are people with special skills and resources, without which learning would not happen so well, or even at all. The focus of interest, as soon as we start to talk about learning, shifts to the process of teaching – if we can get the teaching 'right', learning will happen as a fairly straightforward consequence. Learning as an activity is engaged and driven by teaching, or at least by 'good' teaching. The effect of this institutionalized view is to place just one kind of learning in the foreground. If, as I suggested in the Introduction, there are indeed different compartments to the learning toolkit, such a belief will cause people to neglect the development of those that do not 'fit' within a certain view of education. Stages or kinds of learning which cannot be 'taught', or do not immediately result in a conscious conclusion, become suspect or invisible.

'Learning proceeds calmly'

There is a view which supposes that learning is a rational, 'cognitive' process, and that getting emotional is a sign that the learning process is not taking place 'properly'. In so far as feelings and emotions are involved in learning at all, a mild level of interest is desirable: we only need to be concerned about feelings when they are getting in the way and gumming up the smooth working of the mind. They then constitute a problem to be resolved, so that normal service can be resumed. The solution to this problem should primarily be sought in the learners' own characters, and/or in 'emotional difficulties' they may be experiencing in their lives. Learning can therefore be largely disconnected from the learners' personalities – provided they are 'normal' and 'happy'. When all is going well, personality and emotion can safely be ignored. (A recently published 'teachers' guide to the psychology of learning', for example, has no index entries for emotion, feeling, personality or relationship.)[6] Again, there may indeed be learning processes of this calm, rational kind, but we limit people's sense of learning if we presume that *all* learning has to be like this. We might deprive them, for example, of opportunities to develop the resilience they will need to cope with learning challenges that are emotionally charged, or to handle their own feelings when, as they inevitably will, they experience failure and frustration.

'Proper learning involves understanding'

The traditional idea that 'learning = memorization' is widely dismissed in educated Western circles these days, and has been replaced by the equally lop-sided belief that 'learning = understanding'. Learning that is not discussable, the theory now goes, is second-rate. Children can't just do their sums correctly; they have to 'understand' what they are doing. Automobile salesmen can't just use their native wit to sell cars; they have to attend seminars on 'customer care' in order to talk about what they are doing. There is a presumption that 'explicit is good'. The idea that conscious understanding might be unnecessary, or might even get in the way of other kinds of learning that are equally valuable, is inconceivable on this view. There is, therefore, a risk of this belief inadvertently reducing people's learning power in certain situations.

Effort and ability

What you believe learning is profoundly influences how you think about success and failure. And here cultures differ widely. At one extreme, Asian cultures emphasize effort. They generally assume that anybody can learn more or less anything provided they work hard. Chinese children are encouraged, from an early age, to develop persistence and to expend effort as a matter of course without expecting much praise. If there are inherent differences between learners, they are taken to affect the rate at which one learns, not the ceiling which one can be expected to reach. It is the job of the family/community to ensure that people do achieve, and any sense of failure, and concomitant shame, is shared.

At the other extreme, many Western cultures focus on 'ability' as the major determinant of learning success. Individuals are supposed to vary widely in this commodity, which sets an upper limit on what you can be expected to achieve.

If you failed, perhaps it was because you weren't 'bright' enough. If you achieve less than your presumed 'ability level' (which can be assessed with a dipstick called an IQ test – see note 9 on p.345), a variety of secondary factors are presumed to be at work: family background; disabilities (or 'special needs'), which prevent the achievement of 'full potential'; or lack of effort. Failure, and any publicizing of failure through grades or public punishment, runs the risk, on the 'ability' view, of 'damaging self-esteem', because 'ability' is taken to be an important aspect of personality, and thus an index of personal worth. The sense of shame is different from the Asian one, where one's 'fault' is to have let others down by not trying hard enough. On this Western view, it is one's own personal identity that is at stake. To be lacking in ability is to be wanting as a person. Naturally those who subscribe to, or have been infected by, such a view are keen to resist the idea that they are 'stupid', in both their own and other people's eyes. Substantial learning challenges become seen as occasions for public exposure of 'low ability', with consequent humiliation, rather than as opportunities to strengthen learning muscles. This may lead to educational disaffection or heightened anxiety: a need to withdraw or 'cover up'.

The diagnosis that the culture gives for learning difficulty will determine what is seen as acceptable, sensible or necessary to do about it. Parents and teachers will respond to a child's struggles in different ways. In 'ability'-centred cultures, it is the experience of frustration and failure that triggers self-critical thoughts and makes learning threatening, so it is important for learners to be protected from that experience. Judgements of having failed should be concealed as much as possible – for example by not publishing class-lists, and by constructing various forms of evaluative double-speak in which there appears to be no such thing as 'failure', only varying degrees of success. If the recognition of low learning achievement becomes inevitable, then explanations are offered that avoid the dreaded imputation of 'stupidity': commonly other aspects of the child's behaviour, which prevent them 'reaching their potential', are identified and often 'medicalized'. Face is saved if you are 'suffering from' a condition such as 'dyslexia' or 'attention deficiency and hyperactivity disorder'. Finding learning difficult thus becomes 'not your fault'. You cannot be blamed, any more than someone with measles or a sprained ankle can be blamed for coming last in the egg-and-spoon race. Achievement is to be supported through a mixture of protection from failure, special provision for the diagnosed 'need', 'good teaching', and 'parental support'.

In other cultures very different treatment is prescribed. The learning of Asian children is traditionally 'supported' with a mixture of encouragement, punishment and ridicule. Children are treated harshly in school if they do not work hard, in a way that a Westerner would consider 'Dickensian' and harmful to their development.[7] However, the deeply embedded sense that such treatment is 'for your own good', and the weaker cultural relationship between 'ability' and self-worth, means that Asian children rarely show any lasting effects in terms of resentment or an undermining of 'self-esteem'.

Interestingly, recent research by my colleagues Patricia Broadfoot and Marilyn Osborn at the University of Bristol has revealed that French primary schools show something of the Asian pattern. Children are treated more harshly, and are subjected to more public 'shaming', than their British counterparts, yet they like their teachers and enjoy school more. This apparent paradox is resolved in this way. Provided children (a) believe, deep down, that this treatment is genuinely in the service of improving their learning, (b) believe that they have the ability to succeed if they try, and (c) do not believe that their worth as a person is being impugned, but only their conduct and their performance, they seem to suffer few ill effects. It is the cultural model within which the punishment or humiliation is given meaning that makes the difference.[8]

It is worth exploring the cultural construction of 'ability' in a little more detail, for, as we shall see in the next section, it directly affects how people learn. In Western educational culture, the word 'ability' is used as a synonym for 'intelligence', and is taken to refer to some inner resource which explains or accounts for actual performance. Kelly did well because she 'possesses high ability', or is 'an able child'. Phrases such as 'ability level', 'high ability', 'less able' and so on are used to denote a real, personal characteristic which is generally fixed, limiting, pervasive, predictive, monolithic, measurable and valuable. 'Fixed' means that it is not subject to significant changes over time, and often innately fixed. 'Limiting' means that the 'ability' someone has fixes the ceiling of what they can achieve (other factors possibly intervening to prevent a person achieving up to their 'ability level', as we saw earlier). 'Pervasive' means that this limit is operative across a wide range of subjects and domains, and possibly across 'learning' as a whole. 'Predictive' means that knowing a person's 'ability' enables you to predict their future performance. 'Monolithic' means that 'ability' is a simple, coherent thing: it is not composed of many elements. 'Measurable' means it is possible to discover and quantify 'ability' with the aid of certain diagnostic procedures (such as 'IQ tests').[9] 'Valuable' means that 'high ability' is better than 'low ability', and a person's 'ability level' says something important about what they are worth. In short, on this view people's learning power is largely determined by some central reservoir of general-purpose mental resource, the capacity of which stays much the same across their lifespan. Teaching is about exploiting this 'intelligence' as best we can.

What's wrong with 'intelligence'?

This cultural 'story' about people's capacity for learning and change rests on assumptions that are now known to be false. The ability to solve abstract puzzles does not predict real-life learning and problem-solving – people who routinely solve complex problems in the real world often have rather low IQs. Even within school, students' performance is much more variable over time and across domains than this simple view would predict. The allied idea that people who excel in particular fields do so because they have special ability or 'talent' is refuted by research which shows that the most important variables are practice and commitment.[10]

Robert Sternberg of Yale, one of the world's foremost authorities on 'intelligence', has recently pointed out how a myth such as 'ability' can lead to a society operating in ways that seem to support its validity. Suppose, says Sternberg, that admissions officers to colleges and graduate schools stopped using grade point averages and high scores on IQ-like admissions tests to select students, and started using height. (This criterion has the advantages of being reliably and easily measured, not much affected by special 'coaching', and reasonably hard to fake. It is also already used as an index of advancement: successful US presidential candidates tend to be taller than their opponents.) Under the new system, all the positions in society which depend on educational success would soon come to be occupied by taller people. Those at the bottom of the educational, financial and social pile would be shorter. Being tall would come to seem a natural corollary of success, and shortness of failure. As soon as such a society was established, the originally arbitrary decision of the admissions officers would come to look like the most natural, obvious, necessary procedure in the world. Because tall people do well, it would be perverse not to select for expensive courses of education and training those people who already have the height qualifications.[11]

The practice would be self-fulfilling because short people would simply not be given the opportunity to show whether they could succeed. Just so, Sternberg has discovered, selection on the basis of a spurious, narrow concept of 'intelligence' prevents the many people who have low test scores – but who would have scored highly on other indices of learning or practical creativity – from ever displaying, cultivating or even discovering these qualities. In practical terms, the widespread use, to select people for admission to graduate business schools in the USA, of an IQ-like test called the GMAT, in which people have to do a lot of hard, rational, abstract thinking under pressure, means that those who excel at imagination and intuition are eliminated from the start. When scholars such as Herrnstein and Murray, authors of the influential book *The Bell Curve: Intelligence and Class Structure in American Life*, 'discover' a general correlation between social success and IQ test performance, they claim to have discovered a natural law, when what they have uncovered is merely a self-perpetuating set of cultural practices and beliefs.[12]

Even if you only broaden the notion of 'intelligence' a little, the cracks in its own logic begin to appear. Sternberg assessed students on three different measures of 'ability', which he called retentive, practical and creative, as well as the conventional one, analytical. They were then assigned to one of four introductory psychology classes, each of which emphasized one of these abilities. In the retentive course students were told they would be assessed on their ability to reproduce key points and definitions. In the practical course they tried to apply a theory to a practical example. In the creative course they generated a theory of their own. While in the analytical course they were asked to compare and contrast two existing theories. In a final examination, all the students were tested in each of the four ways. Students whose learning context matched their own preference among the different kinds of learning performed best. Scores on creative and practical forms of 'intelligence' contributed very significantly to their overall performance. And, very interestingly, the students who had high creative and practical scores were a much more ethnically and socioeconomically diverse group than were those who scored high on the conventional IQ-type measures. Sternberg concludes:

> Our current, narrower conceptualizations of abilities create a closed system in which a narrow subset of talented students – those high in memory and analytical abilities – are benefited at all points in the system. They do better on ability tests, learn better in courses where the instruction is geared to them, and then perform better on achievement tests that measure these restricted kinds of learning. . . . Students with creative and practical abilities are essentially 'iced out' of the system, because at no point are they much allowed to let their abilities shine through and help them perform better . . . the result is that career paths may be barred to intellectually talented individuals.[13]

The 'narrowness' of the conventional definition of intelligence, or 'general ability', is conveyed by the type of problems which are used to measure it. In response to the publication of

The Bell Curve, and the apparent legitimacy which it gave to the supposed intellectual superiority of white over black people, the American Psychological Association convened a high-level committee to examine the evidence. In their report, they point out that

> Analytical problems, of the type suitable for test construction, tend to (a) have been formulated by other people, (b) be clearly defined, (c) come with all the information needed to solve them, (d) have only a single right answer which can be reached by only a single method, (e) be disembedded from ordinary experience, and (f) have little or no intrinsic interest. Practical problems, in contrast, tend to (a) require problem recognition and formulation, (b) be poorly defined, (c) require information seeking, (d) have various acceptable solutions, (e) be embedded in and require prior everyday experience, and (f) require motivation and personal involvement.[14]

IQ begins to look more like a rather arcane ability, at which only rather peculiar people would (and would wish to) excel, than a crucial quality for living.

Is there any independent evidence that 'intelligence', defined in this narrow but diffuse kind of way, corresponds to the way the mind actually works? After an exhaustive search for such evidence, Michael Howe of Exeter University concluded: 'There are no strong grounds for believing that identification of someone's measured intelligence justifies any kind of meaningful statement about that individual's qualities, achievements or attributes, or even detailed predictions, except in the . . . rather narrowly defined circumstances that involve or depend upon school education.'[15]

The effects of beliefs on learning

Ordinary people's views about knowledge, learning and ability correspond closely to the picture sketched above.[16] In one survey, a group of Finnish children identified a prototype of an 'intelligent person' as 'an adult male, usually a professor, a scientist or an executive, who is bald, wears eyeglasses and is doing important mental work'. The problem is that such views influence the ways in which people operate as learners. They do not just express these opinions when asked: a substantial number of people act as if they believed them too.

Marlene Schommer at the University of Illinois at Urbana-Champaign has studied the effects of students' beliefs about knowledge and learning on their academic performance. She gave 250 college students a questionnaire designed to assess where they stood on some of the common beliefs about knowledge and learning. One of these was the assumption that 'learning is quick or not at all'. Another was that 'knowledge is generally certain'. Having established where each student stood on these beliefs, she gave them one of two passages to read. In each the concluding paragraph was removed and the students were asked to provide one, spelling out any conclusions they could draw from the information given. They were also given a multiple-choice comprehension test, and asked to rate their confidence in their understanding of the passage.

The results showed that the more the students believed in Quick Learning, the more likely they were to oversimplify their conclusions, ignoring some of the complexities in the original passages; the less well they did on the comprehension test; and the more likely they were to overestimate their own understanding. The more they believed in Certain Knowledge, the more likely they were to draw conclusions that were more definite than the evidence would permit. Thus how well people learn is shown to be a function not only of the learning tools they possess, but of the implicit beliefs which they have picked up. A belief in quick learning leads them to learn in a way that is rushed and skimpy. A belief in the possibility of absolute certainty leads them to ignore important provisos, and to distort information in the direction of their belief.[17]

The effect of beliefs on resilience

It is perhaps learners' implicit beliefs about 'ability' itself that have the most dramatic impact on their learning power. Carol

Dweck, Professor of Psychology at Columbia University, New York, has been investigating what causes people to shy away from learning when it threatens to get difficult: in other words, what undermines their resilience. Her research has found that this fragility in the face of frustration is worryingly common, and in schoolchildren distributed right across the achievement range. Successful students, almost by definition, meet difficulty less often than the unsuccessful, but when they do they are equally likely to withdraw, get upset and/or defensive, and regress to more primitive learning and coping strategies.

However, Dweck did discover that, when looking separately at high- and low-achieving girls and boys, the successful girls are particularly vulnerable. In one of her studies – the one on which I based the example of Emmi and Eliza on p. 2 – Dweck gave a class learning booklets to work through, some with a very difficult chapter inserted in the middle and some without. Students without the insert performed to their normal level of attainment. But in the group with the difficult chapter, the normally successful girls fell back dramatically. 'The staggering thing was that the difficulty didn't just wipe out the difference between able and less able girls,' said Dweck. 'It actually reversed it. I think the brighter girls simply panicked.'[18] Mostly they manage to do well without having to struggle, but when they *do* hit difficulty they tend to go to pieces. All their success has not strengthened their ability to cope with temporary failure.

To understand why this might be so, and to find out what to do about it, Dweck had to dig a little deeper. She asked both fragile and resilient students how they felt when they had to try hard at learning. Resilient students said they liked it, because they felt they were really learning something. Not only might they solve the problem, but they might even get smarter in the process. The fragile students, on the other hand, disliked effort because, they said, it meant they were not very bright.

Herein lies the key. Resilient students have, at the back of their minds, a view of their own learning ability as something expandable. They have not succumbed to the prevalent view of ability as a fixed reservoir of resource. So 'getting smarter' is indeed a real possibility for them, and worth investing effort in. Fragile students, on the other hand, have come to believe in ability as a fixed commodity, so for them the experience of difficulty, and of consequent effort, implied that they had hit the ceiling of their ability – and it wasn't high enough. They were in danger of having to admit that they were 'stupid'. This is a painful conclusion to draw, and, naturally enough they would try to avoid it, employing defensive and diversionary tactics to protect themselves. The crucial difference between the two groups was not so much *whether* they 'tried', but what 'trying' *meant*. One is reminded of Henry Ford's dictum that 'Those who believe they can, and those who believe they can't, are both right.'

Why is it the generally successful girls who are particularly at risk? Dweck suggests that it is because they have had least experience of grappling with difficulty. They may have swanned through the earlier stages of their education and picked up the idea that they were 'clever', but never had to put it to the test. Most learning for them had been relatively easy – and when they did hit difficulty teachers (and perhaps parents too) would let them off the hook at the first signs of distress. Boys, the research shows, are more likely to be encouraged to 'stick with it', so they are able to get used to the experience of staying with learning, even though it is transiently confusing or frustrating, and to discover for themselves that persistence can pay off. Dweck says, 'It doesn't help a child to tackle a difficult task if they succeed consistently on an easy one. It doesn't teach them to persist in the face of obstacles if obstacles are always eliminated from the regime. Knowing they can cope with difficulties is what makes children seek challenges and overcome further problems. . . . Children learn best from slightly difficult tasks which they have to struggle through.'

As we saw earlier, adults who have assimilated the fixed view of ability may encourage brittle children to interpret failure as a negative experience that saps self-esteem, and is best avoided. But, paradoxically, by trying to protect brittle children from failure they deprive them of the only type of experience which might help them develop their resilience. It is by supporting children through difficulty, and by encouraging them to focus their attention on the process rather than the outcome, that such progress is to be made. Well-intentioned collusion with their desire to escape difficulty only reinforces their frailty.

Articulate incompetence

'Lateral thinking' proponent Edward de Bono has argued that people who are – and see themselves as – 'intelligent' on the limited, rational, 'clever' view may well be worse learners than those who do not.[19] For example, he suggests that clever people have the facility to construct a seemingly coherent case for virtually any point of view, and once such a case is made they have a greater investment in supporting and defending the argument than in actually finding out what is going on. Bob Bernstein, CEO of the publishing giant Random House, refers to such people as 'articulate incompetents'. He says: 'That's what frightens me about business schools. They train their students to sound wonderful. But it's necessary to find out if there's any judgement behind their language.'[20]

When the self-image and self-esteem of a person become based on their cleverness, their investment in winning arguments, rather than learning, becomes all the greater. Winning an argument relies as much on picking holes in competing arguments as it does on mounting and defending one's own, and this critical cleverness can often be more immediately satisfying than the more laborious and risky process of developing a well-founded view of your own. And again, self-image needs can reinforce this trait. As de Bono says, 'To prove someone else wrong gives you instant achievement and superiority. To agree makes you seem superfluous and a sycophant. To put forward an idea [of your own] puts you at the mercy of those on whom you depend for evaluation.' Interestingly, he also points out that the sheer physical quickness of the clever mind enables it to pick up and evaluate clues fast, and this tempts it to jump to conclusions. The mind that collects and evaluates its data more slowly may avoid this trap and come to a judgement that integrates a wider range of factors, and is therefore likely to be more satisfying all round. We shall look at the evidence for this in Chapter 9.

This chapter has demonstrated several of the ways in which views about learning and knowing channel or diminish people's learning power. Every culture tends to induct its members into a partial view of the mind and its capabilities. Some Eastern societies develop memory at the expense of creativity. Some Western ones do the reverse. Formal education and training worldwide – at all levels from playschool to business seminar – frequently embody beliefs about knowledge and know-how, and the learning process by which they are obtained, which are limiting and fly in the face of much that we now know about learning. One of the aims of this book is to show just how misguided and ill-founded many of these beliefs are.

What has emerged strongly in this chapter is the negative effect of the widespread belief in 'intelligence' as an all-purpose but limited mental resource; and especially in intellectual 'ability' as the central faculty of mind. In modern society, we misrepresent the nature of intelligence by overvaluing just one of its forms. This belief tends to undermine people's resilience in the face of learning difficulty, and to lead them unnecessarily to restrict their learning options; even, perhaps, to avoid or withdraw from learning altogether. But why is resilience such an important quality in a good, robust learner? To answer this, we have to explore what exactly it means to say that learning is an emotional business, for resilience is, above all else, the ability to tolerate certain kinds of feeling.

TWO

The Feelings of Learning

Learning, of whatever kind, is an adventure. A problem exists for which there is currently no ready-made solution. A challenge is posed for which the requisite skills are not yet established. A plan is disrupted by an unanticipated event. In each case the effect of what one does next is uncertain. Sometimes this uncertainty is purely exhilarating; but sometimes the possibility of incompetence or incomprehension is threatening. The continuing engagement which learning requires may be dangerous. The urge to withdraw and protect yourself becomes stronger. And it is in just these kinds of situation that emotions arise.

This emotional tolerance constitutes the first 'R' of learning: *resilience*.

The basic emotions

There are a number of general types of threat which evolution has equipped us to meet with general kinds of response, known collectively as 'fight or flight'; and each kind of response has an associated characteristic emotional tone. When something goes wrong we make a preliminary assessment of what kind of wrong it is, the details of which are often unconscious, and then prepare ourselves to deal with that category of threat. The way the readiness to respond feels to us is called 'emotion'. Keith Oatley of the Ontario Institute for Studies in Education has proposed, for example, that the readiness to flee (whether one actually does so or not) comprises a whole set of physical reactions which together we experience as *fear*. The feeling of being ready to combat a threat by fighting or a display of aggression we call *anger*. The feeling of emitting, or being about to emit, a general cry for help we could call *distress*. The feeling of dealing with something noxious that has got, or is about to get, inside your body or your mind is called *disgust*. The readiness to withdraw, to lick your wounds, to get used to the hole in your command of life that has been left by loss, to grieve and mourn, we call *sadness*. The extreme case of turning down emotional awareness – of trying to escape not the threatening situation but merely the painful experience of the situation, is the last-ditch reaction of being in *shock*.[1]

The response to threat is essentially emotional. To talk of emotions – at least these basic 'negative' emotions – is to talk of the subjective side of a self-preservative reaction, the objective side of which involves physiological reactions that ready us for one kind of response. At times of disruption or frustration, these negative emotions correspond to ways of getting the sub-systems of the body and mind – digestion and respiration, legs and hands, eyes and ears – to stop what they are doing and all 'pull together'.

'Emotion', as a concept, is associated with the general, all-hands-on-deck aspect of these readiness responses, while 'cognition' refers more to working out the specific knowledge and know-how that are going to be brought to bear. Emotions are, according to these new insights, aspects of a single, vital biological process. When we meet a hitch, when our knowledge and know-how let us down, or when our own goals and interests conflict, feeling afraid (or sad or angry or shocked or disgusted) is part and parcel of the way we are built to respond. Emotions accompany the 'ways of knowing' that evolution has designed to help us out in such situations. The core negative emotions signal that the brain-mind is responding intelligently. It is doing its job, in the face of an upset, an interruption or a temporary loss of comprehension and control.

So emotion is useful, just as physical pain is useful. Because we do not like it we are motivated, at a level way below conscious choice, to reduce it – to put right an adverse situation.

The emotions of learning

The feelings of being unsure of what is going on, and being set to take note of any information that may help to clarify the situation – in other words, to learn – constitute a family of emotions we might call *interest/anxiety/excitement*. The tentative readiness to engage and experiment, to take the risk of staying close that learning requires, generates a range of feelings from interest and absorption at one end to an apprehension that borders on fear, anger, distress, disgust, sadness or shock at the other. As your intuitive assessment of the riskiness of engagement mounts, so does the likelihood of tipping into one of the other threat states. Learning, especially as it becomes more challenging, always operates at the intersection of a variety of options, each of which has a characteristic feeling.

So the feelings of learning are special in that they often occupy an intermediate, ambiguous position between attraction and repulsion. Uncertainty invites an ambivalent response. On the one hand, learning promises greater insight and control. On the other, it might blow up in your face.

The period of attention required to clarify an uncertain situation varies enormously. Sometimes a fraction of a second will be sufficient. Once you are looking in the right direction, it doesn't take long to tell the difference between a Rottweiler and a pussy-cat. But there are many situations which don't reveal themselves so rapidly – and then greater patience, greater tolerance for the discomfort of uncertainty, become important. To know whether this person is the one you wish to spend the rest of your life with; to resolve the intricate cross-currents of a 'mid-life crisis'; to find the proof to Fermat's Last Theorem . . . to deal with these predicaments requires emotional tolerance. Especially where conflicting interests and desires are involved – security versus glory; conservation versus innovation; individual versus community – the kinds of learning that human beings need to do require much more protracted and sophisticated engagement than those of the startled rabbit.

So there is a strong need to understand the place of emotions in learning, and to develop the ability to contain, manage and tolerate them. This is one of the core ingredients of 'emotional intelligence', and nowhere is it more crucial than in the domain of learning.[2] To treat anxiety as if it were itself aversive is to misunderstand what it means. An animal or human being who is able to tolerate some uncertainty, and who does not run and hide at every small hint of the unknown, has a survival advantage over its more cautious cousins – especially when they all find themselves in an environment which is less predictable, less familiar, than the one their evolution has selected them to deal with. As long as the world stays still, studded with the same old resources and dangers as it has been for generations, then the old evolutionary toolkit of responses will do. But as the world becomes more complex and shifting, so either reflex timidity or reflex aggression begin to carry risks, for neither of them allows the kind of engagement – and therefore the kind of increased knowledge and know-how – that learning might deliver. These risks may be less obvious or less dramatic than the risks that are run by learning, but they are no less real. Reckless exploration jeopardizes survival, but so does a persistent refusal to engage with the unknown.

The decision to learn

When faced with the unknown, learning is one option amongst several. And how we make the intuitive decision to select between these options influences our long-term development: our 'quality of life' and, ultimately, our survival. Always growl at strangers and you may end up with no mate or no friends. Always retreat from uncertainty and you will end up the prisoner of a very limited range of knowledge and know-how. Always dive into the unknown, and you are likely to have a short life (but an exciting one). Choosing the option, moment by moment, which is in your own best interests is a crucial aspect of being a good learner.

Whether to engage and learn (and if so how) or whether to disengage and protect oneself (and if so how) may be a very elaborate decision, and it is frequently far from conscious and articulate. The brain is very good at making these rapid cost-benefit analyses of situations, and coming up with the course of action that seems, at that moment, the best. The fact that this process is often largely intuitive does not make it any less rational, nor any less capable of being subtle and complex.

The considerations that go into making that decision are, therefore, of great importance. It matters that the situation is perceived accurately – that the possible threats are neither exaggerated nor underestimated – and that the estimates of the benefits, as well as the costs and risks, are also represented correctly. For it is the subjective evaluations of all these considerations that are weighed in the balance in this decision-making process. A defensive response to a demand for change, for example, is always rational in terms of the way that person weighs up their world. When someone chooses not to learn, it is because they don't feel it is safe enough, or they believe they don't have the skills that it would take, or there isn't enough time, or the possible sacrifices involved are too great, or it simply doesn't matter enough. To explain someone's disinclination to engage with a particular learning challenge by using a term like 'lazy' or 'unmotivated' hardly does justice to this subtle psychological process.

To make this more concrete, we might ask: what kinds of considerations might go into selecting a course of study, for example, or deciding how to go about learning a particular subject? They might include the following.

What would I be learning this *for*? Do I need this paper in order to get into the third-year class that I have set my heart on? Would it impress the selectors if I have done well in it? Will it actually help me practically get better at doing something I want to be able to do? Is it (just) for personal interest, and how interested am I really? What would my tutor say, or my parents? (Is it time to rebel a little, and choose something just for me for a change?)

What will the *experience* of learning this be like? What does the bush telegraph say about the instructors? Are they fun? Do they tend to pick on students who haven't done all the reading? Do I admire them as people? Are my friends likely to choose it? What will the competition be like? Will I get to chat up that gorgeous hunk who was in Microbiology 304?

What are my *resources*? Will I be up to it? Is there a lot of rote learning to be done? What kind of exam does the course have? How good am I at the kinds of learning (and testing) which I anticipate will be required? Do I need to do my best, or can I afford just to get by on this one? Will there be people there who can help me out if the learning gets hard? How much reading is there? How much will I mind if I'm not at the top of the class (as I am used to being)? What strategies do I have to protect myself if I'm having difficulty?

What other *priorities* do I have? Will the effort required interfere with my social life, and how much does this matter? Is it a cool course to choose, or do I run the risk of being thought nerdy? How much time and effort are my other courses (the ones I've got to take) going to require? Can I still fit in volleyball practice and the play I want to be in, or will I have to give something up?

Some of these questions might be fully conscious, such as 'Do I need this for my career?', and may require some deliberate introspection or systematic seeking out of further information. But others, such as 'How do I protect myself from failure, and what are the risks in this class?', are likely to feed into the decision-making process in a more intuitive fashion. And even with those factors that are conscious, the amount of weight they are given is rarely quantified. We may draw up an explicit list of pros and cons, but how much each is worth is usually not spelt out. Like all our decisions, the decision whether to learn, and if so how, is made on a partly conscious, largely intuitive, basis; and it would not be better for being otherwise.

Defences from learning

It is useful, in the interests of emotional self-management, for learners and their teachers to be able to spot, and understand, what happens when the cost-benefit analysis shifts and they move from learning mode into self-protection.

Flight

The tendency to flee may, in extremis, produce actual physical flight. The student runs out of the examination hall. The child backs away from the dog she has been investigating when it begins to growl. The stressed manager calls in sick. But fear may also be accompanied by a different manifestation of flight – by attempts to render yourself unnoticeable. People who don't want to be noticed can wear drab clothes, slink into and out of meetings, and sit where they won't get picked on to answer questions. Educationist James Pye has written about the tragedy of what he calls the 'invisible children' – those who manage to glide through their school careers without attracting anybody's attention, and who teachers have difficulty remembering on parents' evenings.[3] Pye argues that it is these children, rather than those who make themselves difficult or disruptive, who are the real failures of the school system: the ones who learn least, and who enter adult life least equipped to cope with its challenges and uncertainties. At least the naughty ones have learnt how to oppose and subvert. The invisible children may have learnt nothing, except that they are not very good learners, and how to hide.

Fight

Alternatively, one can choose to stand one's ground and 'face down' the threat. A threatened learner can become angry and aggressive, and try to neutralize the learning or make it go away. Disruptive students may try to intimidate their teachers, in the hope that they will retreat and take their 'stupid', 'boring' tasks with them. Cynical delegates to a management training course may denigrate the subject matter or the teaching style, trying to negate any potential learning threat by undermining its legitimacy or its authority. When people feel stressed, asked to do more than they can cope with, surveys show that one of the first and commonest responses is the tendency to become punitive and vindictive, blaming others –

lazy workers, inadequate colleagues, incompetent leadership – in order to fend off any implied criticism of one's own short-comings.[4]

There are more subtle forms of subversion that the reluctant learner might deploy, not least what psychologists have come to call 'passive aggression'. John Holt, a great observer of children's actual (as opposed to presumed) behaviour, notes in his classic book *How Children Fail* the similarity between the demeanour of some students and that of prisoners of war. Holt quotes a survivor of a World War II concentration camp who described how prisoners would adopt, as one of their strategies for preserving their dignity, an air of amiable dull-wittedness, of cooperative and willing incompetence. Told to do some-thing, they listened attentively, nodded their heads eagerly, and asked questions that showed they had not understood a word. When they could not safely do this any longer, they did the opposite of what they had been told, or did it, but as badly as they dared. Holt asks:

> Does not something very close to this happen often in school? Do [children] not, to some extent, escape and frustrate the relentless, insatiable pressure of their elders by withdrawing the most intelligent and creative parts of their minds from the scene? Is this not at least a partial explanation of the extraordinary stupidity that otherwise bright children so often show in school? The stubborn and dogged 'I don't get it' with which they meet the instructions and explanations of their teachers – may it not be a statement of resistance as well as one of panic and flight? I think this is almost certainly so. Under pressure . . . some children may quite deliberately *go stupid*. . . . Most, however, are probably not [so] aware of what they are doing.[5]

Anyone who has observed the almost schizophrenic differ-ence between some children's puddingy demeanour in the classroom, and their bright energy outside it, would be hard put to resist the same conclusion.

Distress

The distress response in the face of threat may show itself as regression. People may give up an attempt to learn and say, 'I can't do it. You do it for me.' School students are prone to adopt this strategy. They know that the teacher will tell them in the end, so they simply outwait (and outwit) them by, as Holt says, 'going stupid'. People may also revert to earlier, more primitive ways of coping that may be quite ineffective, but which again may have the desired side-effect of getting other people to offer comfort and 'fight your battles for you'. Instances of this simplification and regression can be found in all kinds of work situations. For example, British psychoanalyst Isobel Menzies Lyth showed in the 1960s, in a classic study of a big London teaching hospital, how nurses at all levels tended to cope with their anxiety and their feelings of inadequacy by underperforming.[6]

Not trying

A common form of regression is the strategy of 'not trying'. You hide not from the learning task itself, or from the experience of failure, but from the meaning that failure has for you. As we saw in Chapter 1, many people interpret failure as evidence of lack of ability. But you can avoid labelling yourself 'stupid' if you didn't really try. By withdrawing effort you ensure your failure – but you avoid having to conclude that failure means you are stupid.[7]

Give people an alternative way of rationalizing failure, however, and they stop being obliged to deploy this self-protecting, but also self-defeating, response. Studies have shown that the performance of school students who are particularly afraid of failing can be improved by describing the task they are set as 'very difficult'. With a ready-made explanation for possible failure to hand, self-esteem is no longer in jeopardy, and students are free to try as hard as they like. The same defensive logic can be seen when learners are allowed to select the difficulty of their learning tasks. Fragile students can select very hard challenges for themselves, thus building in a face-saving loop-hole in the event of failure. On the other hand they can also select a very easy problem, thereby minimizing the probability of failure. One American female undergraduate, for example, said: 'I never aim too high . . . if you aim for the tree tops you don't have far to fall, whereas if you aim for the stars the disappointment can be too great. So I am careful about the goals I set myself.' A male graduate student – one of the most successful under- graduates, in other words – conceded that he had chosen courses that he knew were 'well within the limits of my ability [since] failing at a course that interested me, but where I was not confident, would have been shattering'.[8]

There is some evidence that this withdrawal of effort to save face is employed slightly differently by male and female students in secondary school and university (and perhaps, by extension, by adult men and women too). Male students who had a fragile sense of their own ability have been found to practise and prepare less for an ego-threatening test: they *really* don't try as hard as they might. Female students in the same predicament tend to work very hard, but to under- estimate, to themselves and to others, the amount of work they have put in. They *pretend* not to try, and thus attempt to have their cake and eat it. The hard work reduces the risk of failure – but if they do fail, they can always blame it on the apparent lack of effort.[9]

Some learners, again predominantly female, risk adopting the strategy of perfectionism – known as 'superstriving' – but without the accompanying laid-back veneer. They really go out on the high wire, but without the safety net of seeming not to try or to care. This is a strategy that exacerbates anxiety in bright students, because, as Martin Covington of the University of California, Berkeley, one of the leading researchers in this area, notes, 'no one can avoid failure indefinitely, for with each new success comes the need to accomplish more in order to experi- ence continued feelings of worthiness; and when failure finally occurs, these superstrivers are in the most threatening position of all, having tried hard and failed anyway'.[10]

The tactic of not trying may enable students to protect their self-esteem in the short term, but stores up more trouble for them down the line. For by not engaging, they have removed the possibility of exercising and strengthening their learning muscles. So their learning power fails to develop while the evidence of failure accumulates, making it increasingly hard to deny that they really are 'stupid'. At the same time, as Covington has discovered, students who withdraw effort also run the risk of labelling themselves 'lazy', effectively swapping one negative self-evaluation for another. The need to save face results, in such cases, in learners shooting themselves in the foot.

Inattention

In extreme cases the threat of learning may tip into a shut-down of feeling, or even, as when people faint on receiving shocking news, of consciousness itself: through the massive release of chemicals called endorphins in the brain we can induce local or general anaesthesia. It seems that human beings have developed the art of selectively editing or attenu-ating their experience – we have discovered the knack of withdrawing conscious awareness from the bits we don't like. Evidence of such denial or repression occurs both in the laboratory and in everyday life.[11]

Not dwelling on awkward things, or even not noticing them at all, is an effective strategy for keeping threat, doubt and learning at bay – tactical inattention offers a 'way of knowing' that may remove anxiety. But in the long run it is both ineffective (it fails to make you more competent) and addic-tive (you have to keep ignoring whatever is troubling you, because you are by definition not getting any better at dealing with it). Yet the modern mind seems to have perfected the ability to ignore threatening uncertainty. It knows how to leap to a conclusion, and how not to notice that it has done so. It knows how to select the evidence to support a conclu-sion that has already been adopted, and how to discount conflicting evidence. It sometimes prefers to argue for its rightness than to admit its possible fallibility. It prides itself on its ability to 'think', yet is often shallow and evasive, throwing up smokescreens and dragging red herrings across the trail of its own supposed logic.[12] There is now an abun-dance of evidence to show how illogical and irrational our much-vaunted faculty of reason is, and how unconscious we are of this fact.[13] As the poet Hilaire Belloc wrote:

Oh! let us never never doubt
What nobody is sure about.[14]

Inner tension

There is another way of reducing the experience of emotion, and that is by reducing the intensity of the experience in the body itself. As we saw at the beginning of this chapter, emotions represent states of readiness for different kinds of survival-related actions. By trying to suppress the physical responses we can thus damp down the associated feeling. But this attempt at internal inhibition may bring with it un-wanted consequenses. Tensing the neck and shoulders to control the anger response leads to aches and pains. Worse than that, clinical studies show that trying to suppress anger may indeed have the opposite effect. The extra physical effort involved actually increases the body's level of agitation, and blood pressure may be raised even higher than the anger response itself has raised it.[15] Chronic tension, too, may deplete the body's resources to the point where the immune system is stressed. Then toxic side-effects come into play, from increased proneness to viral ailments such as colds, flu and herpes through to increases in the rate of spread of cancer from one site in the body to others, in the risk of diabetes and in the severity of asthma attacks.[16] Apart from any other effects, all these serve to undermine still further an indivi-dual's energy for, and willingness to engage with, learning.

Ironic detachment

One modern way of protecting oneself from information or opinion that is uncongenial involves adopting a kind of ironic detachment in which events and experiences are allowed into consciousness, but stripped of any vestiges of personal sig-nificance. Everything is admissible, but nothing can touch 'me', for I have withdrawn my ability to be touched or affected. By declining to engage with issues in terms of values or morality, people are spared the trouble of having to work out where they might stand. But, as with any form of denial, irony is self-perpetuating. The more ironic one is, the more ironic one has to become. One buys a kind of peace, even security, but at the cost of giving up the urge to find or make a set of values and priorities by which to live. Kenneth Gergen suggests in *The Saturated Self* that this ironic stance is forced upon us by the sheer quantity and diversity of the views and experiences to which modern electronic media expose us.[17]

How fear affects learning

In order to learn efficiently, we have to be attending to the right bits of information. We establish a 'cone of attention' which contains everything that is preconsciously judged to be relevant, and excludes everything that is not (more on this in Chapter 4). A feeling of fear can affect this cone in one of three ways. First, it can shift its focus, making us attend to the source of a possible threat rather than the learning topic itself. A junior manager who is being bullied by his boss cannot keep his attention focused on the problem he is trying to solve. Second, fear can narrow the cone, so we suffer from tunnel vision and fail to notice information that matters. A novice driver, nervously gripping the wheel and concentrating on changing gear, fails to register the red traffic light. Or third, it can broaden and diffuse the cone, so that our attention is scattered and we are distracted by non-essentials. When you are a child learning to ride a bike, it is the moment when a parent's anxious cry of concern breaks through into your consciousness that you may fall off.[18]

People who are generally anxious, for example, find a whole range of possibilities, immediate and remote, threatening. Their minds may be swarming with things to worry about and their alarm bells are ringing continuously, which makes it very hard for them to learn about anything else. Sitting in a business seminar, worrying about how his colleagues perceive him and wanting to ask a question that will demonstrate his grasp of the material being presented, an anxiety-prone man is so preoccupied that he can hardly hear what is being said. (Indeed, when he does finally ask his question it may achieve exactly the reverse effect to that desired, having been answered two minutes before while he was mentally distracted.)

His attention becomes both over-focused on identified sources of threat, and scattered as he continually scans for others.[19]

Shame

For a small mammal, what counts as a threat is clearly defined: things that are personally life-threatening such as being too hot or too cold, hungry or thirsty, attacked or injured or ill, isolated from familiar habitat, resources or relatives, or things which jeopardize its ability to reproduce or to raise its off-spring. But human beings have discovered how to proliferate their 'needs' almost without limit. We have added a vast range of other items that 'matter': pride, wealth, reputation, possessions, youth, popularity, memory. And not to have something that matters – not to get your needs met – is to be threatened, and therefore emotional.[20] In New Guinea, the loss of face incurred by having an adult unmarried daughter is almost unbearable – an eventuality to be avoided at almost any cost to either the parents or the unfortunate young woman.[21] In Sydney, the same kind of emotion might be produced by having to sell one's yacht. In Tokyo, the chief executive of a bank, publicly admitting its collapse, might feel something similar.

All these examples hinge on a sense of failure; and in many cultures failure results in a collapse of self-esteem or self-worth. As we saw in Chapter 1, failure becomes a threat to self-esteem because of a person's beliefs. Buried in many people's personal belief systems are implicit theories of what it means to be a mature, worthwhile person – the core values and standards by which we have learnt to judge ourselves as human beings. The effect of these is to set limits on the conditions under which we may feel good about ourselves. When we find ourselves acting, feeling or thinking in ways that are at odds with these standards, we experience that peculiarly human emotion we call shame. It could be argued that shame is a mixture of several, or even all, of the basic emotions. You feel afraid (that someone might find out) and want to run way. You feel anger (with yourself, or with the person or occurrence that triggered the shame) and want to kick yourself, or smash a plate. You feel upset. You want to withdraw and hide. You may find a way of displacing or denying the shame, or distracting yourself from it. Shame is a powerful and complex forfeiture of well-being, exacted in the face of perceived inadequacy or unworthiness.[22]

The beliefs that trigger shame are many and various, but they frequently include the following.

Worthwhile people don't make mistakes. Worth is contingent on competence. Incompetence is unworthy and must be paid for with a loss of self-esteem.

Worthwhile people always know what is going on. Worth is contingent on clarity. Confusion, and feeling out of control, are unworthy and should be paid for with a loss of self-esteem.

Worthwhile people live up to, and within, their images of themselves. Worth is contingent on consistency. Acting un-predictably, out of character, or in defiance of one's prece-dents and principles, is unworthy and must be paid for with a loss of self-esteem.

Worthwhile people don't feel anxious, apprehensive, fraught or fragile. Worth is contingent on feeling cool, calm and col-lected. Feeling nervous, overwhelmed or frustrated should be paid for with a loss of self-esteem.[23]

Here is a big problem, for the experiences which are cen-sured by these beliefs are precisely those which crop up in the course of learning. Learning means acting in ways whose consequences are uncertain – you might be ineffective or make a mistake. It means relinquishing your hold on an inadequate view and daring to 'not know' – to feel confused – while you search out a better understanding. It may mean acting out of character. And it certainly means, as we have seen throughout this chapter, having feelings. All of these have to be tolerable if a person is going to be free to engage with learning challenges.

A person subject to these unconscious programming in-structions will feel undermined and threatened by experi-ences that are necessary concomitants of many forms of learning. Instead of being a precarious transition from a limited competence to an expanded one – difficult enough already – learning can feel like an assault on one's very belief in oneself. People come to feel more threatened by learning than the risk warrants, judge the situation too dangerous to explore, and opt instead for a strategy that is designed to preserve or maintain what they already know, or can do, or are. We misjudge events, so that we flee from, fight or close ourselves up against what is actually safe, nourishing, interesting and within our actual learning power. Resilience and self-confidence are undermined, and we become learning under-achievers.

Self-belief and resilience

One of the beliefs about self that has a particular impact on resilience concerns the degree of control you think you have over events that affect your life. How much does what you do make a difference to how things go? There are many demonstrations of how powerfully this belief affects learning. Students who were good, bad and indifferent at mathematics were divided into those whose belief in their self-efficacy was strong and those for whom it was weak. At all levels of prowess, the students who regarded themselves as efficacious were quicker to discard faulty strategies, solved more problems, chose to have a second go at more of the ones they had initially failed to solve, and did so more accurately.[24]

The practical implications of self-efficacy were underlined by a study of complex decision-making in business organizations by Albert Bandura. Business executives were asked to manage a computer-simulated company. Their job was to learn to be able to meet difficult performance targets by manipulating the resource allocations within the company, and by discovering and implementing certain rules of the corporate culture. At intervals their level of self-belief was measured, as were the kind of thinking they were using and the actual level of performance they had achieved. Prior to the learning phase of the study, the managers underwent a training seminar in which they were introduced to one of the two views of ability that we looked at in Chapter 1. One group was told that research indicated that decision-making ability reflected an unchanging mental aptitude. The second group was told that decision-making reflected a composite of acquirable skills.

Managers in the first group were increasingly beset by self-doubt as they encountered problems during the learning phase: they became more erratic in their thinking, they lowered their aspirations, and their learning deteriorated as time went on. The second group, in contrast, were highly resilient and resourceful. They maintained their self-belief despite difficulties, continued to set themselves challenging goals, tackled problems in a logical and effective way, and discovered more powerful ways of meeting their organizational targets. In a follow-up study, Bandura and his colleagues discovered that a similar alteration in people's learning could also be produced by altering their belief in the flexibility of the organization. People who were led to believe that organizations in general are very hard for individuals to affect quickly lost heart in the simulation, while those who had faith in the responsiveness of organizations tried harder, learnt more and succeeded better.[25]

Self-belief even increases people's ability to choose and construct satisfying life paths for themselves. Just as we tend to avoid situations that we feel ill-equipped to handle, so an increase in self-belief opens up a wider range of options that we feel able to master, and expands life choices. For example, the stronger people's beliefs in their capacities, the more career options they consider as possible, the greater the interest they show in exploring these options, and the better motivated they are to prepare themselves as fully as possible to achieve their selected goals.[26]

Stickability

It took Gertrude Stein twenty years of trying before her first poem was accepted for publication. Stravinsky was run out of town by an enraged audience and the critics after the first performance of *The Rite of Spring*. And the Beatles were refused a contract by Decca Records with the famous evaluation, 'We don't like their sound. Groups of guitars are on their way out.'

Many people who have achieved eminence in a wide variety of fields only did so because of their powers of recuperation and continual reaffirmation of their vision following discouraging experiences such as these.

Staying intelligently engaged with learning challenges that matter to you, despite difficulties and setbacks, is perhaps the most important quality of the good learner. Everyday life, at home as well as at work, is peppered with unforeseen impediments as we pursue our valued goals. And a satisfying resolution of complex personal and moral predicaments rarely comes quickly or easily. Bringing up a child or writing a book are learning projects that require dedication and repeated recovery from error, confusion and disappointment. Clearly a belief in your own ability to make a difference to the course of events is essential to lifelong learning.

Albert Bandura concludes that it is the ability to bounce back that is crucial – not an idealized ability never to fall. But to expect resilience all the time is unrealistic. Everyone has bad days; self-belief naturally waxes and wanes. And this is as true of children as it is of adults. As John Holt says:

> Adults have to be conscious of a rise and fall in children – like the rise and fall of the tide – of courage and confidence. Some days kids have a tiger in their tank. They're just raring to go; they're full of enthusiasm and confidence. If you knock them down, they bounce up. Other days you scratch them and they pour out blood. What you can get them to try, and what you can get them to tolerate in the way of correction or advice, depends enormously on how they feel, on how big their store of confidence and self-respect happens to be at the moment.[27]

Absorption

We should not leave the subject of learning and emotion without acknowledging the importance of the positive feelings of learning. Mihaly Csikszentmihalyi of the University of Chicago has collected many accounts of the kind of learning

experience that involves complete absorption.[28] He has called
this state 'flow' because there is such a good match between
the learner's motivation, her learning power and the demands
of the task that there is simply no room left over to feel self-
conscious, to be aware of any extraneous considerations, or
even to be concerned, in that moment, with success or failure.
The flow is accompanied by a feeling of total concentration
and even excitement. Csikszentmihalyi's research shows how
this intense learning state can occur in any activity given the
optimal conjunction of interest, skill and the intrinsic challenge of the activity itself. Surgeons enter flow while performing complex operations. Sportsmen and women find flow
when their skills are being stretched to the limit. Diane
Roffe-Steinrotter, skiing gold medallist in the 1994 Winter
Olympics, said after her winning run, 'I felt like a waterfall.'[29]

Good school students tend to be those who can gain access
to the state of flow whilst they are studying. When a group of
students at a Chicago high school were asked to keep a record
of their feelings whilst they were studying, the high achievers
claimed to enter this state of pleasing, challenging absorption
about 40 per cent of the time; those who were achieving less
well reported flow only 16 per cent of the time. For them the
more familiar feeling was of self-consciousness, pressure and a
kind of anxiety that was distracting rather than focusing.[30]
These low achievers found their flow principally in social
relationships and physical pursuits. Daniel Goleman, commenting on this study in *Emotional Intelligence*, says: 'Sadly,
the low achievers, by failing to hone the skills that would get
them in flow [when studying], both forfeit the enjoyment of
study and run the risk of limiting the level of intellectual tasks
that will be enjoyable to them in the future.'[31] As Goleman
says, we can learn how to access the flow state, and when we
do so learning becomes more attractive and enjoyable.

This chapter has explored some of the ways in which feelings
are involved with learning. Learning often takes place close to
the emotional point where challenge may tip into threat. It is
therefore very important, if people are to develop their learning power to the maximum, that they understand the necessity, even the value, of emotions in the context of learning;

that they develop the ability to appraise situations accurately, so that they engage with ones that are safe enough and worthwhile enough, and avoid the ones that are genuinely dangerous or not worth it; that they don't magnify unnecessarily the aversiveness of these feelings; and that they develop an increasing ability to tolerate and manage the inevitable feelings of learning. As a continuation from Chapter 1, we have seen how a variety of beliefs can shift the learner's relationship with the feelings of learning for the worse. Concern with beliefs about self-worth and self-efficacy must be added to beliefs about ability and the nature of learning itself if we are to make sure that resilience, the first R of learning power, is to be at its strongest. Having established the emotional background, it is now possible to go on to look at the second of the three Rs: resourcefulness.

THREE

Immersion:
Learning through Experience

Once the foundation stone of resilience has been laid, the *how* of learning can be built on top: the repertoire of learning strategies that comprise the good learner's toolkit. As well as being resilient, learners need to be *resourceful* in the face of uncertainty. They need to know what to do when they don't know what to do. Identifying the major compartments of the toolkit, and exploring what they are good for and how they themselves develop, is what Chapters 3–11 are about.

Animal learning

The first compartment is the one I have called 'immersion': the ability to learn from experience. This is our evolutionary starter pack – the learning ability that we share with other animals; and very smart it is too – even in small mammals and birds, for example. For magpies and mynah birds, roadkill is an easy source of protein, but potentially as hazardous for them as it was for the squashed possum on tonight's menu. Such birds have learnt to judge the speed of traffic precisely, interrupting their dinner only at the last minute to hop out of the way. Pigeons can quickly come to classify widely differing pictures solely on the basis of whether the scene contains a fish (which pigeons do not eat), and can learn to distinguish oak leaves from all other leaves, scenes with or without a body of water in them, and pictures showing a particular person from others containing different people.[1]

If rats eat a new and a familiar food together, and then get sick, they will avoid the new food but continue to eat the familiar one – even though the sickness may begin quite some time after eating.[2] Chimpanzees have learned to count, pushing a panel with the appropriate digit on it when their trainer puts different numbers of sweets on a tray in front of them. Some dogs can be trained to detect and respond to the extremely subtle signs of an imminent epileptic attack in their owners, giving the person precious seconds in which to pull over in the car, sit down or alert a companion.[3]

What all these examples of learning have in common is the ability to detect patterns that recur across a range of contexts and experiences. The most important part of these patterns is what happens over time. If you are able to pick up contingencies between what's happening now and what is going to happen next, this gives you a clear evolutionary advantage. You can capitalize upon these predictions by taking evasive action, or by intervening in the flow of events to your own benefit.

Learning in young children

This same learning ability is the one that starts operating automatically in children even before they are born. Just a few days after birth, a baby will selectively turn towards a rhythmic sound which was played to them while still in the womb. But it is during the first year of the baby's life that this marvellous natural learning ability really gets going – for example, the baby's ability to learn the facial expressions that correspond to different basic emotions, and to adjust their own expression and behaviour accordingly. In one study, babies were shown pictures of four different women – not their mothers – all of whom were wearing the same emotional expression: surprise, perhaps, or happiness. Gradually, as they got used to the pictures, the babies looked at them less and less. However, babies of six months or older increased their attention again when shown a picture of one of the women with a new expression. This showed that they had been able to extract the pattern that corresponded to the emotion from the

patterns that corresponded to the four different faces themselves.[4]

Seven-month-old babies are also able to tell that a certain
emotional expression goes with a certain tone of voice. They
can record patterns that involve combinations of different
senses. Researcher Arlene Walker-Andrews presented her babies with two films side by side, one of which showed an
angry face and the other a happy one. At the same time, they
could hear a soundtrack of either an angry or a happy voice.
The infants reliably chose to spend more time looking at the
face that matched the voice: while listening to the happy
voice they gazed at the happy face; when they heard the angry
voice they switched their attention to the angry face.[5]

The intricacy and quantity of such learning in the first two
years of a child's life is astounding. Children discover all the
detailed ways in which their senses match up with their action
– what kinds of sight are produced by moving the hands in
certain ways; what kinds of sensation are produced by sucking
the toes; what kinds of sound are created by different configurations of the vocal cords. They learn their particular family's
scripts for feeding, bathing, going to sleep and so on. They
learn many of the idiosyncrasies of their family members and
how to adjust their interactions to take account of individuals
and their moods, and they learn how to suss out strangers
more quickly and more effectively. (If I smile, do they smile
back? Do they initiate the kinds of interactions which I am
familiar with, and enjoy?) They learn to recognize the tastes
and sights and smells and sounds of their world, and to take
some of the initiative in exploring them. And they learn how
to orchestrate that extraordinary combination of movements
that constitutes walking. All this and much more.

During these early years learning through sheer immersion
in experience also lays the foundations for the development
of the other main compartments of the learning toolkit. Not
only are children discovering all kinds of ways of predicting
and controlling their world directly; they are also beginning to
learn how to amplify their own learning. They begin to
understand and produce language, not knowing yet how this
will burgeon into a major section of the learning toolkit. They
learn the rudiments of pretend play, again without realizing

that this will grow into the whole learning realm of fantasy and imagination.

Immersion is not just for kids

The development of these other forms of learning will be explored in the following chapters. But one important general point needs making clearly at the outset. The fact that some of our valuable 'ways of learning and knowing' start to develop later does not mean that they are in some sense superior to learning through immersion, or more powerful, and that they should therefore be seen as superseding it, and encouraged to do so. We do not progress upwards through a sequence of ever more powerful learning stages, leaving each one behind as we move on to the next. Rather we add new tools to the toolkit, increasing our repertoire of alternatives and the complexity of the learning we can undertake. And we continue throughout life to practise and develop each of the constituent skills of learning side by side.

However, some very influential voices have suggested otherwise. The great Swiss developmentalist Jean Piaget, for example, identified roughly the same kinds of learning, appearing in the child's development in the same sequence, as I propose; but he made the mistake of assuming that, as each new compartment developed, so the earlier ones became redundant, or were radically transformed so they could be subsumed within the new kind of thinking and learning. In effect, the goal of development was seen as being the appearance of the abstract, analytical intellect, and the earlier modes of mind as a series of stepping-stones to get there. This belief has contributed significantly to the widespread tendency of education (as discussed in Chapter 1) to focus on, value and develop intellectual forms of learning to the neglect of the equally valuable others.

The mistake of infantilizing learning through experience, and glorifying intellect, is still being made. Howard Gardner, Professor of Education at Harvard, Director of the influential Project Zero, and originator of the widespread idea that children are born not with a single intelligence but with seven or eight multiple intelligences, is guilty of this. In his book *The Unschooled Mind*, Gardner introduces us to 'three characters who will accompany us throughout the book'. The first is the 'intuitive learner (sometimes known hereafter as the natural, naive or universal learner), the young child who . . . evolves serviceable theories of the physical world and of the world of other people during the opening years of life'. Note the conjunction of 'intuitive', 'naive' and 'young'. This primitive being is contrasted with the 'traditional student' or 'scholastic learner', aged between seven and twenty, and finally with the 'disciplinary expert', who can be any age and has 'mastered the concepts and skills of a discipline', for example 'students who are able to use the knowledge of their physics class or their history class to illuminate new phenomena'.[6]

At the pinnacle of human development, in Gardner's view, stand the graduate student and the professor, busy applying their academic knowledge in creative ways, eyes fixed firmly on a Fellowship of their professional Academy and a Nobel Prize. At the bottom, gazing upwards in awe, totters the unformed child, concerned only with 'evolving serviceable theories' – intuitive ones, note, not well articulated – of the real world of things and people. The non-intellectual learner's life is seen as not only impoverished but dysfunctional. For Gardner also tells us that children 'who have perfectly adequate intuitive understandings often exhibit great difficulty in mastering the lessons of school. It is these students who exhibit 'learning problems' or "learning disorders" '.[7] There are indeed different ways of going about learning and knowing; but there is no need to arrange them, as Piaget and Gardner do, in a hierarchy of esteem. To do so reflects not a scientific discovery, but a rather uncritical acceptance of Western society's lop-sided love affair with clarity and articulation.

An adult learns to walk

One of the main indications of the fact that learning through immersion is not superseded by other forms of learning is the rediscovery of its importance in adulthood. Let me introduce this idea with a personal example.

A few years ago I was hiking along the beach from one small village on the island of Crete to the next, about a two-hour walk. It was eleven o'clock in the morning: I had left too late and the day was already blisteringly hot. The beach was narrow, stony and sloping, and in places the cliffs fell right into the sea, so I had to paddle. I had a heavy rucksack on my back and an old pair of sandals on my feet. The sandals were necessary because some of the stones were sharp, but when they got wet my feet would slide about and make walking even more difficult. I gradually became aware that the familiar activity of walking had become strange and problematic, and that, for some time before I consciously realized it, I had been paying careful attention in order to make it as successful as possible under these new conditions.

What I had been doing was both refining my perception and modifying my stride. I was picking out those surfaces that made walking easier, and planning my route for the next few metres accordingly. The best stones to walk on, I had discovered, were about 20 centimetres or so across. Sand I sank into; small pebbles got trapped inside my sandals and hurt; slightly bigger ones slid about too much; and big rocks were no good because, though stable, they had to be climbed up and down, and with the rucksack that was hard work. And at the same time as I had been developing these finer than normal discriminations. I had been experimenting with my walking pattern. My stride had become shorter, I was trying to move smoothly to avoid disturbing the stones, and I was keeping out of the water as much as possible to stop the sandals getting slippery.

Some of the general characteristics of this mundane example of learning turned out to be remarkably similar to those of the animal and baby kinds of learning described earlier. It involved detecting patterns and making distinctions, in this case between the way different kinds of surfaces looked, and learning to use these to predict what would happen when I trod on them. I noticed that my learning involved coordinating these perceptual developments with my physical responses. The distinctions I was making were not just those that were 'there' to be found; they were the ones that I could actually respond to and make use of. If I hadn't had the rucksack I would have chosen to follow a trail of the bigger rocks, because climbing up and down would not have been a problem. That day, however, my repertoire of possible movements was more restricted.

But I wasn't just selecting from a ready-made repertoire of ways of walking; I was tuning my walking to suit the terrain. Some new choreography was being developed. Like most learning, this involved not starting from scratch, but taking existing know-how and refining it. I wasn't starting a new page in my learning book so much as writing a variation on a very well-known theme: one that integrated the possibilities I was growing to discern with the capabilities I possessed.

I realized that this process of tuning was cumulative: it developed over time. It involved trial and error, and the slow growth of the ability to consolidate my new pattern of seeing and walking, and to gain more reliable control over it. Not all stones of the same size behaved the same. In order to gain in confidence I had to keep on checking and tuning.

These changes in perception and gait were no mere academic exercise. I had a problem to solve: the walking was uncomfortable, even painful sometimes; I felt clumsy; and I was hot, bothered and thirsty. I wanted to get to the next café just as soon as I could. From all the possible ways of categorizing the stones on the beach, I was busy uncovering one way – not necessarily the only way – that would get me where I wanted to be. From all the possible walks I was capable of producing, I was working on the ones that meshed with my current motivations. This kind of learning is rather Darwinian: I produce 'mutations' – small variations of my normal walking style – and the ones that turn out to be the 'fittest' survive.

Learning to walk seemed to require some awareness, I noticed, but not necessarily very much conscious, deliberate or focal awareness. Of course I was, at some level, being attentive to the beach, to how my walking felt, to the small improvements that I was gradually making; but by the time I 'came to' and realized that I was learning to walk, most of the work had been done. While I had been preoccupied with fantasizing about a cold beer, my brain had been getting on with the job of learning without me. Just as a car driver can 'come to' after twenty minutes' animated conversation with her passenger and realize that the car had been driving itself, so my learning had been proceeding very successfully on 'automatic pilot'. Nor, when I became more fully conscious of what was going on, did I suddenly start learning better or faster.

However, my general state was definitely affecting the efficiency of my learning. Just before I got consciously interested in my learning I had been getting hot and bothered, irritated with the stupid beach and the stupid sandals, wondering how far the stupid café was, wishing I had not decided to pack so much stupid stuff, feeling stupid for having started out so late, and so on. My mind was beginning to shift from intuitive learning into conscious fantasy: wishing the situation were different, rather than looking for ways of accommodating myself to it. I am sure that, under these conditions, my learning had been deteriorating. I was more inclined to kick the stupid stones than to pay attention to them.

I realized, as I thought about it, that this little episode was not particularly unusual. I am involved in such unsung background learning much of the time. Each time I perform an everyday task such as cooking a meal I am refining my intuitive understanding of how long after you put the potatoes on you start the steak; how long the grill takes to get up to full heat; how big I prefer the bits of onion in the pizzaiola sauce; whether a handful of fresh coriander thrown in at the end is an inspired improvisation or a big mistake; and so on.[8]

Immersion in the laboratory

We do not have to rely on such anecdotal evidence, however. There are now many laboratory studies which demonstrate the importance of unreflective, unarticulated learning through experience – just picking up useful patterns by osmosis – in daily life. Dianne Berry of the University of Reading and the late Donald Broadbent of Oxford asked people to take part in a computer game which involved changing the values of a number of variables in order to try to keep within certain bounds the output of a hypothetical sugar-processing factory.

The players were free to vary such factors as the size of the workforce and the level of incentives, and after each play the computer would tell them what level of output had been produced. The relationship between the input variables and the output was controlled by a reasonably complex, and sometimes rather counter-intuitive, equation which the players were not, of course, explicitly told.[9]

Players started out making guesses, but rapidly began to gain control until they were reliably meeting the required target performance. At this point, however, they were unable to say what it was they had learnt: they had acquired the know-how but not the knowledge. It was only after a great many more goes, if at all, that any conscious understanding of what was going on began to come. And it was not until understanding dawned that the players felt fully in control. Their confidence in their competence seemed to track their comprehension rather than their competence itself. They tended to underestimate their own performance and to lack confidence in the perfectly valid hunches which were guiding their actions.

So practical mastery of complex environments can emerge through immersion and experimentation, in the absence of conscious understanding, for adults just as it does for children and animals. It should come as no surprise, for we use this kind of learning all the time and are often able to do things without being able to say why or how. Driving round a city that you haven't lived in for many years, you just have a feeling that the railway station is coming up on the left, or that you need to turn right at the next lights.

What we may not realize so clearly, however, is that learning through immersion can actually be smarter than rational thought. Pawel Lewicki and his colleagues at the University of Tulsa in the United States have reported a very illuminating series of experiments that demonstrate this graphically. In one of these, the student volunteers were shown a long series of photographs of people's faces, and asked to predict 'intuitively' each person's character. The 'right' answer was in fact a complex function of the different facial features, so that someone with a long nose, a ruddy complexion and a crew-cut would be classified as 'kind', for example. Attention was not drawn to these associations, and the participants remained unconscious of them throughout. Nevertheless, they became skilled at using these contingencies to assign the right character to a new face, but could not say why or how they were doing so. Even when the students were told the nature of the game and were offered financial inducements to try to detect and formulate the rules consciously, none of them was able to do so.[10]

Lewicki's studies are different in one crucial respect from the factory experiments of Broadbent and Berry: in the latter, most people were able to work out the problem consciously – in the end. The equation that the computer was using was perfectly comprehensible; it just took a long time for it to come into conscious focus. Here, however, the rules that people were undeniably detecting and using to aid their performance were too complex for them to figure out, even given plenty of time and favourable conditions. Lewicki's studies show that unconscious, natural learning by immersion is able to detect and deal with more complexity than conscious reason can. This is a salutary reminder of the folly of neglecting the non-intellectual compartments of the learning toolkit.

Nor should we assume that such learning only applies to practical topics and physical domains. Paradoxically, intuitive expertise may also emerge slowly and inexplicably in intellectual domains as well. Scholarly kinds of learning often involve gradual mastery of a complex field: the slow dawning of insights and realizations, or an emerging, holistic, intuitive grasp of concepts and their inter-relationships, rather than the methodical accumulation of skills and information. One of the fathers of research on 'learning by osmosis', as he called it, is Arthur Reber of Brooklyn College in New York. In a recent overview of the field, Reber confessed that

It has always been, for me, the most natural way to get a grip on a complex problem. I just never felt comfortable with the overt, sequential struggles that characterized so much of standard learning. . . . What seemed for me to be the most satisfactory of 'learnings' were those that took place [when] one simply steeped oneself in the material,

often in an uncontrolled fashion, and allowed understanding to emerge magically over time. The kind of
knowledge that seemed to result was often not easily
articulated; and most interesting, the process itself
seemed to occur in the absence of the effort to learn
what was in fact learned.[11]

Classroom performance

There are many examples of how people's real-life learning is
influenced by the patterns they have unwittingly picked up
just in the course of living. Take school, for example. Each one
of us has sat through thousands of hours of classroom time,
consciously grappling with our translations and equations but
also witnessing a wide array of performances of 'teaching'.
Looked at from this point of view, lessons are a succession of
episodes in which a variety of characters offer different interpretations of the role of teacher, and we have been the
audience. If learning through experience is, as the evidence
suggests, going on all the time whether we know it or not, it
would not be surprising if each of us had been left with a
largely intuitive set of ideas about what a teacher is: a range of
dispositions and tendencies through which *we* would interpret and respond to classroom behaviour, if we were ever to be
in that position.

Studies by Peter John, a colleague at the University of Bristol
Graduate School of Education, have shown how this residue
of experience influences the learning of student teachers.[12]
Their deep-seated, largely unconscious, images of classroom
life determine how they first go about the business of teaching. This protracted 'apprenticeship of observation', as John
calls it, has often been distilled into composite images of the
'good teacher' and the 'bad teacher': the teacher they would
like to be like (but fear they may not be able to emulate), and
the teacher they would hate to be like (but fear they may have
more in common with than is comfortable). One student
teacher, for example, said: 'I want to be like Mr Gatjik – he
was one of my main reasons why I decided to teach – he was
one of my gurus at school. His lessons were so stimulating . . .

he cared and took time over problems. He would explain things after the class and was always cheerful and enthusiastic about history. You could tell he cared and he knew his subject so well. I'm not sure I can live up to his example.' A bad teacher, on the other hand, 'dictated everything but we still couldn't understand what he said. . . . His lessons were dead lessons. To start with his classroom management was terrible; he would shout at people and threaten them but it still didn't work. . . . He had no teaching techniques – he babbled; he was badly organized and sometimes brought the wrong notes to the lesson. We didn't always tell him, though: we just pretended to write and had a rest.'

Teacher educators often encounter reluctance on the part of their students to think in detail about what they are doing and why, and this stems directly from these intuitive templates: from their form as much as their particular content. For what the pupil audience sees *is* a performance. They see a character on stage, and they judge what they see. They don't see behind the scenes to the rehearsals, plans and doubts that preceded the performance and may underlie it still. They are learning what they, as pupils, enjoy and respond to; not what it is like to be – and especially to learn to be – a teacher. Thus they describe teachers in terms of their own youthful responses to the personalities they have seen portrayed, and in some cases, as Peter John shows, to composite and idealized (or demonized) caricatures. This leads many of them to the view that teaching is about personality, and that good teachers are those who are blessed with limitless knowledge, enthusiasm and empathy – a view which may be intimidating, and which certainly downplays how much there is to learn about the craft of the classroom. They become impatient with any attempt to analyse or theorize classrooms and teaching, and if they do see any need, or possibility, to learn, it is in terms of sure-fire tips and superficial recipes for class control.

Especially if their schooldays have been relatively orthodox and successful, many prospective teachers will have picked up the idea that learning is essentially about the transmission, acquisition, retention and display of 'knowledge'. History, for example – the subject that Peter John's students were learning to teach – was, for many, about 'getting the facts', and a firm grasp of 'knowledge' had to precede any application of it. For instance, one student, after observing a successful classroom role-play, claimed that 'although the children were enjoying themselves and were clearly putting their knowledge to good use, they surely can only do that at the end of a topic because there has to be such a lot of hard-nosed learning of dates, events, places and people before they can go on to interpret those facts in the form of a role-play'. While there is some truth in this, it is very far from the whole truth. It can help children's learning enormously to throw themselves into a topic imaginatively before they have been peppered with 'the facts'.

This knowledge-focused model reinforces teachers' belief that they have to be the fount of all knowledge – a belief that makes student teachers very anxious, and often leads them to focus their efforts at preparation on mugging up the subject rather than thinking about appropriate teaching and learning strategies. Not to know is, for them, to be caught out, to be found wanting, and thus to risk the loss of the pupils' respect. Nor is there any recognition that part of the work of schools, in the age of uncertainty, is to help students develop and practise a whole range of different ways of learning and knowing, not just one. The idea that genuine confusion and uncertainty are part of learning, and that if children are to become good learners they have to get used to operating under such conditions, is, on this model, unintelligible. The idea that it might be useful for teachers to model for children 'what to do when you don't know what to do' would, for many of these students, be unthinkable.

The brain-mind

What gives us and animals this ability to recognize and adapt to the particular patterns that our environments contain is, of course, the brain – or the brain-mind, as cognitive scientists tend to refer to this mysterious conglomerate of nervous tissue and conscious experience. Experience creates lasting changes in the ease with which small electrical charges can jump the tiny junctions called synapses between nerve cells, and thus wears functional grooves and channels along which the brain's activity comes to prefer to flow. When different nerve cells are simultaneously active this process of synaptic facilitation binds them together, so that in future when only part of the pattern is directly activated there is an automatic tendency for the rest to be recruited. So the adaptability of the brain enables it to fill in gaps in experience on the basis of what has happened before, and to anticipate what might be about to happen. When these 'sensory' patterns in the brain get functionally linked into the circuitry that corresponds to our 'priorities' and our 'skills', then the brain becomes able all by itself, as it were, to select actions that have a chance of diverting the course of events in favourable directions.

We might see learning through immersion in experience as occurring via the progressive erosion of interconnected hollows and valleys within a neural landscape. Although genetically precontoured in certain ways, this *brainscape*, as I shall call it, becomes progressively more variegated, and more idiosyncratic, as a result of each person's unique experience. The more firmly a group of features have become functionally stuck together, the deeper the valley they comprise.[13]

The fact that learning by immersion is directly underpinned by the intrinsic modus operandi of the brain has been graphically demonstrated by computer simulations using simplified brain-like systems – so-called neural networks. For example, the sophisticated human ability to recognize and 'read' faces which, as we saw earlier in this chapter, even babies are busily developing, has been mimicked by such an artificial brain. Gary Cottrell and his research group at the University of California at San Diego have created a neural network that can learn to tell a small number of people apart, even though each person's face can appear in an infinite number of different settings, distances, lightings, expressions and so on.[14]

With a 'training set' of 64 different photographs of 11 different faces, plus 13 non-faces, each presented several times, Cottrell's 'brain' reached a level of perfect recognition. Nothing very impressive about that, you might say. After all, the computer could simply have rote remembered each of the correct responses to each of the 77 stimuli. But what happens when you now give the network photos of Andrew with tousled hair and without his glasses, or Bobbie wearing a beret, which it has never seen before? Or an even more severe test: show it completely new people and see if it can tell their gender. The performance was impressive: the network correctly identified 98 per cent of the new shots of familiar people, and got the gender of new people right on 81 per cent of occasions. Even when up to one-fifth of a familiar person's face was blanked out, the network still recognized them almost perfectly.

In a later version of the experiment, Cottrell tried to replicate in his network babies' ability to distinguish between emotional expressions of the same person, as well as between different people. He took photographs of 20 undergraduates, each producing expressions of astonishment, delight, pleasure, relaxation, sleepiness, boredom, misery and anger, and trained the network on these 160 stimuli. After 1000 presentations, the network was able to recognize and distinguish each of the first four 'positive' emotions, as well as anger, with about 80 per cent accuracy. Sleepiness, boredom and misery it was never able to get the hang of – possibly because Cottrell's volunteers turned out to be rather mediocre actors. Nevertheless, the program compares favourably with a six-month-old infant: no mean feat given the vastly different sizes of their respective 'brains'.

Know-how without knowledge

The crucial question about such artificial brains – and real brains, come to that – is: what exactly have they learnt? They have acquired the requisite expertise, just as I did walking on my Cretan beach, but in what form is that knowledge represented? To continue with Cottrell's face recognition program, we can ask how, as a result of its training experience, the network has got wired together. What features of the faces has it extracted? The answer is surprising. You might have thought that the network would gradually come to 'parse' the faces, in the way that we do in everyday speech, into eyes, noses, mouths and shapes, and differentiated the faces in terms of length of nose, distance apart of eyes, size of mouth, round versus oval face shape, and so on.

Not a bit of it. What the network has picked out is a set of holistic features of faces, entire face-like templates, which correspond neither to any of the particular faces which they were shown, nor to any of the features for which ordinary language has words. What the brain 'knows' implicitly is very effective, but it is not represented in such a way that it can be turned into explicit knowledge. Neural networks, in other words, behave just like animals and children and adult experts of all kinds: their know-how develops in the absence of conscious, articulate understanding, and it is internally formatted in a way that cannot readily be explained. No wonder that it is so hard for a dressmaker or a stand-up comedian or a schoolteacher to tell you what it is they know. Know-how and knowledge inhabit different worlds.

To do its delicate work of detecting recurrent patterns, distilling them into useful concepts and generalizations and hooking them up to our developing repertoires of both skills and motivations, the brain needs no supervision. In a baby learning to recognize facial expressions, a medical student learning to recognize tumours on an X-ray, or a wine-buff developing the subtlety of her palate, the brain delivers learning without any conscious intention, deliberation or comprehension. These may come later, or they may come not at all. Whether the lack of explicit understanding is a handicap depends on the specific demands of the situation and the goals of learning. A wine-master may need to be able to articulate her learning. The enthusiastic amateur may very well not. It depends. We shall look later at the relationship between explicit and implicit learning, knowledge and know-how.

For now, though, we need to look in more detail at how this marvellous natural learning ability with which we come genetically endowed develops. First evolution,. and then human culture, have discovered a host of ways in which this basic capability can be augmented and transformed. So the next question is: what are these learning amplifiers, and how do they themselves grow in power and sophistication?

FOUR

Extending Natural Learning: The Basic Amplifiers

The fundamental kind of pattern extraction that the brain performs relies on a certain form of attention. For learning to occur, there must be contact. Patterns of stimulation from the world have to impinge on the nervous system. But the best way in which to discover fresh patterns is for this attention to be unselective, receptive and open: to meet the world without preconceptions. If there are new contingencies to be discovered, this mode will find them. Through gradual strengthening of the repeated circuits in the neural networks of the brain, any patterns that are there simply emerge from a background of 'noise'. This kind of broad, unfocused awareness is, as computer jargon would put it, the default mode of the brain. It is evolutionarily the most basic form of attention. In unfamiliar situations it remains, even for sophisticated adult human beings, the most essential learning tool.[1]

Everyday language does not distinguish clearly between consciousness and awareness, but to talk about this receptive mode of the brain we need to be able to talk of forms of awareness that involve very little consciousness, and sometimes none at all. As Pawel Lewicki's experiments showed, we can pick up patterns, and make good use of them, without any conscious awareness of any learning having taken place. There is now plenty of evidence that information can be registered and retained even when the person is totally unconscious. Patients have been found to recover faster from surgery if given helpful or soothing instructions whilst under general anaesthetic. It is also possible to induce under hypnosis a state of deafness in which the subject is unaware of any sound, and yet you can talk in a normal voice to a so-called hidden observer inside the person, who is perfectly capable of responding to instructions and retaining information.[2]

Evolution, however, has discovered methods and strategies by which the quality of this basic awareness can be intensified or improved. Just as telescopes, telephones and televisions serve as physical tools through which the natural senses can be amplified and extended, so animals – and especially the higher mammals – have evolved a variety of built-in methods for controlling attention, and thus making natural learning faster and more reliable. Once we have established a pattern in the brain, it can be very useful to be able to refine it by narrowing and directing attention more selectively.

Narrowing the focus of attention

One way to modify ambient awareness is by developing 'variable focus' attention, one of the most striking features of the human mind. Sometimes we are broadly aware of a situation – as we enter a crowded room, we take in the ambience in a general way. And sometimes our attention becomes highly focused and selective – we spot an old friend across the room, and suddenly all our attention zooms in on details of what she is looking like, how she has aged, whether she looks happy. Attention runs along a continuum from tight focus, like a spotlight, to low focus, like a floodlight. Spotlight mode segments and analyses; it makes a sharp distinction between what is 'relevant' to the current concern and what is not, and homes in on these preselected variables and facets. Floodlight mode, the 'default' one, illuminates less brightly, but may detect wider patterns and connections. These two ends of the focus dimension correspond to different ways of learning, and we have need of both.[3]

When it comes to learning, spotlight mode is very useful for focusing in on details of familiar scenarios that are discordant or problematic. Instead of waiting for further experience to 'tune' the pattern as a whole, we can attend to just that aspect where further learning seems to be required. Instead of one's attention being spread evenly over whatever is going on, or being grabbed by the most intense source of stimulation, learning is enhanced by focusing specifically on what is strange. My cat Bambosz sleeps through music, the washing machine and gun-fights on the television, but is instantly alert to small noises that do not fit into his scheme of things. He is aware of familiar sounds and smells only enough to be able to categorize them as familiar and safe. But he notices much more intently, and is briefly disconcerted by, a new rug, and seems not to be entirely at ease with it until he has 'killed' it a couple of times. Floodlight attention enables us to detect new patterns. Spotlight attention enables us to fine-tune existing patterns.

Concentration

Attention also varies in the quality of *absorption*. In some situations attention may be paid exclusively to the learning task in hand. The learner is 'locked on', absorbed, 'rapt'. This is the state, as we have seen, that American psychologist Mihaly Csikszentmihalyi refers to as 'flow'. One is oblivious of everything except the film, the music, the daydream, whatever. On the other hand, attention can be less than fully dedicated to the designated task. One's mental resources may be committed not 100 per cent but 60 per cent, with the remainder available to pick up interesting distractions. In an environment that is potentially dangerous and unpredictable, it may be highly advantageous to retain an amount of this ambient free-floating kind of attention. It pays small birds and herbivores, vulnerable when on the ground out in the open, to be very distractible, and people who are constitutionally anxious feel the same.[4] Get lost too much, for too long, in some fascinating activity and you may end up as somebody else's lunch or the butt of a joke.

Focus and absorption are different. 'Focus' refers to the way an amount of attention is distributed across the learning domain; 'absorption' refers to the proportion of total attention that is given to the designated learning task.

Engagement varies, too, in its *robustness* – how likely it is to survive a distraction or a disruption. One person's engage-ment may be quite fragile, hopping from one unstable focus to the next. Or their attention may be fragile in the face of upset or frustration: recall Carol Dweck's 'brittle' students (p. 34). Another person may be much more likely to return to a learning task in such circumstances. Their attention, although still perhaps capable of being called away, is more robust. All these dimensions – focus, absorption and robustness – con-tribute to what is commonly referred to as 'concentration'. The good learner is able without thinking to vary the direction and quality of her concentration to suit the occasion.

The ability to enter a state of undistractible, sustained absorption is a key feature of good learners, and one of their most priceless assets. A family friend said of the young Mozart that 'whatever he was set to learn he gave himself to so completely that he put aside everything else'; and 'as soon as he began to give himself to music, all his senses were as good as dead to other occupations'.[5] Newton, Einstein and Darwin were all characterized by the ability to direct focused and sustained attention on their chosen problems. Darwin, for example, insisted that he was not particularly clever, but that his success came from 'curiosity, determination and sheer hard work, combined with the patience to reflect or ponder for any number of years over any unexplained problem'.

Investigation

Having focused attention in the direction of what is novel, the next most basic set of learning amplifiers are those that intensify the quantity and quality of information coming from that source. Bambosz stops licking his paws and freezes, so that all his attentional resources are dedicated to the channel of sound and there are no distractions. He also swivels his head and ears so that his hearing is most acute in that direction. His eyes widen, to see if there is any tell-tale movement that goes along with the rustle. He doesn't just hear and see, he listens and looks. His nostrils twitch so that faint odours can be caught: he sniffs rather than merely smells.

Babies, too, are natural investigators. Strange objects can be approached and checked out – especially if there are other signals, from its mother, perhaps, that it is safe to do so. Engagement becomes active rather than passive. One 'asks questions' of this novel bit of the world by smiling at it, chewing it, prodding it and so on, so that it will reveal itself more fully, and learning will proceed from puzzlement to mastery more quickly. Animals and babies possess a number of these basic devices that are equivalent to the simple array of tests that student chemists are taught to apply to an unknown substance. Does it dissolve in water or acid? What happens when you heat it? Does it colour a flame?

Adults develop a more sophisticated set of tests that they can apply to other adults – at parties, for example. When I ask 'What do you do?' it is not so much a request for a person to rehearse his curriculum vitae as as invitation to reveal useful information about himself: his accent, his sense of humour, the quality of his eye contact, his tendency to be open or defensive, or the presence or absence of any reciprocal curiosity about me.

An animal that is able to deploy its learning resources selectively and judiciously, and to explore interesting situations in ways that maximize both its safety and the quality of the information it gets, develops its maps and models of the world more rapidly and efficiently, and extends the range of circumstances which it can meet with confidence and control. It needs to fall back less frequently on its non-learning survival strategies of withdrawal, aggression and so on. Judicious investigation, and the learning that accrues, make evolutionary winners. Curiosity may have killed a few cats, but evolution certainly eliminated many more incurious ones.

Imitation

A very powerful amplifier, widely distributed throughout the animal world, is imitation. Many species know the useful learning strategy of apprenticeship: you hang around a more experienced 'elder', watching what they do, what effects it has, and seeing if you can do it too. Juvenile beavers learn dam-building by imitating their parents. A sea-otter learns from its mother to balance a stone on its stomach as an anvil on which to crack open shellfish. By watching her, it finds out what are the best stones and the best shellfish. An orphaned sea-otter can learn these tricks by watching a human diver.

Babies who are only a few days old have been observed to copy facial expressions, and by ten weeks they are mimicking basic emotions such as happiness and anger. A friendly face tends to elicit a matching smile; an angry face, a corresponding frown.[6] Parents tends to encourage imitation as a form of play, but it is not long before its potential as a learning amplifier becomes evident to the child. For example, by watching their elders children learn what kinds of emotional reactions are appropriate to what kinds of objects and events. In the first year or so of life many children (like Ravi in the Introduction), when faced with something they are uncertain about, develop the habit of looking towards their mothers as if for guidance. They have learnt to take their emotional cue from her. A reassuring smile and a soothing tone of voice encourage the child to approach and investigate; an anxious look and an uncertain tone increase the likelihood of the child's withdrawal.[7]

By nine months babies have learnt to follow the line of their mothers' eyes, and to pick out the object of her attention that lies along that line. They can thus interpret her hesitancy or encouragement – her pleasure or distaste – as a comment upon that object in particular, not on the world in general, and tune their own tendencies to approach or withdraw accordingly. The significant people in a child's world are therefore able to influence very strongly the way in which the child applies different survival responses to different kinds of situation, developing a personal repertoire of preferences and aversions. One child may develop a phobia of spiders, but a trusting and sociable attitude towards strangers. Another may pick up an anxious antagonism towards men and a liking for sweet foods. Areas of the child's subsequent learning mobility are being opened up and closed down through their observation and emulation of these emotional reactions.

Observing the emotional reactions of people who are judged to be more experienced than ourselves in a situation, and the way they handle important events, continues to be an essential learning tool throughout life. The child on his first day at a new school, the adult in a new job, the first-time mother – all of these will be busy 'learning the ropes' by watching how others do things. Adults may be able to use more advanced strategies such as asking questions, reading manuals and going on training courses, but their more basic strategies of observation and emulation will still be hard at work – provided they have not been neglected or suppressed.

Off-duty learning: exploring and practising

There are other amplifiers of learning from experience that rely on the availability of leisure: time when you are neither directly engaged in pursuing important goals, nor resting and recuperating. In such recreational time you can go exploring – deliberately seeking out learning challenges to confront. Rats are notorious for their adventurous spirit. Even when all their physical needs are satisfied they will investigate an unfamiliar environment, and will actively work to gain access to new things to explore. Curiosity enables the rat to be not just responsive to the events that come its way, but to be proactive: positively searching for experiences that might have useful information embedded within them. Infants, it goes without saying, are inveterate explorers.

Another thing you can do in your leisure time is practising: attempting to replicate as precisely as possible a skilled action that has been found to be successful, but which is not yet specified clearly enough in the neural networks of the brain to be perfectly reliable. An eight-year-old endlessly bashing a tennis ball against the garage wall is practising. A twenty-three-year-old staying late in the lab, trying to replicate a difficult extraction technique, is practising. A raconteur polishing a new joke in front of the mirror is practising.

The sheer amount of practice seems to be the best predictor of a person's level of expertise. Across a wide range of skills, from musicianship to senior management, surveys show that around ten thousand hours' practice is required for mastery. Even to become a passable soloist on a musical instrument takes some three and a half thousand hours' practice. Contrary to common belief, virtuosi are characterized much more by their dedication than by their innate ability. They do not have some God-given talent that makes learning easy. What they do have behind them is usually a fortuitous set of circumstances that give them the confidence that mastery can be obtained, and therefore the commitment to 'go for it'; and the equally good fortune to have acquired the learning tools and habits that are appropriate for the chosen area of learning.[8]

Trying to repeat flawlessly a difficult passage of the sonata, and to adapt skills to minor variations in conditions, gradually develops the neural circuitry that is responsible for precise, adaptable control. We first cobble together an action that is a crude approximation to the desired one, then spend long hours sanding and smoothing and shaping it, so that it can be produced, in the heat of a recital, in a reliable, fluent and flexible fashion.

Playing

Practising in the narrow sense of repetition makes skills more reliable, but not necessarily more efficient or more adaptable. Once we are able consistently to 'get it right', it may be worth trying out different ways of getting it wrong, to see what happens. There are two reasons why this is a good idea, one obvious and the other more subtle. First, such a precautionary move may anticipate problems that could occur during the 'real-life' execution of the skill, and develop ways of meeting them. Having secured the ability to build a tower of blocks, young children learn more by seeing how insecure they can make it before it topples over. When they are in 'practising mode' the collapse of the tower signals failure, and may cause distress. When they are in 'playing mode' a similar event may be construed as interesting and informative, and even greeted with glee rather than frustration.

Similar kinds of play provide information about the behaviour of people as well as things. Having learnt how to elicit a positive reaction in a parent or elder sibling, children sometimes experiment by 'pushing it' to see how far they can go before things get rough, and what happens when they do. It is important to be able to get things as right as possible, but even more so to be able to right them when they have gone wrong. Adults at work, or as groups of friends, tease each other in this way to check the bounds of their friendship or to see how others react. Teasing becomes a powerful tool for finding out what makes others upset and how they behave when they are. It is a cunning tool for this purpose because, if you do 'go too far' and genuinely distress the other person, you can always tell them: 'It was only a joke!'

The second function of play takes a little more explaining. It has to do with the way know-how is organized in the mind. In both the child's and the adult's life, know-how accretes around repeated scenarios and predicaments – bathtimes, Sunday mornings, visits to Grandma, lectures, board meetings, whatever. These purpose-built packages of competence, crystallized by the brain out of recurrent patterns of experience, are all of a piece – there is no way in which the neural circuitry can be dismantled. And the skills acquired remain closely tied to the details of the situations in which they have been developed. The know-how that learning through immersion delivers is smooth, fast and effective within these familiar parameters; but relatively inflexible when the world becomes more complex, confusing or unrecognizable. And the know-how that lives within one of these 'scripts' cannot be combined, even when it might be useful, with skills that have been honed within a different domain. It is as if the know-how derived from different kinds of activity is stored in separate computer files, and while you are running one you cannot draw on any of the others.

The know-how of animals is mostly of this efficient but inflexible kind. Take the deceptive powers of the plover, for example, which will leave its nest to lead a potential intruder away from its fledglings, but cannot employ a comparable tactic to lead a competitor away from food, from a receptive mate, or from a piece of potential nesting material. In plovers, deception is a skill that is innately restricted to the script of protecting the young. They behave like people who can tell lies only about pilfering fudge, but not about dirtying the carpet, breaking the lamp, or taking money from their mother's purse.[9]

So this type of mental organization can be a handicap, especially under changing and uncertain conditions, and the powerful learner needs ways of overcoming it. In the brainscape, things are connected because they have tended to happen together, in both space and time, in everyday life. Clearly what is needed is a new form of learning which is capable of taking these packages of expertise to bits, exploring their interconnections, and constructing a new layer of know-how composed of more general concepts and combinable skills. For a chimpanzee capable of making this shift, 'sticks for playing with' and 'sticks for catching termites with' can now be grouped together under the general concept of 'sticks', and these concepts can act as the hubs through which several different scenarios can be linked. The knowledge of each script can now become much more widely available, and the power of the brain-mind to solve problems is incremented once again.

Though apes can conceptualize in a rudimentary way, the full exploitation of this new way of organizing knowledge is characteristically human. As cognitive scientist Andy Clark of Washington University puts it, 'the distinctive power of human cognition derives from its capacity to enrich itself from within. . . . On the cognitive bedrock of fluent but limited (because special-purpose) pockets of expertise, human beings have discovered how to erect a more powerful and flexible superstructure of conceptual thought.'[10] And the way we do it is through certain kinds of play.

Clark and developmental psychologist Annette Karmiloff-Smith have explored the appearance of this uniquely human learning mode in young children. Children, it turns out, have an innate tendency to seek greater flexibility and coherence within what they have already learned. What typically happens is that they will draw on their existing know-how, in whatever way they can, to learn to accomplish something 'on-line'. But after they have achieved adequate mastery they will go on through play to explore and even undo what they have just learnt, searching for anything that links this new ability with other pockets of expertise within the brainscape. Children spontaneously indulge in a kind of *learning beyond success*, in which the mind rewrites what it has learnt, segmenting out and rendering explicit concepts and skills that are common to different domains of expertise.

These periods of highly productive play can also give rise to a temporary phase of apparent incompetence in the domain in which successful control has already been achieved. For example, children of four or five are generally capable of drawing 'people' that have the right bits in roughly the right places, but their pictures are stylized and inflexible. If you ask them to draw a 'silly person' or an 'impossible person', they have great difficulty in playing around with the image. Over the next year or so, however, they begin spontaneously to produce their own silly or impossible people, seeming sometimes to have lost even their four-year-old competence. By the time they are eight they may well be able to dismember and adapt figures with ease, which enables them to take on much more complex artistic challenges. Their intermediate loss of competence has been the necessary precursor of a more mature ability.

This ability to learn a pocket of expertise, and then take it apart into a range of more flexible component concepts and skills, begins to make its appearance at around the age of four. But it does not do its work and then drop away – far from it. Such processes of segmentation and crystallization remain invaluable throughout life. For example, a pianist, when practising a new piece, tends to play the notes in sequence, stopping and working on the difficult passages until she can perform the whole piece right through. But at this stage there is often a degree of automaticity about the performance: the young pianist may have difficulty starting a section halfway through, and be unable to play variations on the theme. With more practice still, however, she becomes better able to start in the middle of a phrase, and to create improvisations and embellishments. In the wake of competent performance, with further work, flexibility and creativity emerge.[11] One might say that, in general, this is the difference between proficiency and virtuosity. The expert has achieved a level of mastery that permits playfulness: the ability to respond to unusual challenges, or even to 'break the rules', whilst still staying within the domain. A Picasso and a Pele are able to do things with brush or ball that the journeyman artist or footballer could neither conceive of nor carry off.

So play creates a second plane of interconnections in the mind that allows the know-how of different domains to become available to each other. Skills from different pockets of expertise can be linked, allowing more complicated learning and problem-solving. And it amplifies the extent to which we can solve problems within domains. When expertise fails, it may be possible to identify a crucial element of the expertise and work on that, rather than having to wait while the whole domain is gradually retuned through further experience. If a car breaks down, one tries to isolate the defective part and repair that – if a faulty spark plug can be replaced, the whole engine does not have to be overhauled. With the development of concepts comes the ability to target learning more carefully; to focus attention on the particular component skill or concept that is in need of rethinking. And learning power is thereby enhanced still further.

The experiments with children show two things about the process of segmenting know-how and extracting concepts. First, a 'failed' experiment can be just as informative as one that delivers smooth, quick success. What may look like regression to a concerned parent or teacher may be of inestimable value in the child's development as a learner. Second, this process of learning beyond success takes time; and how much time it takes, and what kinds of activities need to take place for it to happen, cannot be predicted or controlled by anyone, not even the learner herself. It is entirely dependent on what state her brain is in when she starts, and on her own shifting set of priorities. The brain has its reasons, of which the consciousness of the learner knows little, and that of the teacher almost nothing.

From these results we can distil two straightforward educational principles: playful experimentation, though vital, cannot be taught; and its development cannot be hurried. When educational establishments (from pre-school to university) are preoccupied with the rigmarole of teaching (syllabuses, lectures, textbooks and so on), and are always pushing eagerly for the next level of attainment, there is little hope that the brain-mind will develop organically in the way I have been describing. If it is force-fed with information and ideas faster than it can integrate them, it ends up with a mish-mash of half-digested knowledge that may possibly be regurgitated, but which lacks the intricate interconnections that keep the different areas of the naturally evolving brainscape tied together. And the unifying potential of home-grown conceptualization loses out to the impatience of those who, willy-nilly, must 'cover the curriculum'.

We have seen how evolution has developed some built-in ways of augmenting the natural learning power of the brain – through selective attention, the ability to focus and concentrate, actively intensifying sensory information, and investigating and exploring. In leisure periods, practising and playing can further refine the developing stock of concepts and skills. And over the course of the chapter we have moved from strategies that are common to many animals to an appreciation of those that are predominantly associated with people. With play, we stand on the threshold of the exclusively human. One more step is needed, though, and that is the ability to transform play from an external, physical activity to an inner, mental one. When that is accomplished, we enter the second main compartment of the learner's toolkit: the world of imagination.

FIVE

Imagination:
Learning in the Mind's Eye

'Before every shot I go to the movies inside my head. Here is what I see. First, I see the ball where I want it to finish, nice and white and sitting up high on the bright green grass. Then I see the ball going there: its path and trajectory and even its behavior on landing. The next scene shows me making the kind of swing that will turn the previous image into reality. These home movies are a key to my concentration and to my positive approach to every shot.'[1] Thus the great Jack Nicklaus describes one of the core features of his success in his book *Play Better Golf*, and he advises the would-be golf champion to do the same.

In the learner's toolkit imagination is the ability to sense and feel situations which are not physically present, and to explore how they might behave and develop in the mind's eye. In particular, we can investigate our own role in this unfolding, trying on different ways of 'being' and seeing what their imagined repercussions might be. The ability to 'go to the movies in your head' is one of the most powerful learning tools we possess. Whether getting ready for a difficult meeting, seeking a creative solution to a tricky problem, or simply trying to remember a shopping list, imagery is an invaluable resource. Children are adepts in the world of the imagination, and the value and validity of fantasy in their young lives is widely acknowledged. It is less generally realized that the same processes continue to serve as valuable learning strategies throughout life, if they are encouraged and allowed to; and that it is perfectly possible to go on getting better at the use of visualization and imagination as creative learning tools.

Pretend play

Imagination develops first as the internalization of children's 'pretend play'. From about eighteen months children start to engage in pretend play, acting, for instance, as if an empty cup contained milk that was too hot to drink. As we saw in Chapter 4, such play pushes the limits of reality in a number of ways. Metaphorically as well as literally you can play at dressing up, engaging in creative variations on familiar scripts, or introducing elements into one script borrowed from another, to see what happens. To pretend that an upside-down table is a boat, or that a banana is a telephone, you must implicitly accept some aspects of the metaphor and neglect others. The table's legs will serve as masts; the fact that it doesn't actually move we ignore. The shape of the banana is relevant to its use as a phone; its taste is not. So pretend play helps the process of deconstructing objects and events into their component features, and this, in turn, helps link different domains together, and boosts creativity.

Through pretend play and make-believe children are enabled to try out actions and roles that would be either impossible or dangerous in the real world. In that world, when a child plays with genuine fire she may sustain real burns. If she openly expresses genuine fears she may be laughed at. Putting out feelers into the future is a way of mapping out your own possible lines of development, of setting your goals and ambitions. It doesn't take children long to realize what potential this kind of play has for developing their mastery and understanding of the world.

By taking on the roles of others, children also develop their social skills. Through pretend play they can begin to feel their way into the skin of a greater variety of people, situations and emotions, and so extend their range of responses and understandings. If a child can build, inside her own brain-mind, a more delicate and accurate model of how another person will react and feel under various circumstances, she will be able to tune her interactions with them more successfully. If May correctly anticipates the strength of Tony's reaction to her 'borrowing' his toy, she may decide that discretion is the better part of desire on this occasion, resist the impulse to snatch it away, and avoid a major upset. Alternatively she may, on the basis of previous observations, classify Tony as a weak little wimp and take a chance. Even within their second year, children are beginning to be just as happy attributing feelings to a doll, and playing at responding to such feelings, as they are blowing the pretend steam off an empty cup to cool down non-existent coffee.

Pretend play, though, still has its downside. On the one hand, simulations and games do not always mimic the real world accurately, and the learning that results has to remain provisional until it has actually been 'tried in combat'. On the other, even pretend play may not be entirely safe. Acting out your fantasies has two dangers. Even though play is usually somewhat protected, there is still the chance that the rope will break as you swing, Tarzan-like, out over the stream; or that your friends will judge your attempts to be pathetic. And second, you may find that other people steal your good ideas. There are advantages to carrying out some of your fantasy work 'in private'.

And this is where imagination comes in. There is great learning value in making evident to ourselves, in the privacy of our interior play-space, the possibilities and implications latent within our own concepts and beliefs. Without risking public disdain, or giving away precious details of our tentative plans and aspirations, we can try on a range of possible selves and see how they fit. And besides, the inner theatre is much freer of practical constraints than the real world, so our excursions into the realms of the possible can become more creative. With the aid of imagination, and the limitless supplies of literature and drama with which it can be fed, we can travel further out, exploring the improbable and the bizarre as well as the more mundane variations on reality.

But there are cons as well as pros. Imagination may well be less vivid, less detailed, than a fantasy or an experiment that is played out for real. And, in the end, it can only draw out the implications of what we already know. Until they are actually acted out, fantasies do not generate genuine feedback from others. In the mind's eye we can see how our plans are working out and going down only through the perception of our own internalized audiences, which are cloudy mirrors of our own hopes and fears. To the extent that we have not represented the real audience accurately, we shall get unreliable data that may serve only to confirm our pre-existing assumptions. When imagination becomes only a kind of wish-fulfilling daydream (or nightmare), rather than a genuine test-bed, it loses its power as a learning tool.

The imagining brain

Imagination depends on changing the relationship between the level of neural activity in the brain and the senses and muscles to which the brain is connected. When we are physically active in the world, the senses are busy receiving information both from the outside world and from the feedback systems within the body and passing it on to the brain, where it gets channelled and transformed according to the dips and valleys left by prior experience. Likewise, these central channels deliver activity to the muscular systems of the body which makes them move. In 'immersion mode', senses, brain and muscles are all fully activated.

However, it seems that the human nervous system has developed the ability to damp down its own level of activation, so that physical movements can be reduced to a muscular excitation so small that they become invisible to others, yet still create a slight internal sensation of movement. For example, we may not realize that someone else's mood is affecting us physically. Yet Ulf Dimberg from the University of Uppsala in Sweden has shown that when people view a smiling or angry face, their own faces show evidence of the same mood through small changes in the facial muscles: changes that are often invisible to an observer, but which can be detected through electrical sensors.[2] Others have found that the same small activation of facial muscles is produced by asking people to imagine situations with different kinds of emotional tone. When they are asked to imagine a happy scene, activity increases in the muscles that are used to draw back the lips into a smile. When they are asked to visualize a sad or fearful situation, activity is greater in the muscles which cause a furrowing of the brow.[3]

Even more miraculously, the brain can also generate faint copies of the kind of sensory activity which would, in 'immersion mode', be driven from the outside. Nerves can carry from the brain to the sensory organs activity which mimics, in reduced form, that which would have arisen as a response to external stimulation. When people are imagining a visual scene, electrodes can detect these echoes in the muscles that control the movements of the eyes, for instance. It is these peripheral echoes of what is going on in the brainscape that give imagery its physical qualities.

But though the physical sensations of imagery may be faint – indeed there are people who say they are unable to generate internal images at all – the level of activity in the brain itself may be almost as great, when we are using our imagination, as when we are experiencing a real event. And as it is this central circuitry that changes when we learn, imagination, as we shall see, has the possibility to create substantial, long-lasting learning. As far as learning and memory go, the brain treats simulated and direct activity as the same.[4]

So imagination embodies fantasies and ideas and makes them concrete, and by doing so it enables learning to be more finely tuned and more practical. The rest of this chapter describes a number of clear demonstrations of just how practical a learning tool imagination can be – for adults just as much as for children.

Developing skills

Plenty of evidence proves Jack Nicklaus right in believing that visualization aids the development of physical skill. When physical practice is accompanied by regular mental rehearsal, performance increases significantly more than it does with practice alone.[5] Dwight Mendoza and Harvey Wichman asked a group of students to throw darts at a modified board on which the accuracy of their throws could be easily measured. Their score before any kind of practice gave a baseline measure against which to compare any subsequent improvements.

Then the students were divided into three groups. One was to report back for a follow-up test a week later. The second was to undertake two fifteen-minute sessions of practice for each of the next six days, trying to improve their score as much as possible. The third group was to spend the same amount of time sitting quietly and visualizing themselves throwing the darts as successfully as possible. They were instructed to 'feel' the dart in their hand, to 'see' the board, to 'hear' the dart hitting the target, and so on.[6] On the follow-up test, the no-practice group had improved by 5 per cent, the practice group by 34 per cent, and the imaginary practice group by 22 per cent. While direct, physical practice achieved the highest gains, the value of imagination was found to be substantial.

It turns out that feeling as well as seeing, hearing and so on is crucial. If you imagine watching yourself performing a skilled action from the outside, as if you were another person, your skill will be enhanced much less than if you imagine the action from the inside, with all the attendant physical and emotional sensations. Studies of people training in such varied skills as volleyball, karate and gymnastics have shown that improvements are achieved after mental practice only if the image is from a first-person perspective.[7]

Of course what you imagine is crucial. To get better, you have to imagine yourself doing better. The kind of 'worry' in which you vividly imagine yourself doing badly, or things going disastrously wrong, can generate a self-fulfilling pro-phecy. In one study, people practised their golf putting over six days. Before each putt, a third of the subjects were asked to imagine making the putt successfully; a third were asked to imagine just missing it; and the remaining third were given no imagery instruction. Those who imagined the successful putts improved their performance significantly more than the no-imagery group, while the 'missed putt' group performed worst of all.[8]

Amazingly, such 'mental practice' can even increase phy-sical strength. Over a period of four weeks Dave Smith and colleagues at Manchester Metropolitan University trained a group of men to increase the strength with which they could push sideways with the little finger of their right hand. The hand was strapped to a pressure-sensitive block, against which they were asked to make repeated attempts to push the finger out laterally. One group performed the exercise, while another was asked to imagine doing so. After the four weeks the force of the physical practice group had increased by 33 per cent, but those who had merely imagined the exercise also got stronger by over 16 per cent. Recording from the finger muscles showed that the muscular activity did increase somewhat during the periods of active imagination, just as in Dimberg's study of facial empathy (see p. 90). It looks as if the brain is able to reprogram itself effectively even on the basis of minimal bodily activity. It is not the exertion that counts, so much as the opportunity for the neural networks to gain more information with which to develop themselves.[9]

Preparing for demanding tasks

It is not just in the cultivation of physical expertise that imagery has its value. It helps in sorting out tricky situations and planning how best to tackle them. Shelley Taylor and her colleagues at the University of California, Los Angeles, have shown that imagination has a positive effect on students' preparation for examinations.[10] A week before their mid-term exams, first-year undergraduates in the UCLA psychology programme were given some training in the use of 'mental simulations' and asked to practise the technique for five minutes every day. They were instructed to visualize themselves studying in a way that would lead to the achievement of an A grade, and were given prompts such as seeing themselves sitting at their desks or in the library, getting up and turning off the TV, declining a friend's invitation to go out for a drink, and actively reviewing lecture notes. The effect was dramatic. Compared to a control group who did not go through this process, the visualizers started their revision earlier, spent a third longer actually studying, and improved their examination score from 65 per cent to 73 per cent.[11]

This beneficial effect of imagination on learning, however, was only found when the students focused on the actual studying. Another group who were asked to visualize themselves having obtained the A grade, feeling happy, confident and proud, showed no gains compared with the control group. In fact in a second study Taylor found that concentrating on images of success, rather than of studying, had negative effects. Those imagining the successful outcome did worse in the exam, and studied less, even than the control group. In other words simply daydreaming about fame and glory, without visualizing the steps needed to get there, is worse than useless. This is a case where research definitely improves on 'common sense', at least as expressed in self-help books, such as those of Norman Vincent Peale. Peale advises people who want to get ahead to 'hold the image of yourself succeeding, visualize it so vividly, that when [note 'when', not 'if'] the desired success comes, it seems to be merely echoing a reality that already exists in your mind'.[12] Sadly, such visions of glory don't turn out to possess the magical powers we would like them to have. It is imaginatively constructing the journey, not the arriving, that counts.

Estimating the time and effort it will take to learn something or complete a task is a useful ability that many people seem to lack. When Shelley Taylor's students were asked to 'estimate' the time by which one of their project reports would be completed, they showed the same kind of over-optimism: only 14 per cent handed the report in on time. Here again imagining the process can help, by creating a much more detailed 'map' on which the time estimate can be based. After visualizing in this way, the number of students handing in their work when they said they would tripled.

Stress and emotion

Imagery has proved useful in helping people overcome emotional difficulties: an important kind of learning. People who suffer from phobias, for example, are gently encouraged to face the fearful situation and to experience for themselves that it is not as dangerous as they had supposed. However, sometimes this may be impractical – when the feared situation cannot be reproduced for practical reasons, or when the fear is overwhelming. In these cases, encountering the situation in the imagination has proven therapeutic value – provided, again, that the person is able to generate an image that includes their feelings and incipient reactions.[13] In one study, people who showed a dramatic increase in heart rate in response to a request to visualize an unpleasant memory were much more likely to complete their course of therapy successfully than those who did not. Without a visceral response to their fearful images, people were less likely to overcome their phobias.[14]

People facing stressful events in everyday life can benefit from imagery too. In another study by Shelley Taylor, students were asked to focus on a real stressful situation in their lives, visualizing in detail how it arose, how it developed, what actions they had taken, the circumstances surrounding the problem, and how they felt about it. Another group visualized just a happy resolution of the situation, and a third, control, group visualized nothing. One week later the first group of students were feeling more positive about the issue, had taken more active steps to resolve the problem, and had been able to make more successful use of their social supports. The benefits were the same whether the stress was related to studies or relationships. Not only did the use of imagination lead to better planning and more effective coping; it had reduced the amount of negative feeling. Facing up to the emotional difficulties and 'feeling the feelings', even if only in fantasy, seems to enable people to cope in a calmer and more resourceful way. Imagination, in other words, can significantly improve resilience.

Creativity

Imagination also lays the foundations for a particularly vital form of creativity. Pretending that one thing is another enables you to link two separate domains of experience. Pretend play is the basis of metaphorical thinking. 'Let's treat this as if it were that. What possibilities emerge? How far can we push it before we reach the bounds of what can be done or said?' It is not so far from exploring a table's potential to be a pirate ship to seeing what you can say if you pretend that life is a journey, or that learning is a learnable craft like carpentry.

Science is full of stories of the creative power of imagination (though, as we shall see in Chapter 19, this power is as relevant to hard-nosed business executives as it is to scientists and, of course, artists). The general theory of relativity, for instance, developed from Einstein's trying to imagine what it would be like to ride on a ray of light. The Chinese chemist Yuan Tseh Lee won the Nobel Prize for his work on the dynamics of the encounters, during a chemical reaction, between individual molecules. Lee's breakthroughs came from imaginative visualization of these encounters, in many of which he envisaged the molecules having human-like motives and feelings. In a lecture given in Australia in 1996, he argued strongly that science students and others should be given practice and encouragement in the use of these imaginative arts.[15]

People who are able voluntarily to enter the realm of fantasy – to take a theme, and then let an imaginative scenario unfold like a dream or movie – have been found to be more creative than those who cannot. Interestingly, adults with more accessible and more powerful fantasy lives report that they have cultivated their powers of imagination since childhood. As children, they were more likely to have engaged in imaginative play, and to have been able to 'lose themselves' in the fantasy world of a book, than were adults with less vivid or less ready imaginations. It is tempting to read this, conversely, as indicating that some children may be beginning to lose their imaginative birthright even at quite young ages.[16]

There are some conditions, however, in which it is easy for anyone to fall into a state of reverie. Imagery becomes more fluid and vivid in a state of quiet relaxation and with a receptive, non-questing attitude towards the activities of one's own mind. Access to such a state can be gained on falling asleep or on waking up: it seems to be possible to cultivate a disposition to hang in those in-between states, and to allow hypnagogic (falling asleep) and hypnopompic (waking up) imagery to unfold itself. A classic survey by Peter McKellar of the University of Aberdeen in 1954 found that well over half of the 182 students questioned reported these sorts of experience, some of them predominantly auditory, some visual, some physical and some combined.[17] If imagination is as powerful a learning tool as the evidence shows it to be, then knowing how to access it most effectively is important.

One of the most salient characteristics of this drowsy imagery turns out to be its autonomous or uncontrolled quality. Short passages of mental video of random content appear to come and go of their own accord. One subject said: 'When the process is in full swing I feel as if I were a mere spectator at a performance of a rather eccentric kind.' Another respondent described a short sequence of images including a camel on a hilltop, fountain pens being filled, a screen composed of turkey feathers, a rowing eight on a river, and an ice-cream cone. To make full use of this well-spring of creativity, therefore, one needs to be at ease with its modus operandi. Anyone who has difficulty 'letting go' of mental control, or who gets worried when their unconscious throws up bits and pieces that do not make immediate sense, will feel uncomfortable with this learning tool.

Imagination as an aid to memory

When in a state of relaxed reverie, people also experience a degree of detailed access to their own memories which they could not match with their conscious intention. It is as if memories spontaneously appear with a degree of vividness and conviction that they may lack in the normal, busy state of mind. One of the students in Peter McKellar's survey said: 'Occasionally I hear the first movement of Rachmaninov's Third Piano Concerto, which I do not know well enough to construct in my mind when I am fully conscious.' Another reported that, as a young woman, after a day spent picking strawberries, her imagery was 'extremely vivid, in glowing colours (red and green, of course); a formal pattern of strawberry and leaf alternating. I was surprised at the time to find that I could visualize the characteristic leaf pattern so accurately, being usually ignorant on such points.'

This vivid memory of the strawberry leaf reminds us that imagery can also come to the aid of learning in the narrow, 'educational' sense, as in 'I've got to learn these French verbs', meaning 'memorize'. Newspapers and magazines frequently carry advertisements for systems that claim to help you remember people's names, or indeed foreign vocabulary and they all use mnemonic techniques that rely on imagery. Where you have to learn a connection between two or more words or entities that seem to have no meaningful association, you have two choices. Either you repeat them, pair-wise, until through sheer repetition their connection is stamped into the brain; or you concoct some meaningful glue to stick them together. It turns out that the latter, even though it requires a little thought, is more efficient and more reliable.

Suppose you need to learn that 'cabbage' in English is '*choux*' in French. Simply form a visual image of a pair of shoes made out of cabbages. If you are introduced to a Professor Barber at a meeting, imagine her in an old-fashioned hairdresser's chair being shaved with a cut-throat razor. And so on.

Though imagination is born in childhood, its value remains throughout life and its power and flexibility can, if we want it to, steadily increase. We can practise using imagery, learn to relax and let our minds float, and develop a sense of the kinds of situations in which imagination is the learning tool of choice. The widespread idea that as they grow up people can, and should, move through this stage and beyond it to intellectual ways of learning and knowing that make imagination redundant is a fallacy.

SIX

Learning Language:
The Beginnings of Intellect

The first compartment of the learning toolkit contains the tools for learning from direct immersion in experience, which begin to develop in breadth and sophistication during the first year of life. The second compartment contains strategies for learning through imagination, and these begin to proliferate and strengthen from the second year onwards. But alongside these crucial developments in learning power, and inter-twined with them, comes the burgeoning of the third great compartment of the learning mind: intellect, and the ability to use symbolic media of all kinds. In this chapter I shall sketch the way in which language itself is learnt, before turning to look at some of the many ways in which we come to be able to learn through language.

Learning to understand

Children's ability to understand and use language does not arrive out of the blue. It does not, as the influential American linguist and social critic Noam Chomsky erroneously thought, reflect the activity of some mysterious, special-pur-pose 'language acquisition device' pre-wired into the human brain. Rather it arises naturally from the spontaneous activity of the brain's 'natural learning ability': its propensity to modify its own functional connections in the light of recur-rent patterns of experience.

Let's just focus on sound for the moment. Many patterns of

sound are non-linguistic: in the vicinity of a baby cats purr, kettles boil, bathwater gurgles, music plays, traffic passes. But, just as small children are drawn to look at the features and nuances of the human face, so the most interesting and intricate sound patterns are the ones that other people make with their mouths. The average infant is immersed in a sea of speech, both directed at her and simply overheard. And gradually her brain begins to detect repeated cadences and fragments. The child comes not only to tell her mother's face from her father's, but to distinguish the two tones of voice and to make the connections that tie face and voice together. As we saw in Chapter 3, at only a few months old she already associates an angry voice and an angry face, and shows surprise when that association is disrupted. Babies rapidly become alert to the shifting vocal quality that signals approval or disapproval – pleasure, anxiety, reproof and so on – on the part of their carers, as well as to different individuals' voices.

But it is not only general qualities of speech that the child's brain begins to extract. Some much more specific patterns, continually repeated, and reliably associated with certain non-verbal situations, begin to emerge – the first words and phrases that she comes to 'understand'. 'Good girl,' says her mother, again and again, as the infant sucks quietly on breast or bottle, or 'What's the matter?' when she shows signs of distress; and, of course, she hears people's names, including her own. An ever-increasing number of verbal fragments become recognized components of familiar scripts. Mealtimes, bathtimes and bedtimes all have recurrent slogans and commentaries that go along with them, and which come to function as cues of adults' moods, of the next stage in a ritualized sequence – 'Shall we get out now? Time to get dry' – and of the child's part in the unfolding script. Key words and phrases begin to stand out and to signal significant shifts in activity: what is going to happen next, and what the child's role is in the next 'act' of the play.

The ability to join in this kind of communication is given a boost during the second six months of life when the baby learns to discern more specifically what the topic of conversation is. First, her father may pick up the plastic duck and hold it in front of her eyes whilst making a comment about it. Then he points with his finger, and the baby is gently coached to focus her attention not on the finger but on the object to which the finger is pointing. And soon she becomes able even to follow her father's line of sight – to construct, from the direction of his gaze, an imaginary line along which the topic of conversation probably lies: quite a feat of intuitive geometry. Instead of responding to adult speech simply in terms of mood or need, young children come to narrow and direct their own attention so that they 'know' (intuitively and not, of course, consciously) what their carer is talking about. 'Look, there's Billie . . . do you think she's hungry? Let's give her her supper, shall we?' Even if the detail is lost on the one-year-old, she is still able to look where her mother is looking and note the entrance of the family dog.

Over time, the brain picks up the association of the sight, smell and sound of the dog with the frequently repeated speech pattern 'Billie' – and realizes that the sound 'Billie' can function, in its turn, as a way of pointing. Some of the most familiar and well-worn concepts in the brainscape begin to have names: convenient ways for the child to direct others' attention to objects and events that happen to be interesting her. Having already extracted the pattern of multi-sensory and dynamic features that constitute the 'concept' of Billie, the child is now able to access that pattern through its verbal tag. 'Mummy', 'milk', 'sleepy' and a rapidly expanding lexicon of other labels come to denote objects, activities and states of affairs that are present or imminent.

So-called motherese, the language that parents and others use to talk directly to the child, is simple and relates to tangible topics of joint concern. Both mother and child are operating within a network of familiar scripts, so the child knows pretty well what is going on. The child's job is to attach her mother's simplified utterances to the current focus of attention. 'There's Billie.' 'See the ball?' 'That's your hat.' 'Want some milk?' Thus the child's acquisition of vocabulary, and of the rudiments of syntax, is towed along by the joint non-verbal context and activity. Parents do not design motherese to teach grammar; they speak it simply in order to be understood. And when the child does understand what is going on, and is able to join in the conversation effectively, her brain naturally picks out and practises the constructions that are there, embedded in the motherese, waiting to be found.

This means that motherese need only be roughly tuned to the child's current level of linguistic competence. If it contains constructions that are slightly more difficult than the child is ready to learn, that is no matter so long as the surrounding script is strong and clear enough to ensure comprehension. The brain will pick out of the range of constructions in the carer's utterances the one that it is ready to acquire. Provided that what children hear is generally within the range of what they can understand, or are ready to understand, there is no need for adults to tune their language too finely, or to engage in direct, deliberate instruction and correction designed to get children to learn the 'next step'.

The 'teaching' approach to first language learning is not only not necessary; it doesn't work. Studies show that there is only a low correlation between the complexity of adults' child-directed speech and the child's own level of linguistic maturity; and that deliberate attempts to correct children's speech errors are ineffective, as well as being frustrating for the misguided parent-teacher. For example, Katherine Nelson has shown that when children are actively rewarded for pronouncing words correctly and reproved for poor pronunciation, they actually make slower progress than children whose mothers are unconcerned about such matters.[1]

Learning to talk

At the same time as children are learning to recognize words, they are also getting ready to produce them. The ability to recognize words and understand language prepares the ground for the development of talk itself. During her first months of life the baby begins experimenting avidly with the sounds she can produce, and increasing the range and precision of her vocalizations. At about six months all babies babble alike, regardless of the particular language-sea in which they are immersed. They are exploring the scope of their vocal capacities, and also the connections between the ways they move their throat, lips, tongue and lungs, and the kinds of sound that their ears detect.

After six months, however, the baby's vocalizations begin to home in on those sounds that are characteristic of the language by which she is surrounded. A Chinese baby starts to sharpen her control over the subtle tonal glides that are vital in Cantonese, while neglecting the 'click' that will be so important to the Xhosa child, or the distinction between 'l' and 'r' that the European toddler will need to have mastered. Babies prune this universal repertoire down to significant speech sounds in their particular linguistic community, and they do so through observation and imitation. The sensory side of the brain extracts the sound patterns, the action side tries to reproduce them, and the whole learning process is guided by the approval of the baby's audience as her utterances come to sound more and more like the real sounds and words of that language.

Already, in the second six months of life, the baby is beginning to be more than a passive eavesdropper; she is becoming an increasingly skilful conversationalist. Adults and older brothers and sisters engage directly with her babbles, actively looking for, and selectively reinforcing, those that match most closely real words of the language and appropriate comments on events. They attribute to the child more intention and control than she actually has – treating random babbles as if they were deliberate approximations to real words; vague gurgles as if they were communications of pleasure or intent, or sensible comments on current affairs – and in doing so create a context of self-fulfilling expectations. As they reflect back to the child what they thought she meant to say, they create a selective linguistic environment that directs the child's speech development into the 'right' channels. The child, by emulating the speech directed at her, begins to try to say what her elders imagined she was trying to say from the start.

Through these conversations children soon discover that words, as well as being capable of directing other people's attention to what is present, can also be used to comment on things that are not here. Uttering Billie's name when the dog is not around may, from the child's point of view, seem a mistake. But then her mother responds by scooping her up and saying, 'Yes, where's Billie? Shall we go and look for her?' An interesting sequence of events unfolds, which the child discovers can be replicated. She begins to learn that words can be used to make things happen. Language can do more than point: it can be used to comment, complain and demand.

The function of grammar

As children become able to detect more complex relationships between the words they are hearing, their brains discover that the way words hook up also carries meaning, and that they can only be hooked up in certain ways. So as children's vocabulary increases, they are also picking up an increasing variety of linguistic structures that describe different kinds of events. In the non-verbal world of the brainscape, actors perform actions (Billie barks); their actions sometimes have objects (Billie chases the ball); actions sometimes employ instruments (Daddy hits the ball with a bat); actions sometimes have recipients (Daddy throws the ball to Billie); events have locations (Billie runs round the pool); actions sometimes have joint actors (Daddy and Billie are going for a walk); and so on. Each of these types of mini-story has a corresponding linguistic structure – the way words are stuck together signals different types of event or interaction. There are also different types of relationship: category membership (Billie is a terrier); possession of attributes (Billie has a stumpy tail); ownership (Billie is Polly's dog); capability (Billie can jump); disposition (Billie likes to chase cats); and so on. Words can be stuck together to describe general kinds of relationship in the world, as well as the stories of particular events.

Thus words begin to weave together inside children's heads to form stories and semantic relationships: Billie bit the postman yesterday, terriers are noisy dogs, and so on. Simple names knit together into more richly interconnected webs of language. Words are represented in the brain in exactly the same way as non-verbal scripts and concepts: as changes in the way nerve cells are welded together into functional channels and circuits. But because of its special power to label and give access to other conceptual groupings, and to build its own webs of meaning, language can best be represented as a second plane in the overall organization of the brain-mind – the *wordscape*, we might call it – that overlies the first plane, the brainscape, that we met in Chapter 3. We might visualize each name, each identifying tag for an object or an action, as a label attached to the centre of an underlying concept like a pennant planted at the summit of a mountain. Thus the mountainous conceptual terrain of the brainscape comes to be dotted with such flags, and the flags become interconnected into the increasingly intricate strings of verbal bunting that comprise the wordscape.

Initially the wordscape and the brainscape are tied closely together. Each word is either underpinned by a concept, directly connected to the pattern of features that constitutes its corresponding hollow or valley in the brainscape (Mummy, Billie, pool); or it is understood as a signal for a type of relationship (tickles, around, is). The mapping between the planes is very close: it has to be, because that is how language gets going in the first place. It gains its foothold in the brain-mind only because it is parasitic on the scripts and concepts of first-hand experience.

But once the wordscape is established, it can begin to take on more of a life of its own. One can make connections in the wordscape that do not have any direct underpinning in the brainscape – and this is an exciting discovery that is tied closely to the faculties of imagination and pretend play explored earlier. Once it has grown stable enough the wordscape can become partially cut free from its roots, and one is able to talk of things never experienced or even impossible to experience: princesses and dragons, gods and quarks. One can tell stories not just of what happened, but of what might have happened. One can speculate and deduce. Imagination can extend itself by drawing on language. And the foundations of thought and intellect are laid.

Learning to read

Just as speech gives young learners access to the accumulated experience of those around them, so reading and writing open the gateway to other ways of learning and knowing, and thus to greatly enhanced learning and independence. Throughout the world, developing the tools of literacy is seen as the next most important educational priority after learning to speak. But how are adults to help young people best acquire these skills?

Like talking, reading is not a skill that either appears out of thin air or has to be 'trained' from the beginning. There are many pre-literate skills which children need to have acquired during the first six years or so of life, and when these are firmly in place, and the supporting conditions are right, reading proper develops quite easily. It has been estimated that in these circumstances it takes about thirty hours of adult contact before children can take charge of the 'learning to read' adventure for themselves. One expert reading teacher, for example, concludes that 'Most of the students in the classes I had observed had learned enough about reading in their thirty hours so that they could go on exploring and reading, and could become as skilful as they wanted to be on their own.'[2] Even though they were beginners, and still needed help from time to time, they had got the hang of what learning to read was about.

Without the background skills, however, learning to read is fraught with difficulties and dangers. For example, one of the prerequisites is to be able to hear language accurately enough to distinguish between similar sounds, such as 'bad' and 'dad' or 'pop' and 'pot'. Four-year-olds who are not good at these distinctions reliably turn into eight-year-olds who have serious difficulty with their reading. If these at-risk four-year-olds are given the necessary practice in hearing subtle differences, their reading when they are eight is normal.[3] Children who have had plenty of experience of conversation, and especially of songs and rhymes, before they are four will automatically have gained the requisite ability.

It seems as if a secure grasp of the whole business of

communication is essential for the development of reading to proceed smoothly. Where there is a good literacy record, such as in Hungary and Singapore, much attention is paid to laying this foundation at kindergarten and in the first year or so of elementary school. Three-year-olds learn to pay careful attention to non-verbal communication by, for example, playing games in which they have to make a particular response when the teacher or another child winks at them or makes eye contact. They are asked to listen to, remember, and repeat back to the teacher increasingly complex sequences of sounds. Six musical instruments are played to the children: one child is blindfolded while one of the instruments is played again, and she then has to pick it out of the collection by sight.

Once the basics are in place, the trigger for the development of literacy is the experience of lots of written text – and of older people engaging with it in apparently pleasurable, profitable and purposeful ways. The two- and three-year-old need not be short of printed input. Cereal boxes, television captions and advertisements, clothes labels, street signs, junk mail and so on offer plenty of material to attend to and puzzle over. And gradually, as with spoken language, recurrent patterns begin to stand out so that the mass of squiggles begins to make some sense.

As well as print to 'eavesdrop' on, there are rituals in which adult and child can focus more closely on this activity called 'reading'. Children can participate in 'reading' picture books with their parents before they can actually decode written words, even during the first year of life. They get used to snuggling up with a book and can take part in the ceremony of page-turning. The adult inveigles the child into learning her part in the process of putting names to pictures by saying, 'What's that?', and gradually transfers responsibility for naming by keeping track of the child's growing vocabulary and prompting her when she gets stuck. 'It's a dog. I know you know that one.' 'You don't really know what those are, do you? They're mittens. Wrong time of year for those.'[4] And as the child gets more proficient the adult raises his expectations of precision and consistency, and adds commentaries that amplify names into incidents or fragments of knowledge about the world: 'That's right – that's a beehive. Do you know what bees make? They make honey. They get nectar from flowers and use it to make honey, and then they put the honey in the beehive.'

On the back of these well-practised routines for pointing and naming can come an introduction to written words. Instead of asking, 'What's that?', the adult can now point at the adjacent word and ask, 'What does that say?' The pattern of associations that included real dogs, pictures of dogs, dog stories and the sound of the word 'dog' now expands to include a visual squiggle with a characteristic shape. And just as with the learning of spoken language, so learning by immersion begins to focus on the world of these shapes and to pick out the features that distinguish between them. Some individual letters begin to be noticed, especially those, in the first instance, that have clearly identifiable shapes. The first letter of a word provides an important cue.

The simple concrete words of picture books connect to two kinds of pre-existing pattern in the child's brain-mind: the channels in the brainscape that correspond to the concept of the word; and the pattern in the wordscape that corresponds to how the word sounds (and is spoken). As well as learning that the written word 'dog' denotes animals like Billie, the child has to hook up the written pattern with the way the spoken word sounds.

Though at first written words may be recognized 'whole', there are more detailed correspondences to be discovered between the domains of speech and writing. They map on to each other more or less systematically (though the mapping is, in languages such as English, sometimes ambiguous and perverse). Individual letters and groups of letters have characteristic sounds. There are 45 or so sounds that make up spoken English, and some 380 letters or combinations of letters that represent these sounds in written English. Thus the ability to 'say' a written word may reflect either the holistic recognition of a specific pattern, or the use of these general mappings between letters and sound groupings to cobble together a plausible 'guess' at the word's pronunciation. If the child does not recognize the word as a familiar visual pattern, she can break it down into a string of smaller 'bricks' of letter-to-sound correspondence, and build up a guess at the spoken equivalent by translating each letter into sound and then sticking all the sounds together.

Teaching reading

In terms of the natural learning capacity of the brain, the difficulty of learning the mapping that connects letters and sounds should not be exaggerated. Detecting and recording such contingencies is exactly what the brain is designed to do. When reading teachers and textbooks stress how 'difficult' learning to read is, this may reflect their underestimation of the power and subtlety of brain learning, and their neglect of the gradual, cumulative laying of foundations on which the super-structure of formal literacy has to be erected. Drawing on their own implicit beliefs about what learning is, these people may be unconsciously supposing that learning to read is the same kind of deliberate, effortful job as learning foreign vocabulary – but it isn't. When they suggest that careful teaching and sequencing are necessary to prevent the young learner becoming over-whelmed, they may be unwittingly forgetting the gradual, evolutionary, one-step-at-a-time nature of the learning process.[5] Findings such as those of Katherine Nelson (see p. 102), which show that 'teaching' can actually hinder the development of oral language, cast doubt on the wisdom of any approach to early childhood education, or the teaching of literacy, which insists on formal instruction (more on this in Chapter 16).

When learning gets turned into teaching, learning to recognize whole words as patterns becomes the 'look-and-say method', while the discovery of the general mappings between letters and letter groups and sounds becomes 'phonics'. These two methods unfortunately get set up as alternatives by those who don't understand that *both* types of learning are intrinsic to the way the brain is built to learn, and that they are therefore comple-mentary. It is the recognition of whole word patterns that gets the process of learning to read started, and which continues to under-pin the gradual accumulation of written vocabulary. But as the database of particular written word / spoken word pairings ex-pands, the brain can begin to detect and extract the more detailed letter–sound correspondences that connect the two domains.

And these general mappings enable the child to have a shot at pronouncing a word which she has never seen before. In the intermediate stages of learning to read, this is very valuable: it enables you to generate guesses that may help you keep going. But as your 'sight vocabulary' – the words that you can recognize whole – expands, this fall-back strategy needs to be applied less and less often. Even an adult sometimes has to guess at the sound of an unfamiliar word – a foreign place-name, for example – but the process is cumbersome and disrupts the smooth flow of normal reading. Thus the battle between phonics and look-and-say is misconceived. There are two natural learning processes, each of which has its place, its time and its pitfalls, and each of which becomes unhelpful if it is over-promoted or over-taught.

Reading styles

So while phonics is a useful tool to get your reading going in the early stages, and to help you later on the odd occasions when you get stuck, it becomes a handicap if used all the time. There is no need to go from the look of a familiar word to the corresponding concept or meaning via its sound; that can happen automatically. If 'sounding' words to yourself silently as you read becomes routine, it slows you down. One of the main reasons why commercial 'rapid reading' courses enable you to read faster is that they successfully break you of this habit. In one telling demonstration, John Morton of the University of London devised a two-hour speed reading course in which he explained this bad habit to a group of people, encouraged them to believe they could read faster, and gave them some practice at doing so. Over the course of the two hours their reading efficiency – a combined measure of speed and comprehension – increased by 50 per cent.[6] (You need to ensure that comprehension is maintained, of course. Woody Allen once described a speed reading course he had taken. 'It's fantastic. I read *War and Peace* in twenty minutes,' he enthused. 'It's about Russia.')

Reading develops into not just one but a range of different learning tools to suit different purposes and materials. If you read everything in the same way, your reading is not going to be flexible and efficient. Students in higher education often discover that they have never learnt to differentiate between types of reading, and to suit their method to the job. They spend hours trying to grasp every last nuance of a text that only needs skimming, or dash too quickly over material that has to be mastered in detail. Graham Gibbs of the Open University encourages such students to adopt a more varied range of approaches by giving them a list of reading materials, and asking them to pick out of another list of types of reading the best one for each task (see below). It is surprising how easily their learning can be improved with relatively little effort.[7]

READING FLEXIBLY

For each entry in the left-hand column, see if you can identify the best type of reading in the right-hand column.

Type of reading material	*Type of reading*
Sports page of the newspaper	Plotting a route
Instructions on the side of a packet	Looking up facts
Science fiction novel	Quick scan to find a result
A–Z map of Birmingham	Slow step-by-step reading
Complete British Rail timetable	Repeated reading, thinking and rereading
Table of library opening hours	Repeated reading and reciting from memory
Technical photography manual	Fast reading without effort for hours
Crossword clues	Scan quickly to get going, referring to sections as you go along
Rules of the game Monopoly	A quick glance and pin it to the wall for reference
Poem in a school poetry book	Careful slow reading of selected sections and noting things down

(© Technical and Educational Services Ltd, Bristol.)

Study skills:
deliberate strategies for comprehension

An increase in reading flexibility does not, of itself, help you
to understand different material. As understanding hard language is one of the main activities of students in the higher
reaches of formal education, it is from the worlds of high
school and college that much of the work on such 'study skills'
has emerged. There is a voluminous and widely available
literature on how to study better, so I shall merely offer a
few illustrations here.[8]

The main strategy is to mobilize as much as possible of one's
existing knowledge and know-how in order to seek out or
create the coherent integration of ideas that underpins comprehension. Even though a passage of text as a whole may not
yet make sense, there will be words that do, and attached to
these words, through the reader's own wordscape and brainscape, will be other words, experiences and explanations that
connect them to pre-existing webs of meaning. The chances
of comprehension are increased by actively exploiting these
associations.

But how is such an attitude best developed? Not by direct
instruction, it seems. As we shall see in Chapter 7, when we
look more generally at attempts to teach adults and children
to 'think better', it doesn't happen through special-purpose
classes. Teaching study skills as a bolted-on afterthought to a
school curriculum is usually ineffective. It may be enjoyable,
not least because it provides light relief from more earnest
study, but the rules and strategies offered tend not to transfer
into real-life studying. The students may learn new rules, but
in practice they continue to rely on the habits acquired in
their previous experience of learning.[9]

However, if attention is paid to the development of study
skills in the context of real learning challenges, there is a
greater chance of their making a difference. Claire Weinstein
and Vicki Underwood at the University of Texas, Austin, set
up a training programme for fourteen-year-olds which taught
them how to use strategies for improving their comprehension by fleshing out their reading with their own thoughts

and experiences. Two groups of science students, one with this training and one not, studied a passage on the differences between veins and arteries. Both immediately and after a month's delay, the trained group's comprehension and memory were significantly superior to those of the students who had not had the training.[10]

However, though such learning-to-learn on the job is more successful when applied to the same kind of subject-matter, again it tends not to transfer to other domains. So there is something of a dilemma, as study skills expert John Nisbet explains: 'The difficulty is that study skills taught within a subject context may be too specifically tied to the subject, and consequently are not readily transferred to related situations in other subjects. General advice, on the other hand, may be too vague to be applied in any specific context.' Approaches to helping students learn how to learn that have discovered a middle path between these two pitfalls are looked at in Chapter 7.

When students are learning these active comprehension strategies, it may be useful to give them a set of instructions to follow. Although this can seem rigid and formulaic, the instructions merely serve as an aide-mémoire for mental activities that do not at first come naturally. Once the strategies have become second nature, the instructions can be dropped or used more flexibly. One example invokes the mantra SQ3R, standing for Survey, Question, Read, Review, Recall. When approaching a text, take some time, before starting to read in earnest, to get a 'feel' for it: think about the title, read the blurb, scan the contents page. This *survey* should generate some expectations about the content and how it might relate to any task that has been set; and it should also make you ask some *questions* about the content which you hope the book will answer. Then *read* the relevant or prescribed parts, pausing to *review* what you have read, and stopping to see if you can *recall* the main points every so often – more frequently when the going gets harder. In the review and recall phases, try to generate further questions: argue with the author; pick out and identify what you consider to be the main points; see if you can predict where the argument or the story is going; try to restate the argument in your own words. All these activities mobilize your own existing knowledge-base, and your own latent know-how, more fully, and have been shown to increase comprehension and recall significantly. More effective students make more natural use of a wider range of such methods than less effective ones.[11] There is a craft of studentship that can be learnt, practised and developed, though it is often neglected by schools and teachers.

Developing the craft of writing

Like reading, writing consists of many layers and ingredients of skill built upon pre-literate foundations. And, as with learning to read, half the battle is conveying to young people the point of the exercise. This is achieved, first, by a regular diet of seeing their elders writing – paying bills, making shopping lists, doing crossword puzzles and so on – and, second, by being told what writing is, which is a kind of deep-frozen speech. Through writing you can make your speech more effective. You can make your message last longer. You can mull it over and improve it. You can talk to people who aren't physically present or on the other end of a phone. You can reach more people by creating multiple copies. Through example, supplemented with a little light pointing out, the child's curiosity can be naturally piqued and their learning engaged. Without this motivational base, teaching and learning writing is likely to be hard work.

The prerequisites for writing include the development of the fine muscular control that is necessary to hold pencils and form letters. Not all four-year-olds have automatically mastered these skills, and in those countries that are most successful at helping children learn reading and writing time is taken to ensure that they have developed the requisite dexterity. In a typical kindergarten in the Flemish area of Belgium, for instance, three- and four-year-olds are first encouraged to play with making large letter-like shapes in a sand table before moving to a much smaller tray and only then to making marks on paper.[12]

Note-taking

Now let us fast forward again to the high school and college years, where special styles of writing need to be developed as adjuncts to the task of understanding and learning from difficult materials. Hard language has to be held still in order to chew it over, and if such language arises in the form of speech – as in a lecture, for example – it has somehow to be captured and frozen, like a photograph of a speeding car, so that it can be attended to in greater detail. Note-taking is therefore one of the families of study skills with which tutors can help their students.

Taking notes in a class or a lecture involves a sophisticated set of skills. Students need to have not one but a range of skills for different purposes. If detailed hand-outs are available, struggling to scribble everything down is a waste of time. Does the teacher indicate directly, or perhaps indirectly by tone of voice, the key points that have to be captured accurately, and are you alert to these cues? Does it help to try to relate what is being said to your own personal experience, or not? Is it best not to worry about the detail but to try to extract the relationships between the key ideas?

If the answer to the last question is 'yes', have students been given tools such as mind maps or spider diagrams (see over) that are much better suited to the job than connected prose? And having taken the notes, what do you do with them? File them and forget them, hoping that somehow the content will have magically transferred itself to the inside of your head? Spend hours copying them out so they look lovely and neat? Go through them slowly, the same day, and try to extract the main points of the story, or to focus on and follow up the points that you didn't understand? Many students waste a great deal of time and effort taking routine notes of a single kind that are not going to be much help, and which may indeed never get looked at again. Other students fit their note-taking approach – just as we saw they fitted their reading style – to the material and task at hand.

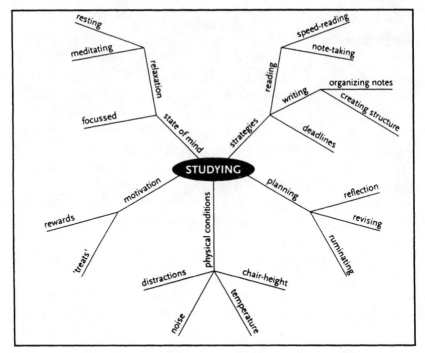

An example of a spider diagram that gives an overall impression
of some of the factors that might influence studying.

Protecting resilience

To return to very young learners, one important consideration
in helping children learn to read and write is to ensure that
you do nothing to damage their existing resilience and resourcefulness – their confidence in their ability to find things
out and master them for themselves. It is possible that parents
and teachers, in their impatience to develop the traditional
three Rs, and their anxiety lest their young charges 'fall
behind', are chivvying and instructing them too much. If
they transmit their own anxieties, they may in fact contribute
to a deterioration in the development of their children's
underlying learning power.

There is something of a self-fulfilling prophecy here. If the
combination of children's natural intelligence and natural
curiosity cannot be trusted to deliver the prize of literacy,
pressure and instruction may indeed be required. If it is true

that all children 'should' be ready to learn to read and write at the same age, and if it is true that the natural learning ability of the brain is inherently unequal to the task, that lack of trust is justified. But if, as the evidence suggests, children are ready for literacy over a range of ages, and if learning through immersion is more powerful than we give it credit for, then formal teaching and instruction may do at least some children more harm than good.

Many authorities, especially in continental Europe and Asia, agree with this risk analysis. They put a great deal of emphasis on developing the prerequisite skills and dispositions in all children, and delay the introduction of formal literacy until six or even seven. Though Hungarian and Swiss children, for example, start learning explicitly to read and write two or even three years later than their English counterparts, they have caught up and passed them within a few months. There is no evidence that 'more able' children are disadvantaged by this late start. By the time they are eight, the top five per cent of pupils in the late-starting countries are comfortably outperforming their English counterparts. The concern to consolidate children's learning confidence, and to take time to get them fully prepared for the different world of formal tuition, pays off too. It seems radically to reduce or even to remove the 'long tail' of pupils, in Britain and the USA for instance, containing a disproportionate number of boys, who fall further and further behind. The sad fact is that such children, forced to engage with reading and writing before they have mastered attention, memory and spoken communication, lose confidence not just in their ability to decode and produce written text, but more generally in their own learning power. As a result they quickly come to see school as a place in which they do not really belong.[13]

Learning to learn to read and write

The over-riding importance of the development of general learning power means that, in learning language as elsewhere, the top priority of a tutor must be 'to help the learner help themselves'. The goal is not just the mastery of writing; it is to help the learner become more robust and self-sufficient in the process. We don't sit the learner down and 'make' them learn twenty spellings a day, testing them till they have got them all right. We offer them a tool for doing it themselves.

We could, for example, give them a stack of cards and ask which words they would like (or need) to be able to spell. On one side of each card they can draw an image that represents or suggests the word, and on the other the word correctly spelt. On the first side they could also write a sentence in which the word would be used – but replaced with a blank. For words that don't have pictures, like 'separate', you can write a sentence like: 'Don't put them together, keep them s . . .'

Learners can then work through their pile of cards, picture side up, attempting to spell the word that is depicted, and then turning the card over to see if they are right. Cards they got right go in one pile; those they still have trouble with go into another, which they can then go through repeatedly, each time weeding out the successful ones. Over time new cards are added, and the growing pile of known cards offers a physical testament to their accomplishment. In this way, the child is simultaneously learning spelling and mastering a learning tool that gives them control over their learning, and which might have other uses – learning foreign vocabulary, or the names of different flies for fly-fishing – in the future.

An example of learning to learn to write comes from a more advanced level: mastering the craft of the kind of writing required for a college seminar paper, for instance. It is an important skill for any aspiring writer to be willing and able to act as their own editor. Beginning writers and poor writers have been shown to be deficient in this respect. It requires the ability to compare what one intended to say with what is actually on the page or the screen, and to read the latter from the point of view of a hypothetical reader. The writer has to learn to put herself in the position of someone who is not privy to her intention. And she may have to develop a number of distinct writing 'voices' for different audiences and purposes.

A number of computer programs are now available that

encourage the development of people's ability to reflect productively on their own writing. One of these so-called revision tutors, called Trace-It, can display a record of the writer's previous revisions of a document, enabling her to observe the kinds of 'mistakes' or 'improvements' which she automatically makes, and thus to develop more awareness of her own writing style, and of areas of existing strength and possible development.[14] Another program prompts the writer with questions such as: 'Does this paragraph have a clear point?', or it highlights any words it finds that are on its 'vague' list, and asks: 'Would it make it clearer if you were to use a more specific word instead?' In one study eleven- to sixteen-year-old students who learned to make use of this program made more corrections than did those not using it, and their revised drafts were of a higher quality.[15]

Literacy in context

In most societies literacy is generally seen as the most essential learning tool for today's young people – the vital foundation for successful lifelong learning. A tremendous amount of money and concern is being dedicated, worldwide, to ensuring that this tool is acquired. Language opens up for people of all ages another enormously powerful compartment of the learning toolkit. Through being able to understand the speech of others, we are able to capitalize on their experience. By listening to people talk, we gain vastly increased access to the accumulated knowledge of the culture. Without language, one's predictions for the future can only reflect the accumulated personal past. With language, one can benefit from the greater control that others have already secured.

By knowing what people in the vicinity are talking about, we are able to direct our attention to salient and informative aspects of the shared world: ones which might not have been obvious enough to grab our attention by themselves. Other people become able to point out things of interest deliberately, thus focusing and intensifying attention, and inviting engagement with different kinds of learning challenge and material. And others, too, are able, through their words, to activate concepts and scenarios in our minds that are not currently switched on by events – thus enabling us to be better prepared for contingencies that we have not yet experienced directly.

And through the power of speech we are able to take fuller control of our own learning. Confronted with something strange or confusing we need neither engage directly and risk injury, nor withdraw and risk missing out on a valuable or interesting learning experience. If there is someone else around, we can ask questions. Language enables us to solicit help and information as and when we feel the need of it; not just to be in receipt of others' spontaneous offerings. And, through increasingly sophisticated forms of conversation, we are able to explore the interface between the understanding and control which we are developing from within and the values and assumptions embedded in the judgements and explanations of others.

But if language is a vital learning tool, it is equally vital that it is seen in a wider context than that of intellectual interest and conventional education. There are other aspects of real-life learning power that have to be protected and developed too: the bedrock of resilience and self-belief, and the other compartments of the learning toolkit. These, in the learning age, are simply too important to risk being neglected or, worse, sacrificed. Learning power comprises both literacy and numeracy, and is ultimately more fundamental than either of them. There are some ways of approaching the development of literacy and numeracy that enhance overall learning power, and some that do not. We have to be sure that the approaches of teachers and institutions are based on this wider concern, and on the best of available information about learning to learn, and not on a narrow identification of teaching with learning, or on an outmoded conception of the human mind.

SEVEN

Learning to Think

Language gains its foothold in the mind as a medium of communication. Its primary function, as a learning tool, is to enable us to absorb ideas and information from our culture and to check and develop our own understandings by expressing them to others. But it quickly develops from being purely a social tool into a psychological one as well. Just as pretend play becomes internalized as imagination, so the discovery that language can be used *sotto voce* makes available the power of verbal thought. Thinking, in the specific sense of 'talking to ourselves', is a very useful learning tool. In this chapter I want to take a look at what thinking is good for; how it works; whether it is actually developed by education as we know it, and whether we can 'teach thinking' more effectively; and whether it is really as powerful and pervasive a tool as we seem to believe.

Concepts: articulating the brainscape

One of the major functions of verbal thought is to make the mindscape even more highly articulated. The word 'articulated' means both 'spoken, turned into language', and 'joint, segmented', as, in English, we refer to an 'articulated lorry', a truck composed of a separable tractor unit and trailer. Language enables us to separate our bundles of expertise and existing concepts into smaller units – features, attributes, component skills – and rearrange them to meet more major kinds of variation than can know-how alone. A new degree of creativity and flexibility becomes available.

Once this has begun to happen, we can use the fine connections of the wordscape to hook up different areas of knowledge and know-how. When learning gets difficult or we become stuck, we can take stock of our resources by sitting back and thinking. By doing so we may find ourselves using words and phrases that make connections with other domains, and when these are activated they may turn out to contain tools or information which can be usefully applied out of context. The process is rather like a CB radio system which allows a truck driver to broadcast a general request for help that can be picked up by anyone who happens to be listening. When you do this publicly, it is called 'asking for help'. When you do it privately, inside your own head, it is called 'thinking'. Thus thinking in language becomes a powerful way of overcoming the limitations of a brain-mind that is initially organized (for good reasons) into separate scripts and packages of knowledge and expertise.

Reasoning

This definition of thinking, however, incorporates a range of mental activities, from the most unconstrained kinds of verbal daydreaming through to forms of thought that are highly disciplined and logical. I shall come back to look at the learning potential of the looser kinds of thinking in Chapter 8, but for now I want to focus on the tighter, harder end of the spectrum, for it is the latter that corresponds most closely to the Western – indeed now practically global – understanding of 'intelligence'. Rational thought is seen as the highest manifestation of intelligence and, by implication, the most powerful learning tool that human beings – and human beings alone – possess. It is so-called hard thinking of this kind, honed through the development of European intellectual culture since the seventeenth century, that has given us our robust understanding of science and the extraordinary proliferation of technology. As we have seen, Jean Piaget's influential theory of child development enshrined 'formal operational thought' – hard thinking – as the pinnacle of intellectual development, and the goal of education. After elementary school, you don't get many marks for unsubstantiated intuition.

At its best, hard thinking derives inescapable conclusions from valid arguments that draw out the implications of premises that accurately and completely capture a state of affairs. It renders complex predicaments into verbal descriptions, and then brings to the surface what is latent in them. Hard thinking likes everything to appear as explicit and clear-cut as possible. 'Show your working' is the pervasive injunction, so it can be checked. If your hard thinking results in a carefully reasoned paper to the board, or a working computer model, so much the better. All the interesting work is done in the well-lit executive office of the deliberate, conscious, rational mind.[1]

Take, as a trivial example, the kind of problem you typically find in the brain-teaser section of a Sunday newspaper. Three playing cards are placed face down on the table in front of you, and you are given the following pieces of information. To the left of a queen there is a jack (knave). To the left of a spade there is a diamond. To the right of a heart there is a king. And to the right of a king there is a spade. What are the three cards, and in what order?

The solution of such problems requires the meticulous combination of separate pieces of information according to well-defined rules, and they are designed to be of a degree of complexity that challenges but does not exceed the educated Westerners' ability to talk to themselves rationally. Though interim results or working hypotheses may need to be recorded with the aid of pen and paper, the bulk of the computational work appears to go on in the conscious mental workspace. And indeed, when people are working on such problems, their ability to think aloud, to externalize their inner talk, is correlated with their ability to solve the problem. In general, the closer to the solution you think you are, the more likely you are to be on the right track. Thought is a valid indicator of imminent success.[2]

The limits of reason

Valuable, and much vaunted, though the tool of rationality is, people are not as good at it as they would like to think. Their ability to be logical is often subverted by their stronger desire to be right. We tend to select, and accept relatively uncritically, evidence or arguments that seem to confirm what we believe, or would like to be true; and to neglect or explain away that which is uncomfortable.[3] Educationist John Holt reported a similar phenomenon when playing a game with schoolchildren. He thought of a number between 1 and 1000, and the students had to find out what it was by asking yes/no questions. They might, quite logically, start by asking: 'Is it bigger than 500?' If Holt said 'yes', they cheered; if he said 'no', they groaned – even though they got exactly the same information from both answers.[4]

Though countless tests have shown that horoscopes are incapable of making factual predictions with above-chance accuracy, 78 per cent of women and 70 per cent of men in the USA take them seriously, and seek out interpretations for vague statements that 'prove' how clearly they apply to themselves. More than 99 per cent of college students believe in at least one of the following: channelling, clairvoyance, precognition, telepathy, psychic surgery, psychic healing, healing crystals, psychokinesis, astral travel, levitation, the Bermuda Triangle, UFOs, plant consciousness, auras and ghosts.[5] Give them twelve unlabelled horoscopes, ask them to choose the one that is 'theirs', show that there is no correlation between their choice and their actual birth-sign, and substantial numbers will still leave the class with their belief in astrology intact. (Such persistence is easy to rationalize. For many believers, the laws of the paranormal do not have to work all the time, and they are particularly likely to suspend themselves if they feel they are being put to the test by sceptical scientists. Thus rational or scientific disconfirmation has no validity for them.)[6]

The well-known fact that many ailments clear up of themselves fails to dent people's faith in the efficacy of the medication they were taking at the time of spontaneous remission. As

Sir Peter Medawar describes it: 'If a person (a) is poorly, (b) receives treatment intended to make him better, and (c) gets better, then no power of reasoning known to medical science can convince him that it may not have been the treatment that restored his health.'[7] People frequently find such single, vivid examples more compelling as evidence than the most carefully conducted survey, and discount the latter by referring to two popular beliefs: that 'science (like the government) is not to be trusted', and 'there are lies, damned lies, and statistics'.[8]

Does education help us to think?

We would expect education to help people to guard against such pitfalls and give them tools for sharpening their wits. And in some ways it clearly does. Someone who has mastered the use of formal logic or of what are known as Venn diagrams is better equipped to distinguish between the validity of an argument and the plausibility of its conclusions. It can be tricky to sort out in your head the logic of syllogisms such as 'Some police officers are freemasons; no liars are freemasons; therefore no police officers are liars'. But by representing the three 'sets' as overlapping circles in a Venn diagram it becomes visually obvious that the conclusion is invalid. But such tools, if they are to be of practical value, have to be used not just in examination rooms but spontaneously and appropriately – and they are often not.

David Perkins at Harvard has evaluated the effect of education on people's ability to construct valid arguments in informal contexts. He took large groups of people with varying amounts of formal education and asked them to make notes for a discussion on topics such as 'Does violence on TV influence the likelihood of violence in real life?', or 'Would a refundable 20-cent deposit on soft drink cans and bottles reduce the amount of litter?' The notes were scored in terms of their overall length; the number of different lines of argument considered; the consideration of objections to the preferred line; and the overall quality of the argument. Six groups were surveyed: high school, college and graduate students, each at

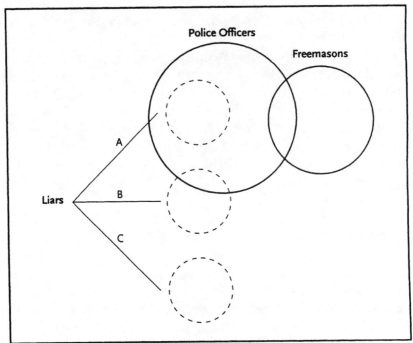

A Venn diagram helps to solve logical problems. Here, the set of liars could
be in any one of the relationships A, B or C to the set of police officers. If
it is either A or B, the conclusion that 'no police officers are liars' is invalid.

the beginning and completing stages of their studies. Properly, Perkins looked for any changes in informal reasoning
within these groups rather then between them. Obviously
graduate students in general score higher than college students, who score higher than high school students.

Within each type of education, however, length of exposure
made surprisingly little difference. Five years of high school
made only a marginal difference to students' reasoning. The
comparisons for students in higher education are even more
disappointing. Over four years of undergraduate study, not
one of the four measures described improved significantly.
Over four years of postgraduate study, only the tendency to
consider counter-arguments increased significantly. While
eleven-year-olds are spontaneously producing less than two
different lines of argument, ten or more further years of
education have increased the equivalent score for beginning
graduate students to just over three. However adept such elite

students have become at specialist reasoning, precious little of it seems to spill over into their everyday thinking. Perkins concludes that: 'broadly speaking, most educational practice does little to prepare students for reasoning out open-ended issues', and he titled his paper: 'Post-primary education has little impact on informal reasoning'.[9]

If part of the problem is that over time students' thinking has not improved as much as we might have suspected, the other part is that they do not, in the heat of the moment, apply all the strategies that they do in fact possess. Keith Stanovich of the Ontario Institute for Studies in Education has even ironically identified a widespread clinical syndrome which he refers to as dysrationalia, the key feature of which is 'a level of rationality, as demonstrated in thinking and behavior, that is significantly below the level of the individual's intellectual capability'.[10] Despite their ability to do better when reminded, people's thinking generally tends to be hasty (impulsive, coming to premature conclusions without examining all the evidence); narrow (failing to challenge assumptions and explore alternative points of view); fuzzy (careless and imprecise, tolerant of ill-defined and ambiguous concepts); and sprawling (generally disorganized and unfocused, not adding up to a coherent argument).[11]

Teaching thinking

It is disappointing to learn how little impact schooling has on people's real-life thinking; but that does not mean that it is impossible to help people develop their thinking skills. In recent years, programmes at all levels of education have been devised with the aim of enhancing the quality of students' thinking. In the information age, everyone needs to be able to evaluate the flood of information that pours into their homes and offices through every electronic, communication and print medium they possess. What do such courses do? And do they work?

Thinking programmes train students in logical thinking and problem-solving, highlighting the nature of the thinking process rather than the particular content being addressed. Some of the earlier – and less successful – attempts tried to remove content as much as possible by using abstract puzzles and very general strategies. For example, students would be set brainteaser-type problems and invited to focus on such strategies as looking for evidence, generating analogies, seeking counter-examples, exploring a specific instance, checking for illicit assumptions and so on.

While such abstraction did indeed make it easier to focus on the structure of arguments, the problem was that any gains in thinking did not tend to transfer into spontaneous use either in the classroom or the real world. As with the attempts to teach study skills described in Chapter 6, there is something of a Catch 22 situation. Try to encourage transferability of skills by making the teaching content and methods highly abstract and generic, and you run the risk of any learning-to-learn lacking bite in terms of specific kinds of problems. Try to teach thinking in the context of a particular subject, however, and any improvements may be tied to those specific contexts and materials. Cracking the problem of how to teach for transfer of the skills involved has proved a major challenge.

The situation has not been helped by entrepreneurs making grand claims for proprietary methods that are not substantiated by objective evaluation. Ray Nickerson, one of the most respected researchers in the area of teaching thinking, warns of 'unsubstantiated claims, one-sided assessments, and excessive promotionalism', and he concludes that 'The field needs more self-criticism. It is a bit paradoxical that some developers of programs to teach critical thinking have had less than severely critical attitudes towards their own work.'[12] Many of the published evaluations have been based on short trials with small numbers, and using measures of limited validity. And there is the ubiquitous risk of the so-called Hawthorne Effect – apparent improvements in thinking that are not due to the nature of the teaching programme, but simply reflect the novelty of the situation. If you bombard students with a lot of attention and some unusual and entertaining activities, it is not surprising that something happens; nor is it surprising that such gains often fizzle out soon after the intensive instruction ceases.[13]

To give just one example, the CoRT Thinking Programme devised by Edward de Bono has been evaluated both by him and by independent researchers in Britain, Australia and Venezuela. Of his own evaluation, de Bono says:

Some of the larger, more global objectives of the thinking programmes indicate positive changes in the general nature of many students regarding intelligent behaviour . . . the confidence of those who have been trained in thinking, the focus of their thinking, their structured approach and breadth of consideration. Teachers often sum up these factors as 'maturity' in commenting about these children who come to their classrooms after some training in thinking.[14]

An independent evaluation by the UK Schools Council, covering the use of the CoRT materials with ten-year-olds, found that the feedback from the students was 'generally favourable', but that evidence of improved quality of thinking was not statistically significant.[15] An evaluation of fifteen-year-old students using CoRT in science lessons in Australia found that, when they were tested on the same kinds of 'general interest' problems that they had used in the training sessions, their thinking improved, but that there were no gains in their science examination performance compared to groups who had not used CoRT.[16] Finally, modified versions of the CoRT programme have been widely used and evaluated in Venezuelan schools. In one evaluation, a group of 320 ten- to eleven-year-olds received Learning to Think instruction twice a week, and after three years did indeed show significant improvement on the kinds of problems with which they had become familiar (such as 'Produce a list of rules for parents to follow in the daily care of their children', or 'What would happen if the supply of water was cut off for a month in a major city?'). However, 'whether the CoRT training would help students solve problems that are different in character from those on which they were trained is unclear. Whether CoRT has enhanced the thinking of the students in other subject areas or in out-of-school situations also remains to be studied.'[17]

Thinking programmes that work

More recently, programmes have been developed that take a rather broader view of what 'good, hard thinking' entails.

Most of the earlier ones saw their purpose as the deliberate training of thinking skills, and it may have been this narrow focus that accounted for the disappointing results. For good thinking is more than a matter of skill: it involves the disposition to think in different kinds of ways in different kinds of situation; the self-knowledge to monitor and manage one's own thinking effectively; and the awareness that different pockets of knowledge and know-how are relevant in specific cases. Programmes that aim to improve these more general concepts, as well as the repertoire of skills and strategies, seem to be more successful.[18]

For example, Diane Halpern of California State University at San Bernardino has recently devised a very promising critical thinking programme that incorporates all these dimensions. Critical thinking, she argues, is 'purposeful, reasoned and goal-directed. It is the kind of thinking involved in solving problems, formulating inferences, calculating likelihoods and making decisions. Critical thinkers use these skills appropriately, without prompting, and usually with conscious intent in a variety of settings.' The first element of Halpern's four-part programme focuses on developing the right disposition. To think well, one must be not only able but ready and willing. For example, discussions on the nature of hard thinking encourage students to understand that this kind of learning involves processes that are conscious and effortful. Through such understanding, they learn to expect hard thinking to be, at least some of the time, just that – hard – and thus not to feel dispirited, or to abandon it, when it becomes so.

Students also practise recognizing the kinds of problems which warrant such hard thinking and those that do not. What is worthwhile in responding to a diagnosis of cancer is probably not in choosing where to eat. Halpern argues that critical thinkers need the dispositions to engage in and persist with complex thinking tasks; to control initial judgements and impulses whilst conducting a more measured analysis; to question assumptions and taken-for-granted beliefs; to try alternative learning strategies when stuck; and to engage in rational discussion with other interested parties whose points of view and priorities may be different.

Then there is the skills training component, which is similar to many of those programmes discussed already. Skills to be developed include recognizing and discounting the sloppy use of language; analysing the validity of arguments; separating relevant from irrelevant considerations; unearthing unstated assumptions; assessing the validity and reliability of empirical claims; and generating and evaluating alternative action plans. Each of these is addressed explicitly, and illustrated through realistic examples.

The third element is the ability to recognize when to use each of these skills and strategies. As we saw in Chapter 6, it's no use having a sophisticated toolkit if you don't know what each tool is for. Thus teaching thinking involves exploring the scope and limitations of the component skills, partly through the open-ended investigation of complex problems – finding out what works and what doesn't – and partly through explicit discussion and tuition. Teaching for transfer involves practising not just on one type of problem but on as wide a range as possible; and it involves trying to unearth the underlying or structural features of situations which can be used as the trigger for a particular approach. (We shall go into the idea of transfer in more detail in Chapter 12.)

The fourth ingredient of critical thinking is sometimes referred to as 'metacognition': the self-awareness that we can use to guide our own thinking processes. There are ways of encouraging the development of people's self-awareness so that they manage their minds more productively and deploy their resources most effectively, and they are discussed fully in Chapter 11. When these four ingredients are woven into a coherent critical thinking training programme, substantial, transferable and lasting improvements can be brought about.

General vs specific thinking tools

Effective programmes also take a more enlightened view of the relationship between learning tools that are specific to a particular domain or a certain kind of problem, and those that are more generic. We need both. When we are working within a familiar domain, the most effective tools are purpose-built for that kind of material. The chess grandmaster, the architect, the theatre director, the teacher and the systems analyst all rely on very specific forms of thinking with which to develop their mastery of their home domain. But at times they will be faced with a problem that is unusual, or even unprecedented, and then the normal ways of learning may not give an adequate purchase. It is at such times – when you don't know (exactly) what to do – that you may have to fall back on a more general-purpose kind of strategy that will kick-start your learning back into life. As Ray Nickerson and his colleagues put it:

> No matter to what extent experts may depend on a repertoire of [familiar scripts and strategies] in handling routine problems, they must spend much of their time working at the edge of their competence on fresh types of problems not so well covered by their repertoires. It may be that there, general principles, which admittedly are not that powerful in comparison with the more particular knowledge and skills applicable to specific familiar problems, make the difference between skilled and unskilled performance. They are all that the expert has to fall back on.[19]

Some of the strategies that we need at the margins of competence may indeed be of 'rational' form. We can fall back on hard thinking – purposeful, deliberate and clear – to try to give us a handle on the situation. We can keep talking to ourselves, albeit in more general ways: 'Come on, think! There must be a way through this. Can you generate a more abstract representation of the problem? What assumptions have you been making? Can you break the problem down into sub-problems which might be easier to solve one at a time?' And so on. This kind of thinking works when the basic parameters of the problem remain more or less the same. To think hard, one has to be able to think clearly, with precision, and to do that one needs concepts with agreed definitions. Unfortunately, not all learning challenges come so neatly packaged and defined. As we shall see in Chapter 9, when hard thinking runs out of steam it may well be soft thinking that comes to the rescue.

EIGHT

The Uses of Language: Skills, Stories and Memories

Before we turn to the concept of soft thinking, we need to complete the story of the relationship between language and learning. As well as helping us to maximize the flexibility and availability of our own knowledge in the course of problem-solving, language also aids learning in a number of other ways. The ability to talk to ourselves supports the development of physical skills. Listening to and telling stories helps people to make sense of challenging and puzzling situations. And language also enables us to develop our powers of memory.

The internalized coach

Talking to ourselves can guide the development of practical skills. Through language novices in any field, instead of continually depending on instruction from another more experienced source, can guide and correct themselves. They become their own internalized coach, recalling the tutor's prompts and tips and using them to direct their own learning. Rules, maxims and targets that originated from manuals or real-life instructors can be used as memorized yardsticks of achievement, or instructions for action, to channel and evaluate the person's own intuitive experiments: their 'playing' and 'practising'. This is how 'instruction' works, it appears. Explicit rules do not automatically dissolve into spontaneous, intuitive competence, like a sugar cube into a cup of coffee.

Rather they provide the basis for a self-correcting monitoring or editing function. When we think about our performance as we are engaged in it, we hear the mentor's voice in our own minds.

In learning simple skills, the natural consequences of your actions give you clear enough feedback. The tower of bricks stays up or it falls down. The cat purrs or it scratches. But in learning complex expertise, many layers may need to be stacked up, and many sub-skills to be in place, before success is apparent. The learner-driver or the learner-pianist needs to take on trust the tutor's instructions, and try to act in accordance with them, even though they may not appear to produce much immediate progress, or their rationale is not clear. Learning some skills is like constructing an arch. A wall you can build brick by brick, and it will stay up as it goes. But an arch will not stay up until all the bricks are in place: remove one and the whole collapses. So to build an arch you need to construct so-called falsework underneath it, to keep the constituent stones temporarily in place. Once the last brick has been cemented in, the falsework can be taken away and the arch remains. Instructions are like falsework.

Stephen Krashen of the University of Southern California has shown how this internalized coach functions in the learning of foreign languages. The bulk of adults' language learning, if they are constantly hearing the language spoken, occurs automatically – just as it does for a child learning its first language. The natural pattern detection ability of the brain begins to pick out the recurring configurations of sounds and words, and to begin to build comprehension and production on the basis of these neural circuits. Provided the learner is attentive and the input is comprehensible, adults' natural learning ability will serve them well. In general adults, again like children, don't learn to speak by understanding the rules and then applying them, nor by being systematically corrected. Such deliberate correction has been shown to have little or no effect on the developing mastery of either a first or a foreign language.[1]

Older children and adults, though, can make use of some explicit comprehension of the rules of the new language to check their own productions. A word or an expression may come to mind, but before – or after – it is uttered, a conscious monitoring-and-editing process may intervene to detect and remove any 'bugs' in the sentence. Having written 'recieve', a learner of English as a second language may recite to herself 'i before e except after c', and correct her spelling. For native English speakers learning a European language like French or German, such a conscious checking process often accompanies a lingering insecurity about the gender of nouns or the agreement of verb endings.

People differ markedly in the skill with which they deploy the self-correcting strategy of thinking about what they are doing. Some people hardly use it at all. Even when they have achieved a high level of fluency, they may persist in making simple grammatical errors that they don't notice. Others, however, may become chronic overusers of the monitor, pausing to check every detail of a sentence in their heads before they utter it. Such self-consciousness becomes counter-productive, of course. The anxious student becomes increasingly tongue-tied as she checks every utterance for tenses and endings before she dare deliver it (just as the child carrying a full cup of hot tea becomes increasingly clumsy as she nervously tries to 'be careful', to 'look where you are going', to 'hold it steady'). And while they are busy inside their heads making sure that everything they want to say is correct, such self-critical conversationalists are probably missing the ensuing contributions from other people – by the time they are ready to deliver their polished prose the moment has passed.

There are different reasons why people overuse the editor. The pressures of the situation may make you try too hard, and in doing so you fall into the error of self-consciousness. Or the person themselves may be constitutionally hesitant and self-conscious, distrustful of their own spontaneity and intuition. But it may also be because they have been taught in a way that mistakenly exaggerates the importance of conscious comprehension and underestimates the amount of non-intellectual practice needed. Getting the balance right between intuitive experimentation and conscious deliberation is vital. Think too little and you may be stuck with bad habits. Think too much and you may become paralysed with self-consciousness.

Conscious editing is a relatively slow process and takes up a good deal of attention. It's no use trying to observe too many rules at once. Checking whether an action conforms to a prescription is attention-demanding, and most people cannot work with more than one or two such prescriptions at any one time. Good mentors know this; bad mentors tend to swamp their students with advice and wonder why they look demoralized.

In the heat of the moment it is often preferable to get it roughly right than to freeze into immobility. In periods of off-duty time, on the other hand, as we saw in Chapter 4, it can pay you to dismantle the constructions you spontaneously threw together and see how they might be improved. Here, thinking can help. In a session with the tennis coach the emphasis may be on getting the backhand right, and not, for the time being, on winning the point. Trying to remember to 'cock your wrist earlier' can help during practice but hinder in an actual match.

If an instruction or rule is to be useful it has to be known and to be capable of being brought to mind. But some rules are difficult to make explicit. As you progress in learning a language, for example, the sequence through which know-how progresses is not the same as the order of difficulty of articulating the rules. As Stephen Krashen says: 'The rules we can learn and carry around in our heads for use as an [editor] are not those that are earliest acquired, nor are they those that are [most] important for communication. Rather, they are the simple rules, rules that are easiest to describe and remember.' So there is a chance that what you are thinking about is not actually relevant to the learning that you want to happen.

Stories

Language makes it possible to express our own ideas and to understand other people's. But there is more to language than literal comprehension. Language gives us contrasting ways of organizing experience and making meaning. Conceptual understanding is one. Listening to and telling stories is another.

Stories are not 'true' in the same way that conceptual

understanding purports to be true. When we explain to someone how to spend time under the sea using scuba equipment,
or describe the double-helical structure of the DNA molecule,
we are attempting to say something about the way the world
is. Even if we acknowledge that what we are talking about is
just one among many ways of describing things, we are
attempting, to the best of our ability, to depict things as they
are. When we tell stories, on the other hand, we may be
attempting to say something that is true *to* life, but not
necessarily true *of* life.

Where explanations are direct and logical, stories make
their points elliptically and show the human side. The world
of struggle, conflict, doubt, ingenuity, desire and frustration is
depicted. Situations change and develop over time. Barriers
are overcome and lessons learnt. But the moral is implicit. It is
much harder to disagree with a story than with an opinion.
Yet, to the extent that we identify with the events and the
characters, stories have enormous power to teach about life,
albeit indirectly, and great potential as learning tools. When
Peter Pan tries to persuade Wendy to return with him to Never
Never Land he tells her that, if she does, she can teach the Lost
Boys there how to tell stories – and if they knew how to do so
they might be able to grow up.[2]

Stories help people learn in a variety of ways. Telling stories
about your own life is a vital source of meaning and coherence. They can consolidate a sense of competence and identity. Stories give concrete life to philosophies and value
systems against which one can measure oneself. Stories embody tales of learning that can inspire and inform. Stories and
fantasies enable children and adults alike to put experimental
flesh on the bones of their own aspirations, and see and feel
what alternative futures may be like.

Children in all societies are told stories from their earliest
days; through them they learn both the nature and function
of story-telling, and the cultural values and patterns which the
stories enact. Children's stories and fairy tales embody the
guiding myths and values of their particular culture, and offer
powerful examples of how these values are threatened: how
one goes astray; how people learn and grow through their
transgressions and misfortunes; and how order is restored. For

an eleven-year-old Australian, the teenage dramas of *Neigh-bours* repeatedly demonstrate the mischief and unhappiness caused by acting on unchecked imaginings about other people's motives, intentions and feelings; by being led astray by people who are less scrupulous or mature; and by not thinking of the consequences of impulsive action. When Darren is seduced into an 'innocent' goodbye kiss by a girl with a bad reputation, and happens to be caught on film, Libbie chucks him, tearfully explaining that 'I love you, but I cannot trust you any more.' Darren should have thought. When a Xhosa mother tells her child his night-time *intsomi*, the traditional improvised cautionary tale, he is being shown the trials and terrors that befall those who do not follow the values and customs of the tribe, and the rewards of those who uphold the traditions.[3]

Many of the great stories, however, are sagas of dissidence. The *Iliad, The Gulag Archipelago* and *Moby Dick* celebrate the hero's courage and integrity. Such stories offer us models of people (or people-surrogates) learning: facing uncertainty, unpopularity, adversity and conflict; finding resources both in themselves and in their surroundings; showing resilience and ingenuity; and emerging chastened or transformed – 'older and wiser'. From Ulysses to Tom and Jerry, stories depict the nature of the learning journey, and of learning to learn, in all their graphic variety. In the face of difficulty stories offer hope, encouragement and insight.

But children have to learn how to create stories, too; and different societies have different ideas not only about the kinds of stories that can or should be told, but about how to tell them. While some of the features of narrative are universal, others vary widely between and even within cultures. What gives a story much of its interest, and its educational power, is the inner life of the actors as they struggle and inter-relate: insights to which we may be given direct access, or which we may be required to infer. Much of the tension of a good story comes from this inference process, and how convincingly inner worlds are conveyed depends on the craft and the culture of the story-teller. Children have to learn what makes a 'good story'.

The ability of children to follow the basic sequence of

events in a story develops very early. But it takes longer for them to learn to remember and re-create the underlying 'plot structures', and to move from simply recounting events to giving accounts in terms of the feelings and intentions of the characters. This is something that has to be acquired through practice rather than direct instruction. Children are not usually told: 'Think what the story was about. Think about the main characters, and what they goals and motives are. Now reconstruct the plot in line with these intentions in your own words. Just give the main structure of the story – don't worry about every last incidental detail.'

Yet as adults coax children into recounting stories and incidents, they are also coaching them in doing exactly this. They say: 'What did you do at school today?' or 'What did you watch on TV last night?' If not very much is forthcoming, they might prompt by asking: 'Well, who was in the story?' or 'Did you play with Tania?', and then: 'So what happened after that?', or 'Why did Tania get upset?' Implicitly the questions serve to indicate what is considered central to a story and what peripheral, and through their use adults achieve two things. They are able to support the child in producing a better approximation to a 'good story' than she would have been able to do on her own. And they are enabling the child gradually to absorb these prompts and hints into her own way of thinking, so that she becomes more able to be her own narrative coach.

Barbara Galbraith, an elementary schoolteacher working with linguist Gordon Wells in Toronto, demonstrates this process as she helps six-year-olds trying to reconstruct a story which they have all read. Galbraith gently elicits the main events from the children by asking questions. As she picks up on certain details and not others, and gently asks for certain kinds of clarification, she does not tell the children the structure of the story, but rather guides or scaffolds their conversation so that they develop the craft of plot reconstruction, learning what to put in the foreground and what to sideline, as they go along.[4]

The criteria for what counts as a 'good story', and the conventions used to create 'good stories', are, as I say, different according to culture and community. Children who have grown up with one set of criteria and conventions have difficulty if transplanted to a culture with a different set of tacit ideas about story-telling. A detailed study by American cultural anthropologist Shirley Brice Heath has revealed what trouble these conflicting approaches can cause when children from differing backgrounds go to school. In one community, for example, a child learns, through observation and imitation, that a good story is one that is above all dramatic and entertaining. Story-tellers are expected to exaggerate and embellish as they regale others with choice incidents from the day. In a different social group, however, what counted as creative, playful ornamentation for the first may be judged as showing off or even lying. When children from these two cultures meet a teacher who holds yet a third set of narrative values – with very different ideas about what are appropriate and inappropriate topics for a five-year-old's story, or about their optimal length and structure – both of them are going to be in trouble, through no fault of their own.[5]

Critical literacy, the ability to make visible, and questionable, the conventions through which accounts of events are rendered into narrative, is a more advanced ability that children may – or may not – develop as their familiarity with different forms of dramatic structure deepens. Under the tutelage of parents and teachers, children may begin to become aware of these conventions, and to inquire explicitly into how stories are constructed, and why: in whose interests is it to present matters in one particular way rather than another? The British tell quite different stories about what they call 'the Falklands War' from those that have circulated in Argentina. Maori teachers and elders tell different stories about the land from New Zealanders of European descent.

As we saw with the acquisition of language, learning through direct exposition requires skills of comprehension which take time to develop. Paradoxically, children's skills of indirect or implicit learning develop much faster. After all, ever since they have begun to understand language, one of their main tasks has been to infer what others around them mean by what they say. Rarely do we spell everything out, either in normal conversation or in stories – we rely enormously on the listener to fill in the gaps from their own knowledge. And if they don't already have that knowledge their job is to try to infer what it must have to be (on the assumption that the speaker was talking sense). Thus children become past-masters at intuitively figuring out the presuppositions of what they hear; and smart teaching capitalizes upon that expertise. Their facility with indirect forms of learning may even decline later if they are not continually valued and exercised. Howard Gardner and Ellen Winner at Harvard have found that three- and four-year-olds are more adept at producing and understanding appropriate metaphors for a situation, for example, then seven- or eleven-year-olds, who in turn are more fluent than college students.[6]

When a person's involvement with a narrative becomes visible rather than vicarious, reading turns into theatre. Through acting out stories we are able to take on other roles and personalities, to loosen the bonds of too tight a self-image and expand the range of our 'possible selves'. Here is Justin, an eleven-year-old student at the Barbara Taylor School in Brooklyn, New York, trying on a different way of dealing with his frustration.

Justin was lying still on the rug surrounded by several children and an adult kneeling beside him peering at his bare stomach (his shirt had been hiked up to his neck). Len, the adult 'learning director', was holding a paper tube upright above Justin's belly button. Caught by the scene and the students' rapt attention, I asked what was happening. 'We're performing an operation,' they told me, 'the surgical removal of immaturity.'

Later that day, Justin and Len performed a commercial break during a circus scene created by Alice (age eight) and Julia, another learning director. Len and Justin entered the stage walking. Len said, 'Justin, you won't be going to your speech therapist today.' Justin stopped in his tracks, yelled, cried, and fell to the ground in a screaming temper tantrum. Len looked up at the audience for a moment, took some wads of paper out of the manila envelope he was holding and said, while he arched them towards Justin's mouth, 'The miracle cure – "Matchore Partz (Mature Parts)".' Justin 'swallowed the pills'. He stood up and he and Len began the scene again. Len: 'Justin, you won't be going to your speech therapist today.' Justin looked up at him and calmly said, 'Oh well, I guess I'd better go home then.' The audience applauded.

Lois Holzman, the recorder of these stories, explains that Justin had for years been plagued by such temper tantrums, and had become stuck with this counter-productive response to frustration. He knew only one way of reacting – what Holzman calls 'the picture that holds us captive'. Through adopting a different persona the grip of that single image of ourselves can be loosened, and learning can be freed. 'It is through performance – through doing what is beyond us (if only for that moment) – that we learn to do the varied things that we do not [yet] know how to do.'[7]

In a sense, as Holzman is implying, people see their own lives as stories: a lifelong narrative with a single hero or heroine. The human need to gain a sense of personal momentum, history and control by developing such a story is so pervasive that the wherewithal to create it may even have been enshrined in the brain. Michael Gazzaniga, the American neuroscientist who, with Nobel Laureate Roger Sperry, pioneered the study of the differences between the two hemispheres of the brain, has proposed that the left side of the brain (in normal right-handed people) contains a special-purpose module, the 'narrator', whose job it is to look at the thoughts, experiences and behaviours that are the products of all the other bits of the brain and make sense of them in terms of the on-going narrative of the owner's life.[8]

It is, in other words, part of our biological design specification not just to look for guidance and learning in the stories we are told, but continually to create our own. Some people have even suggested that much contemporary unhappiness is due to the fact that people in modern hi-tech societies now receive neither strong myths and stories from their culture nor the ability to construct their own.[9] When their own internal narrators break down or lose the plot, they may be threatened with a collapse of meaning and purpose which may manifest as depression or anxiety. If we are not to be given ready-made credible stories to live by, it becomes all the more important to support the development of the narrator: to nurture the ability to create stories and inhabit the world of narrative.

Memory

Language also functions as a learning tool in the development of memory retrieval strategies. We have already seen how the active use of imagery can aid memory by creating mental pictures that link different ideas (like a foreign word and its translation) together. But verbal thought is a useful tool too, as when we improve retrieval by consciously grouping items into larger categories, or by stringing them together into stories. And whereas some remembering strategies have to be actively taught and learnt, others are picked up from a child's elders in the course of everyday activity.

Anything which improves comprehension also improves memory. Trying to remember things that don't make much sense is a thankless task, and the effort of searching for some kind of meaningful 'glue' is usually well repaid. One study showed how an active approach produces dramatic gains in memory, as well as comprehension, even in young children. Five-year-olds were given 21 pairs of objects to look at, and later asked to see if they could recall the second member of each pair on being shown the first. When the children were simply asked to name each object when it was presented, they remembered only one out of the 21 pairs. When they were asked to make up a sentence that joined the two objects together – for example, 'The soap is hiding in the shoe' – they recalled about eight out of 21. However, when they were asked to make up a question about the two objects – 'Why is the soap hiding in the shoe?', or 'What is the soap doing under the shoe?' – they recalled on average 16 out of 21. With exactly the same time to attend to the objects, the children's activity increased recall from almost none to very nearly all.[10] In another study, high school students who had made an effort to add some meaningful glue at the times of study recalled, on average, 90 per cent in this final test. Students who had not recalled around 20 per cent.[11] The beneficial effects of these strategies is powerful indeed.

A powerful illustration of the craft of memory in action is provided by the actor Anthony Hopkins, who is renowned for his ability to remember lines. (While filming *Amistad* he so overawed the crew with his one-take delivery of a seven-page speech that director Steven Spielberg could not bring himself to call him 'Tony' and insisted on addressing him as 'Sir Anthony' throughout the shoot!) But Hopkins' facility masks an array of effective techniques. He reads each line over three hundred times, annotating the script with the number of times he has read each section so far. As his recall improves he makes a cross in the margin, then a star out of the cross, and then puts a ring round the star. The script is covered with his hand-drawn images, executed in multicoloured felt tip: landscapes, faces, incidents ranging from the Gothic to the futuristic. The lines themselves are highlighted in green, yellow, blue – and orange and red for the violent scenes. Hopkins' prodigious memory is not an innate talent; it reflects consummate mastery of the skills of a particular kind of learning.[12]

Some awareness of what kinds of things are generally hard to remember, or the times when unaided memory is likely to fail, can also be useful. If you are aware of what kinds of things you are bad at remembering, this self-knowledge can be used to trigger a variety of self-supporting strategies. If you tend to forget to put the garbage out on Tuesday when it is collected, write a note to yourself and stick it where you will see it; or put the waste-bin in the middle of the kitchen floor before you go to bed on Monday night. If you have to call someone when you get home, and know that you are likely to forget, create an image of yourself doing something that you will automatically do on arrival and link it somehow to that person's face, or to the act of picking up the phone.

Finally let me return to strategies that rely on doing less rather than more: on *not* trying to remember. In the famous tip-of-the-tongue state, a word or name that you know perfectly well stubbornly refuses to come to mind. The more you try, the more it refuses, and the more strongly wrong alternatives seem to crowd in. You can either give up completely and trust that the unconscious will deliver it up to you when it is good and ready; or you can come at it sideways by allowing your mind, of its own accord, to generate all kinds of spontaneous associations to the target, and associations to these associations. Sometimes the accumulation of these fragments will generate enough neural activation in the general vicinity of the recalcitrant word for it to pop into your mind.

The deliberate relaxing of the mind seems to have more general benefits for memory. In one demonstration, Ralph Haber and Matthew Erdelyi very briefly flashed a detailed Wild West scene in front of volunteers who were asked to draw what they could immediately. Some of the subjects were then given a period of relaxation, designed to calm and quieten mental activity, after which they were asked, without being shown the picture a second time, to recall it again. These second drawings were rated by independent judges to be more detailed and more accurate than their first attempts, even though, with the passage of time, one would normally expect the second attempt to be worse.[13] Many of us are familiar with the corollary of this relationship between memory and relaxation – when stress makes us forget something that we know perfectly well. The actor 'drying' on stage is an obvious example.

We have touched on the benefits of giving up trying and allowing the mind to do it by itself before, in our discussion of the value of reverie in creativity, and, indeed, in the brain's ability to pick up patterns automatically through effortless immersion in experience. But these are not just incidental phenomena of the mind. They are absolutely essential to lifelong learning, and deserve a more systematic treatment. The obsession of Western culture with focused consciousness and rational argument as the ubiquitous tools of learning and problem-solving needs rebalancing. Chapter 9 explores the value of 'soft' strategies for thinking and learning.

NINE

Intuition:
The Power of Soft Thinking

There are many learning predicaments in which the search is not for a new way of solving a problem as conceived, but for a new way of conceiving the problem. The creativity of the architect, the theatre director or the psychotherapist often lies not in the construction of a clever solution, but in a new way of thinking about the situation. Many professionals do not inhabit a world of technical rationality, with an unobstructed overview of the conceptual terrain. Rather they find themselves in the lowlands, in which the view is foggy, the ground boggy and the problem ill-defined.[1] In such cases, where genuine creativity rather than proficient problem-solving is required, hard thinking runs out of steam. Now we must turn to the fourth compartment of the learning toolkit: intuition or soft thinking.

When hard thinking is not enough

Many creative figures have argued forcibly that hard thinking – talking to yourself in a purposeful and deliberate manner – is not the medium of innovation; indeed it may get in the way. Arthur Koestler, for example, explains in his monumental work *The Act of Creation* that language and logic embody 'constraints which are necessary to maintain the discipline of routine thought, but which may become an impediment to the creative leap. . . . Words are a blessing which can turn into a curse. They crystallize thought; they give articulation and precision to vague images and hazy intuitions. But a crystal is no longer fluid.'[2] Faced with predicaments which the normal channels of conceptualization are not able to represent, the crystalline categories of the wordscape may themselves need to be put back into solution, and novel forms of mental organization allowed to gel.

Einstein famously said, of his own creative process, that 'the words or the language, as they are written or spoken, do not seem to play any role in my mechanism of thought. . . . In a stage where words intervene at all, they are, in my case, purely auditive. [They] have to be sought for laboriously only in a secondary stage [to produce a] logical construction in words or other kinds of signs which can be communicated to others.' These reflective comments were made in a letter to the mathematician Jacques Hadamard, who instituted a major survey of the working methods of scientists and mathematicians living and working in the USA in the 1940s. Hadamard concluded that 'practically all of them . . . avoid not only the use of mental words but also, just as I do, the mental use of algebraic or other precise signs. . . . I insist that words are totally absent from my mind when I really think . . . and I fully agree with Schopenhauer when he writes "thoughts die the moment they are embodied in words".'[3]

Insights, hunches and complete guesses

In creativity the result frequently comes before the proof. First comes the insight, and then the figuring out: not the other way round, as hard thinking would have it. Hermann von Helmholtz, one of the great mathematical physicists of the nineteenth century, said in 1881 of another, Michael Faraday, that he found 'a large number of general theorems, the methodical deduction of which requires the highest powers of mathematical analysis . . . by a kind of intuition, with the security of instinct, without the help of a single mathematical formula'.[4]

You don't have to be an acknowledged genius to be able to make use of such non-verbal ways of learning. Frances Vaughan in *Awakening Intuition* reports several similar experiences in ordinary high school students. For example, one young woman wrote:

I was a low B student. I was confused and ill at ease in the [algebra] class. I didn't understand what was going on, and each day when I walked into the room I felt painfully embarrassed. Then one day we were given an objective [multiple-choice], city-wide test, and I scored highest in our school and third in the city. When taking the test I was aware that I couldn't figure out the problems . . . resigned myself to failure and decided to go ahead and guess at the answers. As I was guessing I realized I could just tell which one was the right answer. . . . I relaxed, felt my stomach muscles unknot, and felt almost giddy with laughter. When the test results were announced, I was shocked, embarrassed, and pleased. I felt confused and scared. How could I have guessed that well? . . . However, I learnt that when I didn't know the answers on tests I could just let go, relax, and guess or write down whatever came into my head, and I often was right.[5]

The fact that guesses can have more validity than we think they do has been demonstrated under controlled conditions. In a study by Kenneth Bowers and colleagues at the University of Waterloo in Canada, a group of people were shown a list of fifteen words, one by one, all of which shared an associated word which it was their job to try to identify. After each cue word was presented they were asked to write down a candidate, even though they might think it was a complete guess, and to rate their confidence in it. Typically people would get the associated word on about the twelfth or thirteenth cue word. When their preceding candidates were evaluated by independent judges they were found to be homing in on the target, even when the person had no confidence in them at all. Again, the guesses had more validity than their authors were willing to give them credit for. The implication is that if, like the mathematics student, we were willing to pay greater heed to such guesses we might all be able to make better use of the unconscious machinations of the brain-mind.[6]

There are a number of lines of evidence to show that access to the workings of our own minds is increased when we are relaxed and 'not trying'. The Haber and Erdelyi experiment described on p. 145 shows how we can improve access to our memory stores when in a relaxed state. The same benefit of not trying is also seen in perception. When a target letter is flashed briefly on to a computer screen at a duration which would normally be visible, and is then followed a few milliseconds later by a pattern of some kind, the latter masks the former, making it less likely to be consciously identified. Paradoxically, this masking effect can be reduced by *not* trying to identify the first stimulus. Some people are naturally at ease with this passive attitude, and when encouraged to adopt it do better than people who are busily trying to 'see what's there'. In the words of one of the subjects, he was 'just sort of placidly sitting there and the more relaxed I was the more the words just came'. Sorting out the possible explanations will take further research; but the fact that the phenomenon of 'not being able to see for looking' has been demonstrated in the laboratory is of considerable significance.[7]

Trying too hard: how to squash creativity

But it is in the field of creativity itself that the most dramatic benefits of not trying have been observed. Anecdotal evidence is not hard to come by. Mozart wrote: 'When I am, as it were, completely myself, entirely alone and of good cheer . . . it is on such occasions that my ideas flow best and most abundantly. Whence and how they come I know not; nor can I force them.' Rudyard Kipling said: 'My Daemon was with me in the Jungle Books, Kim and both Puck books, and good care I took to walk delicately, lest he should withdraw. . . . When your Daemon is in charge, do not try to think consciously. Drift; wait; obey.'[8] Paul Cézanne, echoing Hadamard and Schopenhauer, simply said: 'If I think, everything is lost.'

Trying has a number of effects, any of which can undermine creativity. First, as we have just seen, it can make us less sensitive to subtle sources of information, both those in perception and those within our own memories. Second, it tends to involve the ego, the part of us that worries about appearance and performance, and thus to make us feel anxious and under pressure. In any field we know how such pressure leads to self-consciousness, tension and a loss of expertise. Third, pressure tends to pull us back into hard thinking. We start trying to remember the rules, and to fall back on those tried and tested ways of thinking that, in an unusual situation, may be precisely the ones which we should be questioning. In a social situation – a business meeting or a seminar, for example – that feeling of being under pressure, of trying to make a good impression, tends to lead people to play it safe, and that, of course, is the opposite of creativity.

Even quite mild degrees of stress may be sufficient to stifle creativity and inhibit learning. Arthur Combs and Charles Taylor gave people the task of learning to encrypt some sentences according to the kind of simple code, substituting numbers for letters, that spies in children's comics tend to use. Some of the sentences they had to work on were neutral ('The campus grew quite drab in winter'), while others were of a more negative, personal nature ('My family does not respect my judgment'). Some of the neutral sentences were preceded by the experimenter saying mildly: 'Come on, can't you do it a little bit faster?' The personal sentences were encoded more slowly and with more mistakes, but the worst situation was when a neutral sentence was accompanied by time pressure. Even though the degree of creativity required in this task was of a low order, it is still a case of more haste, less speed.[9]

It seems not to matter whether the feeling of effort is induced by a threat or a positive incentive: the effect on creativity can be just as bad. Carl Vesti showed people sets of three complicated pictures and asked them to pick the odd one out. When he looked at how well they did, and how much they had improved over a series of tests, he found that those who were offered the bigger financial rewards for success performed less well, and learnt less, than those who received only a token payment. Note that Vesti's tasks did not involve logical thinking or serial, bit-by-bit learning. Rather they were exactly the kind of challenge that involves holistic perception and sensitivity: insight rather than analysis.[10]

This brings us to the last disadvantage of trying too hard: effort and pressure tend to narrow the focus of attention. Too much stick or too many carrots often restrict attention to what is pre-judged to be pertinent to the task as conceived, and to exclude everything rated as irrelevant. When the task itself is routine, and does conform to expectations, well and good –

thinking and learning do indeed become focused and efficient. But when the problem is non-routine, this preconscious selection may be quite misleading. Information is prematurely excluded, or invalid assumptions imported, so the likelihood of spotting the creative solution is reduced.

Most obviously, this restriction of attention affects perception itself – even in animals. When rats and monkeys have to learn a skill in order to get food, their learning of that specific task improves if they are hungry; but the more hungry they are, the less they learn about their environment in general. When a different task is set – one which relies on patterns in their world which had previously been part of the incidental wallpaper – the animals who were less hungry before learn it quicker. Their cone of attention, as I called it in Chapter 4, had been wider than the bare necessities of the original task, and they had been able to take in more information 'just in case'. Make the search for a solution too intense, and you cannot afford to adopt this broader attitude.[11]

In just the same way, people who are given bigger rewards for detecting visual targets on a screen tend to concentrate on those in the centre and neglect the peripheral ones – even though both are rewarded equally – to the detriment of their overall performance. Even when people are asked just to imagine that there is a substantial bet riding on their performance, their perception becomes coarser and they literally lose sight of subtle features that are essential to the task.[12]

But tunnel vision can be inner as well as outer, making people less likely to spot new opportunities as they arise, and to persist with conventional ways of solving problems even though these are no longer optimal. In a classic demonstration, Abraham and Edith Luchins gave people a series of problems in which they had to imagine being equipped with jars of differing capacities, and having to use them to arrive at a designated quantity of water. For example, you might be given jars of 37, 17 and 6 pint capacities, and have to end up with 8 pints. After some trial and error, you discover that it can be done by filling the 37 pint jar to the brim, and from that filling the 17 pint jar once and the 6 pint jar twice, leaving 8 pints in the big jar. The next few problems involve different numbers, but can all be solved by the same strategy. But then comes the critical trial. You are asked to make 20 pints from 49, 23 and 3 pint jars. The question is: do you carry on with the familiar solution (which does work), or do you realize that this time you can simply fill the smallest from the middle? It turns out that the more pressure people are under, the less likely they are to make the creative leap and spot easier and more elegant solutions when they become available. Their problem-solving has become mindless.[13]

This is not an academic problem – it limits creativity in all kinds of fields. Sigmund Freud, in his 'Recommendations to physicians practising psychoanalysis', explains to would-be psychotherapists the perils of this preconscious assumption-making process. The technique of psychoanalysis, he said,

> consists simply in not directing one's notice to anything in particular, and in maintaining the same 'evenly-suspended attention' . . . in the face of all that one hears. In this way we avoid a danger. For as soon as anyone deliberately concentrates his attention to a certain degree, he begins to select from the material before him; one point will be fixed in his mind with particular clearness and some other will be correspondingly disregarded, and in making this selection he will be following his expectations or inclinations. This however is precisely what must not be done.[14]

There is evidence that this broadening and narrowing of the cone of attention is mirrored in the actual workings of the brain. Remember the metaphor of the brainscape as a heavily contoured landscape, with the hollows and valleys corresponding to familiar concepts and well-worn chains of associations? Unlike a real landscape, this terrain is capable of being twisted and shaped, from moment to moment, by changing expectations: more bouncy castle than mountain range. Research has shown that as one area of the brain becomes active, creating an epicentre of excitation, a stockade of inhibitory activity can be thrown up around its edges to prevent its becoming too diffuse. In this way the brain is able to corral its own activity, making its trains of associations more or less precise and well-defined. It is as if the structural brainscape of valleys and basins could, on the one hand, be functionally sharpened, via these inhibitory rings, so that the brain behaves as if it were composed of steep-sided canyons; or, on the other, loosened to allow trains of activation to spread more broadly.[15]

In hard thinking mode, the brain functions like Venice: it constitutes an intricate network of well-defined canals, highlighting what is conventional or plausible. It responds quickly, efficiently and reliably to the normal run of events. But soft, creative thinking, as we have seen, needs a brain that is more like a river delta, in which different currents of thought are able to blend into each other. In tight-focus mode, the brain-mind draws quick, clever cartoons of the world; in broad-focus mode, it creates watercolours on wet paper, in which the paints bleed and swirl together in unexpected ways – many of them uninteresting or even ugly, some of them beautiful, fresh and startling.

Creative individuals have the knack of allowing their brain-minds to move between these two modes as appropriate. As the nineteenth-century French mathematician Henri Poincaré said, 'It is by logic that we prove, but it is by intuition we discover', and the well-equipped learner needs access to both worlds. Colin Martindale at the University of Maine has used electroencephalogram (EEG) technology to monitor the level of arousal in people's brains when they are engaged in either analytical or creative tasks. The higher the level of arousal, the more Venice-like is the brain's modus operandi; the lower that level (within the limits of wakefulness, obviously), the more delta-like. Martindale divided his subjects into those who were generally more creative and those who were less so. What he found was that the arousal level went up for both groups when they were working on the analytical tasks, and stayed at that level for the uncreative subjects when they were engaging with the creative task. But on the creative task the arousal level of the more creative people actually fell to below normal. They had retained the art of allowing their brains to go soft, and thus to generate less conventional ideas, whilst at the same time being able to switch back into hard thinking in order to test or elaborate these ideas.[16]

A parallel concept is involved in 'seeing' three-dimensional stereograms, such as Magic Eye pictures. To perceive the hidden figure the eyes have to be softly focused, and you have to wait, receptively, for the brain to resolve the squiggles into a 3-D shape. Sharply focused vision will prevent the shape emerging. But once it has clearly appeared, paradoxically, you can then inspect the scene in detail. Creativity works in just the same way.

Learning to think softly

It is possible to get trapped in the low-focus mode, so that even mundane events continually trigger a mental firework display of associations. In his book *The Mind of a Mnemonist*, the Russian neurologist A. R. Luria described a case of a man who was severely incapacitated by such rampant, gratuitous creativity.[17] The brain has developed the ability to corral its own activity for good reason. But it is more common for people to suffer from the opposite problem, getting stuck in the narrow, analytical mode and losing the fluidity of thought and attention that the creative process needs.

However, there is evidence that soft thinking can be regained and developed. One can learn to be more creative by cultivating states of mind that are relaxed and patient, yet quietly attentive and receptive to impressions, patterns and associations. At one level, this is quite easy: you just slow down. Milton Rokeach has shown that, when people are working on the Luchins' jars problems (see p. 151), they are more likely to spot the elegant alternative if instructed to wait for a minute before writing down their answer.[18] Sidney Parnes, one of the pioneers in teaching creativity, has shown that people tend to produce more creative ideas if they are required to keep on thinking after the first flush of more obvious ideas has passed. He asked University of Buffalo students to spend either five or fifteen minutes thinking up novel uses for an ordinary wire coat-hanger. Ideas produced during the last five minutes of the fifteen-minute period were judged to be the most interesting. It is as if the brain naturally follows its more conventional routes first; but if required to persist with the problem it has to allow its activity to 'pool' around the key concept, thus creating the possibility of more gradually discovering less obvious routes (as a stream will find new directions of flow if its original course is dammed).[19]

The ability to hold a problem in mind without actively, purposefully deliberating on it – perhaps even for years – is one of the keys to soft thinking. As mathematician and philosopher George Spencer Brown says in his book *Laws of Form*, 'To arrive at the simplest truth, as Newton knew and practised, requires years of contemplation. Not activity. Not reasoning. Not calculating. Not busy behavior of any kind. Not reading. Not talking. Not making an effort. Not thinking. Simply *bearing in mind* what it is that one needs to know.'[20]

More colloquially, it means being able to put a recalcitrant problem on the back burner without letting it fall down the back of the cooker. In this way, our first impressions and taken-for-granted assumptions have a chance to drop away. Instead of the situation being, in effect, an automatic projection of our own experiences and expectations, we suspend

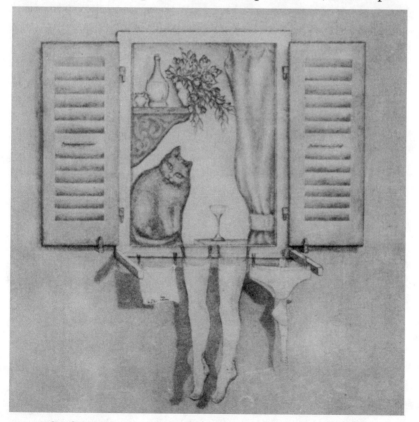

Our first impressions will cause to misinterpret this image. But if we allow the image to work on our senses we see it for what it really is.

judgement and allow *it* to impress itself upon our senses in more detail and with greater intricacy and richness. The illustration below uses a visual illusion to make the point.

Soft thinking needs to happen in its own time. We can create conducive conditions for it to work, if we are sensitive to them. One of the most important of these is the need to allow time at the front end of the learning process, before becoming focused on issues of analysis, planning and execution. Try to hurry through this stage, and the quality of both the learning process and the creative solution are jeopardized.

In one study, fine art students at the Art Institute in Chicago were given a wide range of objects from which to compose a still life. The researchers monitored carefully the differing ways in which they went about the task, and had the finished paintings rated in terms of originality, technical skill and overall aesthetic value. The best were produced by those students who took longer to decide on their composition, often changing their minds even after they had made considerable progress with the painting itself. They played with more objects, and in more imaginative ways, before choosing which they wanted to paint, and their choices were more unusual. When the whole group of students were followed up seven years later, the most successful artists were those who had adopted the more playful, patient and imaginative ways of working.[21]

Yet the encouragement of such fruitful patience and playfulness can be neglected in the pressure to achieve results. As the nineteenth-century French painter Théodore Géricault complained, 'The Academy . . . in desiring to produce precocious fruits, denies itself those which a slower ripening would have made tasty.' There are those today who would argue that the drive for higher standards in schools makes children too busy to think.

The conditions of creativity:
boredom, anxiety and rotting apples

The low boredom threshold of many young people may be attributed, in part, to the loss of this ability to let events reveal their creative possibilities. 'Being bored is one of the privileges of childhood,' says journalist Diana Hinds as she entreats parents (and teachers) not to give in to children's demands for constant stimulation and entertainment. 'The child who has learnt to play, and who has sufficient resources and sufficient space to be bored in . . . has the unique opportunity to be bored in a productive way. Out of this boredom comes, eventually, play – the ordinary, good enough, undirected play that is the work of childhood. . . . So addicted, indeed, are some parents to this relentless diet that the prospect of a single day in the holidays with no activity or outing planned fills them with horror: how on earth will they manage to pass the time?' Sebastian Kraemer, consultant child and family psychiatrist at the Tavistock Clinic in London, says simply that boredom 'is the basis of creativity, and central to our lives'.[22]

Allowing time and space for soft thinking is partly a matter of the external conditions. Too much pressure for results and justifications, and a climate of insecurity and personal criticism, militate against it. On the other hand, conditions that are conducive to relaxed, patient, receptive attention may be found in solitary meditation, country walks and the mental drifting that sometimes occurs on the borderlands between sleep and wakefulness (the kind of reverie discussed in Chapter 5). Such conditions can also be intensely personal. The poet and dramatist Friedrich von Schiller liked to fill his writing desk with rotting apples, claiming that the aroma stimulated his creativity. Ralph Waldo Emerson had to leave home and family for months at a time and do his writing in the anonymity of a hotel room.

Milton Rokeach, in the study quoted on p. 154 about the benefits of slowing down people's answers to the Luchins' jars problems, found that some people could not benefit from the enforced delay: they made up their minds as quickly as possible, and that was that. 'Some individuals, because of past experiences with frustrating situations involving delay of need satisfaction, become generally incapable of tolerating frustrating situations. To allay anxiety, such individuals learn to react relatively quickly to new problems. . . . The inevitable consequence is behavioral rigidity.'[23]

Listening to the body: learning to focus

In a large-scale study of psychiatric patients Eugene Gendlin and colleagues at the University of Chicago discovered a key factor in their potential for recuperation. Patients who talked in a fluent, articulate way were less likely to make headway than those who sometimes talked in a much more hesitant, introspective fashion. It was as if these 'successful' patients were struggling to capture in words something which they were sensing only vaguely in terms of more or less clear images and body sensations. They were listening attentively to a part of themselves, often located in the torso, and trying to give voice to what that in- or pre-articulate 'voice' was trying to communicate. There would be long pauses in their narratives, and when they managed to find the right words or images to capture the feeling, there was invariably a physical sense of release and recognition that would free their inner inquiry to progress a stage further.[24]

Gendlin dubbed this process 'focusing', and perhaps his most important discovery is that, although people initially differ markedly in the extent to which they focus spontaneously, it is a skill that can be readily acquired over a few days with some tuition and guided practice. Learning to shift the focus of attention from the head to the body, and slowing the time scale of learning, needs coaching, just as any skill does, to prevent the beginner mistaking the instructions or getting into bad habits. You have to learn, for example, that when articulate answers come quickly to mind you must discount them and return your awareness to the more nebulous, intuitive 'felt sense', as Gendlin calls it, that is the source of genuinely fresh understanding. This sense, says Gendlin, usually takes about thirty seconds to a minute to form, and has the feel of a gradually developing photographic print: an image slowly forming, not an argument being assembled or a story being told.

Focusing involves the same process of increasing perceptual acuity as that which underlies the wine-taster's developing palate or the physician's awareness of different heart-beat sounds. It is, apparently, just as straightforward to refine our sensitivity to inner, bodily patterns of emotional experience as it is to the bouquet of a burgundy or the murmurs of a heart. Indeed there is evidence that soft thinking in general has this kind of holistic, patient, perceptual quality to it. The best predictors of people's skill at solving insight problems – those that require a creative leap – are their ability to recognize out-of-focus images, and to spot figures embedded in more complex pictures.[25]

This sensitivity is clearly valuable in everyday learning and problem-solving. Any complex predicament can be sensed and explored through the medium of intuition as well as through language and reason. Whether to take a new job, get married, have children or accommodate an elderly parent: all such issues and decisions involve feelings, values and perceptions that are not easy to put into words, and time devoted to gently examining the non-verbal signals that attend them is time rationally spent.[26]

The voices of intuition

Learning power is enhanced by learning to listen to the different voices of intuition. They are not necessarily 'right', any more than tightly reasoned argument necessarily leads to wise conclusions; but they enable us to extract the maximum of meaning from what we already know. The key to this learning is the realization that clear articulation is but one of the voices in which our knowledge and our know-how speak to us, and not always the most appropriate one. The others, however, may be faint, and some are unfashionable; so it can take a little practice to hear them. Most of them have already been touched on in this chapter, but it might be useful to summarize them.

First, there are the physical *feelings* which we have just been discussing: a sense of unease as we contemplate a problem or a solution; a feeling in our bones that one course of action will work out better than another. There are what we might call *insights*, in which a creative idea bursts forth, more or less well articulated and fully fledged, out of the blue. There are *images and dreams* that bring insights in the form of visual and other sensory pictures and metaphors. There are *guesses*, much less certain forms of intuition, in which ideas pop into our heads without any confident feeling of 'rightness', but which may in fact be more soundly based than we think. There are intimations of understanding that we might call *inklings*: fleeting thoughts that flash across the edge of consciousness and are often gone before we can get a good look at them. Some intuitions bubble up as *promptings* or *hunches*: impulses about which way to go, or an almost magnetic feeling of being attracted towards or repelled by certain lines of inquiry, certain practical directions or indeed certain people. And finally, intuition also manifests through an *aesthetic sense*. Scientists and mathematicians routinely talk of proofs and theories in aesthetic terms: not just a logical proof but an elegant proof; not just an interesting theory but a beautiful one.

The resistance to soft thinking

Soft thinking is the most neglected compartment of the learning toolkit, even more than learning through immersion and imagination. These at least have an acknowledged place in the developing life of the child, if not in the adult. But the gentle arts of nurturing intuition seem to go unrecognized in contemporary Euro-American culture. Information, speed, logic, analysis: these are the current gods of cognition. If you don't know what to do, get a bigger hard drive and a faster chip – as if data on its own could provide answers to any of the interesting 'why' and 'how' and 'whether' questions of life, as well as to the 'what'.

Intuition is disdained as lazy, sloppy and primitive: a second-rate way of knowing that we have, as a culture, thankfully outgrown. For example, the attitude that learning is – or should be – fast, clear and well-defined is rife in education. A popular book for parents and teachers, for example, proclaims that 'The feeling of intuition is actually nothing more than the by-product of a very sloppy learning situation. It can be induced merely by presenting a concept in such a way that the learner must spend an unnecessary amount of time trying to learn it. The intuitive feeling can be eliminated by improving the presentation, thereby reducing the amount of time required to learn the concept.'[27]

Giving students problems that require them to ruminate and mull, and the time to do so, is seen as slack teaching and wasteful of precious time. The model of learning that informs such views is wholly focused on the product, the achievement, and has no sense of how tasks do or do not cumulatively extend learners' resilience, resourcefulness and – the third R which we have yet to explore – their powers of reflection.

Over the last four centuries, the craft of hard thinking has indeed been developed to a point of extraordinary sophistication, and with enormous success; but in the process, this rampant cognitive cuckoo has kicked all the other birds out of the nest. To develop technical rationality to such a high point, perhaps it has been necessary to believe that it constitutes the pre-eminent form of learning and knowing; that the human mind is specifically designed for that kind of thought; and that we humans are in essence centres of analysis and articulation. When Descartes declared, in 1637, 'cogito, ergo sum', he was suggesting that we exist primarily, even exclusively, as conscious, deliberate, articulate beings. In a couple of decades he, Mersennes, Locke and other philosophers sold European culture on a model of the mind as essentially conscious and rational, and on a model of the self as the chief executive of such a mind. Intelligence, conscious reason and human identity became roped together into a single package, and thus the idea of unconscious intelligence, and of a sense of self which embraced it, became rapidly and literally unintelligible.

When the notion of the unconscious – of aspects of our functioning to which we, as conscious agents, have no access and over which we have no control – reasserted itself, it could only do so on the terms which the rationalism of the seventeenth century, had set. Unconscious forces, whatever they were, had to be not intelligent, not 'rational', and not 'me'. In the nineteenth century Freud and others were ready to reassert a conception of the unconscious that was duly wild, emotional, subversive and alien. The hot dark corner of psychopathology became mistaken for the whole cool cellar. It is only relatively recently that cognitive science has been adding its considerable empirical weight to the unfashionable testimony of poets, anthropologists, historians and theologians, to remind – re-mind – us of the resources of ingenuity that are available if we make time and space for them.

TEN

Complex Learning: The Toolkit in Action

So far, we have considered the different compartments of the learning toolkit as if they were separate. I have discussed learning through direct immersion in experience largely in isolation from learning through language and through analytical thinking on the one hand, and from the use of leisurely intuition and active imagination on the other. But of course these tools develop side by side, and complex learning challenges may demand a concerted variety of approaches, just as a complex mechanical problem calls for a sophisticated repertoire of physical tools. In this chapter I shall explore some of the ways in which these learning modes interact, sometimes cooperatively, but sometimes in ways that subvert each other.

Intellectual creativity

In Chapter 9, I was at pains to reassert the vital importance of soft thinking. Having a well-developed intellect does not necessarily guarantee that you will also be skilled at the use of imagination, intuition or the direct pick-up of patterns through immersion in experience. Indeed, too much pressure, and too great a need for continual clarity and mental control, can suppress the creative process. But in the context of complex real-life learning, the different learning modes have to work together.

Scientists, for example, need acute powers of inspection –

the ability to allow themselves to be tutored by their experience whether that be reams of computer print-out from a radio telescope, or months of patient scrutiny of a colony of wild gorillas. They need intuition – a sharp nose for interesting problems, critical details and likely avenues of investigation. They need imagination, the power of the 'mind's eye', to find ways of capturing such patterns of results in metaphors and webs of associations. And they need intellect to test, sharpen, and formulate their insights in rigorous and comprehensible form.

In fact the most widely used description of scientific creativity divides it into four stages: preparation, incubation, illumination and verification. The initial phase of an investigation often starts with a seed of dissatisfaction with existing understanding. This seed may be the detection of a critical flaw in the reasoning or the methodology of a piece of published research – a very rational, hard thinking kind of process; or it may be a much more nebulous hunch about something, or the piquing of interest by a small detail that does not seem to fit with conventional theories. *Preparation* for the ensuing inquiry may involve some information-gathering (comprehending and even remembering the relevant literature); practising techniques of experimentation or analysis that might be necessary; analysing concepts and uncovering ambiguities in the questions one is asking, and hidden assumptions in existing formulations; and making some rather unfocused preliminary observations to get a better feel for the phenomenon. Some of this activity is highly purposeful and analytical. Some of it might be much more leisurely and receptive.

Often the process at this stage is highly social. One survey of the working habits of creative people concluded: 'When we look at the complete "life span" of a creative insight in our subjects' experience, the moment of insight [itself] appears as but one short flash in a complex, time-consuming, fundamentally social process. The periods of hard work that precede and follow are deeply rooted in interaction with colleagues.' A physicist, for example, said that 'science is a very gregarious business. . . . It's only by interacting with other people in the building that you get anything interesting done; it's essentially a communal enterprise.'[1]

Kevin Dunbar, a psychologist at McGill University in Montreal, has observed closely what it is that distinguished the most successful research laboratories from the less successful ones. The quality of the group discussions turned out to be crucial. In the most creative laboratories, there was a general air of support – people wanted to help each other, and the team as a whole, to produce the best possible results. This sense of group collaboration, focused on the quality of the research itself, was trusted by the individual members. But within this, conversations about each other's ideas and findings were often highly analytical and even critical. People would not let each other get away with sloppy thinking or procedures, and would force their colleagues to improve or discard ideas that did not measure up. They would sometimes emerge from team meetings bruised or deflated. However, the fact that they knew the attacks were not personal, and were aimed at the greater good, enabled them to take the criticisms on board and respond to them without becoming defensive or despondent.[2]

Good-quality research was also correlated with members of the team possessing different but overlapping research backgrounds. Their experiences and interests were similar enough to allow accurate communication, but varied enough to enable different individuals to bring differing information and perspectives to the task. This variety also enabled people to construct and offer different analogies, and analogical thinking was found to be a major tool for advancing understanding. In the good labs, surprising results and odd phenomena tended not to be discarded as a nuisance, or explained away, but became objects of discussion, to see if there might be something of interest to be explored.

However, if the problem is a meaty one, sooner or later there comes a feeling of impasse. All one's conscious efforts so far have failed to crack it, and at this point it may be advantageous to put it on the back burner and allow intuition and *incubation* a chance. There is evidence that incubation works best only when this stage of impasse has been reached. One cannot, unfortunately, avoid the hard work of preparation by giving up prematurely and hoping that the unconscious will do it all for you. As Louis Pasteur succinctly said, 'Fortune favours the prepared mind.' Because of the preliminary work the problem's representation in the brain is, as it were, magnetized, so that, even when one is not thinking about it directly, remote associations that happen to float across the mind, or even incidental details of daily life such as a snatch of overheard conversation, or a chance observation, can be temporarily connected to it by a channel of activation.[3]

Occasionally a novel chain of associations may couple the problem to a remote area of the network that turns out to be very productive. An analogy is found that provides a key, or perhaps a hub, through which the different parts of the problem are now able to achieve some coherence. A small detail, which may not even be noticed in itself, precipitates a dramatic shift in the channels of the neural network – like the shout that releases an avalanche that was waiting to happen – and a moment of *illumination* is experienced. (As we saw in Chapter 9, this insight may be abrupt, but it can also be slow and subtle.)

At the incubation stage, too much communication can be a hindrance. Despite the conventional wisdom of some management trainers that group brainstorming is an effective way of generating ideas, more objective research has recently suggested otherwise. People working in groups often produce ideas that are fewer in number and lower in quality than the same individuals working for a period alone. When people engaging in group problem-solving share their thoughts and information too quickly, none of them has a chance to develop an independent viewpoint before it is subject to influence by the thoughts and experiences of others. Under such conditions, it has been shown that people tend to converge too rapidly on a solution, or at least on an agreed way of conceptualizing the problem, that may be less than optimal. When you insert periods of more solitary thinking (whether hard or soft) between the discussions, you tend to get higher-quality ideas and solutions.[4]

In addition, despite the brainstorming injunction to suspend the critical faculties, temporarily, during the generative phase, there often remains a subtle culture of judgement and consequent apprehension and reticence. Individuals may 'coast' in a group, sitting back and leaving the work, and the risk, to others. And the need to attend to other people's ideas at the same time as you are trying to come up with your own can overload short-term memory, and you forget what you were going to say. It is harder to catch the creative gleam when a lot is going on around you.[5]

Finally comes the stage of *verification*, which is typically more effortful, focused and again social. Does this brilliant idea actually hold water? What further tests are needed to establish its validity? What findings are left unaccounted for, and can the new model be made to fit? What lines of reasoning need to be filled in to convince those who will judge the worth of the solution? How would it best be developed, refined and communicated?

Creative people of all stripes talk about the need for this interplay between hard thinking, soft thinking and observation. A renowned sculptor, interviewed in the survey of creative people referred to on p. 96, said: 'You have a few good idea, your head begins to swim for a few minutes, you get excited, you have a "moment", and you make your model; and then for weeks and months afterwards you just work on it. . . . The germ of an idea doesn't make a sculpture that stands up . . . so the next stage is the hard work.'[6]

As we saw in Chapter 9, creative people are able to move easily between hard and soft thinking, and they can do so with different rhythms. They may just take small pauses of a few seconds or so in which to allow their brain to go soft during a focused discussion or train of thought. When you take a moment to collect your thoughts before responding to a question, for instance, you may not be frantically scratching around for an answer but just allowing your mind to settle. When people are asked to think aloud continually whilst trying to solve problems that require a degree of creative insight, their performance suffers: verbal fluency impedes creativity. Conversely, people whose minds go blank for a few moments, and who have short periods in which they can find nothing to report about their own mental process, are more likely to receive illumination.[7]

Slightly longer are what we might call hunch breaks, deliberate periods of a few minutes that allow the mind to relax in the middle of a protracted period of focused problem-solving such as a long meeting. Steven Smith of Texas A&M University has found that one of the commonest reasons for getting blocked whilst solving problems is that our thinking has got stuck in an unhelpful groove, and we don't realize it. If periods of hard thinking are interspersed with off-task breaks these wrong-headed assumptions have a chance to dissipate, and when we return there is a greater chance of seeing the problem in a fresh, more productive light.[8]

The third tempo of the learning rhythm involves playtime: time set aside every day for quiet observation, and for soft as well as hard thinking. Another respondent in the survey discussed on p. 96, a writer, spoke for many when she said: 'In the morning, that's when I really like intellectual activity, very, very finely focused intellectual activities. . . . And then after lunch is always a time where I like to slack off; maybe snooze for fifteen minutes, maybe take a bike ride. . . . I mean, who knows when you might suddenly have a terrific "Aha!" idea: I don't know! Mostly it happens to me when I'm gardening . . . or doing something steadying with my hands . . .' Overall, the interviewers concluded that 'Many of the individuals we interviewed structured their day to include a period of solitary idle time that follows a period of hard work. . . . Without this solitary quiet time, they would never have their most important ideas.'

The longest cycle is the one that embraces holiday periods as well as work. There are many stories of people getting their insights on vacation, when the seeds of ideas from other fields can blow across the surface of the mind and take root. Brian Arthur, a Stanford economist, has worked out a new theory of market competition that challenges the law of diminishing returns. Conventional wisdom has it that the growth of companies must be self-limiting – but what if a business were, by luck or judgement, to get so far ahead of the competition that it could effectively 'tilt' the whole market, and lock it into its own products and agendas? Arthur's approach was initially disdained, and it took him ten years to get his first paper published. Yet he anticipated the explosive growth of Microsoft by several years, and his theories help to explain what has happened in the software industry and what the effects on the global economy may be.

And where did he find his revolutionary idea? On the beach. During an eight-week break in Hawaii Arthur was teaching demography – his subject then – in the mornings and going to the beach to read and surf in the afternoons. He found himself reading a book about molecular biology, and became fascinated by the idea of certain biochemical reactions in which an enzyme, far from getting used up, actually produces more of itself, and so catalyses the reaction increasingly strongly. Such an enzyme reaction races away, whilst other reactions, which were a priori equally possible, fall by the wayside. 'What if', Arthur said to himself, 'all this were to apply to economics?' The seeds of his analysis of the runaways in the information technology industry were sown.[9]

When not to think (too hard)

Most of the examples in this chapter so far have concerned problems that are essentially intellectual, such as the development of scientific or economic theories. But an obvious context in which articulation might interfere with problem-solving is when significant portions of the data on which the problem is based are themselves hard or impossible to verbalize. Think of making an aesthetic choice, for example, such as choosing a picture to hang on the study wall. In such cases, where most people would be hard put to capture all the relevant considerations in words, we might expect to find conscious, deliberate thinking getting in the way. In a series of studies Jonathan Schooler of the University of Pittsburgh gave groups of people such choices to make, and asked some of them to think very carefully about their decisions so that they could explain and justify them later. The other groups were asked to make their choices intuitively. Over a range of tasks the result was clear: when people were later asked to reflect on their choices, those who had chosen most deliberately were less satisfied. If we are required to focus on only those features of the situation that can be verbalized, we should not be surprised if we end up feeling that something has been left out of the equation.[10]

These and other studies suggest some general guidelines

about when it is a good idea to give the intellect a rest. First, when you recognize that you have hit a block or an impasse. Second, when it looks as if the solution to the problem might involve a kind of perceptual reorganization. Third, when the block may be one of your own unconscious assumptions. Fourth, when a significant part of the data for the problem is not easy to put into words. Fifth, when there may be a significant disparity between the extent of your relevant experience and your ability to articulate it. Sixth, when the parameters of the situation are not clearly defined, so that you don't know what concepts or considerations are going to be relevant or useful. Seventh, when the situation involves too much complexity: too many factors varying too fast or interacting in ways too complicated for the intellect to grasp.

Practical intelligence

But switching off the analytical mind may be easier said than done. People of a scholarly bent can find themselves taking an analytical approach to problems that over-complicates and obscures what is essentially a simple situation. The brilliant logician Alan Turing used to get around Cambridge on his elderly bicycle, and every so often the chain would fall off. After a while, it dawned on him that the intervals between breakdowns were suspiciously regular, and he decided to investigate.

> On counting the revolutions of the front wheel, he found exact regularity: after a certain number of turns, the chain fell off. He took to counting the turns so as to be able to execute a manoeuvre that kept the chain on. Tiring of this, he fixed a counter on to the wheel. Later he analyzed the mathematical relationship between the number of spokes in the front wheel, the number of links in the chain, and the number of cogs in the pedal: he discovered that the mishap occurred for a unique configuration of wheel, chain and pedals. On examining the machine, he found that it happened when a particular damaged link

came into contact with a particular bent spoke. The spoke
was duly straightened . . .

and the problem was solved. Turing's sophisticated, tortuous
and impeccable logic had led him, after several weeks, to a
realization that any bike mechanic would have arrived at in
seconds.[11] In many practical, real-life situations, intellect
counts for less than we might have thought. There is now
a great deal of research which shows that people's practical
intelligence has little to do with their IQ or other measures of
formal reasoning ability.

In an experiment similar to that of the Luchins' jars described on p. 151, psychologist Sylvia Scribner observed the
practical intelligence of a group of workers at a dairy in
Baltimore, who were making up mixed crates of different
kinds of milk for distribution.

Her research showed that the assemblers were adept at
making up complex assortments of different-sized cartons
to complete the orders they received, even though on paper
sophisticated mathematics was involved – indeed, they were
perfectly able to fill several orders simultaneously. She found
that these workers were amongst the least educated in the
whole dairy, yet were able to perform these complicated
intuitive calculations more successfully than the better-edu-
cated, and higher-IQ, white-collar clerks who occasionally
filled in when one of the assemblers was absent. There was
no relationship between this mental skill and any of their
high school test scores, including IQ and arithmetic. Their
intricate problem-solving ability had developed purely as a
result of experience – learning through attentive immersion in
the situation, coupled with observation of the old hands and a
few well-chosen tips.[12]

Dietrich Dorner and his colleagues at Augsburg, Germany,
have explored the way in which people approach a life-like
simulation of the economy of a mythical town called Lohhausen. It has all the complex problems of a real city: infla-
tion, unemployment, variable levels of local taxation, upkeep
of the infrastructure, environmental concerns, influence of
national government policies on, for example, privatization
of the utilities, and so on. There are over a thousand variables

of varying importance, and the players' success is measured in terms of the state of the books at the end of the game. Having devised a way of measuring the cognitive complexity of the strategies that people use to cope with this task, Dorner has consistently failed to discover any relationship between this measure and IQ. If IQ is supposed to be a measure of some general-purpose reasoning ability, this is extraordinary. We can only conclude that 'intelligence' is much more situation-specific than the IQ approach assumes.[13]

The relationship between knowledge and know-how

The fact that we can be astute without being clever, and clever without being astute, invites us to ask how these two sides of the mind are related in the brain. We know we can't point to one area of the brain which looks after intuition and practical intelligence and another that deals with academic knowledge and verbal reasoning. (It is now quite clear that the popular attribution of all things creative and intuitive to the 'right brain' and everything verbal and logical the 'left brain' is far too simplistic.) But there is some evidence about which part of the brain is needed to tie the two together.

Antonio Damasio of the Salk Institute in California has examined the way in which the relationship between knowledge and know-how is affected by damage to the frontal lobes of the cerebral cortex. In his study people were presented with four decks of cards, face down, and on each go had to choose the top card of one of the decks to turn over. Each card won or lost a small or large sum of money. Only gradually did it become apparent that the decks were constituted differently – two of them contained a higher proportion of cards that signified a heavy loss. People without brain damage slowly focused in on the two better packs, initially on the basis of what they described as a 'feeling', a 'hunch', or even a complete guess. Only much later were they able to justify their strategy and to describe the situation. Having gone through the intuitive stage, they ended up both being able to explain what was going on and to make advantageous choices.

Patients with frontal lobe damage, however, differed in an intriguing way. They too ended up being able to explain the difference between the two decks and to describe an optimal strategy for playing the game; they had 'the knowledge'. But when it came to choosing a card they persisted in selecting cards from the inferior decks. This inability to link their rational knowledge to their practical know-how was prefigured by a complete absence of those shadowy, uncertain feelings that were characteristic of the learning of the non-brain-damaged group. Their intuition was missing. Damasio concludes that it is our intuitive know-how that underpins our ability to make use of the conscious knowledge that we have. Without this underlying erosion of the brainscape, and the practical, physical control which it makes possible, our knowledge, however accurate, remains impotent.[14]

The idea that explicit knowledge and intellectual dexterity are necessary for the development of practical intelligence and skill no longer passes muster. True, the 'talking to yourself', the internalized coaching discussed in Chapter 8, remains a useful way of supporting your own learning. But that involves only the temporary use of strategic hints and reminders, not the kind of thorough-going intellectual comprehension of which educators sometimes seem so fond. As learners gain in proficiency, their skills become embedded in the neural networks of the brainscape and self-talk becomes useful on fewer and fewer occasions. The verbal scaffolding is then required only when you hit a glitch, or are momentarily at a loss. In this intermediate stage of learning you may still flip occasionally from a smooth, unreflective and intuitive way of operating back into a more conscious, articulate and laborious back-up mode. Conscious thinking provides only a kind of support which can be dismantled when it has done its job.

Before they have mastered the knack of talking to themselves *sotto voce*, children do a lot of self-coaching out loud while tacking difficult tasks. As they become more proficient speakers and thinkers, this process goes underground; and as they become more proficient at particular crafts, the need for such explicit guidance drops away. The goal of most skills is, after all, to do it well; not to discuss it or think about it. For a practitioner – unlike a pundit or an academic – comprehension is only a means to an end.

When thinking interferes with expertise

Not only is conscious thinking often irrelevant to the acquisition and expression of expertise; it sometimes positively interferes. We saw one example in Chapter 8: the self-consciousness that can afflict an inexpert speaker of a foreign language by too earnest an attempt to monitor and correct what they want to say. When the voice of the inner coach becomes too critical or obtrusive, performance can collapse. Timothy Gallwey, author of *The Inner Game of Tennis*, was one of the first sports coaches to appreciate the negative power of this kind of self-critical mind chatter.[15] We can even explain it in brain terms. The more anxious and upset one becomes with one's own performance, the less neural activation there is left over to generate the skilful engagement of the muscles, or the accurate perception of the senses.

But you don't even have to get into such a state for thinking to undermine your expertise. You may need no more than to start trying to remember all the good advice which you have diligently assimilated. If too much brain activity is drawn off into thinking and remembering, not enough activation is left for the non-verbal parts of the brain-mind, and performance which was formerly elegant and fluid becomes clumsy and jerky. This raises the intriguing possibility that people who have learnt a skill without any accompanying theorizing or explicit understanding might actually be better off, under conditions which might bring about self-consciousness, than people who have understood their actions. When they are under pressure, or being judged, the latter might try to fall back on their knowledge and, in doing so, inadvertently undermine their know-how. The former, having no such understanding, cannot be tempted to adopt this counter-productive strategy – and their skill might therefore hold up better.

This is just what R. S. Masters at the University of York observed when he taught groups of novices to putt. Some of these groups were given precise instructions, taken from reputable golf coaching manuals, which they were told to follow as carefully as possible. Others were given no instructions, and practiced their putting whilst having to call out random letters every second, so they could not think about what they were doing even if they wanted to. Then both groups were put under pressure. They were told that an eminent professional golfer was coming to judge their competence, and that sizeable financial rewards and penalties would depend on these judgements. All groups showed an increased heart rate when they were being tested, showing that they were finding the situation stressful. But the performance of the group who had learnt with the instructions deteriorated much more markedly than the others'. As Masters sums it up: 'If, in passing from novice to expert . . . explicit learning can be minimized, the performer will have less conscious knowledge of the rules for execution of the skill, and will be less able to reinvest his or her knowledge in times of stress . . . result[ing] in a lower incidence of skill breakdown. . . . In practical terms, the performer will be less likely to choke.'[16]

Trying to understand what you are doing whilst you are learning can, in some circumstances, even obstruct the learning itself. Take the Rubik cube: the puzzle which requires you to twist the sides of the cube around in order to get all the mini-cubes of the same colour on to the same face. The puzzle is too complicated to be figured out logically; there are too many possibilities to keep in mind. As a beginner you cannot consciously work out what twist to apply at any moment. But if you mess about with it for a while, your hands begin to develop habits and hunches which are quite without conscious justification. To learn how to do the Rubik cube, therefore, you have to trust and tolerate this process of learning by immersion. Children have been adept at mastering the cube because they are quite at home with this kind of learning. Their parents have often found it infuriating because they themselves were not comfortable with such a 'mindless' approach: they wanted to figure it out, but couldn't. Their resilience was undermined, their resourcefulness diminished, and consequently their learning impeded, by their adherence to an intellectual approach.

Well-intentioned tuition can exacerbate this effect. Dianne

Berry and Donald Broadbent have shown that preliminary instructions can invite people into a figuring-out frame of mind which, as with the Rubik cube, may be unhelpful. Especially when the learning task is complicated and/or counter-intuitive, the immersion approach may be preferable and an intellectual mind-set may get in the way. In general these researchers have widely found that teaching tends to improve people's ability to answer questions about what they are doing, but not to improve their expertise. These studies show that accumulating knowledge and developing know-how are in fact two different kinds of learning that may run side by side, may sometimes interact positively, but may also compete with and undermine each other.[17]

The mentality of madness

At its most general, over-reliance on conscious deliberation combined with distrust of intuition and spontaneity borders on mental illness. American clinical psychologist Louis Sass has recently argued that schizophrenia is just an extension of the modus operandi of the philosopher, the calculator, the compulsive deliberator: the person for whom hard thinking has become a way of life. If we try too hard to find certainty and security in analytical understanding, our world falls apart. Sass's patients say: 'I have to do everything step by step, nothing is automatic now. Everything has to be considered.' And: 'I used to cope with all this internally, but my intellectual parts became the whole of me.' He concludes that 'madness . . . is the endpoint of the trajectory [that] consciousness follows when it separates from the body and the passions, and from the social and practical world, and turns in upon itself'.[18]

Iain McGilchrist, in a comprehensive review of Sass's work, comments on the way in which sufferers from schizophrenia perceive the world in terms strongly reminiscent of my distinction between tight- and loose-focus attention.

It seems that something interferes with the broad scope of attention whereby many of our thoughts and perceptions are experienced as a whole. Instead, there is often an intense, narrow focusing of attention on some quite everyday object or event, which renders it strange, inhuman, perhaps terrifying. Detail is emphasised at the expense of the whole. Understanding what something denotes is not normally impaired, but connotative meaning may be completely lost. Predicted patterns are neglected, and the usual assumptions about what is going to happen, on the basis of what *has* happened, are not made. The net effect is to produce a sense of alienation from others, from one's feelings and even from one's own body.[19]

The ecologist Gregory Bateson used to illustrate this precariousness with the example of a male patient standing in the hospital cafeteria queue, and a cheerful woman behind the counter saying: 'And what can I do for you, my love?' Staring at her like a rabbit in car headlights, he dropped his tray with a clatter and blundered in panic from the room. He had experienced her friendly, innocent remark, suggested Bateson, as a yawning pit full of nameless uncertainties over which he was suspended by a thread. Was she making fun of him? Was it a sexual advance? Was she offering the care for which he was looking? How to respond? How not to make a dreadful fool of himself? Other people seem, inexplicably, to be able to deal confidently with such treacherous events – but how do they do it? How come they march firmly across dry land, while I am for ever skating over thin ice?[20]

Sass's analysis of contemporary culture goes so far as to suggest that we are living in a world that is itself borderline or 'schizotypal'.

Some aspects of late 20th-century life in the developed world – the distancing effect of technology and bureaucracy on our apprehension of others, the barrage of disparate information and surrogate experience – reproduce traits that are easily identified in schizophrenics: the tendency to abstraction, or to hyper-consciousness, the concentration on detail rather than the whole, the perception of people and objects as mechanical entities.

These indeed are the most obvious emergent forms of attention in Western societies . . .

How the planes of the mind relate

The inter-relationships between the four compartments of the learning toolkit – immersion, imagination, intellect and intuition – turn out to be much more intricate, and interesting, than the popular idea of the mind would allow. In practice they assist each other in a variety of ways. And the two forms of erudition to which they give rise – knowledge and know-how, the wordscape and the brainscape – also have a complicated relationship. Though the wordscape originally grows out of the brainscape, once they are established they start to interact in novel ways.

Know-how can make its way up into the worlds of concepts and words. I may from time to time have an insight, a spontaneous bubbling up into language of a pattern not previously recognized or articulated – though the vast majority of what I have learnt about people, gravity, water, justice, cooking and the behaviour of cats stays firmly below ground, exquisitely functional and absolutely inaccessible to word or even thought.

As well as experience bubbling up into language, language percolates down into experience. People can describe to the young learner concepts like a 'unicorn' or 'the King of France' which have no real existence in the world of bare experience. With the aid of her imagination, she can blend together previously unconnected concepts and properties, creating new neural circuitry for herself. And through their tuition and instruction, other people's perspectives and priorities can influence what she attends to and what sense she makes of her experience, and thus channel the growth of the brainscape itself. The influence of culture and the influence of direct experience become inextricably entwined. Through language she describes the world as she experiences it, but the very way she experiences it is informed by the language that she has learnt to speak: the way in which the language itself is grammatically structured, and the things that can be said within those structures. Even her emotions will depend on the culture in which she grows up.

But there are many occasions on which talk does not cause such an embodied change. There are many things we have learnt through language that affect connections within the wordscape, but which do not filter down and cause corresponding changes in the brainscape. I remember that 'procrastination is the thief of time'. I even believe that it is true. I try not to put things off that have got to be done. I may even proclaim the evils of procrastination to others, fluently and persuasively. And yet I still procrastinate. It is notoriously difficult to walk your talk, and we know we are all hypocrites in one way or another.

Thus the planes of the child's brain-mind, though originally quite congruent, begin to shear apart. The wordscape comes to contain facts, ideas and opinions for which there is no experiential substrate in the scape. We can learn at one level without automatically linking that change to the other level. The dislocation of lived experience and language, intuition and intellect, know-how and knowledge, enables us to believe things that we do not embody, and to have areas of competence that are not yet represented in our self-image – what we consciously 'know' about ourselves. We are capable of becoming laminated without being integrated. We can articulate things that we know not to be true. Alongside the boon of communication comes the more dubious ability to deceive others and to deceive ourselves.

The brainscape's modules of competence will always contain fine-grain connections that have not crystallized into general-purpose concepts, let alone into verbal propositions. The lessons of experience can never be completely rendered into words, for words are themselves abstractions across experience – or they find their meaning not through the experience that underlies them, but solely in terms of the positions they occupy in the wordscape. As in a dictionary, much of our vocabulary is defined in terms of other words. If I try hard, I may be able to construct a form of words – a poem, perhaps – that will evoke in you a reasonable copy of my own experience. But often the attempt to talk about 'the human condition' peters out into endless trails of ideas that keep leading across the wordscape, but never manage to drop vertically down into the mines of personal meaning.

One of the most powerful functions of imagination, as we have seen, is to mediate between the worlds of intuitive expertise and explicit comprehension. Resolutions and intentions that remain at the level of verbal propositions have a notoriously weak effect on behaviour. But turn those good intentions into vivid images of the goal, and of the means to achieve it, and a bridge is built between the different planes of operation. Likewise a great deal of physical, as well as imaginative, practice may be needed to re-embed some acquired theory, however wise, into the level of practical proficiency. Thus learning is as much about the way in which information is represented internally – how it is converted between different formats; how it is disembedded from particular contexts, occasions and purposes of use; and how it becomes hooked up to the senses and the muscles – as it is about acquiring more 'stuff'. The neglect of these processes of inner transformation is one of the main ways in which learning has been oversimplified and consequently misunderstood.

ELEVEN

Becoming Reflective: The Consciousness of Good Learning

Now we come to the third R of good learning: reflection. To be resilient and resourceful is not enough. Certainly learning power needs a foundation of emotional tolerance for the vicissitudes of learning. And certainly, on that foundation has to be built a broad and flexible repertoire of learning skills and strategies – the knowing what to do when you don't know what to do. But good learners also need to be strategic. They need to know their own minds; to be aware of their strengths and weaknesses; to be able to take stock of their own learning and to plan and manage it effectively. They need to be open-minded, willing and able to see through the appearances of familiarity to the learning opportunities hidden behind them. They need, in a word, to have the disposition, and the ability, to be reflective. In this chapter I shall explore some of the main facets of reflection, and show how these higher-order learning qualities can themselves be learnt and cultivated.

Open minds and closed minds

As we saw way back in Chapter 1, people's learning depends not so much on the challenges and uncertainties that their world contains, but on how these are perceived. Even the most familiar environment is full of things that can be treated as problematic – if we see them as such. 'How come electricity and water go safely together in kettles but not in bathrooms?' 'What are you thinking?' 'I'm very worried about Jim . . .' To be open-minded is not to be swamped or paralysed by questions (as was the schizophrenic patient in Chapter 10), but to be ready to see learning invitations when they occur. With a closed mind, any discomfiting discrepancies from 'normal' are simply disregarded. The subjective world remains cosy, familiar and therefore learning-free – whether it is or not.

Bottom-up and top-down

To understand the difference between an open mind and a closed one, and the way to develop the quality of openness, we need to look at how perception itself works. Perception involves two reciprocal processes. Imagine yourself kidnapped, blindfolded and carried into a strange room, where the mask is removed. The moment your sense-doors are opened, information starts streaming inward along the sensory neural pathways towards the brain, where simple features such as colour, shape, brightness, movement and location are extracted, and begin to be bound together into waves of activation that flow along the channels that have been worn into the brainscape by experience. This inflow of activity from the periphery of the nervous system towards the centre, and from more simple to more complex conceptual kinds of features, is called *bottom-up* processing. The sensory evidence homes in on the identification of what kinds of objects your new world contains.

But we rarely find ourselves in situations where we do not know what we are going to see when we open our eyes. Even in my example, your brain will not be completely unprepared. Clues in the hard feel of the floor under your feet, the way your footsteps echo, the coldness and stillness of the air, the smell of damp and the sound of old-fashioned bolts being drawn will have prepared your eyes to see a dungeon rather than a cosy living room. In normal life such clues as to what will happen next are very strong. We see in terms of our past experience and current expectations, as well as in terms of brute sensation. As sensory clues begin selectively to activate certain scripts and concepts, these start to function as unconscious hypotheses which then reach back down the neural pathways and influence the sensory processing that is taking place. By priming those features which would be present –

grim-faced jailer, barred window, bare stone walls – if our preconscious guess is right, we effectively bias the sensory analysis towards the selective detection of just those predicted features. And if the neural circuitry corresponding to those diagnostic features does indeed 'fire', then we consider our hypothesis confirmed. This use of knowledge, context and expectation to funnel the inflow of activation is called *top-down* processing.

Mindful or mindless?

Top-down processing is highly efficient when what is there is what you expected. You can cut out a lot of unnecessary work and arrive at a state of recognition more quickly. 'Ah! One of those. And I know what to do with those: I boil them for four minutes (or smile at them, or try them on for size, or run away, or ask for their phone number).' In familiar situations, and under pressure to respond quickly, it makes sense to use as much top-down processing as you can. The risk, though, is that you will tend to see only what you expect to see, and see things as more familiar than they really are. To have a closed mind is to have developed the top-down habit to the point where your perception is continually skimpy and hasty. Learning happens only when bottom-up processing is allowed to proceed in a way that is not completely channelled and pre-empted by top-down expectations and assumptions. Just as the successful science laboratory is the one that takes the odd result seriously, so is the successful mother or manager, product designer or program developer. To perceive in such a way that your neural networks can grow and change is to live mindfully. To perceive in such a way that aberrant data is filtered out before it can cause any surprises is to live mindlessly.

Examples of mindlessness are not hard to come by. Both its pros and cons are illustrated by the tendency to complete another person's train of thought. Sometimes our ability to anticipate what someone is going to say, or is struggling to say, even before they themselves may know what it is, is a valuable form in empathy. Through our sensitivity to clues such as changes in body language or tone of voice (of which they may not be aware) we are able to engage our top-down understanding and fill in the gaps. But such empathy may also be false or premature. We paste our own hasty projections on top of the other person's hesitant reality.

Some mindlessness reflects an inability to see the straws in the wind. Spouses may not notice how their partners are changing, or the signals of dissatisfaction that they are emitting increasingly strongly. When the partner finally walks out the one left behind is astonished. A company may similarly ignore the signs of changing markets, persistently treating them, if they are perceived at all, as temporary blips in a natural order which will soon be comfortably re-established – and then the company goes under. Such resistance to learning is often associated with a hardening of the categories. If you assume that it is the sole business of your typewriter company to make typewriters you are in for a nasty surprise when the word-processor comes along. But if you had been mindful enough to think of your typewriters not as particular types of machine, but as devices that fulfil a more general function – a means to a broader class of ends – then you might now be a major player in the laptop market. As Theodore Levitt said in his classic 1960 article entitled 'Marketing myopia' in the *Harvard Business Review*, 'The railroads are in trouble . . . because they let [airlines] take customers away from them . . . [by assuming] themselves to be in the railroad business rather than in the transportation business.'[1]

What predisposes people to open- or closed-mindedness? Mindlessness can simply be the result of short-term expectations. People's inability to see the simple solution to the Luchins' jars problems (p. 151), after they have solved several in a more complicated way, is an example of short-term mindlessness. There are many tricks and jokes that rely on the same effect.

A: 'A woman goes into a pet shop to buy a goldfish, but when the proprietor appears he indicates that he is deaf. Not being able to see any fish of the type she wants, what does she do?'
B (brightly): 'That's easy; she goes like this [miming a fish's mouth opening and closing slowly, and wiggling his hand like a fish swimming].'

A: 'Right. Now the next day the same woman wants a puppy and goes into another pet shop. But this time the owner is blind. What does she do?'
B (smugly): 'Easy again. She goes "Woof! Woof!" '
A (even more smugly): 'No, she doesn't. She says: "Hello. I'd like a dog, please." '

Sometimes the cause of mindlessness is simply the familiarity of the situation. You fall into old habits without thinking. This is especially pernicious if you have only ever experienced a single way of operating, leaving you with the unconscious assumption that your way is natural and inevitable. The elderly head of the family firm typically reacts to 'new-fangled' management ideas as if they were 'crazy'. Or, to take a less hackneyed example, the prognosis for an alcoholic is much better if they experienced a variety of role models as they were undergoing their apprenticeship as drinkers than if they knew only one (if they were a child at home with an alcoholic parent, for example).[2]

'Could be' thinking

But mindlessness can also be due to a general disposition to assume that there is only one way of looking at something, or of behaving, inculcated by past experience. Ellen Langer of Harvard has evidence that one of the most common approaches to teaching can inadvertently lead to just such a closed, anti-learning cast of mind. If you have been repeatedly told, implicitly or explicitly, that there is basically only one way of looking at things, there is no point in thinking about how you might look at them differently. But if you were told that this is just one way of looking at things, there is some point in you taking control of your learning and exercising your discretion, your critical faculties and your creativity.

Following this line of thought, Langer explored the effect on students' learning of two kinds of teaching, which conveyed the impression that the subject-matter was either 'absolute' (i.e. true and therefore non-negotiable) or 'conditional' (i.e. a theory or perspective, and therefore open to question and interpretation). In one test, she asked high school students to read a passage about the ways in which city neighbourhoods evolve. The passage was written slightly differently for three equivalent groups. For the first, the approach was presented as definitive: this is the way neighbourhoods develop. For the second, the approach was presented conditionally, using terms such as 'could be' and 'may be'. For the third group, the passage was written in absolute terms, but introduced as 'one possible model'. After checking that all groups had understood the passages factually, they were asked to apply the information to a hypothetical case which did not fit the approach very neatly; and to generate new ideas about how neighbourhoods might develop. The 'could be' group was significantly more creative in these tasks than either of the other two. In a similar study ten-year-olds wrote poems that were more creative when they were given instructions in the 'could be' format.[3]

Students of all ages seem well able to handle the inherent uncertainty that such conditional framing entails – provided the teacher uses the conditional language to imply that the uncertainty is an inherent attribute of the information conveyed, and not of their own insecurity as teachers. To people who question whether younger children are able to handle this uncertainty, Langer replies: 'It could be [NB practising what she has been preaching] that children taught conditionally are *more* secure because they are better prepared for negative or unexpected outcomes.' She is suggesting that children brought up to feel comfortable with 'it depends' will be better learners, in a world that is increasingly unstable and equivocal, than those of us who were brought up to think in terms of absolutes.

Could it be that people who have faced greater uncertainty, even though this might have caused them hardship, are better prepared to deal mindfully with novel situations? Ellen Langer reasoned that people who suffer from dyslexia typically face the uncertainty, in reading, of not knowing whether a particular squiggle, 'd', say, corresponds to a spoken 'd' or 'b'. When she repeated her experiments with a group of dyslexic people, they showed a greater ability to handle information flexibly even when it was presented in absolute terms.[4] There is even a suggestion that more creative schoolchildren come from homes in which greater amounts of uncertainty are tolerated. The mothers of children who score highly on standard tests of creativity, for example, admit to many more uncertainties about their own child-rearing practices and philosophies.[5]

Contemplation: dwelling on the world

It is particularly when situations are complex and ambiguous, or when we are in danger of being fooled by our own minds, that the willingness to be reflective comes into its own. The ability to switch from top-down into bottom-up mode, and simply contemplate a situation without, for the moment, trying to come to a conclusion about it, is an essential learning aid. We saw some examples of this in Chapter 9: the way the picture of the woman in the window reorganizes under sustained scrutiny; and the superior creativity of the art students who attended more closely and slowly to the material of their still life.

This ability is no mere aesthetic luxury: it is the essential ingredient of many practical arts. The ability to discern small detail with a quiet eye, to allow a delicate, complex image of a situation to emerge slowly, and to let this picture interact with the fine structure of accumulated experience: that is the mental process that underlies many acts of real-life connoisseurship. The tracker, squatting by the side of a trail, examining a bent leaf and an almost imperceptible hoof-print, is able to make inferences about the age, size and condition of an animal that passed many hours before: inferences that seem like magic to an untutored eye. A farmer telling an ailing horse by the condition of its hocks and an architect developing an idea for a house from the lie of the land are both relying on a kind of contemplation in which deliberate, articulate thought plays only a minor role.[6]

Different fields require different balances between the analysis of data and the pondering of clues. And the person whose work takes them across the boundaries between different 'trades' needs to develop a flexible repertoire of learning methods and an intuitive appreciation of when each is best used. The Russian neurologist A. R. Luria, in describing his change from experimental to clinical work, drew an analogy with police detection to make this point. 'At first I found it difficult to change from the logic of ordinary experimental investigation, which was imprinted on me, to the logic of clinical work. It took a while to learn to pay attention to those small events that can become a turning point in such investigations. The procedures and reasoning of such investigations seemed more like those used by detectives solving a crime than like the problem-solving behaviour that prevails among psychologists and physiologists.'[7]

Practising contemplation

But how can the disposition and the art of contemplation be cultivated? Anything that induces a quiet and sustained attention to detail will do: for instance poetry, fishing and meditation. 'With an eye made quiet by the power of harmony, and the deep power of joy, we see into the heart of things,' said Wordsworth, in 'Tintern Abbey'. Jacques Maritain says it is the job of the poets to 'hear the passwords and secrets that are stammering in things', and they do so 'by a kind of unifying repose . . . to which they have to consent, and which they can cultivate, first of all, by removing obstacles and silencing concepts'.[8]

Poems are vehicles for encouraging us to enter – to practise entering – the same state of unquesting, non-intellectual mindfulness as the poet had when inspired. English teacher George Whalley talks of experiencing a poem before we can understand it, and by this he means 'paying attention to it as though it were not primarily a mental abstraction, but as though it were designed to be grasped directly by the senses, inviting us to function in the perceptual mode'. A poem is therefore not to be read as a cryptic message to be decoded – for that is to shrink it, or massage it, to fit the normal categories of thought; and if the message could have been said simply in the first place, the poem would not have been needed. To help students develop the feel of this contempla-tive knowing there must be 'strong imperatives against "in-terpretation" and against "thinking about" the poem', says Whalley. 'By quietness and submission, a reader . . . can treat the poem as a self-unravelling clue.'[9]

Thus to study poetry is to make use of, and sharpen, a very valuable learning tool. In his radio talks to schoolchildren about poetry in the 1960s, Ted Hughes recommended some techniques for cultivating this poetic sensibility. 'Practice in simple concentration on a small, simple object is the most valuable of all mental exercises,' he said. 'Any object will do. Five minutes at a time is long enough, and one minute is enough to begin with.' Having got used to this kind of contemplation, and whilst engaged in such concentration, you begin to write descriptive phrases that are 'detailed, scientific in their objectivity and microscopic attentiveness', not worrying about narrative or sentence structure, but giving each phrase a new line. With practice, you can begin to 'extend the associations out from the object in every direc-tion, as widely as possible, keeping the chosen object as the centre and anchor of all your statements'.

It is as if the observed object were a baited hook, dropped quietly into the mind, and bits of one's own knowledge rose to it, in their own time, like fish in a pond. Your job, like that of the fisherman, is to sit quietly and attentively on the bank, seeing what comes up. Ted Hughes, a fisherman himself, saw a direct link between real fishing and the metaphorical fishing of the poet. When you are fishing

> all the little nagging impulses that are normally distracting your mind dissolve. . . . Your whole being rests lightly on your float, but not drowsily: very alert, so that the least twitch of the float arrives like an electric shock. And you are not only watching the float. You are aware, in a horizonless and slightly mesmerized way, like listening to the double bass in orchestral music, of the fish below there in the dark. So . . . fishing with a float is a sort of mental exercise in concentration on a small point, while at the same time letting your imagination work freely to collect everything that might concern that still point.[10]

Yet another method of cultivating contemplation is meditation, particularly the mental training known as mindfulness practice. Though it derives from the contemplative Buddhist traditions of South-East Asia, it is a highly accessible, practical and non-mystical way of developing contemplation and open-mindedness. The practice involves the attempt, over recurrent periods of half an hour or so, to focus one's attention as fully as possible on whatever experience arises in the present moment, and to discourage the mind's tendency to elaborate these experiences with layers of judgements, evaluations, associations, stories and fantasies. You practise not hanging on to pleasant memories, not pushing unpleasant feelings away, and not getting involved in the familiar activities of solving problems, planning for the future or rewriting the past. Instead, you try to maintain a clear-sighted, welcoming yet dispassionate attitude towards whatever comes, observing thoughts and feelings as they arise, and as they fade away, as if they were natural phenomena like the passing weather. Of course you keep getting swept away, leaping on to the back of a passing thought and galloping off into the worlds of regrets, recriminations, plans and hopes. But with practice you learn to resist the impulse to take thoughts for real, and see them, like itches and bird-calls, as evanescent, even impersonal, phenomena.[11]

The documented effects of such training include the ability to sustain attention on the sensory world without getting distracted, and without overlaying it with (unacknowledged) projections and associations of one's own mind. One group of meditators showed much less 'projection' than people normally do when they were asked what they 'saw' in Rorschach ink-blot pictures – meaningless shapes that commonly invite such projections. To them, the ink-blot looked like an ink-blot. One of them said: 'The meditation has wiped out all the interpretative stuff on top of the raw perception.'[12] There is evidence from other sources that mindfulness training makes perception more acute. It increases the extent to which people can become totally absorbed in a scene. It enhances their ability to detect figures that are embedded in other, more complex, pictures. There is some suggestion that the increased acuity leads, as you might expect, to a subjective sense of perception 'slowing down' (a phenomenon also associated with the use of marijuana and certain other drugs).[13] And such meditation has also been shown to increase people's ability to pick up and 'read' the subtle cues of body language in a way that significantly increases their empathy.[14]

But does mindfulness training pay off in terms of real-life learning? John Miller's students seem to think so – though it may take some time. Miller is a professor at the Ontario Institute for Studies in Education, where he offers graduate-level courses in which students can learn meditation and explore its effect on their development as students and professionals. The experience of one such student, Jane, seemed to speak for the others. At the start of the programme, she found it difficult. In her Day 3 diary, she wrote: 'I need to learn to relax, but it's not something that comes easily to me!' After a couple of weeks she reported a common experience of beginning meditators: the feeling that her mind had become busier and busier, coupled with the realization that this reflected a growing awareness of what had always been the case. 'I'm surprised how busy my mind is: so many thoughts fighting for attention.' After five weeks Jane was noticing some practical benefits. 'My ability to concentrate on my work after meditating seems greater. . . . Today I noticed an alertness, an attention to my work which I began after meditating.' By the eighth week, she even surprised herself by 'beginning to consider the possibility that I might actually continue this practice after the course. Not that I'm a skeptical person, but I just wasn't getting much out of it until recently. It always seemed to work against my "intense", busy nature and lifestyle. I'm now beginning to see the benefits and to appreciate the difference it might make in my daily life.' The next day she wrote: 'The irony is that meditation is maybe something that fits who I am after all. I like this focused, relaxed feeling. . . . This is not what I expected at all!'[15]

Self-knowledge: learning by mulling things over

Being reflective means looking inward as well as out, making explicit to ourselves the meanings and implications that may be latent within our store of originally unreflective know-how. In periods of reflection, in this sense, one chews the cud of experience, ruminating on experiences and impressions to see what larger significance they might have. At the same time, ideas and theories that have been registered intellectually can be re-examined in the light of personal history. Does this new perspective offer useful insights that develop my understanding of my lived experience? And, at the same time, does my experience suggest modifications to or developments of the framework? Reflection is essentially an off-line search for greater coherence between knowledge and know-how.

And this is quite a different kind of learning from simply trying to grasp someone else's ideas. Jacqui, a management consultant, for example, recalls how, at university:

> I learnt plenty of strategies for reading academic books. I would pick at them; copy large chunks that seemed relevant to the essay I currently had to be working on; and then carefully assemble the chunks of people's writing into a shape that seemed best to meet what my tutor was looking for, so that he would give me an adequate grade. . . . Now, twenty years later, it is different. The strategies I learnt to deal with learning from books do not work any more. Now I want to *really* understand; but I have no idea how to go about tackling the book in order to make sense of it.

She has been brought to the realization that the old learning tools are not up to the new job and to a question: how to develop better strategies?

Through her ponderings Jacqui was able to understand her complex relationship to studying, and, by recognizing them, to guard against her tendencies to feel disempowered, resentful or envious. She needed time to feel around an idea, test it, customize it and perhaps even, eventually, reject it. Thus the development of learning power through individual reflection.

Self-directed learning

There is a strong world-wide movement to place this kind of reflective learning at the centre, especially of adult education. The effort to make explicit what is latent in one's own experience is seen as being of essential value. By making things explicit one is enabled to take a critical stand towards them, and to see that there are indeed alternatives to what had seemed, implicitly, to be inevitable. Reflection breeds choice. One seminal article, for example, claims that self-directed learners ought to be able to 'examine themselves, their culture and their milieu in order to understand how to separate what they feel from what they should feel, what they value from what they should value, and what they want from what they should want. They develop critical thinking, individual in-itiative, and a sense of themselves as co-creators of the culture that shapes them . . .'[16]

What is required is the ability to take an aspect of your functioning that has been tacit and bring it to light, crystal-lizing out the values and beliefs on which it is based and holding them up for conscious scrutiny. Where previously these assumptions had been invisibly woven into your sub-jectivity, embedded in the ways you think and feel, you are now invited to make your beliefs objects of knowing and learning. What was taken for granted as natural and inevita-ble, largely comprised of the unexamined beliefs of your culture and your childhood, is made equivocal.

In discovering that the way your parents saw the world to be was just one model among many, and that you have the freedom to change it or reject it, you become a renegade from that culture. This post-modern journey, of learning to adopt the ironic stance, to see through that which had seemed substantial and eternal, is difficult, exciting, destabilizing and lonely. Bringing to conscious light the premises on which your roles as son or daughter, parent, partner, employee, student, woman or man, have been based, may feel, as

Harvard educationalist Robert Kegan has said, 'more like mutiny than a merely exhilarating expedition to discover new lands'. It is easy to underestimate the difficulties and costs of this transformation. As Kegan says, self-direction, in this sense, is a

> bloodless word that fails to capture the human wrenching of the soul from its cultural surround. . . . [Such educators] are asking many of them [their students] to change the whole way they understand themselves, their world and the relationship between the two. They are asking many of them to put at risk the loyalties and devotions that have made up the very foundations of their lives. We acquire 'personal authority', after all, only by relativizing – that is, only by fundamentally altering – our relationship to public authority.[17]

Yet the supermarket of lifestyle options to which the media expose us daily, and the increasing visibility of different races, classes and cultures to each other, makes it almost impossible to retain unquestioned faith in 'the one true way'. And many adult educators now see it explicitly as their job to encourage that development of critical literacy and self-conscious choice. The goal of producing self-directed learners is widely espoused.

Reflection and self-direction depend on complex composites of learning skills and qualities that themselves have to be learnt. People have to learn how to reflect, just as they have to learn how to make best use of their imagination and their literacy. Students do not come with reflection pre-installed; it needs demonstrating, coaching, practising and shaping. Yet the literature of adult and professional education is full of expressions of frustration, disappointment and even disdain by tutors, for many students do not share their enthusiasm and commitment. Some tutors seem not to appreciate that, if they want their students to reflect, they have to be shown how. And they may also underestimate the difficulty of what they are asking for in terms of mental and emotional maturity.

An example of how to help students develop this self-awareness is provided by the Harvard educator William Perry. Perry offered adult students a course in reading skills that, he claimed, would help them cope with the burden of course materials which they had to study. He showed them films of blurred text across which a clear 'window' hopped, forcing them to scan at a preset rate. Then the size of the window and the speed of its hops were gradually increased, training their eyeballs to move faster. He distributed pages of text and told the students not to read them, but to skim them in order to find the answer to a given question. He gave them other texts, which they had to skim to get just a vague idea what they were about. Such exercises (like the two-hour rapid reading course described on p. 110) do increase students' reading speed.

But Perry's exercises had a subtext: to get the students to see for themselves that reading was not a single activity but a complex mixture; not a self-evident concept but one with many different possible meanings; and not controlled by the text but by them. What he had actually been doing was not so much teaching them how to read better, but transforming their relationship to the authority of books. Invited to place their own questions behind the wheel of their learning, many of the students felt rather scared. They were being encouraged to leave a place of dependency and security for one in which they took control of their own learning. As Perry says: 'They come to see that "better reading" is not a challenge to their intelligence [or "skill"], but to their courage.'[18]

Dancing with the task: management and metacognition

What makes Perry's innocuous-sounding course difficult and challenging is that he is inviting students to overthrow a model of education as (relatively) passive absorption to which most of them had grown accustomed at school. They are being asked to accept responsibility where they thought they had none. The article on self-directed learning from which I quoted above goes on: 'Self-directed learners set their own goals and standards, with or without help from experts. They use experts, institutions and other resources to pursue these goals. . . . [They] are both able and willing to take responsibility for their learning, direction and productivity. They exercise skills in time-management, project management, goal-setting, self-evaluation, peer critique, information-gathering, and use of educational resources.'

To people who are unused to it, such responsibility, though empowering, may feel unwelcome. They may need a mixture of manageable pressure and gentle support to move in the direction of greater independence. But they also need to know how to take on the role of being their own learning organizer and learning coach. And this requires the cultivation of a different sort of reflection. When a skilled artisan tackles a complex job, she needs more than courage and her toolkit. She needs a strategic plan; she needs to be able to monitor whether the work, as it unfolds, is going according to plan; and she needs the flexibility to change her tack when it is required. She needs, in other words, to be an adept manager of her craft. Good learners, too, need to have their learning skills organized in such a way that they can dance with the task, adapting their approach as they hit snags and discover short-cuts, resources and unanticipated possibilities.

Sometimes, this management occurs through a kind of conscious reflection. We sit back and think about the situation, analyse it and devise alternative ways of proceeding. We can articulate the task or the nature of the difficulty, articulate the resources we have available, and marry the two. The activity of thinking about our own thinking and learning has come to be known as *metacognition*. And there is no reason why its development should wait until adulthood: young children are quite capable of starting out on this part of the lifelong learning journey.

Children who develop their reading capability most quickly tend to be those who are able to talk most fluently about how they read, and what they do when they hit difficulty. Kathy Hall at Leeds Metropolitan University has talked to children about their reading – *how*, as well as *what*, they read – and discovered that some of them are highly articulate about their own mental processes. They are able to describe in detail their own strengths and weaknesses, and the learning strategies which they employ to get out of trouble. Linda is a nine-year-old rated as above average in her class for reading. She clearly knows where she stands – 'I'm quite a good reader' – and what she likes: 'I mostly like adventure stories . . . [and] nice gentle stories for bedtime.' She has theories about how she became a good reader: 'Practice. I just practise and practise at home' and ideas (that agree with the research) about the importance of pre-reading. 'I think a good speaker also makes a good reader . . . being able to speak at a very young age. . . . When you can say really good words and think up them (sic) and write your own stories – that's what makes a good reader.'

Linda knows what to do when she doesn't know what to do, and can explain it too. When she comes across a word she can't read, 'I'd split it in half: say it's something like "minute", I say "min" and "ute". [Or] I look at the first, the middle and the last letter. If I can't figure it out from that, I simply do the same again, but I do something else as well – I don't just give up and ask me Mum. I read the word before and the word after and see if that helps me a little.' If a whole sentence foxes her, she uses a similar approach. 'I'd look at the sentence before and after.' When asked about a whole book that she couldn't immediately read, she revealed some other learning tools. 'I'd look at the pictures – "Dr Xargle's Book of Earthlets", say – and make a story up from that. If there weren't any pictures, I wouldn't give up then. I'd pick up the story as much as possible from like the blurb at the back. I'd just read the blurb and decide, and then say what it's about in my mind [and] fill in the bits I don't understand.' Linda clearly doesn't like to be beaten, and has enough confidence in her general ability and her reading repair kit to be a very tenacious and self-directing learner.[19]

As with other learning tools, the skills of self-management do not need to remain conscious and deliberate. Within a year or so, Linda's strategies may be so well integrated into her intuitive reading expertise that she may no longer be able to articulate what it is she does. It will have become second nature. It is sometimes assumed that the more conscious, the more deliberate, the more thoughtful we are, the better. But the good learner is not necessarily one who is constantly thinking about her learning strategies, and what to do next. Her mental system may have evolved, as a result of her informal life experience and her education, so that her broad repertoire of learning strategies is hooked up together in such a way that the system as a whole just does the right thing as often as possible. Some reflection and deliberation may be needed to adjust the system from time to time, but conscious thinking does not need to be the default mode of learning. As the philosopher Alfred North Whitehead said:

> It is a profoundly erroneous truism, repeated by all copy-books and by eminent people when they are making speeches, that we should cultivate the habit of thinking of what we are doing. The precise opposite is the case. [Intelligence] advances by extending the number of important operations which we can perform *without* thinking about them. Operations of thought are like cavalry charges in battle – they are strictly limited in number, they require fresh horses, and must only be made at decisive moments.[20]

TWELVE

Learning When:
The Problem of Transfer

On the old view, the story of learning to learn would stop here. All the difficulty lay in the process of acquisition: that's what learning was all about. Once the knowledge or the know-how was inside your head, and assuming it hadn't faded away or been overwritten in the meantime, you ought to be able to fish it out whenever it was subsequently needed. This was because in the traditional models, the mind's contents and abilities were assumed to be general-purpose. When you had learnt something 'properly' you would be able to use it whenever and wherever it might turn out to be relevant.

The myth of general-purpose cognition

This meant that transfer was not, in principle, a problem. You could practise a skill (logical analysis, say) in any context (a schoolroom) on any material (algebra or Latin) and then you would 'have it', so that when the need for it arose in a different setting (tracing a fault in an engine or doing jury service) it would be there, ready and waiting. For example, one of the founding fathers of modern psychology, E. L. Thorndike, wrote in 1924: 'Accuracy, quickness, discrimination, memory, attention, concentration, judgment, reasoning, etc., stand for some real and elemental abilities which are the same no matter what material they work upon; . . . in a more or less mysterious way learning to do one thing well will make one do better things that in appearance have no community with it.'[1]

Jean Piaget's model of mental development, which as we saw in Chapter 1 has greatly influenced elementary education, relied on this kind of view. As children got older, he said, so a number of mental revolutions took place, in which their faculties of learning and reasoning were transformed across the board. The particular contents of a problem were rather irrelevant – it didn't matter if the counters were red or green, if an interview with a child took place in a laboratory or in their home, or if the task was phrased in terms of butterflies or triangles; so long as the underlying logical demands of the task were the same, you should get the same result. So your choice of teaching methods and materials was not critical, provided they exercised the right ability. And you could test what a child knew by asking them any question which logically called for that piece of knowledge or ability. Examinations could legitimately be thought of as dipsticks which you could just push into children's minds, and they would reliably tell you what was in there.

Despite its abiding influence on education and training at all levels, we now know that this view of the mind and the way it develops is quite wrong, and the assumptions about teaching, learning and testing to which it gave rise therefore unfounded. The particular wrapping in which a learning task appears may alter dramatically how, and how well, people go about it, and what abilities they consequently appear to possess. Mental skills do not float around freely inside the head, like goldfish in a bowl, waiting to be hooked by any passing problem to which they are germane. When they are learnt, and as they are used, they are inevitably tied to a specification of when and how they are to be used. And if a new task does not hook them it tells us something about the nature of that specification and the way those abilities are indexed, not about whether the person actually possesses them or not. We cannot infer from the fact that people did not do something, under certain conditions, that they cannot do it. Here is some of the evidence.

Mental tools are situation-specific

One of Piaget's famous tests involved laying out two rows of counters, and asking children if each row contained the same number. If the counters in the two rows were spaced evenly, four-year-olds could tell by the length of the rows whether they contained the same number. However, if they both contained six counters, say, but one row was bunched up more than the other, young children would say that the short row contained fewer counters than the long row. Piaget inferred from this that these young children could not differentiate between number and size, whereas their eight-year-old sisters and brothers could.

Margaret Donaldson and her colleagues at the University of Edinburgh, however, showed that this conclusion did not hold water. When they were working with the children they introduced a character called Naughty Teddy. They would lay out two evenly spaced rows of beads, and then Naughty Teddy would appear and mess up one of the rows, pushing the beads closer together or spreading them out. They found that when it was Naughty Teddy, rather than the experimenter, who altered the layout the younger children had no difficulty in stating that the total number of beads had remained the same. When the apparent change seems to result from an accident – an event with which children are very familiar – they are able to tell what has really changed and what has not. When an adult – and a stranger at that – deliberately makes a difference to the way something looks they are on less certain ground, and have to fall back on trying to infer what this grown-up is doing. The problem becomes not so much a cognitive one as a social one: what does this person want me to say? And the younger children tend to read the situation in a way that leads them to the wrong response.[2]

Another of Piaget's classic tests involved pouring out two obviously equal amounts of orange juice into two identical squat beakers, and then pouring one of these into another beaker that was taller and thinner. In this clinical version of the task, the younger children again tended to say that there was more juice in the tall container. But when you embed the same logical task within a more meaningful scenario, things change. Introduce two animal characters, one a low-slung hippo who cannot reach up to drink, and the other a rigid giraffe who cannot bend down. Give the original short beaker to the hippo and the tall one to the giraffe, and the children turn out to be quite happy that the distribution of the orange juice is fair. As in the previous example, the difference between the older and the younger children lies not in whether they possess the ability to recognize sameness despite superficial change, but in the extent to which that ability is tied to a certain type of scenario with which they are personally familiar: whether this insight has become, as a result of wider experience, more 'disembedded', as Margaret Donaldson calls it. The older children can spontaneously see the sameness in a strange situation. The younger ones cannot yet do so.[3]

Even a change in a word or two may shift people from one way of approaching a problem to another. In a study of high school science students were told that two equal amounts of water were combined, and they were asked to say what the resulting temperature was. In one version, when they were told that it was two lots of 'cold' water mixed together, they rightly responded that the temperature of the mixture would be the same. In a second version they were informed that it was two lots of water each at 10 degrees Celsius added together. In this case there was a marked tendency to say that the resultant temperature would be 20 degrees. Call the water 'cold' and I'll use my common sense. Introduce numbers, and talk about 'adding' the two lots of water together, and I unconsciously switch into 'sums' mode, throw away my experience, and obligingly give you a silly answer. Interestingly, some students, when confronted with the apparent discrepancy between their answers to the two versions, changed their originally correct answer to the first problem, saying, 'Oh, no. The mixture must be twice as cold.' Assuming that, as this is physics it must involve sums, they reason that if you add two lots of 'cold' together, the answer must be 'double cold'.[4]

The power of numbers to seduce people into acting stupidly is extraordinary. Kurt Reusser asked 97 five- and six-year-olds in the United States: 'There are 26 sheep and 10 goats on a ship. How old is the captain?' To this question 76 of them responded that he was 36 years old. On the slightly 'harder' problem: 'There are 125 sheep in a flock and the shepherd has 5 dogs. How old is he?', Reusser got similar results, though glimmers of common sense did occasionally intrude. One typical child reasoned aloud: '125 + 5 = 130. This is too big [i.e. shepherds don't get that old]. And 125 – 5 = 120 . . . that's still too big. 125 ÷ 5 is 25: that works! I think the shepherd is 25 years old.'[5]

Contexts switch strategies

The power of both context and content to change the way people approach a problem has been explored by Stephen Ceci and Urie Bronfenbrenner, using real-life situations. They asked ten-year-old and fourteen-year-old boys and girls to keep track of time, and to this end set them one of two tasks. In the first a batch of cupcakes were baking, and the children were asked to take them out of the oven in thirty minutes. In the second a motorcycle battery was charging, and they were asked to be sure to disconnect the battery in thirty minutes. Each child was left on his or her own with a big wall clock and a video game they could play to while away the time. Some of the children carried out the task in the familiar setting of their own home; others travelled to Ceci's lab to do it. In each case, the children were observed to see how they solved the pro-blem of monitoring the passage of time.[6]

Whether they were at home or in the lab made a big difference. At home the children checked the clock frequently at the beginning of the half-hour as if setting their own internal clocks. Then they immersed themselves in the video game and only surfaced in the last few minutes, returning to making frequent checks when the time was nearly up. This is obviously an efficient strategy as it frees one's attention to get on with other things. Having checked that their own sub-jective estimate of the passage of time matched the movement of the clock hands, the children were willing to trust their intuition and allow the unconscious to take over the job of monitoring the passing of time.

In the unfamiliar setting of a university psychological laboratory, on the other hand, very few of the children were willing to trust this strategy. Instead they watched the clock throughout the thirty minutes, and were consequently much less able to play with the game. Interestingly, one group did tend to behave in the lab as they did at home – the older boys when engaged in the cupcake task. It was clear from their demeanour that they were the most relaxed group under these conditions – not because they felt most at home in the laboratory, but because they considered baking an activity not worth bothering with! Though they actually performed the task as well as any of the other groups, their insouciant air enabled them to take advantage of the intuitive strategy that the others, feeling more on their best behaviour, were unwilling to trust. The implications for the presumed validity of school examinations are clear.

Mood and state

Learning is tied to our internal state at the time of learning, as well as to the external conditions. Geoff Lowe of the University of Hull has shown that learning is tied to the presence or absence of alcohol in the body, for example. Undergraduates were given a map and asked to learn by heart a route from A to B. Twenty-four hours later they returned to the lab and tried to recall all the turns and street names involved. Half of the students had been given a large vodka and orange twenty minutes before the original learning; the other half had had the orange juice on its own. When they came back the next day, half of the originally 'drunk' group were again given the vodka before the test, so they were 'drunk' again when they tried to recall the route. The other half of this group, however, had only the orange juice, so they were 'drunk' during the original learning but 'sober' during the test. The group who were originally 'sober' were also split in two at the time of the test, half being given the alcohol and half the pure juice.

There were therefore four groups to be compared: drunk-drunk, drunk-sober, sober-drunk and sober-sober. The doses of alcohol were not large enough to affect the original learning of the 'drunk' group, who took the same length of time to learn the route as the sober group. But when it came to the recall test, both the sober-sober and the drunk-drunk groups outperformed the other two sub-groups. The results show that memory is better if you are in the same condition during learning and retrieval. When you are learning the route your brain-mind is also recording the physiological state that accompanies the learning, and this comes to form part of the 'index' for that learning. If that part of the index is missing at recall time, the learning is harder to activate and make use of.[7]

There is evidence that even a change in mood can interfere with retrieval. Though some researchers have disputed the generality of the finding, Gordon Bower has demonstrated that words learnt when a person was in a sad mood were better recalled when they were again sad; words learnt when they were happy were likewise remembered better in a happy rather than a sad state.[8]

The conclusion from all these studies is inescapable. When we are trying to understand how people learn, we cannot assume that we are watching a disembodied intellect meeting a logical task. The interaction between person and situation is much wider and more multidimensional than that. People take in the whole scene, including details that may from a logical point of view seem small or irrelevant, and bring to bear the specific package of knowledge and know-how that seems to them to offer the best fit. This choice, and the kinds of learning that ensue, may be very different from that which appears to be optimal, or even obvious, to an objective observer. People's history and their humanity, their feelings and their foibles, reach right into the heart of their learning.

Over-generalizing

If people approach a piece of learning in a way that surprises or disappoints their teachers, it is not because they are being stupid or lazy but because they are taking into account, consciously or unconsciously, factors that matter to them but which may be invisible to outsiders. Someone may be failing, or looking as if they don't know how to do something, not because they don't really know, but because they don't yet realize that *this* is a situation in which it is appropriate to try *that*, and not to use *the other*. You may fail to apply something when it is in fact relevant; or you may assume that some general rule or procedure applies when in fact it doesn't.

Take rounding up and rounding down of decimals. You may have been taught at school that 7.8 is 8 to the nearest whole number, and that 10.4 approximates to 10 and not to 11. Yet there are many situations in which you will get into trouble if you follow these rules. Suppose you are deciding how much wallpaper you will need for the bedroom. You measure the height and the width of the walls. You find out how wide and how long each roll of wallpaper is. You get out your calculator and do your sums and you find that you need 10.43 rolls. An automatic rounder-downer is going to end up with an embarrassingly bare hole in the corner of one wall.

Learning the domains

So learning the domain to which each of your learning strategies applies is a major part of learning to learn. You may have the most sophisticated toolkit in the world, but if you don't know what each tool is for you aren't going to get the job done. Relevance – the domain of applicability of each skill – has to be discovered. It is not magically 'given'. Learning involves learning not only what and how, but also when and where and why.

This gradual alteration of the sense of purpose and occasion of some knowledge or know-how often happens quite automatically, as part of normal learning through immersion. When faced with a situation that looks like a slight variation on a familiar theme, the brain-mind says to itself: 'Ah! It's probably another one of those.' It then calls up the module that is familiar with whatever those are, and contains the experience, the expectations, the explanations and the expertise to deal with them. If the situation pans out more or less as anticipated, the index for that module is simply amended to include any new features of the situation. Thus a nearly-five-year-old may approach her primary schoolteacher as if he were going to be a minor variant of her father. The student teacher approaches her first class as if it were going to be rather like the classes that she herself inhabited as a pupil. They may be right or they may be wrong; only experience will tell. Sometimes new know-how is needed; sometimes a simple adjustment to the index of what you already knew.

But such perceptions of relevance do not always occur automatically. Some people can do mathematics at school, or in an office, or when working up a spreadsheet, but never transfer those skills to the context of shopping. Others may be highly efficient and reliable when giving change to customers at their market stall, but quite unable to do the same sums when sitting down with paper and pencil. In these cases, we need to consider more powerful ways of encouraging people to discover the maximum relevance of what they know. The psychologist George Kelly used to talk about the 'focus of convenience' and the 'range of convenience' of our mental tools. The focus of convenience comprises the setting and purposes in which and for which a skill, or a way of looking at the world, was learnt in the first place. The range of convenience of that tool is the wider circle of circumstances to which it has been found to apply. So how do we help people extend the range of convenience of their learning tools?[9]

Teaching for learning transfer

There are a number of ploys that parents and teachers can use to help learners explore the transferability of what they know. First, you have to encourage them to play with it, in the sense in which I used the word in Chapter 4. You experiment with its use, finding out by trial and error when it works and when it doesn't. If you want to be able to disembed your metal tools from their original foci of convenience you have to push the boundaries, to explore for yourself the scope and limitations of their use. There are some contexts in which it works perfectly well to use a screwdriver as if it were a chisel, and others when it does not. It is useful to find out when its use can be extended (in scraping small spots of paint off a window, for example), and when it can't (cutting a slot in a doorframe for a lock). This, in turn, implies the need for a mindful, 'let's see' kind of attitude, in which you are always prepared to find out that the tentative use is in fact an overuse and to try something else. With this exploratory attitude towards the differing powers of your own mind, even a misapplication is informative – cause not for disappointment, let alone recrimination, but simply for an updating of the index.

When I decided to go on a week's course on writing fiction I assumed that having had several non-fiction books published would stand me in good stead. Of course, I was expecting to have to learn some new techniques. I had never thought about characters or dialogue before. But basically I knew how to write. It therefore came as a shock to discover that many of my deep-seated attitudes and habits were anathema when it came to writing fiction. I was used to explaining people's actions and motives, and here was my tutor saying, 'Show, don't tell', and sending me away to try again. My existing writing style had to be thoroughly scrutinized and dismantled before I was able to write fiction even as well as people who had never written anything more than a letter and a school essay before. I have now begun to write passable fiction, and – the main point here – to be clearer about when my different voices are appropriate.

From this it is obvious that variety must be deliberately created in the contents, contexts and purposes for which each capability is used. If a particular way of thinking is taught in only one context, it will stay mentally wrapped up in those details and will not disembed. And this variety should help people discover not just forms of valid transfer that are based on superficial, perceptual similarities between situations, but less obvious, more 'structural' ones too. Diane Halpern, whose work on teaching thinking we looked at in Chapter 7, uses the example of learning to think critically about what are called sunk costs. An old car needs a large sum of money to be spent on it if it is to pass its road-worthiness test. Whether the money is well-spent or not depends on a host of factors such as one's general cash-flow situation, the current value of the car, its value after the repairs, its likely lifespan, and so on. What is not relevant is how much you have spent on it already. Yet it is tempting to want to pay for the repairs just

because you have already invested so much in its mainte-
nance. Rationally, these sunk costs should play no part in the
present decision.[10]

The goal of teaching for transfer would be achieved if, having
worked through the argument about the car, you were then
able to recognize the sunk costs trap when it appears in totally
different settings: say, when a politician urges parliament to
spend another million on a defence system because so much
has been invested in it already. If this recognition is to happen
spontaneously, information about sunk costs has to be extracted from the practice problems and represented in the
brain-mind in a more generic form. This is encouraged when
learners are presented with the issue in a variety of guises, and
actively encouraged to seek out the similarities for themselves.

Since learning tools tend to stay cocooned it is important
that at the learning stage you choose contexts, materials and
purposes which match as closely as possible any contexts,
materials and purposes for which you might want that tool in
the future. On the old model of the mind, the disparity
between the circumstances of acquisition and those of eventual use didn't matter. Now we know it does – very much. So if
you are a mathematics teacher it helps your students if you
think in advance about the uses to which a particular mathematical skill may be put in real life, and create learning
situations which simulate these as closely as possible. When
you accept that knowledge and know-how are not free-floating, you have to take this concern with their anticipated
contexts of actual use very seriously as you are teaching them.
'What are we teaching this *for?*' and '*When* are they going to
have to use it?' are questions that no teacher can afford to
duck if they want to be truly effective. When learning is of
academic interest, in the pejorative sense, it is because instructors have not accepted the responsibility to think
through the contexts of eventual use, and teach accordingly.

These concerns affect trainers and consultants as well as
school and university teachers. People are continually attending short courses designed to teach them the skills of team-
building or leadership or negotiation or counselling. The
trainer explains why the particular skill is important, what
its basic principles are, how to do it, and then delegates try it

out in a simulation. In the classic example, a group of mid-career managers on a team-building course are bidden to take off their jackets, loosen their ties, get down on the floor with four of their colleagues, two milk bottles and a packet of spaghetti, and build a bridge. After the simulation they take part in a plenary session with the other teams, and discuss why one group worked well together and another didn't. At the end of the course, delegates fill in feedback forms on which they say what a good time they have had and how useful it has been – and then they go back to work and everything proceeds pretty much as it always did.

The problem is that the simulation is so remote from the real context and real concerns of the workplace that no transfer takes place. If it is to stand a chance the simulation must be much more realistic and diverse, and continuing workplace-based support is needed to keep reminding people *when* they are in a setting where their new skills can be applied, encouraging them to do so, and helping them iron out the inevitable teething troubles. When learning is initially disembedded, remote from the context of eventual use, it has to be helped to re-embed or it will not take root.[11]

It can save time if you seek out the critical features that govern the appropriate use of the tool. However, that is not usually enough in itself. Explicit comprehension has to be dissolved back into intuitive expertise; and for this, personal exploration and practice are required.

General learning strategies?

There is no such thing as a completely general-purpose learning tool; but all the contents of the mind vary in the extent to which they have become disembedded. There are, unquestionably, kinds of relatively general learning strategies that practitioners in particular domains gradually discover and disembed, or are taught and gradually re-embed. Experts in any field sometimes encounter problems that, even for them, are perplexing, and when they do, they need something to fall back on.

John Clement of the University of Massachusetts, Amhurst, has explored what creative physicists do in such a situation. When their rich stock of ready-made expertise and specific problem-solving techniques grinds to a halt, they possess a store of general learning tools they use. They may consciously look for an analogy, maybe a more remote one, with a system they understand better; try to dig up any potential mis-ana-logies buried in the way they have been approaching the problem to date; construct intuitive mental models of the situation based on visual or bodily imagination, to see if they give a clue as to how the unknown system might behave under various conditions; use hypothetical 'extreme cases', to get a handle on how the system might behave if various parameters were pushed to zero or infinity; or construct a simpler version of the system and investigate that.[12]

But such strategies are no use if they do not come to mind when needed, and for that they need to have been more than taught and understood. The problem as encountered needs to trigger the use of the tool either directly, or via a thought or memory. It is that automatic triggering that is crucial. And for those functional links to have been made takes time and practice. Even to have generated the idea of the strategy for yourself does not guarantee it will come to mind again. Some intense reflection, or even a fortuitous conjunction of circum-stances, may result in the bubbling up of a learning insight. But such insights can be captured as memories without re-taining strong enough links with their roots to make a func-tional difference. If you are reminded of them explicitly they may wake up and do their work; but they don't (yet) recognize the call to arms of direct experience.

In an example of this, Gavriel Salomon and Tamar Glober-son showed that college students who were urged to formulate for themselves an abstract principle linking two problems did not spontaneously make use of this principle, when they were given a third, equivalent problem, any more than did students who had been taught the principle explicitly. However, when both groups were urged to 'search their memories for an appropriate principle which they may have encountered be-fore', the former group showed much more impressive trans-fer. They could find the learning aid when prompted, but it had not yet been indexed to the critical features of the problems themselves.[13]

The research on the way knowledge and know-how are embedded in an intuitive cocoon of presumed relevance, and on how that cocoon can be changed as a result of experience and of teaching, provides a particularly clear illustration of the power of the new science of learning to change the way we think about development and education at all levels. The need to pay attention to the details of the teaching situation, and the context in which the learning will be eventually used, poses one such challenge. The dubious nature of any form of dipstick assessment of what someone is presumed to know is another. If performance depends so much on details of mood, setting and material, any inferences of general knowledge or ability have to be highly suspect. This is not just a practical irritation. It strikes right to the core of our cultural beliefs about the mind.

THIRTEEN

Learner-Plus: Making Use of Technology

What does it take to be a good cook? You need practical know-how: skills to bake without burning; to chop and slice and mix and stir. You need mental skills – to scale up a recipe for four to a dinner party for ten; to figure out what happens to two-thirds of a cup of flour when you are halving the quantities. You need knowledge: how long an egg takes to boil; which ingredients to avoid if your guests are on a low-fat diet. And you need more general qualities and dispositions: patience, when cooking meringues or setting a custard; flexibility and resilience, to cope with setbacks and interruptions; creative flair, to give an unexpected twist to a familiar dish.

But all the experience and all the character in the world will not enable you to prepare a meal if you have not got a kitchen. As well as a store of memories, skills and qualities, a cook needs real, physical resources and ingredients: pans and knives; sources of heat and water; a grater and some scales; maybe even a calculator and a phone. To manifest your cooking talents, you need equipment. And if you want to know how good a cook someone is, you do not sit them in the middle of a bare, strange room and say, 'Show me.' You provide them with a kitchen.

Outer (as well as inner) tools

The same is true for learning. So far we have concentrated on the inner resources of the learner: her temperament, her skills and her knowledge. I have used the idea of a learning toolkit as a metaphor for the many ways in which the human brain can learn to augment its inherent capacities and overcome some of its limitations. But learners in general need physical tools and material resources. You can't learn to write without a pen and paper, or, at a more advanced level, without a dictionary and a thesaurus. Human beings' minds and memories are limited, just as their strength or their vision is. It would make no sense to take away their libraries and note-books and say, 'Tell me what you know.' The 'intelligent unit' that constitutes a learner is 'learner-plus'.

People doing real learning and solving real problems in real life are almost always relying on what has come to be called distributed cognition. An engineer brings to a bridge-building project her knowledge and her know-how, but she also brings her reference books, tables of material strengths, formulae about stress on beams, building regulations, and descriptions, specifications, images and working papers about the project itself. She uses computer programs to calculate the structural loads, to keep accounts, to write reports, to generate 3-D models of the bridge and test it under various conditions. She makes use of databases, tables of contents, indexes and other retrieval systems to call up information as and when she needs it. She works surrounded by printouts, notes and sketches. And she interacts with other people, drawing on their ideas and expertise. She phones up friends. She has meetings.

She does not just find herself in an environment on which she can capitalize; in part she creates that environment, and her extended learning power is a reflection of the resources with which she has cumulatively equipped herself, and the skill with which she exploits them. Just as she has invested in acquiring her internal skills and knowledge, so too she has invested in her computer programs, her reference books and her network of contacts. She may have deliberately taken a job, or appointed her associates, in order to gain access to resources that she anticipates she may need. And just as neo-Darwinism sees animals not as passive victims of their environments but as co-creators of their niches, so too the learner needs to be both receptive to the resources available in situations which are not of her own choosing or devising, and

instrumental in choosing and devising congenial surroundings when she can. Over time, she builds and equips her
problem-solving workshop, outer as well as inner, and does so
with more or less skill, and more or less enthusiasm. She
enhances her learning power by accumulating, organizing
and capitalizing intelligently upon the outside world.

Take long multiplication as a simple example. Our neural
networks can learn to recognize and complete patterns such as
8×7, or 5×4. Old-fashioned elementary school practices like
'chanting your times tables' are efficient ways of wearing these
useful grooves into the neural landscape. But this learning
method runs out of steam when you are faced with 259×783.
Instead, we calculate. This means we break the task down into
sub-tasks until we reach a level that the remembered patterns
of the brainscape can deal with, and then reassemble these
into an answer. The trouble is that our short-term memories
are not good at holding on to the pieces as they arrive and
putting them back together. So what do we do? We use pen
and paper as a device for off-loading the memory job. If we
have a calculator, we can off-load the whole computation.

Off-loading mental effort

Technological tools can often take some of the mental burden
off the operator, allowing them access to kinds of problems
and kinds of learning which information-processing constraints had previously concealed. The spreadsheets, statistical
packages and graphical utilities which are used with computers dramatically overcome limitations of memory and thinking speed, enabling the novice to engage with more complex
issues. For example, users can simulate ecological, economic
and other kinds of complicated systems. Freed of the need to
commit anything to memory, students are able to generate
and explore their most creative or bizarre hypotheses about
the relationships between different species and their habitats,
or between a variety of economic variables. They are therefore
able to encompass relationships that had previously been
only within the range of an expert.

Good tools work well because they fit both us and the job. A pair of scissors is an excellent tool because it both fits the shape, the manipulative capacities and the strength of the human hand, and it transforms the hand's natural ability to prod and tear, on appropriate occasions, into the ability to make neat, straight cuts in paper and fabric, to cut string and open bubble packs, and so on. The blind person's stick uses the ability to grip as the basis for augmenting the ability to feel. The abacus uses our abilities to grasp and to see to augment our ability to do sums.

One of the most valuable tools for off-loading cognitive effort is physical space itself. Consider the problem faced by a cook scaling down a recipe for four that calls for two-thirds of a cup of cottage cheese. She only wants to make enough for three. How does she get three-quarters of two-thirds? If she were adept at arithmetic she would quickly discover that what she wanted was, conveniently, half a cup. But if she were not? She should simply dump the two-thirds of a cup of cottage cheese on a board, pat it into a circular mound, make two cuts in the mound (top to bottom, and side to side) to divide it equally into four, put one of the quarters back and use the rest. In this case, a smart solution uses physical space to capitalize on cottage cheese's helpful properties: it will stay put, and when you cut it it stays cut. You could not use this solution to get three-quarters of two-thirds of a bottle of whisky.

The way we arrange or manipulate things in space can make our cognitive lives easier. Scrabble-players and anagram-solvers use real space to support their thinking. By physically ordering and reordering the letters, different possibilities are encouraged to make themselves known. My study floor functions as a space for displaying and organizing the structure of this book and the most important resources that are going to be needed for each chapter. Where possible, these papers are partially overlapped, rather than piled up right on top of each other, so that I can see their headings. I cannot always remember where I filed (when I was working on a different chapter) the particular paper that I now want to get hold of – but my physical layout, coupled with the visual memory of what the first page looked like, often helps me to solve very quickly what would otherwise have taken ages searching through boxes and piles. This ability to solve the problem of flexible retrieval by using a combination of physical space and visual recognition, by the way, is something you cannot do on a computer screen. For jobs such as the one I have just described, it is just too small.

But learning tools are not just solid physical objects and spaces. Language, as cognitive scientist Andy Clark says, 'is in many ways the ultimate artefact'.[1] It takes our abilities to gurgle and hear, and turns them into an extraordinary device that transforms our ability to think and communicate with each other. A written draft is a tool for improving the structure and balance of a lecture. A poem is a tool for exploring meanings and feelings that fall between the cracks of normal language, and which are therefore hard to talk about. And there are many other symbolic tools, too. A sketch is a tool for thinking about an extension to the house. A balance sheet is a tool for planning and running a business. The Dewey-Decimal system is a tool for organizing and accessing a library.

Tool-spotting

We can improve our relationship with tools in three ways. We can invent smart new tools for particular jobs. We can learn to use existing tools more effectively. And, most fundamentally, we can become better able to see what tools there are around us. Just as our inner tools, our learning strategies, are no use if we do not realize their relevance to the current challenge, so outer tools are of no use if we do not recognize their existence and their potential. At any moment the environment contains an array of learning challenges (many of which we ignore), and likewise it contains resources and supports. Objects and events afford possibilities, and if we (or any other species) look around with eyes tuned by our current range of interests and priorities we may spot something that will help. To a human being a chair affords sitting; to a cat it affords sleeping and claw-sharpening; to a woodworm it affords eating and nesting.

Some very basic affordances have become evolutionarily wired-in. Even tiny babies understand the relationship between visual opacity and locomotor impenetrability – if you can't see through it, you can't go through it; and if you can, you can. Infants are reluctant to crawl towards their mothers across plate glass, while they react with surprise when a solid-looking toy that is actually a hologram turns out to be intangible. But many possibilities have to be discovered – both those that are physical (chairs *and* tables afford sitting) and those that are cultural (*we* don't sit on tables).

Whether you spot affordances depends on a number of factors. Obviously, if you haven't yet discovered or been shown a tool's potential, you can't use it effectively. If you don't know what a spanner is for, you may end up using it only as a clumsy kind of hammer. Or you may spot a tool, and be perfectly well aware of its possibilities, but simply be prevented from making use of it. You can't get to it (you know that Mummy keeps the key to the shed on the top shelf, but you're not big enough to reach). You can't afford it (the conference is in Auckland, but no one will give you a grant to go). You don't have the time (you want to keep on reading the book but you have to be up early). Or your culture forbids or inhibits your access (your mates would ridicule you if you went to the dressmaking evening class).

The ability to realize how something can be used depends also on your state of mind, and on the way in which the situation inclines you to see, or not see, different possibilities. Several other studies described earlier in this book have demonstrated that one's ability to escape from the usual forms of categorization depends on being in a relaxed, receptive, inquisitive frame of mind. In such a state the answer itself may appear; but relaxation also helps you spot a potential problem-solving tool. When people are tense and trying too hard, they are less likely to spot the unusual but appropriate affordance.

Most importantly for the development of learning power, the ability to spot affordances depends on a general disposition to look for them. People who are not well-off often have this aspect of intelligence much more finely developed than those whose relative affluence has made them mentally lazy. In some cultures, automobiles are often the site of intense ingenuity. If you are motivated, you can see that a bent wire coat-hanger may afford the qualities of a perfectly satisfactory replacement aerial; that part of the radiator grille from an old car affords the necessary properties of a splint for a broken leg; or that old motor tyres afford the requisite combination of flexibility and toughness that is required of a pair of sandals. The well-off can afford not to be bothered with such low-tech affordances. But even in their world, when it comes to ingenuity in the face of fierce commercial competition it is the R&D department which spots the new affordance of an existing material that may gain the edge over its competitors. Looking for new affordances is an important disposition in good learners. Realizing that learning habitually proceeds with the aid of external tools makes it clear that good learners need to be disposed to look around for them, and to be inquisitive about the range of possibilities that existing resources may have.

Tool-making

Tools do not just amplify an individual's real-world intelligence; they embody intelligence themselves. They are ways of making stable and widely available a 'smart' way of tackling a particular job. And in doing so, they enshrine a particular culture's history and its values. 'This is a job worth doing', they say, 'and this is a good way of doing it.' Euclidean geometry, for example, is a tool that has a revered place in Western culture. It is not, however, the only way of describing space and the properties of shapes and contours that can inhabit that space. Euclidean geometry is an essential tool for carpenters and landscape architects, but it does not do for astrophysicists: on a celestial scale, space is curved, and other geometries work better. Yet schools quite rightly privilege Euclidean geometry, partly because it is easy to teach and has some interesting properties that are readily accessible, partly because of its status in Western culture, and partly because it is a useful tool for engineering, home-improving and other jobs and activities that our culture values and supports.

Tool-learning

Many tools are ready-made, but to make use of them we have to learn how to use them. To capitalize on a word processor, a graphical calculator or the world-wide web, an investment of learning time is required. Manuals have to be studied, tutorials worked through, capabilities explored. But once that investment has been made, the object of learning becomes a tool that makes different kinds of exploration and learning possible, and can lead to increased performance.

In 1896, when pole-vaulting became an Olympic sport, the vaulters used heavy, inflexible poles made of hickory, ash or spruce. The record vault was 3.3 metres. In the 1900 Games bamboo poles were used for the first time, and over the next fifty years, as both technology and skill evolved, the record rose to over 3.8 metres. But the introduction first of alloy poles, and then in the 1960s of fibreglass, with their much greater strength and flexibility, made possible an entirely new vaulting style and as a result the record was smashed by a metre or so. With continual improvements in both the poles and the techniques which they afford, top-class modern vaulters can now regularly exceed heights of 5 metres.[2] Vehement denunciations of the new poles by former record-holders may not have been unconnected with the fact that they couldn't get the hang of the new technology. The truth, unwelcome to some, is that a new area of learning is opened up by a change of tool, and a different kind of expertise, no less intricate than the previous one, is brought into being. The expertise makes creative use of the tool, just as the tool shapes the development of expertise.

Autonomy or addiction?

So physical and symbolic tools have two effects: they alter what people using the tool can achieve, and they influence the way in which their inner learning toolkit develops. In the context of enhancing people's long-term learning power we have to be very aware of the latter as well as the former. For technology could undermine learning power as well as expand it. Such tools might, for example, make people lazy or dependent, or render their own intelligence redundant. What if computerized systems for medical diagnosis become so smart that they reduce the need for clinical skill and human judgement, reducing the doctor to the status of a technician? While the performance of the system as a whole might improve on that of the unaided physician, the capability of the person on her own could be undermined to the extent that, deprived of her technology, she might be less competent than before.

In the best of all possible worlds, you are good at amplifying your arithmetical ability by intelligent and creative use of a calculator or a spreadsheet, *and* good at doing the mental arithmetic that enables you still to function when the computer crashes. Even more importantly, your own expertise enables you to have an intuitive feel for arithmetic operations, so that you know when the tool comes out with an impossible or implausible result.

Thus from a developmental point of view, we may have to be selective about which tools promote overall empowerment rather than dependency. The best tool for aiding medical diagnosis is probably going to be different from the best tool for helping junior doctors develop their diagnostic skills. And we also need to understand when and how tool-use develops rather than undermines learning power. We have, in other words, to be concerned about the learning conditions that encourage positive effects of technology, as well as the effects that can be achieved with it.

A crucial factor seems to be whether engagement with the tool is mindful or mindless. Whether I learn how to spell a new word correctly when my computer spell-checker highlights its mis-spelling and offers me a menu of alternatives depends critically on what mental state I am in at that moment. Sometimes I spell-check absent-mindedly, selecting the right replacement almost without noticing. But sometimes, when I am more alert, I do my corrections mindfully, and then the alterations are more likely to stick in my mind. As a result of mindless engagement, the application of the tool becomes routine and circumscribed; its use is mechanical. But mindful engagement with the tool enmeshes what is learnt with a wider network of resources and approaches, to give flexibility and perspective. As you are mastering its operation, you are also asking (or being encouraged by a tutor to ask) questions about how and why it does what it does.

Some studies show that people do indeed tend to develop a more flexible and reflective approach to tool-use when the conditions under which they are learning instruct or encourage them to think. Douglas Clements and Dominic Gullo at Kent State University in Ohio explored the different effects on children's cognitive development of giving them a ready-made computer program to use, as opposed to teaching them how to program the computer.[3] Two groups of six-year-olds had two forty-minute sessions a week on a computer for twelve weeks. One group, working in twos and threes per machine, used computer-aided instruction (CAI) programs to work on their sums and their spelling. The other, also in small sub-groups, began to learn the programming language Logo. Logo programs control the movement around the screen of a small 'turtle'. The turtle leaves a persisting 'trail', a visual record of its journey, when it is told to do so, enabling the children to draw pictures. Basic instructions tell the turtle where to start, how far to go and in what direction.

As they became more sophisticated the children were able to create sub-routines that could be combined into programs to draw increasingly ambitious pictures. For example, they could decide they wanted to draw a stylized house, with a chimney, leaded windows and a front path, and were then guided by the teacher to think about how they could break this down into separate drawing operations. They wrote their instructions to the turtle, and saw what happened. When, as was often the case, the result was unanticipated, the teacher encouraged them to de-bug their sub-routines by asking such questions as: 'What did we want the turtle to do?'; 'What did we tell it to do?'; 'What did it do?'; 'How could we tell it differently?'; 'What would those instructions look like if you were the turtle?'; and so on. Gradually they developed a super-program that would draw the whole house, while at the same time mindfully developing an increasingly sophisticated dialogue with the computer.

All the children were given a variety of tests at the beginning and end of the twelve-week course. These included a test of how reflective or impulsive they were when facing a complex predicament; how creative they were, in terms of realizing different ways of looking at the situation; and how well they were able to monitor their own level of understanding of a situation. In this last test they were told how to perform a magic trick, but a crucial piece of information was missed out. The children were then asked a series of increasingly directive questions designed to see how much prompting it took before they realized that they did not understand what to do. They were also tested to see how well they could describe a route from A to B on a street map.

The results showed that the Logo group, but not the CAI group, seemed to have become better learners, in a variety of ways, as a result of their mindful engagement with the turtle. The Logo group had become more reflective: they took twice as long to look at the complex pictures, and made half the errors, compared with their pre-test scores. The fluency and the originality of their creative ideas increased significantly. They were very much quicker than the CAI group at diagnosing and reporting their own lack of comprehension of the magic-trick task. And the Logo group were better at using the map to generate clear, systematic directions. Getting the turtle to do what they wanted it to do required careful, patient looking and thinking, and, as a result of the mindful way in which they were encouraged to approach the task, these habits seemed to have rubbed off on their learning more generally.

Mediacy

Some of the most powerful and pervasive tools of modern culture are, of course, those of information and communication technology: computers, televisions, films, the Internet and so on. To make use of these media, we have to learn how to use them. But, as we have seen, while we master them they also come to master us. As we learn how to interpret and use their conventions, our own development is channelled and skewed. For instance, different representational formats capture different aspects of the 'real world', present it in different ways, and demand of us different mental capacities if we are to make use of them. Looking at a photograph, we think we see what is there, depicted more or less accurately and neutrally – but an African bushman and an Inuit midwife would surprise us by what they do – and don't – see in what to us is so straightforward. Styles of filming have changed tremendously over the history of the cinema, and what seems transparent to today's ten-year-olds may look horribly jerky and contrived to their mothers. Abrupt cuts from close-ups to long-shots require the viewer to fill in the gaps, and indeed children who have a better-developed mastery of relating parts to wholes are better equipped to make sense of such discontinuities.[4]

Children who are consistently exposed to different forms of visual technique or information technology develop the mental habits, attitudes and tolerances that those practices call into play. One young student commented: 'I have learned to think of my life as a series of frames partly overlapping and dissolving into each other.' Prolonged exposure to 'busy' forms of media such as music videos tends to cultivate fast, erratic, even chaotic ways of handling information. It can decrease children's ability to concentrate and persevere with a single line of thought, and lead to a preference for jumping around and following different tacks.

The Internet may similarly affect the development of the mind. It is claimed that the world-wide web is a congenial piece of technology because it mimics the network structure of the brain itself, and superficially that may be true. Both neural networks and a computer web are woven out of relationships. But these connections can be of different kinds, and in the human brain-mind they are indeed variegated and sophisticated, as we have seen. One can move through the mind's various planes on the basis of perceptual, conceptual, contextual, humorous, emotional and logical associations, and mix these to create many different kinds of associative patterns of thought. The Internet, by contrast, is put together by human beings on the basis of a much more limited set of connections which are accessed and followed at the whim of the operator.

Many programs are indeed based on superficial association and visual fascination. Because computer displays primarily invoke vision (and secondarily sound), they are constructed (as television is) around images that are intrinsically visually attractive (or shocking), and visual associations that are clever or arresting. On this basis, it is easy to start by looking up the life-cycle of the African elephant on the web, and quickly find yourself involved with the battles of Napoleon, the political situation in Turkey or the antiques trade in London. Whilst there is nothing intrinsically wrong with such explorations – indeed they can throw up very fruitful or amusing juxtaposi-tions – their predominance may relegate more purposeful or rationally driven modes of thought. Surfing can be creative but it can very easily become facile and disconnected, a jumble of baubles and trinkets that grab the attention fleet-ingly and are gone. A heavy diet of fast cutting between fragmentary images, or mindless grazing of dramatic ones, is likely to increase the appetite for such kinds of stimulation and selectively develop the mental facilities needed to track them, and a mental organization that is built around such flimsy associations – a syndrome that Gavriel Salomon of the University of Haifa has dubbed 'the butterfly defect'. Asks Salomon: 'Would not interaction with such a technology strengthen the preference for mental networking as free as-sociation, at the expense of a more demanding, disciplined web? . . . The potential consequences . . . of this possibility for education have to be seriously considered.'[5]

The most widespread applications of information technol-ogy powerfully and insidiously invite us to think of learning in terms of the acquisition and manipulation of information. Info-evangelists such as Bill Gates seem to talk as if the endless accumulation of up-to-the-minute information were the an-swer to all the world's ills, from the transnational to the personal, though any student of ethnic wrangling or even of domestic troubles could tell us otherwise. Yet, if it is true that everything comes to look like a nail to a man who only has a hammer, it is equally the case that everything will come to look like information to a person who only has (or pre-dominantly relies upon) a laptop. If we succumb to the metaphor of the mind as a computer, we shrink our sense of what learning is and neglect opportunities to develop other kinds of learning tools. Access to avalanches of information, loosely interconnected by threads of casual associations, does not of itself bring about the transformation of that information into knowledge or wise judgement, nor the development of the requisite skills and dispositions for doing so. It is the business of education to foster the development of the ability to select, integrate and evaluate theories and opinions, not to drown in information – however glitzy.

Ability and education – again

If people are, in real life, learners-plus, we have to think again about how we design educational organizations and workplaces so that they both capitalize on people's inclination to amplify their personal, portable intelligence by surrounding themselves with tools and resources, and foster the development of the skills and dispositions involved in tool-learning, tool-spotting and tool-making. Good learners need to become resourceful, in the particular sense of making good use of external resources. As Roy Pea of Northwestern University in Illinois says: 'In the world outside school, part of knowing how to learn and solve complex problems involves knowing how to . . . deftly use the features of the physical and media environments to one's advantage.'[6] A central goal of the teacher, tutor or coach therefore becomes helping the learner to exploit the resources of their environment: to be perceptive about the possibilities for support that exist around them, and ingenious in making use of them.

This realization has yet to percolate into the practices of conventional education, which persists in operating as if intelligence were still all in the head. Despite the increasing use of discussion, and some collaborative project work, the conduct, and especially the assessment, of education remains resolutely individualized. We still insist, come exam time, on taking the pole-vaulter's fibreglass pole away, giving him at best a walking stick, and saying, 'Now show me how high you can jump.' As David Perkins of the Harvard Graduate School of Education says: 'Schools mount a persistent campaign to make the person-plus a person-solo [or, at best, person-plus-pen-and-paper]. . . . If part of the mission of schools is to prepare students for out-of-school performance, this perseveration on the person-nearly-solo . . . does little to acquaint students with the art [of being resourceful].'[7] It is not just that learning-solo is so unusual as to be almost unnatural. And it is not just that whatever is learnt in this mode is unlikely to transfer into real-life situations that are invariably interactive. It is that learning-solo neglects a whole potential area for developing people's learning power, and tacitly reinforces a debilitating view of the human mind and its capabilities.

For the realization that human learners routinely rely on external as well as internalized tools administers the coup de grâce to the traditional notion of 'ability'. We have seen that the idea of intelligence as pre-eminently conscious, rational and articulate is undermined by evidence of the vital importance of the other, non-intellectual, compartments of the learning toolkit, and by demonstrations that hard thinking isn't very relevant to many of the smart things that real people do. The belief that a person's learning power is fixed by some kind of general-purpose intelligence has had to give way to the idea of a flexible and learnable repertoire of mental strategies. We have seen that the idea that intelligence is purely cognitive – that it can be divorced from people's qualities, values, beliefs, dispositions and personalities – is also invalid. Ability is a function of the whole person. And now we see that intelligence isn't even a personal possession, but rather a floating conglomerate of resources that are external as well as internal.

We have to see ability in a new light – as an ecological concept. Ability is person plus the opportunities for assistance which their environment affords, plus their skill at detecting, creating and managing these resources. We certainly do build up and carry with us a stock of skills and attitudes that make us better or worse learners; but the way these manifest in any real, messy situation depends on what else we can lay our hands on. If we don't understand intelligence in this way, if we persist in thinking that it is all in the head, we shall neglect an important aspect of learning power and its potential for development. Only if we see our minds as tool-using will we develop the habit of looking around and seeing what help there is to hand.

FOURTEEN

Cultures of Learning: How Habits of Mind Are Transmitted

In Chapter 13 I intentionally downplayed the most obvious learning resource of all: other people. The most important tools that learners can and do make use of are not inanimate but social. It is other people who are most instrumental in teaching us the tools of our particular culture. In this chapter, I want to explore three of the social and cultural dimensions of learning. The first is how we learn *from* people: the ways in which we pick up our learning skills, styles and strategies from those around us. The second is how we learn *through* people: in their company we assimilate the more pervasive values and assumptions about learning and knowing that characterize different cultures. And the third is how we learn *with* people: how learning, problem-solving and decision-making are shared in groups.

Learning from others

Many of our learning tools are first encountered in a social context, and our experience of those tools, and what we learn about them and from them, is guided and mediated by other people, especially those who are more experienced with those tools than we are. Parents show their children how to hold and turn the pages of a book, or how to wield a baseball bat properly. Teachers show novice string players how to play pizzicato, or math students how to wield the 'tool' of differential calculus. Our dependence on our elders for all kinds of initiation and induction is too obvious to need stressing. But exactly what they teach us, and how they do it, deserves further consideration.

An enormous amount is learnt through the basic tools of immersion: watching, copying and practising, perhaps with a modicum of explanation and feedback from an elder. Much of this simply involves younger or less experienced people picking up habits from their elders in an entirely informal and implicit fashion. Just as children pick up their family's speech patterns quite unconsciously, so too, in the absence of any explicit intention or tuition, do they learn many of their manners, skills and reactions.

As more and less experienced individuals engage in interesting, non-trivial challenges together, the former models and displays particular ways of going about such things and the latter appropriates them for herself. Sometimes, for instance, a parent will naturally organize their joint activity in such a way that the child can act in ways that are currently beyond her own unassisted competence. The parent may simplify the situation so that it becomes more manageable. He may add a bit of strength, a bit of encouragement, a bit of knowledge or a bit of know-how at just the right moment, and in just the right amount, which enables the apprentice to keep going where she might have got stuck; to surpass her unaided ability. The baby takes her first steps when she is supported and steadied by older hands. She persists longer with her block-stacking when her older brother is leaning over her shoulder saying, 'Come on – you can do it!' The emotional and practical support of others enables her to reach further out beyond her current borders of competence and comprehension, tackle bigger challenges, and so learn faster.

'Scaffolding' the learner's learning

A vital part of these apprenticeships involves the passing on of tools for, and attitudes towards, learning itself. As novices pick up the elders' ways of doing things, they also pick up their ways of learning. In what contexts do the elders permit themselves to feel and to show uncertainty? And how are problems faced? As the newcomers master the learning tools that are being offered to them, incorporating them into their intuitive modus operandi, so they come to be able to extend their competence for themselves. Ways of learning that first needed modelling and reminding now become part of their spontaneous learning power.[1]

Here, for example, is a snatch of everyday conversation between a six-year-old and her father. Lucy has lost her favourite toy rabbit, and seeks to enlist Daddy's help in finding it. He asks her where she last saw the rabbit. Lucy says, 'I can't remember.' He then asks her a series of questions about where she has been, and offers hypotheses as to the possible location of the toy.

'Did you have Bunnie in your room?'

'No.'

'Have you been outside this morning?'

'No.'

'Have you been in the play-room?'

'Yes.'

'Did you leave it in the play-room, maybe?'

'I don't think so.'

'Next door?'

'Haven't been next door.'

'Did you go in the car to the shops with Mummy?'

'Uh-huh [nodding "yes"].'

'Did you leave it in the car?'

'Oh, yes. I think I did', and Lucy trots off to retrieve the errant rabbit.[2]

Daddy is involving Lucy in a joint problem-solving exercise: they are doing the remembering together as a team. He is also modelling for her a useful strategy for tracking down lost things. You call to mind places where you have been, and see if these memories contain useful records of the presence or absence of the lost object. Before this strategy clicks into place automatically when needed, it may have to be stimulated and guided by talking yourself through it. Lucy will register the dialogue that she is having with her father, so that on future occasions she will be able to talk to herself in the same way. What started out as a social interaction ends up as a psychological tool. And if the memory of this useful conversation does not spring to mind by itself, her father may need to give her a nudge – he can say two weeks later when she has lost her hat, 'Do you remember how we found Bunnie the other day? . . . Now what did we do then?' – and his reminder may be sufficient for her to take over much more of the problem-solving work for herself.

There are thus a number of stages that people go through on their way from ignorance of a tool to intuitive, spontaneous proficiency in its use. First they have to have mastered any necessary precursors of the new tool. Lucy would not be ready to acquire the memory strategy if she were not already able to call to mind the recent past, and if she were not able to sustain a complicated conversation. Then you have to meet the tool in the course of getting things done with other people. Your primary goal is not to learn anything; you want to get the programme videoed, the gene isolated, the rabbit found. But in working on the problem you surpass yourself: you discover new strategies, and new uses for old strategies. You pick up ideas from those around you by eavesdropping on them, watching them and talking to them. And you become en-gaged in collaborative kinds of learning that sow the seeds of future individual powers.

But though you may have discovered a new tool and used it once, that does not mean that it will come to mind again. So prompts are needed: reminders that you do have this tool; it might be relevant again here; and this is how you do it. Children between the ages of five and ten are hugely expand-ing their learning repertoires through interaction and infor-mal tuition, and they need to keep track of much that is only half-mastered. This is why they are prolific users of private speech – children talk to themselves, especially when they are alone and trying to perform some difficult task. And it is those children who make the greatest number of self-directing comments who make the fastest learning progress.[3] Private speech enables them to call to mind ways of conceptualizing, thinking and learning that are still in transition from the social to the fully psychological. By talking to themselves they are able to play the supervisory role of the other person, and reinstate the social conditions under which the tenuous skill was first encountered. And, as we saw in Chapter 6, language acts as an internal CB radio system that makes the know-how of different scripts and modules more available to each other.

Structured apprenticeships

Learning through immersion also occurs in more structured settings. Jean Lave has studied the variety of different forms that such apprenticeships can take. Some of them are close to the master–apprentice relationship which characterized the craft guilds of medieval Europe, with their strict hierarchies, set tasks and absolute obedience to the master. But not all are so rigid.[4]

For example, young men and women in Liberia in West Africa learn the craft of tailoring in the traditional way. In Tailors' Alley in the capital, Monrovia, 120 master tailors ply their trade, watched by as many apprentices at different stages of their learning. First, the new apprentice just watches as garments are cut, stitched and finished. Then he is allowed to practise the finishing touches: sewing on buttons, hemming cuffs and pressing. (In the early stages of learning, it is important that apprentices tackle jobs where they cannot do much damage. To mess up the cutting process is to waste valuable cloth.) He continues to observe all stages until he feels ready to cut and sew his first garment, usually something low-status and simple. He waits until the shop is closed and the masters have gone home, and then, perhaps guided and egged on by other apprentices, has a shot at it. If he gets it more or less right, he is allowed to practise making the same kind of clothing until he can do it quickly and reliably. Then he moves on to increasingly complex garments until he is finally qualified to make men's two-piece suits with elaborately tailored jackets. Throughout the apprenticeship, which takes around five years, there is very little instruction and no formal evaluation.

Joining a culture

Formal apprenticeships focus on the development of a particular kind of expertise, but the learning involves more than technical skill. There are concomitant changes in perception, attention, interpretation, language and values. The apprentice tailor is learning which operations require careful attention and which can be treated as routine. He is getting to grips with the names, weights, feels and appropriate uses of different materials. He is finding out how to weigh up customers, to make flattering suggestions, to deal with accounts. He is learning not just to make good clothes, but the whole neb-ulous, vital set of values and behaviours involved in being a master tailor.

Much of this kind of cultural apprenticeship proceeds im-plicitly. The elders may have no intention of taking on the role of model, instructor or initiator, yet be fulfilling these functions none the less. The oncology specialist thinks she is passing on technical knowledge to her students, but she is also, often unwittingly, teaching them what it is to be a consultant. How does she treat her patients? The relatives? The nurses? What kinds of language does she use for each group? How does she respond to requests for more informa-tion, or challenges to her authority. What does she treat as sacred, and what can be the subject of irreverence? And so on. Medical training teaches students medicine; but it also teaches them – all the more powerfully because this part of the curriculum is usually hidden – to become doctors.[5]

Learning through others

Most importantly in the present context, the elders transmit values and beliefs about learning itself. As we saw in Chapter 1, good learners need to hold beliefs about the nature of learning, and about themselves as learners, which enable them to maximize their learning potential. And not all beliefs are so benign. If you believe that learning is fast or not at all, there is no point in taking time to chew over something difficult. If you believe that knowledge is certain, you will tend to fight shy of any ambiguity. If you believe that all learning results in clear comprehension, you will tend not to value learning that you cannot yet identify. But if such beliefs have substantial practical implications for the ways in which people learn, where do they come from? Clearly the seeds of people's learning beliefs are sown in the cultures they inhabit as children. Educating good learners must therefore include socialization into an enabling, rather than disabling, set of beliefs about learning and knowing.

Jacquelynne Eccles at the University of Michigan has been engaged in a long programme of research which explores how young people acquire their learning-related beliefs. The kinds of learning choices that they make, for example – the things they think they are capable of tackling successfully – are strongly influenced by parents' assumptions and attitudes. Indeed, in some cases the beliefs that parents pass on to their children, through off-the-cuff reactions to their achievements, have a greater influence on the children's future than direct evidence of their own ability. A large group of twelve-year-olds in Michigan were quizzed about how good they thought they were in mathematics and English in school, how hard they thought those subjects were, and how well they thought they were going to do in them. These beliefs were then correlated with their parents' attitudes, and with their past and future performance in those subjects. It turned out that parents' opinions were stronger predictors of their children's attitudes and their performance than were the actual grades which the children had received.[6]

One specific example of these self-fulfilling prophecies concerns the different explanations that parents give for their sons' and daughters' achievement in mathematics. The mothers in the sample tended to attribute their daughters' success to hard work, while they credited their sons with ability. (Interestingly, the fathers generally showed much less gender stereotyping.) The maternal influence is strong: the girls come to attribute themselves with lower ability, and assume that their success is due to effort. It has been suggested that the fathers' more balanced assessment of their daughters' ability in mathematics and science can play a significant role in their subsequent success in stereotypically male careers. Strangely, in English the position is reversed in relation to ability and hard work.

Eccles has found that mothers' tendency to subscribe to, and pass on, these gender-related views reflects their exposure to the expression of such views in the media. Here, in micro-cosm, is the process of cultural transmission at work. Views at large in the culture partly reflect, and partly influence, the learning-related folk theories that are held (consciously or not) by parents; and they, in their turn, pass these on to their children through the ways in which they interpret, comment on and account for their children's performance. Such views become installed in children's views of themselves, of the nature of learning and knowing, and of what it takes to learn different things; and these self-images and implicit theories then manifest in the private interpretations the children make of their own behaviour, in the ways they go about learning itself, and in the possible choices and futures which they see as being open to them.

Cultures of learning

Each family, each classroom, each office has its ways of responding to problems or uncertainties which rub off on new arrivals as they learn the ropes. When we enter a new culture, and as we learn to become one of its proficient, accepted members, we swallow the learning tools, views and values which are embodied in its ways of working. Im-bibing beliefs, priorities and assumptions through our basic learning processes, we become part of the culture, and it becomes part of us, its views so embedded in the way we see and think and learn that they become invisible. In the world of work, the French refer to this as the *déformation professionelle*. Learning literally looks different to an accoun-tant, an artist and a teacher. Priorities have been absorbed which make different kinds of challenge, and different inter-pretations of things, pop out of the background. But the *déformations* are *familiale* and *culturelle* as well. It is not just the ways we learn, the learning tools that are privileged or neglected by particular societies, but the whole way we look at learning and knowing that is affected.

What is a culture? It is a group of people who act as if they shared some common set of beliefs. The Welsh and the Inuit are cultures, but so too are a Brooklyn youth club, a school class and a school staffroom, a church, Tailors' Alley, cognitive scientists, crack dealers and trainspotters. To be a member of a culture you have to subscribe to a certain view of the world, value certain things above other things, and do certain things in a certain way.

How do a culture's assumptions manifest themselves? They appear most obviously in its declared purposes and interests: to make money, win the Nobel Prize, increase national prosperity, pass the exam, give glory to God. There may be purposes that are undeclared as well: to meet potential lovers, to fight, to avoid boredom. The purposes generate values and priorities, which again may be overt or covert. We value what furthers our goals; we disdain what goes against them. Values manifest as a set of core evaluations within the culture: what counts as good, bad, cool, stupid, funny, creative, naughty, criminal, kind and so on. In one workplace culture, it may be generally cool to be cynical, to do the bare minimum and to disparage any signs of creativity or enthusiasm as immaturity or brown-nosing. In another, it may be the cynics who are on the back foot and the enthusiasts who create the dominant ethos. Cultures have a variety of formal and informal ways of policing their core values and beliefs. If you break the rules you can be excommunicated, sent to Coventry, not invited to the pub on Friday evening, not get your jokes laughed at, or be driven mad or sick.

What we value is what we notice. We notice what meets our needs and threatens our interests, and ignore almost everything else. Trainspotters don't give much heed to pigeons. Ambitious students don't pay much attention to an 'interesting' diversion in a lesson if it isn't going to come up at exam time. This example reminds us that cultures are nested inside each other: a school is at one level a culture, but at another it may be better seen as a loose and unstable coalition of very different sub-cultures (in the staffroom as well as amongst the students).

Cultures manifest in physical structures and scheduled activities. Most schools have classrooms, playgrounds and libraries; most businesses have offices, reception areas and so on. The culture of school in general is evident in the structures of lessons, holidays, exams, homework and so on; and the culture of a specific school is seen in how these different spaces and activities are valued, arranged, maintained and interpreted. Here assembly is an empty ritual, while homework is treated as vital; there, the reverse.

Cultures have roles and badges. Schools have teachers and students. A football supporters' club has a treasurer, good members and hooligans. An office has its flirt and its nerd, as well as it cleaners and its directors. Status is signalled by the quality of the carpet on your office floor, whether you can make international calls on your phone, whether you have a designated parking space, and how the janitor greets you. Uniforms may be tightly proscribed: wearing a suit on Friday may be almost as bad as wearing jeans on Tuesday.

And cultures manifest their beliefs and values in talk: what we say we are up to; how we explain forms of breakdown or deviance; the cumulative oral history of the place – the 'golden days', and 'the time when . . . ; the kinds of technical language and jargon that are used – the acronyms that are used to signal insider knowledge, the difference between doctor–doctor and doctor–patient vocabularies.

What we say and what we do: espoused vs embodied beliefs

There is an important difference between what people say about their culture, and what they act as if they believed. The former are called 'espoused beliefs', the latter 'embodied beliefs'. The essence of a culture is the belief system which it embodies. Sometimes people are able to say very little about what their culture is, what it stands for and how it works. They might even resist any attempt to make the core values explicit, or deny them if they are. Sometimes cultures have plenty of espoused theories about what they are up to. And when they do, the espoused beliefs may or may not reflect accurately those that are embodied in the way the culture actually works. Let me give some examples of these different degrees of self-knowledge in a culture.

Dorothy Holland and Debra Skinner have studied the way in which close male–female relationships are construed within a representative culture of women college students. From interviews and observations, Holland and Skinner have deduced that this culture acts as if it believed the following model:

> The male demonstrates his appreciation of the female's personal qualities and accomplishments by concerning himself with her needs and wants, and she, in turn, acts on his attraction to her by permitting a close, intimate relationship, and by openly expressing her admiration and affection for him. In the prototypical relationship, the two parties are equally attractive and equally attracted to one another. However, if the discrepancy in relative attractiveness is not great, adjustments are possible. A relatively unattractive male can compensate for his lesser standing by making extraordinary efforts to treat the woman well and make her happy. A relatively unattractive female can compensate by scaling down her expectations of good treatment.

It is a safe bet that few if any female students think of their relationships in these terms, and many would utterly reject the idea that such a simplistic model could capture at all this intimate world. Nevertheless, it fits what they say and do. The model does not exist explicitly in these women's heads, yet they make use of it to evaluate each other's relationships and to identify categories of men who do not conform to the model. For example, there are males who are attractive and popular but who don't play by the rules. They take advantage of their attractiveness to gain affection and intimacy (most obviously, sex), but do not reciprocate with the caring, loyalty and attention which the model demands. An attractive woman in such a relationship loses status, as she is being treated in a way that only befits a less attractive person. Such men are often called 'studs' or 'jocks': terms that can carry ambivalent feelings of both censure and admiration.

Conversely, there are males who are not attractive to women and not adept at pleasing them, but who pursue more attractive women – women who, because of their attractiveness, can do better. These men have little chance of success, but their persistent attentions threaten to devalue the female's attraction. To avoid the threatened lowering of prestige, she may be forced to reject him in stronger terms than she may actually feel. Such males are called, pejoratively, 'jerks', 'nerds' and so on.[7]

Newcomers cannot be taught the beliefs and values of the culture directly when they are unarticulated. Nevertheless such embodied theories are conveyed, and very efficiently, in more covert ways. Apprentices to the community pick up the common beliefs implicitly, by learning to make the 'right' kinds of judgements, and to use the current jargon in approved ways. At the same time as people are learning the (invisible) ropes, they may also be learning to give accounts and descriptions of what goes on on the basis of another set of beliefs, an espoused theory that overlaps only partly, or not at all, with the embodied theory. The espoused theory is much more conscious and articulate; it represents what we 'believe' in the conventional sense of the public 'creed'. Consciously, our company espouses a clear policy of equal opportunities, and we really believe we are close to eradicating sexism and racism. But unconsciously they may still exist, operating strongly through the promotions procedure, which somehow never seems to be able to find women or black people who are good enough; and through the kinds of ('well-meant', 'innocent') jokes which we still laugh at (and expect women and ethnic minorities to laugh at too, or they 'lack a sense of humour').

Examples of such disparities are not hard to find. The fact that people get more colds during the winter is 'explained' by a variety of folk theories. There are more 'germs' around. They attack us more when we are cold or wet. Our resistance is lower. In fact, so common cold researchers tell us, the main cause is the reduction of ventilation in homes, offices, trains, buses and so on. When it is cold we close all the windows and doors to keep warm, but one of the side-effects is to reduce the exchange of air between inside and outside, and thus to increase the concentration of the cold virus inside. It is this increased concentration that matters. Yet the popular theories persist unabashed. And it is not obvious that such slippage between the brainscape and the wordscape itself matters terribly. Each does its job, and it is only when a scientist comes along that the disparity is brought to light and questioned.

Learning with people

Learning and problem-solving are very often team efforts. The lone innovator is the exception rather than the rule. We saw in Chapter 10 that the scientist's moment of insight, for example, is almost always embedded in a much longer social process, and that the most productive research laboratories rely on mutual support and vigorous communal debate. At work, most people find themselves contributing to collective enterprises through an intricate web of letters, phone calls, e-mails, draft documents, meetings and memos. Much of the day is spent responding to requests for information and opinions, and initiating our own.

The success of such group intelligence depends, of course, on the quality of communication within the system (and between the system and its environment). The best way of organizing these webs of communication, however, is not so obvious. Take the distinction between centralized and devolved control of problem-solving. In the conventional organization, there is an individual or an office that manages and directs. It receives digests of relevant information, makes informed and intelligent decisions, and then constructs plans and issues orders. Others, the workforce, need to communicate between themselves only well enough to ensure that the requisite information is supplied to the board, and that orders are implemented correctly and effectively. The successful cogs are the ones who do as they are told. But this conventional, hierarchical wisdom has come under scrutiny of late, with many organizations realizing that it breeds a culture which is rigid, unresponsive and uncreative. In many companies the old layers of middle management have been stripped out, and replaced by more autonomous teams who have greater flexibility and responsibility. They learn and decide together in a more interactive and democratic fashion. The coherence of their efforts is created not by the presence of an overseer, but through listening and responding to what their team-mates are doing.

Edwin Hutchins, anthropologist, cognitive scientist and ocean yachtsman, has studied the way naval navigation teams solve complex problems.[8] The US Navy has a set of intricate procedures for determining the precise position of a ship as it cruises offshore or comes into harbour. The basic procedure involves finding three landmarks on the coast that correspond to identifiable points on a chart; determining the angles of the lines of sight from the ship to these landmarks; and then computing the point of intersection of the lines on the chart. A team of six or seven people contributes to this enterprise.

From his meticulous observations of this procedure Hutchins draws the conclusion that the team works as a true team. There is no one person who governs the process; no one person who ever possesses all the information; no one person who has all the skills. The work gets done because each member of the team does something precise in response to a specific signal, and then broadcasts another signal which triggers someone else to carry out the next move in the cycle. The team can 'organize its behavior', says Hutchins, 'in an appropriate sequence without there being a global script or plan anywhere in the system. Each crew member only needs to know what to do when certain conditions are produced in the environment.'[9] Hutchins' research gives support to those in the business world who believe that teams can function effectively and intelligently with far less management than has often been assumed. Such centralized control may even be inefficient and counterproductive.

It is not just how communication is organized that influences a team's learning and problem-solving. The speed and ease with which members can talk to each other also turns out to influence the quality of the team's performance in unexpected ways. Suppose a group has to come to a consensus about how to proceed: a management think-tank deciding whether to invest in product development or marketing, for instance, or a jury considering its verdict. The members of the group start out with different views and perspectives. But what type of communication is most likely to generate an optimal solution? Obviously, if communication is very slow and inefficient, the members will not be able to listen to each other's views and come to a consensus. Less obviously, it turns out that they are likely to agree on a less than optimal solution if communication is too full and instantaneous.

Hutchins has shown in a number of studies and simulations that, with too much communication, people can quickly line up behind a plausible interpretation of the situation and become resistant to any evidence or argument that might threaten it. Even if a series of pieces of counter-evidence appears, they can be discounted one by one and their composite weight goes unrecognized. Hutchins explains: 'Because they are in continual communication, there is no opportunity for any of them [individually] to form an interpretation that differs much from that of the others.' Learning with other people works best, it seems, when their sharing of progress and information is periodic rather than continual.[10]

As communication is increasingly made electronically, it is important that its style and speed suits the job in hand. Where decisions rely on a steady stream of accurate information (as in the example of the navigators), e-mail or an open phone line may be best. When more complex decisions need to be made more slowly, Hutchins' research suggests that it may be advantageous to change the form of communication. Faster is not always better, and good old-fashioned 'snail mail' may create just the pondering time that is required.

Richard Bolland and colleagues have been designing a piece of computer software called Spider that supports this kind of distributed learning. Decisions often require managers from different departments and divisions in a company to participate in joint exploration and decision-making teams. They need to be able to communicate in a common format which enables them to understand each other's perspectives and concerns; yet also to have the time and ability to question priorities and assumptions. Spider encourages them to represent their positions through a linked set of spreadsheets, cognitive maps, graphs and notes. They can make these available either selectively or generally, and invite responses from the recipients. However, each interpretation remains under the control of its author; the generation of an agreed position has to await more comprehensive involvement such as at a meeting. So differences are initially preserved, even while team members are scrutinizing and challenging each other's positions. Preliminary results from trials with a large international manufacturing company are positive. It seems as if the Spider environment is conductive to good, collective problem-solving.[11]

The distinction between the beliefs and values which a culture professes, and those which its institutions and habits embody, is an important one when we come to look at national or global culture. Particularly during times of change, the rhetoric of learning may alter whilst the reality stays very much the same. I suspect this may be the case at the present time. Around the world there is much talk of the importance of learning and the creation of learning societies. The need for people to be equipped to handle increasing uncertainties is widely recognized. The question is: do the responses that are being proposed really meet that need? Or are they leaving in place too much that is unexamined, and based more on traditional provisions than on current requirements. It is to this question that we now turn.

FIFTEEN

The Age of Uncertainty: Why Learning Power Matters Now

One Saturday evening at a little after midnight I woke up from a doze to find my TV set in the middle of a game show that I later learnt was called *Carnal Knowledge*. Two young couples were pitted against each other, and the game involved seeing if one member could anticipate what their partner would answer to a range of questions. Other shows use a similar format, so I thought I knew what was going on – until I registered what the questions were. A young woman was asked, 'Which of your friends do you think your partner would most like to have sex with?' Then the young man was asked, 'In which of the following locations would your partner be most likely to give you oral sex: in the office; in a taxi; or while you were driving?'

Was this a bit of harmless late-night fun? Was it another brave step towards sexual liberation? Was it mildly tasteless and tacky? Was it a disgusting trivialization of sexuality? I wasn't sure where I stood. Was it, I mused further, socially acceptable, or even actually possible, for anyone under the age of seventy to be disgusted by anything any more? I was being made aware of how my capacity for revulsion has been superseded by a rather bland, ironic sophistication. I felt simultaneously the freedom and the disconcerting responsibility of being able to choose how to evaluate my experience. I found part of me envying my parents' generation, who lived securely inside a single, unquestionable worldview that told them clearly what was right and what was wrong.[1]

Previewing another television programme, a front-page article in *The Independent* newspaper announced that new parents Lee and Rosie had invited a friend, Sue, together with a celebrity chef, to prepare a pâté from the baby's placenta which they served to a party of twenty of their friends. 'We are always recycling things in this household,' said Rosie's mother, 'so we thought it would be quite appropriate. We had a toast and then passed the dish around and asked people if they would like to share in our gene-pool.' The cooks flash-fried strips of the placenta with shallots and blended two-thirds into a puree. The rest was flambéed in brandy and then sage and lime juice were added. 'It was quite gamey but without a long aftertaste,' said Sue. 'Of course there are certain taboos I had to think through . . . but I was stunned how palatable it was.'

It is an unusual world in which the flouting of such deep-seated taboos is presented as casual entertainment – one which dares you to be shocked and challenges you to make a response. Daily we are invited to see dead animals and cans of shit as art; drunken and violent celebrities as heroes; painfully thin fashion models as heroin chic. Both adults and children are presented with material that says: 'OK, what do you make of that, then?' What do *you* make of that? Not what do your community, your parents or your church make of that; but you, as an individual. It's make-up-your-mind time; but on what basis, and with what tools?

If cognitive science is telling us that we possess more learning power than we think, and showing us how that potential can be developed, the nature of contemporary society surely tells us that this option is no mere academic possibility but a vital necessity. Before we go on in the last few chapters to look at some of the ways in which our culture is (and occasionally is not) responding to this need, it will be useful to take stock here of how the pressures on individuals to be good learners arise. Exactly why is learning power such an important social issue right now? This book so far has been about the 'how' of learning; in this chapter I want to pause to consider the 'why'.

Automatic and stick-shift cultures

In his book *In Over Our Heads: The Mental Demands of Modern Life*, Harvard educationist Robert Kegan describes our transition from what he calls an 'automatic' to a 'stick-shift' culture.[2] In an automatic culture, the accepted rules, rituals and understandings of the society function like the automatic gearbox in a car. When you get to a certain speed, the car 'decides' to change gear. You, the driver, don't have to think about it. You don't have control – the car does. In a stable, traditional, homogeneous society you don't have the individual responsibility to decide what the transition from girl to woman, bachelor to husband, or wife to mother mean; nor, to a large extent, whether, when and how to make that transition. What is normal, what is disgusting, what is admirable, what is harmless fun, what is inspiring, what comes next: these judgements are built-in, unquestionable. They are part of the apparatus by which one lives, not objects of scrutiny or equivocation. But in a stick-shift culture, as in a car with a manual gearbox, the onus is on you to decide. Beliefs, value and lifestyles are up for grabs. You have, to a significant extent, both the opportunity and the onus to invent – perhaps to keep reinventing – yourself, and this freedom is distributed widely, regardless of wealth or birth.

Throughout the world, cultures are changing from automatic to manual in a host of different ways, some of which I shall explore in this chapter. Sociologists and post-modernists talk easily of the collapse of certainty and the rise of the risk society. The decline of deference to traditional sources of authority, whether religious, legal, civic, medical, educational or just parental is well known. The question is: now that we are all required to make up a sensible and satisfying life for ourselves, by engaging personally and intelligently with unprecedented forms of complexity, what can we do to help ourselves, and each other, be equal to the challenge? In such societies you have to have skills and tolerances that the 'automatic' citizen simply does not need, and therefore does not miss. You need to be able to handle intelligently far greater degrees of responsibility and uncertainty. You need to be a good learner.

Work

Perhaps the area of life in which the importance of personal learning power has escalated most obviously is the world of work. This world has changed, even in the last decade of the twentieth century, out of all recognition. One of the main reasons is the huge increase in the number and size of global corporations and in the mobility of their capital. The merger of car giants Chrysler and Daimler-Benz in 1998 created a company with an £80 billion annual revenue and whose loyalties, in terms of geography and nationality, are far from clear. Such transnational companies are willing and able to chase the most profitable ratio of skills to costs around the globe, making regional workforces anxious and vulnerable.

In 1997 a huge microprocessor plant, owned by electronics giant Siemens, was opened in the North-East of England. People moved there from all over the UK, attracted by the high salaries and promise of stable employment in a thriving industry. The plant was hailed as a flagship for the revival of an area economically depressed by the collapse of its traditional industries of coal-mining, ship-building and fishing. Fifteen months later, Siemens announced the closure of the plant to its stunned workforce. The UK could no longer compete with the 'suicidal pricing' of Asian competitors, and the Siemens billions were on their way to Korea or Malaysia.[3]

The implications of such trends for individuals' working lives, as well as for national economies, are immense. Robert Reich, Brandeis University professor and ex-chief adviser on the learning society to the Clinton administration, introduces his book *The Work of Nations* with this succinct summary:

We are living through a transformation that will re-arrange the politics and economics of the coming century. There will be no *national* products or technologies, no national corporations, no national industries. There will no longer be national economics, at least as we have come to understand that concept. All that will remain rooted within national borders are the people who comprise a nation. Each nation's primary assets will be its citizens' skills and insights. Each nation's primary political task will be to cope with the centrifugal forces of the global economy which tear at the ties binding citizens together – bestowing ever greater wealth on the most skilled and insightful, while consigning the less skilled to a declining standard of living. As borders become ever more meaningless in economic terms, those citizens best positioned to thrive in the world market are tempted to slip the bonds of national allegiance, and by doing so disengage themselves from their less favoured fellows.[4]

While the income of the richest fifth of US citizens increased by about 9 per cent between 1977 and 1990, the income of the poorest fifth fell by about 5 per cent. In 1960, the chief executive of a large company was taking home twelve times the wage of an average factory worker; by 1990, the differential had increased to seventy times. The less mobile and less fortunate, predicts Reich, may not accept with docility this huge discrepancy in rewards. 'Those who bear a disproportionate share of the burdens and risks of growth, but enjoy few, if any, of the benefits, will not passively accept their fates. Unless they feel some stake in economic growth, they are likely to withdraw their tacit support.'

One response to these trends, the one argued by Reich, is to promote a renewed sense of community. The other is to ensure that as many people as possible are good learners: able to acquire the skills and to come up with the ideas that will make employers want to hire them, or will enable them to create and organize work for themselves. On this view, it is learning that is the key. Bluntly, the poor and the marginal of the twenty-first century will be those who cannot or will not engage in lifelong learning. And on a national scale the successful economies, in the increasingly cut-throat global marketplace, will be those that find forms of education to produce workforces that are adaptable, innovative and all-round smart.

Of course, the kinds of jobs available have changed dramatically. The new work is mental, not manual, and the new labourer needs to like brain-work and be good at it. But profound changes are also occurring in the very structure of work – in the way in which people think of work and manage their working lives. The new age is irreversibly entrepreneurial. No longer does one train for a vocation or profession and confidently practise it until one retires. Neither unions nor governments can any longer hold out the promise of a job for life. People have to be prepared to retrain perhaps several times over the course of their working lives, constantly seeking ways of investing, as the current jargon has it, in their 'cognitive capital'.

It is not just that people are having to prepare themselves to take a series of jobs. Increasingly they have to have a much more fluid conception of work, often doing several jobs – or at least having several sources of revenue – side by side. In my area of Britain, nearly half the adult workforce – people who are economically active – no longer have a single, full-time job; and the figure is rising fast. Some have a number of part-time jobs. Some are consultants of various kinds. Some work only part of the year. Some supplement their earned income with interest on savings or rent from property – they live in a caravan over the summer and rent out their houses to holiday-makers, for instance. Routinely, local officials no longer talk of a person's salary but of the various 'income streams' that together constitute enough revenue to live on. Again on the gearbox analogy such a life is manual rather than automatic. Each individual (and her or his family) has to decide what 'enough' means. Many have downsized their standard of living in the interests of improving the quality of life. Talk of voluntary simplicity is no green rhetoric but a practical reality – a deliberate life choice.[5]

The skills of managing such a variegated working life for oneself – as opposed to simply turning up, day after day, at the same office and doing what someone else has decided you shall do – are enormous. The 'people skills' of networking, self-presentation, joint project development and so on become central; the ability to handle new and different kinds of pressure, anxiety and uncertainty becomes paramount.[6] You need to know your own strengths and weaknesses, to decide what you need to learn next: maybe to select the next job on the basis of what it will teach you, rather than (or as well as) what it will pay. The number of people who, by design or necessity, find themselves in such a position is growing dramatically; and they need resilience, resourcefulness and reflectiveness by the bucketload if they are to make a good go of it.

Belonging

The shift in the nature of work requires more than a new set of practical learning skills, though. Along with a number of other, interlocking changes in society it strikes at the heart of human identity. Everyone needs an implicit answer to the questions: 'Who am I? What is my place in the scheme of things?' In traditional, automatic societies, that sense of belonging used largely to be provided through the roles that people fulfilled; the rituals, sacred and secular, in which they took part; and the relationships that were nurtured and reinforced every day. You were what other people, and the structures of your community, continually told you that you were: God-fearing husband, respected doctor, favourite daughter, fallen woman. You might have felt stifled by such powerful, immutable definitions – indeed much of Western literature over the last two centuries has explored and celebrated the attempt to break these bounds – but you knew who you were. Work, at least for men, played a key role in establishing the sense of self.

The global economy, and the consequent development of Reich's highly skilled elite of 'global knowledge workers', is just one of the factors that has led to the destabilization of identity. Others include the rapid rise of affordable air travel, the collapse of traditional heavy industries such as steel-making and coal-mining, the growth of telecommunications and the ethnic pluralization of societies. These and more combine to make it easy and attractive for people from opposite sides of the world to meet, offer each other jobs, compare moral frameworks and fall in love.

American sociologist Kenneth Gergen has argued in his book *The Saturated Self* that the rapid growth of worldwide telecommunication systems has also had a profound effect on people's sense of themselves.[7] Not only do we have personal contact with people dispersed over a wide area, we also have contact with a vastly increased range of different types of people and ways of being. Through newspapers, magazines, television and now the world-wide web we can fill our inner world with a much larger and more varied cast of characters, each one of whom could potentially be a role model or an example of how to deal with a particular life predicament. For every predicament – bereavement, for example – there will be not one but a variety of incompatible models in the back of our minds to choose from. Should I grieve like Queen Elizabeth, or like Elton John, or like Oprah Winfrey, or like an Ulster widow? Under such an onslaught of images, models and possibilities Gergen suggests of identity, as Yeats did of society, that 'things fall apart, the centre cannot hold'. How do we choose between so many options? How is it possible to find an authenticity? We are in danger of drowning in a plethora of possibilities. On what basis, then, do we make ourselves up? How do we learn who to be?

With the collapse of job security, the rise of global mobility, the proliferation of moral frameworks and the weakening and dispersing of family ties, ready-made answers to the questions of identity and belonging are less available and less convincing. Other solutions have to be sought: for instance to shed your lineage and become your personal history, your memory, your achievements, the accumulated life choices you have made – your own 'story'. Along with this goes the tendency to redefine yourself in terms of internal, portable, psychological characteristics: likes and dislikes; personality traits; knowledge and opinions. Before speaking at a public meeting, a traditional New Zealand Maori would establish his credentials by reciting his ancestry and his people's historical connection with certain significant places. Now, on our conference badges, even our surnames have disappeared. The modern businessperson is able to pack her identity into her hand luggage and be ready to step off the plane in Atlanta, Auckland, Ankara or Addis Ababa, feeling – *being* – the same person.[8]

The choices from which one can create oneself have, with the aid of technologies of all kinds, proliferated enormously. As well as where and how to live, there are options that simply were not available to previous generations. With the help of contraception, as many as one in five women in the industrialized world are now choosing to be childless. A career-minded couple can have some of the woman's eggs frozen so they can have a baby 'when they are ready'. Cloning techniques bring closer the possibility of making babies without a male participation and lesbian couples may soon, therefore, be able to have their own – their very own – baby. With hormones and surgery you can swap your physical gender, or decide to be of no identifiable gender at all. You can decide to stay 'young' with the help of HRT and a discreet tuck. You can enhance your chances of becoming a world-beating athlete with the help of some steroids. Homo- or bisexuality are routine lifestyle options. So much freedom to explore; so many costumes of identity to try on.

Sources of authority

In the face of such complexity, responsibility and opportunity, where are we to look for help in making sense of, and responding appropriately to, the vicissitudes of life? Not any longer, for most of us, to the traditional sources of external authority. The Churches are being challenged by exotic, mystical and secular movements that purport to offer more contemporary or congenial forms of salvation. Just as I can choose whether to be hetero- or homosexual, so I can decide to be Buddhist, Moslem or Jewish; to take as my guide a medium or a guru. There is no agreed moral uniform to slip into, but dozens of ready-to-wear suits in a bewildering range of sizes and styles.

Nor, it seems, do most of us look for guidance to the leaders of secular society. Politicians, judges, chiefs of police, prominent businessmen and women: investigative journalism is all too happy to whip away the respectable veneer and expose the fat cats and the hypocrites. There have been too many well-documented miscarriages of justice; too many pillars of the establishment caught with their trousers down. Those who dare to take a public moral stand are often derided for being pompous or pretentious. A diet of exposés has, so the surveys say, made cynics of us all. No more heroes; only anti-heroes and rugged individualists.

The two new contenders for the role of external authority
are science and 'information'. So successful have the claims of
science been that at one time it was seen not as an approach to
knowing the world, or as a body of concepts and theories, but
as direct, unmediated truth. Science was accepted as 'a way of
doing without conceptual schemes altogether – an instrument
for showing the world directly and impartially, without the
drawback of any single perspective'.[9] Unlike the authority of
Church and State, fatally weakened by public recognition of
the fallibility and self-interest of their agents and ministers,
that of science appeared for a while to be impregnable.

But there are a number of well-rehearsed reasons to adopt a
more sceptical attitude towards that presumption. The speed
with which scientific theories supersede each other is now
evident. The history of science is littered with the bleached
carcasses of findings and theories, once the last word and now
disdained; some initially dismissed as crackpot, then accepted
as valid and true before being finally overthrown. The British
scientist James Lovelock's findings on the effects of CFCs on
the ozone layer, for example, were long rejected by the
scientific establishment as impossible. So certain were orthodox scientists that Lovelock was wrong that the instruments
they used to measure the chemical composition of the strato-
sphere were deliberately programmed to reject the very read-
ings that would have corroborated his research.[10] The claim
that scientific knowledge is independent of human bias and
self-interest is now thoroughly discredited.[11] What gets accepted as scientific truth reflects social machination and
personal ambition as much as it does the workings of im-
partial intellect and objective examination.

The idea of uncertainty is now installed even in the theoretical heart of science itself. The nuclear physicist Werner
Heisenberg tells us that we cannot in principle know everything about a fundamental particle. The act of trying to
measure its properties itself introduces perturbations, so that
as we nail down one variable (momentum, say) another
(position) becomes commensurately vague. And once we
get beyond the mathematically tractable world of simple
mechanical systems, where the old certainties were apparently so secure, and inquire into the complex and chaotic

worlds of the weather, or even of living organisms, we find that their interlocking systems of feedback and feed-forward make prediction and control impossible. If science, for all its sophistication, cannot advise us with much confidence whether to take an umbrella or not, it surely cannot help us very much in the even more complex world of social living and learning.

Individual rationality

Having reluctantly abandoned the idea that any external authority will solve the problem of how to live, we are thrust back on our own inner resources. Instead of seeking reassurance by subscribing to a collective system of belief, it might be feasible to fabricate one's own. It is now more common in the Western world for people to believe that they have fashioned their own worldview than it is for them to admit cheerfully that their belief systems have been taken, unquestioningly, from their parents, their Church or their teachers. To make up one's own mind is the thing to do. Even if we end up adopting a communal or conventional system of belief, it is a matter of importance that we chose it for ourselves, rather than just slipping into it as we suppose our less critical, more compliant forebears did.

The problem is that the view of the individual mind, the tool we have for making sense, that has evolved in European cultures over the last two millennia is essentially an intellectual one.[12] As we saw in Chapter 9, our predominant cultural assumption is that intelligence involves conscious, articulate and preferably rational thought, and thus the idea of learning is reduced to intellectual learning. The very idea of any form of intelligence that is unconscious, or ungoverned by conscious deliberation, becomes unintelligible. Eventually, we may find ourselves in the cramped position of believing that intelligence *is* thinking, and so not to be thinking is to be unintelligent. Not to be busy collecting information, collating thoughts and producing opinions and conclusions is, ipso facto, to be stupid.

So being knowledgeable becomes self-motivating. Having

and expressing opinions becomes an important element in the construction of identity. And ignorance becomes a reason for shame or apprehension. Instead of perplexity being seen as a tolerable and potentially productive state, it becomes anathema. Not to understand one's own actions; not to be able to explain, justify and defend one's choices and opinions; not to have an opinion: these become matters of personal failure. To be knowledgeable and opinionated are the badges of someone who has sorted things out, who knows her own mind. Whether these conclusions form a genuinely satisfying basis for living is of less significance than the fluency with which one can articulate them.

When all confusion is experienced as aversive and debilitating, uncertainty leads to insecurity. When we are sure of something we say, 'I'm positive!' Being certain is a positive thing to be, and, by obvious implication, being unsure is negative. A decisive manager is one who can be relied upon to escape from uncertainty as quickly as possible. Doubt, on this view, can only cause us to be censured – or to hang back when what is called for is strong, decisive thinking and acting.

It would hardly be an exaggeration, therefore, to see the modern predicament as one in which a large and increasing proportion of the populace is faced with deep learning opportunities and challenges that go far beyond the need to learn Japanese or Windows 98, and even beyond learning to cope with redundancy and divorce. We have to learn to make our own way through a complex world without the benefit of an accepted, trustworthy route map – indeed with a profusion of different and conflicting maps – and with only one compartment of the toolkit available when we break down. This predicament tests our powers of learning and discernment to the limit. Can we find satisfying patterns and models in the welter of images with which we are daily drenched? Can we sniff out and take up the most valuable learning possibilities and leave the rest? And most importantly, can we develop our learning powers, as individuals and as communities, so that we meet those challenges and invitations with as much intelligence as we can muster?

SIXTEEN

Learning to Learn:
The Early Years

The vignette of Ravi and Ben with which this book opened, together with other studies also by Jerome Kagan, show that the foundations of good learning are laid very early in life.[1] But they are not genetically fixed. In these studies, about half the children who had been very timid during their second year had become significantly more adventurous by the time they were three and a half. Only 50 per cent of children retain the same pattern between the ages of 7 and 14; 35 per cent have changed somewhat, while 15 per cent have changed in a major way, becoming either much more timid or much more adventurous. Children may perhaps have some innate pre-disposition towards resilience and adventurousness, or the lack of them; but early experience has a major influence on whether these traits are consolidated or weakened. We shall now begin to look at the implications of the new science of learning for the way we can help learning power develop.

In this chapter we focus on the early years of home life, playschool and elementary school. The foundation laid then – predominantly that of resilience – strongly influences children's subsequent learning careers. On top of it can develop a general confidence in their learning powers, the disposition to look for learning opportunities, and the ability to stick with learning and to bounce back from frustration or failure. With these assets, children's mastery of particular learning domains will rapidly expand. But more importantly still, as they go about tackling a host of different learning jobs they develop their repertoire of learning tools.

The enemies of resilience: being good

If we are to help children develop their ability to enjoy learning challenges, to persist in the face of difficulty and to deal with frustration, one of the most important things to know is what undermines it. All the encouragement in the world is not going to do any good if adults inadvertently behave in a way that subverts their good intentions. Research by Patricia Smiley and Carol Dweck has clearly demonstrated one of the things that can undermine resilience.[2] Working with preschoolers attempting to solve jigsaw puzzles they found wide differences in four-year-olds' resilience which, unchecked, could carry through into adolescence and beyond. Some children consistently chose easy puzzles, showed signs of distress if they were unable to complete one, and later avoided any incomplete puzzle. Others selected challenging tasks, did not seem to mind failing, and were happy to have a second go at a previously uncompleted puzzle. Interestingly, children's anticipation of their own success did not necessarily predict which group a child would belong to: there were several children who chose the hard puzzles, and enjoyed grappling with them, even though they had estimated their chances of success as low. Nor did a child's actual puzzle-solving ability determine whether they would make the learning choice or the safe choice. Some good solvers preferred to stick with the puzzle they knew they could solve; some poor solvers nevertheless wanted to return to the unsolved puzzles.

Even by the age of four, some children are so locked into the 'mistakes mean I'm stupid' view that they find it hard to own up to difficulty, or to making mistakes, at all. An adult asks Martin: 'Do you ever make mistakes?' Martin says: 'No.' Adult: 'When you make dinosaurs, does it ever go wrong?' Martin: 'No.' Adult: 'Never goes wrong?' Martin: 'No.' Others have learnt to shy away from the risk of failure. Susie says: 'I don't do anything that's hard for me . . . If my big sister does something really hard, I won't do it.' And Trevor advises: 'If you make a mistake you should just leave it.'[3]

It is important to keep in mind that it is the strength of children's learning power that is at stake, not their actual achievement. When what is demanded is routine performance, or learning that involves minimal risk and uncertainty, timid children will do as well as adventurous ones – maybe even better. In Jerome Kagan's studies, the two groups of children did not react differently when the level of uncertainty was low. It was only as 'what to do' became increasingly uncertain that the differences in resilience began to emerge. If children are more able to tolerate the uncertainty that learning involves, the more adventurous they will be, the quicker they will learn, and the more they will strengthen their own learning muscles.

But what lies behind these differences? This and other studies by Dweck suggest that those children who shy away from the harder challenges do so because their priority is to look good, and one way to do so is to be right, to offer adults evidence of competence and conspicuous success – even if to do so means sacrificing an opportunity to develop their learning power. The other children don't mind being less successful if it means they stand a chance of learning something new. For example, when the timid children are asked to imagine what might happen to a child who fails in some way they anticipate more criticism, more upset feelings and more likelihood of punishment than do the more robust children. They evaluate a temporary failing or setback as more serious than it is and as having more long-lasting repercussions.[4] It is this association between being good and being right that blooms, for many children, into the compulsion to prove their ability, to be seen to be bright, that we saw in Chapter 1. Crudely, to be right is to be bright, and to be bright is to be good.

For such children success has become a crucial indicator of their worth to others, and thence of their self-worth. During the elementary school years, children who have learnt to fear the negative judgement of others tend to internalize the critical voice. Instead of worrying about the social consequences of transgression, the same judgements are now installed in the beliefs and values that they carry around with them, bundled into their self-image. For timid children, adventurousness can thus become suppressed at source, and their antipathy to risky learning becomes even harder to shake. That is why the establishing of a learning-positive attitude is so crucial in the early years.[5]

For the four-year-old, being disapproved of is a significant threat. And there are a range of ways of risking censure or rejection. You can be naughty, disobeying rules of conduct which adults believe they have made clear. You can be baby-ish, behaving in a way that adults judge to be appropriate to a developmental level that you are supposed to have grown out of. You can be seen as bad by acting too much or too often in a way that is characteristic of the opposite sex. But, of over-riding importance to timid children, you can also be bad by being ignorant of what you are expected to know, inept at what you are expected to be able to do. Tragically, for a large number of children learning, with its attendant risks, comes to jeopardize 'goodness', and so their adventurous spirits have to be reined in. The cultures of some families, schools and workplaces invite people to see failure as evidence of stupidity and ignorance as a source of shame.

Of course there is a healthy balance to be struck between being a learner – choosing the challenging option – and being a performer – choosing the option that will make you look good. It is as dangerous for a child always to jeopardize approval in the search for growth as it is always to do the reverse. If a four-year-old wants to be taken on a trip to the shops, it may be sensible to display as much 'goodness' as possible. The optimal state is not to be a reckless adventurer but to be able to make good tactical choices – good in terms of your own genuine best interests – about when to gamble and when to play it safe. Good learners are not always in learning mode, but they are ready, willing and able to move into learning mode when the conditions are right. Unfortunately, Dweck's research shows that up to half of all four-year-olds have already begun to get stuck in the cautious mode. What can be done to prevent these patterns starting, and where they have, to reverse them, before they become too firmly estab-lished?

Early intervention programmes

In the 1980s and 1990s a number of so-called early intervention programmes, of which Head Start and High/Scope are the best known, have been implemented in the United States and elsewhere. They are designed to help young children who have not had a very auspicious start in life to be able to benefit as fully as possible from school. Various kinds of intensive stimulation, teaching and support are involved, sometimes by trained professionals, sometimes by the child's own carers. Evaluations have shown that the long-term effects of these programmes are often disappointing. Gains made while they are running tend to fizzle out unless the programme starts early, continues for several years, is intensive, and is supported by the child's own milieu during and, most importantly, afterwards.[6]

However, there are some indications of lasting benefits. Weikart and his colleagues tracked the progress, up to the age of twenty-seven, of the 'graduates' of a number of pre-school programmes, including their own High/Scope programme. Compared to similar groups of people who had not experienced one of these programmes, the medium-term effects were negligible. Though there were some immediate gains in terms of reading and writing, these had disappeared within a year or so of the children leaving the programmes. But when the High/Scope groups were followed through into their teens, and certain social and emotional measures were taken, gains began to re-emerge. By the time the High/Scope graduates were twenty-seven they were more likely to have stayed on at school and to have obtained and held down a job, and less likely to have committed a crime. When he looked at the details of his results, Weikart concluded: 'The essential process connecting early childhood experience to patterns of improved success in school and the community seemed to be the development of habits, traits and dispositions that allowed the child to interact positively with other people and with tasks. This process was based neither on permanently improved intellectual performance nor on academic knowledge.'[7]

Similar long-term effects have also been reported by a group of Swedish researchers. Broberg and his colleagues followed a group of 146 children from birth to nine years old, and examined the relationships between their early experiences and their later learning dispositions and abilities. The best predictors of their long-term development were the quality of the interactions which they had with adults: their parents and, even more strongly, their pre-school carers and teachers.[8]

Broberg suggests that the main reason why early experience has such a significant and sustained effect on children's development as learners is because it sows the seeds of learning-positive or learning-negative dispositions, which then set up self-perpetuating and self-reinforcing spirals in development. The child who is encouraged to explore, and is helped by her carers to have a safe, enjoyable and successful time, begins to develop the habit of seeking and enjoying challenges and thereby exercising her learning muscles. The child who has become more fearful of uncertainty tends to withdraw from learning, and thus to pass up opportunities to strengthen her learning power – and these two patterns become self-fulfilling prophecies.

Every child is, of course, an idiosyncratic mixture of brave and timid, and her engagement in learning will fluctuate with the nature of the challenge, the presence of support and her own moods. But overall these early dispositions translate into what Broberg calls 'niche-picking' – the effective creation by the child of a more or less challenging environment for herself, and therefore a speeding up or slowing down of her own development.

What makes a good learner?

So what kind of early environment sets these learning-positive habits and attitudes in place? Isabella and Mihaly Csikszent-mihalyi in Chicago have discovered that adolescents who were the best learners shared similar backgrounds. They came from homes which, predictably enough, valued learning and education, and where there was plenty of stimulation. But less obviously, their homes also offered structure and support. There had been clear rules which were reliably respected (and, where necessary, enforced), and regular routines in which the youngsters took an increasingly responsible part. Within such a clearly structured family life there was freedom for children to make decisions and pursue their interests, and a secure web of social support. They could get help and reassurance if they needed it, but they learnt increasingly to do without it. There was a natural expectation that people would get on with their duties and their own learning projects without continual supervision or constant cajoling or encouragement (an attitude, interestingly, not unlike that of the typical Asian family as noted in Chapter 1).[9]

On the other hand, teenagers whose attention span was short and scattered tended to come from homes that lacked clear family rituals and responsibilities, and where rules were arbitrary, unclear or not consistently applied. In these families, the habit of getting on with the current job was not developed. Instead a lot of energy went into disputing what was expected, and squabbling about whose turn it was to do a routine chore, trying to evade responsibilities and feeling resentful. Requests for assistance or comfort were not reliably responded to, and emotional upset in one family member could trigger sulking, attention-seeking, or criticism in others.[10]

Security

Thus the first foundation of good learning is an environment which provides clear, consistent patterns which the natural learning ability of the young child's brain can pick up and make use of. Parents must convey a basic security which enables children to believe that their world is comprehensible, predictable and therefore controllable. This basic security makes it worthwhile for children to invest their own efforts and talents in making meaning for themselves.

Children begin to develop this sense of their own efficacy from the word go. As the baby sucks, so the world reliably responds with warm milk. She pats the breast, and her mother tenderly squeezes her back. She pauses in her sucking and coos; her mother coos back. As she engages with the world in a burgeoning variety of ways, regular, reliable and useful patterns of response begin to emerge from what the psychologist William James referred to as the original 'blooming, buzzing confusion'. She learns she can intervene in the course of events, often to her own advantage. She can sometimes make things happen. And if sufficient sources of control begin to appear, distilled naturally out of the confusion by her own brain, she gradually gets the idea that her developing repertoire of learning strategies can be used to seek and generate such control. She observes; she experiments; she plays with different responses to see what will happen. Learning is fuelled by the embodied belief that patterns do exist, can be found, and are worth discovering.

Without an early diet of discoverable patterns, though, this basis for learning does not get established. Infants whose lives are chaotic, such as those left without human interaction in the orphanages of Ceauçescu's Romania, may learn only that there is nothing to be learnt. There is also evidence that the development of babies whose mothers are suffering from post-natal depression may be adversely affected. Typically the mother is unresponsive to the baby: she attends to it when she feels willing or able to, not when the baby needs it. This lack of reciprocity means that the child can fail to develop the essential faith in order, and the disposition to forage for it.[11] The same disabling of learning may occur with parents who are over-indulgent with their children, flooding them with attention and treats that are unconnected with what the children themselves are doing or wanting.[12]

Stimulation

But if the world is too stable and predictable, once it has been attended to and its secrets discovered it offers no further stimulus to learning. Basic security must therefore be balanced with an increasing menu of interesting and challenging learning options. This does not mean that children's worlds have to be exquisitely engineered to contain precise challenges that they are ready for. This would be impossible in principle and undesirable in practice. As we saw with the development of language, rough tuning is sufficient: it offers a range of possibilities which the child's own changing mixture of interest and capability can select from. That is how children's minds have been designed by evolution to work. Given a safe, varied and accessible world, the patterns that the brain is ready to pick up depend on those which it has already detected and its current state of activation. Learning is essentially open-ended, and offering diversity within security respects that.

Through these interactions, adults and older siblings also channel the development of the young learner's interests. The objects, rituals and experiences with which adults populate their worlds will determine what children learn, and thus, implicitly, what they come to think of as worth learning about. Parents' values and attitudes are conveyed through the objects around them, those which they consider appropriate for children to play with, and the methods of engagement and exploration which they permit or encourage.

Little boys and little girls are notoriously susceptible to the skills, attitudes and interests judged appropriate to their gender. Depending on the activity, parents participate in different ways with their sons from how they do with their daughters. Some unsurprising biases are revealed. They work jointly on a computer, and play computer games, more with sons than with daughters, for example. Parents encourage their daughters to read more than their sons, and read with their daughters more.[13]

The objects, experiences and forms of interaction that carers can offer their children clearly reflect not just their idiosyncrasies, but also more general characteristics such as their ethnic and cultural background and their socioeconomic status. Poverty limits the nature and variety of 'educational' objects and experiences that can be provided, and determines the neighbourhood resources which can be drawn upon. A child whose mother cannot afford child care, toys, holidays or a car, and who cannot get to parks, zoos and libraries, lives in a world that affords very different opportunities for learning from one who does have access to these things. The foundations of a learning life are determined by financial and political considerations as well as psychological ones.

Support

More critical than children's material world, though, is the nature of their interactions with those around them: parents, carers, elder sisters and brothers. But what is it, exactly, about these early contacts that angles the developmental trajectory in one direction rather than another? Margaret Carr, one of the architects of Te Whaariki, New Zealand's innovative 'curriculum' for early childhood, concludes that the key factor is whether those interactions are responsive and reciprocal. The evidence is that adults who are involved in the children's world, responsive to their interests and efforts, produce children who are more inquisitive, more robust in the face of uncertainty, and have better peer relations.[14]

This is as important for those who are responsible for early childhood education as it is for families. Carr's collaborator Anne Smith sums up the evidence on the New Zealand preschool situation:

> In good quality centres [adults] focus on the children, respond to their initiations, and real reciprocity exists between the child and the staff member. In poor quality centres . . . staff do not interact much with the children, who are left to amuse themselves. The main interactions staff have with children [in the bad centres] are negative, with children being reprimanded and controlled continually. Staff members do not respond when children get into difficulties. . . . The extent to which adults participate with children in joint attention or involvement with objects, activities or ideas . . . has many important functions in early development.[15]

Crucially, these interactions boost the development of persistence, and more generally of the ability to handle the continual interweaving of learning with feeling – both positive and, up to a point, negative. One American study, for example, concludes that 'an adult's joy, enthusiasm and interest will increase or maintain a child's attention, creating a shared context and making learning possible. Indeed, secure attachments, revolving around positive affect, are related to children's greater attention, patience and persistence in cognitive tasks.'[16] Such responsive relationships support the development of the children's language through involving them in conversation. They also develop the child's ability to join productively with others in cooperative learning tasks – a major precondition for the further development of their learning power.

If parents have a rigid, prescriptive view of what is appropriate for children of a certain age and gender, and are unwilling to modify it when it fails to mesh with the child's own nature, then the child's development is at risk in the following way. Most of us tend to like and value things we feel capable of engaging with. Learning and interest lock together, so we engage with things that interest us, and become more interested in the things we have been successful at mastering (even if only as a beginner). Things we are not good at, or do not feel confident about learning, we tend to disparage or ignore. But in the face of unresponsive parents with an intransigent regime of rituals and learning tasks, children are not able to use this strategy for protecting their self-image and self-esteem. They are not able to withdraw from, or lower the perceived value of, activities which they are not good at or interested in, and are thus forced to engage with them in a state of distress and self-criticism – which runs the serious risk of undermining their resilience and self-belief.[17]

However, it is equally important that parents and carers do not over-support children, especially when they get into learning difficulty. Rushing in and rescuing children prematurely deprives them of the opportunity to flex their learning muscles, and also to get used to the emotions that naturally accompany such difficulties: frustration, confusion, apprehension and so on. Doreen Arcus, an associate of Jerome Kagan's, has demonstrated that mothers who are too anxious to protect and comfort their infants tend to encourage the development of timid reactions to learning difficulty. She videoed mothers and babies over a number of home visits, and worked out what proportion of the total time each mother spent holding her baby was in response to the child's distress. It appears from her results that mothers who over-protect their children from frustration, anxiety and distress actually exacerbate the infant's frailty in the face of uncertainty, and produce the opposite effect from the one intended.[18]

Interestingly, Arcus also looked at the mothers' tendency to set consistent limits on their children's behaviour, making it clear when their explorations were becoming dangerous or unacceptable. Without being punished, the infants were given unequivocal signals of when to stop. Arcus measured the proportion of such transgressions which were actually met with a clear prohibition. Children of mothers who were clear and assiduous in their limit-setting were more resilient and robust than those of mothers who were more laisser-faire or inconsistent. All the mothers of robust, adventurous toddlers rated obedience a desirable quality in children. All the mothers of timid, fragile children rated obedience as unimportant. It would appear that such limit-setting sends an important message to children: that their mother is monitoring their experiments, and intervening to protect them from dangers which they themselves cannot discern. This sense of being gently overseen by a benign but firm supervisor enables them to be less cautious or fearful on their own account, because they have faith that they will come to no great harm. These results reinforce the idea that an adventurous spirit develops only within a context of clearly communicated, consistently enforced expectations.

Holding back

It is also essential that parents, in their desire to protect their children from distress, don't jump in and solve their learning problems for them. Allowing children to grapple with difficulty for a while, even to experience a bearable amount of distress, teaches them that this is not something to worry about or be ashamed of. The converse is well-known: parents can transmit their anxieties to children very easily. As we have seen, children quickly develop the ability to read other people's emotional expressions, and from them to gain a vicarious evaluation of the situation. A mother who reacts with revulsion to a spider, or with agitation to a broken glass of milk, is demonstrating to the child that spiders are disgusting, breakages are disasters. Likewise, if a child on the verge of tears because her tower of bricks has just fallen over looks up and sees a warm, calm expression on her mother's face, she learns that her distress is not itself a cause for alarm. If her mother runs over, picks her up and says in a very concerned voice, 'There, there, my poppet. It's all right', she learns that her distress *is* something to be worried about.

Children are often themselves very sensitive to, and resentful of, too much help; too much rescuing; too much information. Not infrequently parents are puzzled by fierce rejections of their well-meant help. As they often put it, 'My little two-year-old (or three- or four-) was having some kind of problem with something the other day and I went over to help her or him and the child turned on me with rage and said, "Leave me alone! Don't do it. Let *me* do it!" What happened?'[19] When basically resilient children get stuck, what they often want is the merest nudge; the minimum help that will get them going again, not the full weight of an adult's accumulated knowledge and expertise. John Holt recounts the old story of the five-year-old who went to her mother in the kitchen and said, 'Mummy, how do traffic lights work?' Her mother, busy cooking, said, 'I don't know, darling. Why don't you go and ask Daddy?' To which the little girl replied, 'I don't want to know *that* much about it.'

Too much praise or reward can have a similar effect. A group of nursery children who were happily playing with materials of their own choice, crayonning, say, were approached by an adult who told them that they would be awarded a 'Good Player' certificate if they carried on. The result was to make their play less active and less creative. Children whose drawings and paintings were regularly praised by a teacher started to produce work that was increasingly conventional and unoriginal. In other studies, children who were rewarded for doing their own thing lost interest in the activity when the rewards were later discontinued.[20] John Holt describes the destructive effect on resilience of too much praise:

My first elementary-school teaching was at a school that believed in supporting children with lots of praise. By the time I came to know them in fifth grade, all but a few of the children were so totally dependent on continued adult approval that they were terrified of not getting it, terrified of making mistakes. The practice of that school – and since then I have seen many others like it – had exactly the opposite results from those intended. Every teacher in that school was intent on nurturing each child's self-esteem, but despite their intentions, their stream of praise had an extremely destructive effect on most of the children. Though affluent, high-IQ, and favoured in all possible ways, they were pathetically lacking in self-confidence.[21]

Being a learning coach

Children's learning is best encouraged when an adult actually takes part with them in an activity, and when interactions arise from the child's self-initiated actions. As we saw in Chapter 14, through engaging together in an enjoyable task the adult is able to offer hints and nudges that enable the child to do things that they could not have done on their own – and thus to experience and learn how to do them. The logic of learning is almost the reverse of the familiar one of 'teach them what to do and then they can do it'. Through the adult's scaffolding, the child can do what they 'can't do', and thus feel themselves using, with help, the tools and strategies that they will come to master for themselves.

Here is an example of good scaffolding.[22] Simon, three and a half, is at his playgroup and wants to work on a jigsaw puzzle. The group leader, Karen, tips the pieces out of the box for him. She tells him he'll need to get them all the right way up, then leaves him for a few minutes. When she comes back, Simon points to one of the pieces and asks, 'Does this go at the top?' Karen tells him it does. 'Look at the top of the clock again. That's the one that comes right at the very top. Look, the big hand's on it. Can you see? Right, start off with that.' Simon gets to grips with the task: 'Then . . . then that one goes in there and that one goes in there!' Karen encourages him further: 'That's right. Now you've got the idea.' Later, Simon signals for help: 'I've got some gaps.' Karen tells him: 'Look on the floor – there might be some pieces there.'

In this way, adults supply the 'glue' that holds children's learning activities together, enabling them to experience greater success whilst still having plenty to struggle with, and still retaining 'ownership' of their learning project. Adults may suggest ways of breaking down a demanding task into manageable units. They may highlight things that it would be helpful for the child to pay attention to, while leaving the child a manageable amount of work to do ('Look on the floor . . .'). They may draw attention to the effects of the child's actions, and to the actions themselves ('Now you've got the idea.'). They may remind him of actions he can do but which are part of his passive repertoire, not coming spontaneously to mind at the right time.

In addition, they may modulate the child's emotional involvement with the task. They provide encouragement to persist when they think success is probably within the child's grasp. ('Come on, Jackie, you know that word . . .'). They may confirm that the task is difficult, and thus reassure the child that he is not silly for finding it so. They may soothe the child, stopping him from perhaps becoming over-excited and blowing it. Adults can share and celebrate moments of triumph. And by their interest and involvement, they validate the worthwhileness of the activity. Through such conversations adults can also reflect back to the child what he is doing and formulate it in language, thus modelling and encouraging the ability to verbalize activity, and demonstrating the usefulness of musing aloud. And they can intersperse this with invitations and opportunities for the child to offer his own commentaries.

Finally, adults can guide and encourage the child's control of the emerging 'game', responding positively to workable suggestions and elaborations which the child spontaneously offers. Young children tend to be monopolized by what lies immediately before their eyes. If they are to become truly effective learners, they need to be able to lift themselves out of immediate happenings in order to weigh up possibilities, plan their actions and evaluate their efforts. (Jigsaw puzzles offer opportunities for this strategic planning: finding the corner pieces first; making the border; sorting all the 'sky' pieces together.) This is precisely the sort of activity the skilled learning coach encourages and draws out.

The learning coach's eye stays firmly on the expansion of children's learning power. It doesn't matter so much whether this morning's fascination is with jigsaw puzzles whilst the afternoon's is with next door's new kitten, and tomorrow's is with naming the characters in a story-book. It doesn't even matter if they are not interested in books or sums yet; there is plenty of learning-to-learn that can be done in the meantime. The top priority is to guide activity, model approaches and offer suggestions so that children keep expanding their stock of things to do when they don't know what to do, and their ability to stay intelligently engaged with difficult and novel predicaments.[23]

Encouraging mistakes

Learning power develops as children grapple with challenges that are currently at the limits of their competence, and as they do so they inevitably get stuck and make mistakes. The context of their learning must therefore allow for this at least some of the time. They have to be able to work on problems where mistakes are not too costly in either material or social terms. When young people are carrying out real tasks, particularly in poor societies, getting it right may indeed be more important than developing learning power. The performance of a child caring for the family livestock has to be flawless, or the consequences may be dire.

But sometimes children's carers may err on the side of 'correctness' out of habit or belief rather than actual necessity, and then the development of learning power can be held back without good cause. In one study, six-year-old children in rural Brazil were observed working either with their mothers or their teachers on a learning task which involved using toy figures to re-create a scene which they were shown. When they were working with their teachers, the children were encouraged to study the model scene for themselves more than twice as often as they were by their mothers. On over half the occasions, the mothers actually picked up the correct figure and gave it to the child; teachers rarely did this. Mothers' top priority was to perform the task correctly. Teachers' top priority was to encourage maximum learning and independence in the children. To develop learning power, parents need to be thinking and behaving more like these teachers.[24]

In the USA, it appears that parents hold more mixed views about their children's learning. When Carole Ames and Jennifer Archer at the University of Illinois at Urbana-Champaign asked mothers of elementary school-age children which of two projects they thought would be better for their child, 'one where they'll learn a lot of new things but also make a lot of mistakes', or 'one that would involve a minimum of struggle and a strong likelihood of success', they split, roughly 50:50, into those who valued success, wanting their children to get good grades and be doing better than others; and those who valued effort, wanting their children to be working hard and fully engaged. 'Success' mothers were more likely to attribute their children's positive achievements to ability; the 'effort' mothers were more likely to explain it in terms of hard work. As we saw in Chapter 1, it is easy to see how these beliefs might directly influence children's development. As they talk to them about their school work, react to their efforts, offer more encouragement for some activities than for others, reinforce certain of the children's spontaneous ways of understanding their world but not others, so their views are being broadcast, picked up and installed in children's own belief systems.[25]

Modelling learning

As we saw in Chapter 4, children learn a great deal simply by observing how those around them go about things. It would seem only common sense, therefore, to make sure that children see those around them modelling the capabilities, qualities and dispositions of good learning. To help them get the hang of learning, they need to be able to watch people doing it – and preferably doing it happily and well. (Albert Einstein once observed that 'the only rational method of educating is to be an example'. And he added, as a last resort, 'If you can't help it, be a warning example.')

Children like to be around people doing interesting, grown-up things, and to be able to play some small part in these enterprises: cooking, cleaning the car, gardening, repairing things. But more than that, they benefit from being around people learning. Only by seeing the struggles and uncertainties that people go through, and the real time that difficult projects can take, can they pick up accurate images of what learning may involve. If they don't get used to the fact that learning takes time and can be frustrating, when they get stuck they will be more inclined to think that something has gone wrong, with the world or with their own capabilities, rather than to recognize that this is just the way learning sometimes is. Parents can easily be visible learners: learning to use a new domestic appliance; learning how to use a new computer; learning to play the flute.

As a writer, for example, I could show my older children all the drafting, exploring and note-taking that is invisible in a finished book. I could explain a little about what is happening at each stage of the process, from the first glimmering of an idea to the correction of the proofs and the eventual publication. If I were a teacher I could keep all my scraps of notes, materials, quotations and drafts, and make a poster showing all the stages that a sustained piece of writing has to go through. This would at least have the merit of showing students what many of them simply have no other way of knowing or appreciating: the sheer amount of time, effort and experimentation that goes into a piece of serious writing.

Growing up too fast?

The idea that children need to engage with meaningful learning challenges does not, of course, imply that we should remove all protection and allow them to wrangle with whatever comes their way. Just as toddlers need to trust that they are being shielded from things that are too dangerous, so too do eight- or twelve-year-olds. Many children are exposed to adult dilemmas and behaviours which they do not have the tools to deal with, and which they therefore find overwhelming or frightening. There is a difference between encouraging them to venture progressively further out from the shores of the known, and giving them the tools and qualities to do so, and taking them far out to sea and pushing them overboard.

A month or so after my disorienting experience with the sex quiz *Carnal Knowledge* (screened, as I said, around midnight on a Saturday) I was giving a talk to a conference of primary headteachers on the subject of preparing young people to deal with the uncertainties they would be facing. On the spur of the moment, I asked them what proportion of their ten-year-olds would be likely to be watching television at midnight on a weekend. They agreed that 50 per cent would be a realistic estimate. On that basis, thousands of youngsters across the UK could have seen that show. How many of them would have had the tools to inquire into what they were being fed, rather than respond defensively, for example by suppressing their own emotional reactions? (There is evidence that the damage done to young people by watching violent videos is not direct, but reflects their picking up, from the elders around them, an attitude of casual acceptance. They learn by observation that their natural revulsion or fear is unnecessary, or, worse, is 'stupid' or 'babyish', so they become numbed down, as well as dumbed down, by the experience.)[26]

So the idea that we must be preparing young people to deal well with uncertainty, and to be ready to make up their own minds about complex dilemmas, is not opposed to the idea that children need structure, protection and guidance. Of course we must give children as sure a footing as we can. But these days a moral framework has to be the launch-pad for a child's inquiries and explorations, not a rigidly enforced code of ethics that precludes such learning. The issue is one of timing and transition – of when and how much to hand over responsibility, and encourage inquiry – not whether to or not.

SEVENTEEN

Schooling for Learning

Everyone agrees that schools are important. British Prime Minister Tony Blair famously said on taking office that his top three priorities were 'Education, Education and Education'. In a 1998 speech to the Education World Congress in Washington, US President Bill Clinton declared:

> Where once we focused our development efforts on the construction of factories and power plants, today we must invest more in the power of the human mind, in the potential of every single one of our children. A world-class education for all children is essential to combating the fear, the ignorance, the prejudice that undermine freedom all across the globe today. It is essential to creating a worldwide middle class. It is essential to global prosperity. It is essential to fulfilling the most basic needs of the human body and spirit. That is why the twenty-first century must be the century of education and of the teacher.[1]

School failure

Yet it is equally widely accepted, around the globe, that schooling in general is very far from delivering the quality of education that is needed. Even in many of the industrialized nations, basic levels of literacy and numeracy are unacceptably low. Globally there are estimated to be nearly 900 million adult illiterates. In Britain almost 15 per cent of school-leavers and adults have limited literacy skills, while 20 per cent of adults have limited numeracy skills. In the USA, the latest survey shows that over 20 per cent of adults score only in the lowest categories of literacy and numeracy, lacking the ability to perform the most basic arithmetical operations or to locate a simple item of information in a short piece of text. Only about a fifth of the population could solve mathematical problems requiring two or more steps, or integrate information from more complex passages of text.[2]

The fundamental problem of adult illiteracy and innumeracy is not so much that people have not acquired these skills. It is that they have come to believe they cannot. Having missed the boat once, they have given up. Many of them, despite an acute awareness of the fact that their employability and their enjoyment of life are handicapped, feel unable to do anything about it. They feel ignorant, ashamed and inept. Underneath the visible problems with reading and writing lies the deeper problem of 'illearnacy': an acquired disabling of learning courage and learning initiative. Kelvin from the introduction to this book (see p. 5) is a typical example.

Even those who do well on conventional examinations can display an alarming lack of common sense when asked to use those skills in out-of-school contexts. In the third National Assessment of Educational Progress (NAEP) in the United States, a national sample of students were asked: 'If 1128 soldiers need to be bussed to their training site, and each bus holds 36 soldiers, how many buses do they need?' Seventy per cent correctly divided 36 into 1128 and came up with '31 remainder 12'. However, less than a third of those students went on to conclude that the answer to the question was '32 buses'. Rather more of those who had done the calculation correctly said they needed '31 remainder 12 buses', and 18 per cent said they needed '31 buses'.[3] And qualifications are no guarantee of practical competence. The chairman of a large employment agency was quoted in 1997 as saying: 'Everyone's got [qualifications] these days but I can't find people with sufficient skills that I feel confident of putting them forward to my clients.'[4]

Young people's attitudes to education

In terms of their ability to cope with the wider demands of adulthood, young people certainly do not feel well prepared by their schooling. Typical of Western youth are the attitudes revealed by a national survey commissioned by the British Industrial Society in 1997. Two-thirds of sixteen- to twenty-five-year-olds said that school had not prepared them for life in the real world.[5] One eighteen-year-old Moslem man spoke for many when he said: 'The things you learn in school are to do with education and to get jobs. You're not really using them in actual real life. . . . [Even when school is "successful"] I think there is a gap. . . . In school everything works like clockwork, you know; you go to your lessons, you do your work, you learn all your information, and it sticks in your head, you do your exams and you get all the information you can possibly get. . . . Real life is not like that.'

A nineteen-year-old Chinese woman said: 'Up to a point [mathematics is] all right, but then again . . . I think, what's the point? I don't need it in later life. You just wonder why you bother.' While a young mother from London said: 'You learn to read and write in the infants and juniors – and then the rest of it, to be honest, most of it I can't even remember now.' Of those young people still in full-time compulsory education, 36 per cent of eleven-year-olds, rising to a massive 60 per cent of sixteen-year-olds, say they are 'bored by' or 'not interested in' school work.

The report characterizes young people's lives, at the end of the millennium, in terms of insecurity: an acutely felt mis-match between the demands of an increasingly uncertain world and the resources with which they meet it. One young woman said of her husband: 'There's no security . . . my husband can't take a job for three months . . . he's twenty-four and he's in the age group where he can't be trained up because he's too old . . . he's in the building trade but he has got no other type of training, so trained jobs won't touch him. So nobody wants him; he's on the scrap heap.' An eighteen-year-old said: 'The thing that I'm scared of is, say I got laid off, I've got nothing, nothing to help me get another job, if you know what I mean? I've got no other skill. . . . I'd have to try and start up on my own. . . . I'd never get another job.' The feeling of being unprepared for uncertainty is rife in these young people.

The report concludes:

> Most [young people] fear that their world will generally become more challenging, and some have a bleak view of future opportunities and trends. . . . Their lives are riddled with insecurity, and traditional aspirations seem inappropriate in the context of the world as young people experience it. Values seem to work against each other rather than reinforcing individuals' lives. At school they are under pressure to achieve. They are told they need qualifications in order to get a good job. . . . Meanwhile media reports and the experience of unemployed family and friends suggest that job security is an illusion. . . . Insecurity becomes an integral part of growing up.

Parents and teachers

Teachers, too, know that all is not well. On several occasions in the late 1990s when I have been invited to talk to groups of them about the future of education I have started by taking a straw poll of those who thought that schools, as they are, do a good job of equipping the majority of young people for 'lifelong learning'; currently proposed reforms would make them so; or we were a long way off. Out of a total of some three hundred respondents so far, nobody thought schools were fine, two thought they could be fixed up, and the rest thought that they were missing the target by a mile.

Parents as well are voting with their feet, withdrawing their children from school at an unprecedented rate and opting to educate them at home, or in collaboration with like-minded families. In the USA 1.5 million families are now home-schooling, with the number increasing by 15 per cent every year. Soon this could amount to 10 per cent of the school-age population. In the UK, some ten thousand families home-school with a start-up rate of a hundred a month.[6] Professor

David Hargreaves, the doyen of British educationists, has
predicted that this trend is about to explode, with thousands
of families turning their back on schools and making alternative arrangement for their children's education. Companies
will offer perks to their employees which will make it easier for
them to educate their children at home, leaving state schools
eventually to provide little more than custodial education for
students whose parents cannot or will not take them out.
Many firms already provide medical benefits, leisure facilities
and crèches for their workforce. 'It is but a small step',
Hargreaves argues, 'for them to intervene, as an investment,
in primary and secondary education, whether in the form of
schools, some specializing in the area of the business itself, or
in the form of technological support or peripatetic tutors. . . .
Indeed, many employees will [be ready to] forgo a portion of
their salaries for these educational benefits, which simply
become a replacement of the company car or other conventional perks.'[7]

The response from within

From within the educational establishment, the 'obvious' responses to its deficiencies are to do what you have been doing,
but harder, or earlier, or better, or with greater 'purity', or
slightly differently. So we are seeing in education, at the
moment, a huge variety of such tinkerings. To watch the
manoeuvrings of politicians and educationists is to be irresist-
ibly reminded of heated seating-plan discussions on the *Tita-
nic*. Debates rage about precisely how to teach reading and
mathematics. Unflattering parallels are drawn between one
country and another. The kind of traditional methods used
in Singapore produce a much higher proportion of twelve-year-
olds who can handle fractions correctly, so European governments are rushing to tighten guidelines on the teaching of
mathematics that make a definite break with progressive ideas.

Meanwhile, back in Singapore the pendulum has already
started to swing in the opposite direction. Worried that
learning by rote and unquestioning obedience have created
a generation of brilliant conformists who pass exams with

ease but cannot think for themselves, Singapore's schools and universities have started a Thinking Programme. When Chua-Lim Yen Ching, principal of Zhonghua secondary school, enters his classroom for the morning's English lesson, the students stand and bow in the traditional manner. But within minutes the orderly rows of teenage boys and girls have dissolved into cheerful, chattering work-groups, reminiscent of the liberal-style classrooms which Western governments are trying to stamp out. 'We have to teach children decision-making skills', says Chua-im, 'and encourage creative thought, academic scepticism, originality and innovation.'[8]

In the USA, teachers are taking seriously students' complaints about being bored and the curriculum's lack of relevance to real life. Six of the staff at Elsie Robertson High School in Lancaster, Texas, made use of a mathematics worksheet which had been circulating nationwide for a while to 'let students know', according to math head Scott Martin, 'that we have a sense of what goes on in the world'. The worksheet contained the following problems.

José has 2 ounces of cocaine. He sells an 8-ball to Jackson for $320 and 2 grams to Billy for $85 a gram. What is the street value of the balance of the cocaine if he doesn't cut it?

Rufus pimps for three girls. If their price is $65 for each trick, how many tricks will each girl have to turn so that Rufus can pay for his $800-per-day crack habit?

Whether this material recruited students' interest or enhanced their achievement is not recorded. The teachers who used it were suspended without pay. The gimmicky (and/or ironic) attempt to repackage the same tired old arithmetic seems to betray a certain desperation.[9]

Meanwhile 'education action zones', funded by private business and encouraged to run at a profit, are to be introduced in deprived inner-city areas of Britain, as they have been in the States. Schools will be taken over by 'rescue teams', made up predominantly of businessmen, who will have the power to sideline local councillors and school governors, dispense with the national curriculum, ignore teachers' pay

scales and recruit £100,000-a-year superheads. This despite
the fact that the experiments in the USA on which the plan is
based have met with very mixed success. Education Alternatives Inc., given a $135 million contract to run nine schools in
run-down Baltimore in 1992, was thrown out in 1995 having
falsified exam reports and managed to increase the truancy
rate significantly.

A rival company, Edison, has introduced its own commercial TV channel, Channel One, into schools. In return for
receiving expensive television sets free of charge, the schools
sign contracts by which students are obliged to watch two
minutes of advertisements for junk food, cameras and fizzy
drinks for every ten-minute programme package. A study in
Michigan found that students on the receiving end of Channel One were more likely to agree that 'money is everything',
'a nice car is more important than school', 'wealthy people are
happier than the poor', and 'designer labels make a difference'.[10]

From inside the 'box' of education, all this looks like new
wine. From outside, what is mainly visible is the old bottles.
The commercialization and commodification of education
leave the contents, methods and structures of the past endlessly tinkered with but substantially unaltered. Slogans are
vigorously traded, but the underlying assumptions about the
nature of learning remain unquestioned. Left firmly in place is
the belief in the primacy of knowledge over know-how; the
reliance on a very restricted range of learning modes; the
neglect of the fact that this pedagogy privileges those whose
home life has accustomed them to these modes early and
necessarily disadvantages others; the belief in 'ability', and the
neglect of learning to learn; the unwitting undermining of
resilience, resourcefulness and reflection; and the assumption
that transfer of learning takes place automatically.

How we teach what we don't know[11]

Education is what adults deem necessary to provide for the
young – over and above that which can be trusted to happen
naturally in the process of growing up – in order to prepare

them to live well in the world that they, as adults in their turn, will enter. In a stable culture the educating adults can look at the world that they themselves inhabit, ruminate on the arts of living which that world requires, and turn them into a curriculum. However, when the future is as unpredictable as ours – when all we know about the year 2020 is that we know precious little about it – this educational strategy won't work. To persist in preparing children for a fantasy world is at best self-indulgent, and at worst criminally negligent.

In an uncertain situation, the only useful – and defensible – thing to do is try to prepare young people to deal well with uncertainty. As John Holt said as far back as the 1960s: 'Since we cannot know what knowledge will be most needed in the future, it is senseless to try to teach it in advance. Instead, we should try to turn out people who love learning so much and learn so well that they will be able to learn whatever needs to be learned.'[12] That has to be the central curriculum objective of the learning society, not just in rhetoric but in reality. We have to remember that the end of education is to enable young people, when they are grown up, to live happy, responsible and successful lives. If teaching them to multiply fractions is genuinely a means to that end, then let us do it. But we must not vaguely wish or hope that it is such a means; nor must we fervently believe it, for that makes the future of education a battleground rather than an inquiry. The nineteenth-century American essayist Alexis de Toqueville once defined a fanatic as someone who redoubles his efforts when he has forgotten what he is fighting for. We cannot really start to decide what education should be unless we first remember what fundamentally it is for.

The way ahead

Happily schools are not beyond redemption, and there are many examples to prove it. Around the globe, innovative educators are finding ways to do more than tinker with the curriculum. Here are just a few examples of the lessons that are being learnt.

Increasing emotional self-management

In *Emotional Intelligence*, Daniel Goleman describes the lessons in 'self science' that form a core part of the curriculum at the Nueva Learning Center in San Francisco. As the register is called at the beginning of a lesson, a group of fifth-graders respond to the call of their name not with the conventional 'Yes' or 'Here', but with a number from one to ten that indicates how high (10) or low (1) their energy or their spirits are, and a word that catches the flavour of it. Jessica says, '10; I'm jazzed.' Patrick says, '9; excited.' Nicole says, '10; peaceful.' Anyone with a low number is invited – not pressurized – to talk about why their spirits are low, or what is troubling them. With the guidance and modelling of their teacher, the group has gradually learnt to listen to and respect different concerns.

Some of the components of the so-called self-science curriculum are *self-awareness*: observing yourself and recognizing your feelings; building a vocabulary for feelings; knowing the relationship between thoughts, feelings and reactions; *managing feelings*: monitoring 'self-talk' to catch negative messages such as internal put-downs; realizing what is behind a feeling (for example, hurt that underlies anger); finding ways to handle fears and anxieties, anger and sadness; *handling stress*: learning the value of exercise, guided imagery and relaxation methods.

By paying attention to feelings, students are led to adopt ways of responding to their emotional reactions that are more skilful, both personally and socially. Just as children at home learn from the models and conversations that surround them, so do they in school. It is not so hard to become conscious of some of the common dynamics that tend to clog up learning, and to make them an explicit part of learning conversations.[13]

Building resilience with real problems

The constant need to move on, and to document progress, in normal schools means that education tends to be cut up into bite-sized tasks that take just a few minutes, at most, to complete. This constant regime of small exercises systematically denies children opportunities to experience making slow progress on complicated, ill-formulated tasks – to find out what that feels like; to take pleasure in this cumulative progress; and to strengthen the learning muscles that such sustained engagement requires. It has been shown that, faced with genuinely hard problems, even those students who are relatively successful at conventional tasks tend to give up after just a few minutes, unable to retain any kind of thoughtful and persistent intelligence in the face of frustration. They do not develop resilience.[14]

Mike Forret, a physics educator at the University of Waikato in New Zealand, has found that students develop their persistence and resilience if given time to work, preferably in small groups, on a genuinely difficult problem which they have chosen, and to which, very importantly, the teacher does not know the answer. They are so used to going through the motions of learning, knowing that there is a standard solution which the teacher is holding back now but will eventually deliver, that quite a different quality of engagement emerges when this is not the case. Mike was involved in creating a series of videos on technology for the New Zealand Ministry of Education, and a small group of fourteen-year-old boys, who had studied an introductory unit on electronics, volunteered to be filmed as they grappled with a problem over the course of a day and a half – an eternity, in school terms, to spend on a single topic. The boys, all unexceptional students, chose a tough problem for themselves: designing an electric circuit to turn on your house lights when you open the front door at night (but not during the day), and to leave them on when the door is closed, until turned off at a switch.

As the boys played with relays, switches and the light-dependent resistor on a circuit board, their circuit gradually became more complicated. When they hit a problem that they could not solve after some experimentation and discussion, they would often leave it and work on a different part of the circuit. Gradually, through trial and error and a lot of conversation and argument, they created a satisfactory solution. At the end of the sessions, when Mike asked one of the boys what he thought he had got out of this learning experience, he said: 'Perseverance; being able to have a problem you couldn't do and actually working through and solving it and being able to. Because quite often you get a problem you can't do, you tell the teacher and they help you with it. But with this one it was actually up to us to solve the problem.'

One of the other boys agreed that the feeling of being on their own was important. 'No one knowing the answer was good.' Mike asked if this was similar to learning approaches that they met elsewhere on the curriculum. The first boy said: 'We do nothing like this at all in any of the other subjects, nothing of this calibre. It's all watered-down stuff.' Mike inquired what he meant by 'watered-down'. 'It's nothing hard; it's like . . . it may take you twenty minutes to half-an-hour – everything is aimed to be solved in half a period . . . and usually nothing major if you know what you are doing.'

Through this genuine challenge – one which gripped them, because they had created and adopted it for themselves – the boys have learnt a lot about electronics. They have been practising some important real-life learning skills too: not just those of logical thinking, discussion, listening and learning to give and take criticism without taking it personally, but also, through Mike Forret's skilful probing, to articulate and reflect upon their own learning processes.[15]

Developing imagination

Justin, the eleven-year-old who underwent the 'surgical removal of immaturity, in Chapter 5, is a student at the Barbara Taylor School, which since 1994 has been located in a store-front in Brooklyn, New York. In many ways it is typical of a long tradition of small, independent progressive schools, but what makes it distinctive is its emphasis on the use of imagination and drama. We learn, says Lois Holzman, one of the school's directors, by play-acting: we throw ourselves imaginatively into a role, and if it fits we can grow into it. We project imaginative grappling hooks into the future, and then haul ourselves, through play, towards them. Adolescence is notoriously a time for trying out many different ways of being, and seeing how they go down with family and friends. At the Barbara Taylor School, this is one of the main educational tools. People learn through imagination, and as they do so, they cultivate imagination as a learning tool.[16]

Even quite conventional kinds of learning may involve performance. Over lunch Charles was teasing Alice, both of them eight, about not being able to spell. 'How come she can't even spell "cat"?' he asked, and someone else asked him how come he could. 'My mother told me to watch the game shows on TV,' he said, 'and that's how I got so good.' Did Charles think that Alice might be able to learn by watching game shows, too? Yes, he thought she could. And did Alice want to learn? Yes, she did. Suddenly, the school was buzzing with ideas on how to organize spelling 'game shows' for Alice, and by the time lunch was over a team had assembled itself to create, write and produce some shows. Over the next few days, these performances became an integral part of the school day. Alice learned how to spell a lot of words. But everyone learned more than that: they learned something about *how* spelling could be learnt; and they learned something about the feel, the process and the identity of being a learner. As we have seen, the role of imagination in learning is not restricted to drama or creative writing as encapsulated subjects. It is a useful tool in an infinite variety of different settings.

Teachers as learners

Souhegan High School in New England opened in 1992 and has seven hundred pupils. Every member of the school's teaching faculty had made a commitment to putting into practice the ideal of the school as 'a community of learners where a spirit of inquiry, reflection and risk-taking prevails'. The teachers had been selected on two main criteria: commitment to the students, the school's ideals, and each other; and 'a willingness to goof' in order to learn. 'The challenge', said the principal, 'is to avoid retreating to the comfortable.' Turning the normal safety-first culture on its head, the humanities division leader said of one of her new staff, 'Joe is a good example of the kind of teacher who will flourish [here]. . . . He's willing to risk trying new things, and to risk learning from his colleagues. . . . The teachers who don't have that openness, who are still trying to impose on their students and on their teammates an old system . . . will have the most difficult time.'[17]

The teaching staff's willingness to live with some uncertainty, and to allow creative resolutions to emerge over time, is illustrated by the issue of whether students were going to call teachers by their first names. In a conventional school culture, the impulse would be for somebody to decide – the principal, the management team, or perhaps the staff as a whole – and then for a policy to be agreed and carried out by all. A neat, and preferably quick, solution would be desirable. One teacher describes how it was handled, rather differently, at Souhegan:

> Teachers had a lot of different opinions. So then we took it to the kids on the transition team. And the kids ultimately said, it doesn't make any difference at all. Why don't you let teachers decide, let students decide, everyone deal with what they're comfortable with. So I thought OK, I don't care either way. I figured that I would say, my name is Mrs Elise Watson, use any combination of these words that you feel comfortable with. I figured that the first kid would set the precedent for everyone. Everyone would listen for the first kid's choice and then fall in line. And that's not what happened. What amazes me is that some kids call me Elise, some kids call me Mrs Watson – within the same class.

In such ways the teachers' willingness to take their time, to live with uncertainty, and not to buy conventional solutions or even familiar ways of framing the problem is transparent to the students. They see that the institution is a changing manifestation of human ideas and decisions which can always be treated as provisional. Just as Ellen Langer's students (p. 184) were more creative when they were told that the view they had been given was 'one way of thinking about' how city neighbourhoods develop, so Souhegan is a 'could be' school, encouraging all concerned, by the very way it runs, to think about how things might be otherwise.

Communities of inquiry

Ann Brown at Harvard has researched the effects on children's learning of establishing what she calls communities of inquiry in the classroom. Working mostly with elementary school children, she divides a class of thirty into about six teams, and gets each team to research a different aspect of an overall topic. For example, a project that seems to recruit the interest of nine- to ten-year-olds involves the relationship between animals and their habitats. Brown will ask the children to gather information about different kinds of habitat, and on the basis of that knowledge invent a novel conjunction of resources and perils. Then the job of the class as a whole is to design a new animal that fits the invented habitat. One team will explore the different types of defence mechanism that different animals use. Another researches predator–prey relationships. A third investigates different ways of gaining protection from the elements. A fourth looks at the reproductive strategies of different species. A fifth explores animal communication. And the sixth group might research different ways in which animals gather their food. Where possible, the children are involved in the process of designing the topic, setting up the research teams and deciding how to go about collecting and organizing their information. During the research phase of a project the teacher acts as a consultant, helping them locate resources and refine the questions they are asking, and giving them a nudge when they get bogged down.

Interspersed with this research are class meetings of two kinds. (Brown's observations suggest that it helps the children if the shifts between these different kinds of activity are clearly and explicitly marked.) First there may be occasional keynote or benchmark meetings in which the whole class comes together to listen to an invited expert or to plan strategy and discuss progress. However, there are more regular meetings of jigsaw groups, made up of one delegate from each research team, in which each delegate shares with the others the progress that her team has made. Each research team has only one piece of the 'jigsaw puzzle' which the whole class is putting together, and as they are pursuing their own subtopic they are aware that they will have to communicate their results to others, and that their progress depends in part on the findings of the other teams. Eventually the children reach an agreed solution and create a presentation of their research and their conclusions, showing how the different strands interweave.

The learning-to-learn that these projects stimulate is multi-faceted. The children are learning to cooperate and communicate in their research teams. They are learning the skills of research itself: deciding what information they need, how to get it and the best ways of capturing and communicating it, both within their teams and to the jigsaw groups. In some classrooms, the children are able to ask questions or request information from graduate students at the local university via e-mail and videoconferencing. In this way they are developing not just their IT skills, but their confidence and competence at communicating across a wide spectrum of ages and expertise. They are learning to grapple with problems that are relatively open-ended, and to generate and refine questions. They are discovering that learning involves judgement, interpretation and imagination, as well as accurate comprehension and retention. They are beginning to think and talk about their own learning; to be able to stop, take stock, evaluate progress and plan their learning strategically. Across a whole range of measures of children's learning, thinking and communicating, Ann Brown's evaluations of her communities of inquiry reveal impressive and lasting gains. Clearly she has been successful at creating cultures that embody rather different beliefs about knowledge and priorities for learning than those of a more conventional classroom; yet she has done so in a way which means that the infrastructure of schools does not have to be radically altered.

In Ann Brown's words, communities of inquiry are places 'that emphasise the active strategic nature of learning', where 'children routinely engage in a search for understanding and effort after meaning', and in which they develop 'insight into their own strengths and weaknesses and access to their own repertoires of strategies for learning'. Such classrooms create 'an atmosphere of wondering, querying, and worrying about knowledge', in which, 'initially, young learners are trapped into these thinking activities through the [research teams and jigsaw groups], where everyone must think aloud, thus making the invisible visible. But over time, it becomes second nature [to them] to appreciate good questions and critically evaluate answers.' And in communities of inquiry, 'members are critically dependent on each other. . . . Expertise is deliberately distributed. . . . No one is an island; no one knows it all; collaborative learning is necessary for survival. This interdependence promotes an atmosphere of joint responsibility, mutual respect, and a sense of personal and group identity.' And if anyone believes that six- or eight-year-olds (with appropriate support, modelling and coaching) are incapable of such disciplined interaction and sophisticated learning, that is just their implicit theories about childhood talking: the evidence is here.[18]

Thinking about learning

One of the longest-running and best-documented experiments in teaching for learning power is the Project for the Enhancement of Effective Learning (PEEL) in the Australian state of Victoria. Now running in more than thirty schools, PEEL aims to get students to ask questions, to recognize and say when they don't understand, to think about their own learning and to listen to and learn from each other. Founder Ian Mitchell's first task was to create classroom cultures within which students felt that there was time for their questions, that they were taken seriously, and that it was OK to find things hard or to feel confused. From this he could invite students to reinvest the effort in trying to understand which many of them had withdrawn, and to take back the responsibility for their own learning which many of them had found it tactically advantageous to give away.[19]

This was not easy. Mitchell's research revealed that many students were not used to asking real questions. 'Teachers are so busy trying to get through the work that they never have time to answer your questions,' said one student. 'You're different; you're not afraid if we ask questions,' said another. When Mitchell asked a student called Michael, 'Why don't you ask questions in class?', he replied, 'Because I don't know how to. I've never done it before.' Asked why he didn't try, Michael said, 'I'm afraid they won't be any good.'

Some students' resistance to real thinking and ownership of

their learning, even when they found themselves in conducive circumstances, turned out to be strong. About two
months after Mitchell had started his PEEL teaching, three
fifteen-year-olds came into his office and said: 'We've been
talking about this PEEL thing, and we think we've got it
worked out.' 'Good,' said Mitchell, who smelt a breakthrough.
'You want us to think more in class ["yes"], to ask more
questions ["yes!"], to link one lesson to another ["Yes!!" with
increasing excitement].' The boys' spokesman paused, and
then said: 'Right. Well, we don't want to do that. It's too
much work. We'd rather you went back to telling us the
answers!'

Despite such moments of depression the PEEL teachers
persevered and began to identify quite precisely the classroom
behaviours that distinguished between good and bad learners.
Students who had trouble learning tended to attend to communications superficially, to give up attending prematurely,
and to direct their attention to incidental rather than central
features of what was being said or what they were reading.
They followed instruction blindly and mechanically, seemed
unaware of their own misconceptions, and did not think
about the meanings and implications of what they were
studying. And they often lacked the concepts and vocabulary
for talking about learning itself. Polly, who had been trying to
design a way of stopping an ice block melting, was asked,
'What have you learnt by doing this?' She replied, 'I don't
know what you are talking about.'

More important, though, were the behaviours and attitudes
that led to good learning. Good students often knew when
they did not fully understand something, and were more
prepared to involve others in helping them sort it out. They
checked what they were doing against the designated task,
and used their common sense to assess their answers and their
progress. They checked what the teacher said for mistakes or
ambiguities. They offered suggestions and ideas, and were
willing to express disagreements. They were more likely to
invest time in planning their learning, and actively sought
links between different lessons, between different subjects
and with their own experience.

The PEEL teachers have built up an extensive repertoire of

techniques for encouraging the development of these attitudes and practices which, in terms of the conventional classroom, offer an interesting mixture of the radical and the commonplace. For example, teachers make deliberate mistakes to keep students on their toes, and compliment those who spot them first; hand out a passage without a heading or sub-headings, and ask students (solo or in groups) to suggest some and explain; give students more information or more equipment than they need, and get them to prune what is not relevant; get students to make 'mind maps' of their main concepts of an area as a basis for generating questions; stop in the middle of an experiment, or a poem, or a piece of history, get students to predict what comes next, and then discuss whether they were right or wrong and why; have a discussion in which every contribution has to start with an explicit link to a previous student contribution; get students to take it in turns to make an inventory of their classmates' good learning behaviours.

One interesting teaching strategy is to involve students in assessing their own learning. For example, one mathematics teacher got a class of seventeen-year-olds to devise a test for the unit of work they were just completing. He divided the class into four groups of five and asked each group to produce five questions for the test, with solutions. In his learning journal he described how the exercise turned out. 'The lesson before, students were complaining about how long and involved some of the problems were, and that they didn't understand this part or that part and so on. But during this lesson all of these worries seemed to disappear as other members of the group were using their expertise to explain steps and procedures to each other. . . . Each group worked away very enthusiastically and without fail came up with five questions representative of the range of work covered.' 'After the test, the students marked each other's work as one of the original question-setters went through it on the blackboard. The teacher concluded: 'It worked very well, and I will definitely do it again.'

Some ages and classes will respond to strategies like this better and more responsibly than others, but for teachers interested in being learning coaches this is not grounds for despair. They see their job as enhancing effective learning from wherever a class or an individual happens to be. It is a developmental agenda, with each step functioning as the precursor of another. Learning power is built up layer by layer. With one class it may be a struggle – and an eventual triumph – to get pairs of student to discuss what happens next in a story for one minute without drifting off or messing about. But that step modelled, scaffolded, practised and secured provides the platform on which more demanding kinds of interaction can gradually be built.

Mitchell's evaluations of PEEL classrooms show that such teaching strategies and changes of attitude are highly effective in increasing the number of good learning behaviours per lesson. Students who have experienced several years of PEEL teaching talk more in lessons; more of them talk; and much more of the talk is student-initiated and content-focused rather than merely responding to teachers' questions or dealing with management issues and instruction: 27 per cent of the total talk was of this kind in PEEL classes, as against about 4 per cent in comparable classrooms. In PEEL classes, students listen and respond to the contributions of other students four times as much as in other classes. As a result of PEEL teachers holding back and allowing student discussion to develop, the students become more used to, and tolerant of, periods of confusion. An unsolicited note from a fifteen-year-old to Ian Mitchell seems to capture much of the change.

> I've noticed something in our science classes. I can't exactly put it into words, but it seems to be a whole lot different from any other class in regards to activity (i.e. like 'student involvement' I think some teachers call it). . . . It's a feeling that everyone's sort of *doing* more. Sure there are people who still sit there and dream and/or scribble in the back of their binder books (I've probably got a guilty look on my face right now!) but people are *talking* more, even if it is arguing and disagreeing. . . . This is something I've noticed and I just thought you'd like to know (seeing as you're interested in that kind of thing!) Yours, Jenny Goldsmith.

Reflection

One of the recurrent elements of the PEEL approach is to get both teachers and students to write a learning log, a personal record of thoughts and impressions that relate to their own learning. We have just seen an example of a teacher's log: the account of getting students to create their own examination. Katie, fifteen, provides the students' perspective. After a science lesson on forces she wrote: 'I didn't really enjoy it because I thought it was boring and really hard to understand. . . . It was useless because I couldn't contribute – or wouldn't?' The next lesson, however, had a different feel for her. 'Today I participated well as my view on the debate was used for a class vote. I found . . . I could easily work out the answers because I was interested. . . . I enjoyed the lesson because we were learning about things that were around us and they happened every day.' Out of such continual reflection on students' own learning grow insights, interests and plans for the future.

Learning logs can also be used with much younger students. Hilary Dyer, an ex-student of mine, invited a class of five-to seven-year-olds to write or dictate their reflections on lessons two or three times a week. They were prompted with the openers 'I learned . . .', 'I found it easy/hard to . . .' and 'I enjoyed . . .', and their replies were used as a basis for a conversation about their learning progress with the teacher and their classmates.

Sian, a bright five-year-old, made up in self-awareness what she lacked as a speller. Hilary wrote to her in her log, 'I wonder why we find some things easy or hard. Please write about it.' Sian replied: 'I do not no wiy I find things hard but one day I will learn, and I'm not shur wiy things aro easy for me. But they just aro and it is hard for me to think wiy it is easy for me.' Later Hilary asked: 'Tell me, do you think learning is done the same at home and at school?' Sian said: 'No, because I do difrt thngs at home than at school. I think I learn eyse easier at school than at home because I do mur things at school.' Sian wrote that she had 'bean wating to No how the Best way to laene is, and the eysistist', and, when prompted, answered her own question by saying: 'I think the eest and the best way to laene is not to gese and think; that will help you to learn the best way.' Hilary concluded: 'From an early age (five upwards) children are able to engage meaningfully in dialogue about their own learning, and can use frameworks offered by the teacher to . . . access their own intuitive understanding of themselves as learners. . . . This seems to indicate that teachers could now desist from treating children as passengers in the voyage of their own learning . . . and treat young learners as pilots.'[20]

We saw in Chapter 11 that children's progress in reading reflects their ability to articulate their own reading strategies. What was not mentioned there was the extent to which the development of children's metacognitive knowledge is influenced by their teachers. Two teaching strategies in particular would appear to encourage this development. One is for the teacher herself to make strategic thinking public by thinking out loud whilst modelling the task. For example, she reads with the children and, appearing to get stuck on a hard word, talks herself through various strategies. Second, she can raise a public dialogue with the children that focuses on the processes of reading. There are many ways in which teachers can encourage learners to pay attention to their own learning strategies, and to articulate both what they currently do, and possible alternatives.[21]

Responsibility

Many of the examples in this chapter, whether focused on the development of resilience, resourcefulness or reflection, involve a common ingredient: giving learners greater responsibility for the initiation, direction, control and evaluation of their own learning. Just as a doctor or an engineer learns their craft by gradually taking on more and more responsibility, so do learners in general. Finding ways to give young people experience of guiding their own learning is not a legacy from some liberal, child-centred ideology; it creates the practical conditions under which learning power develops.

There are many practical examples of the effects of giving responsibility. In one study, elementary school teachers found that children's reading improved significantly when they were given a greater degree of responsibility for selecting and planning their own learning activities. The improvements were greatest in the classes of teachers who had been most successful at putting the new procedures into effect. In another study teachers determined what learning was to take place, but six-year-olds were encouraged to work out for themselves the schedule they would adopt to complete the tasks. As a result their learning improved, and the proportion of assignments that were completed successfully increased considerably. In a third study, twelve- to fourteen-year-old students were explicitly taught about the concept of self-belief. They were invited to think of themselves as origins, people who are in charge of their own lives, rather than as pawns, people who believe they have little control. As a result their perceptions of themselves changed for the better, and their schoolwork improved as well.[22]

All around the world practical examples and experiments can be seen which explore how learning power can be developed through schooling. To help students become better learners does not mean abandoning the concerns of the traditional curriculum; it means finding ways of attending to the *process* of learning at the same time as one is working on any particular *content*. Some of the ideas reviewed here are quite challenging, and could at the moment only be implemented in specialized circumstances. But many of the others are being put into practice in situations that range from the orthodox to the inauspicious. There is no reason why any teacher could not begin to shift her classroom, little by little, from tomorrow.

EIGHTEEN

Higher Education: The College beyond Knowledge

Nowhere is the confusion between the development of learning power and the consumption of intellectual education more apparent than in colleges and universities. Originally founded as centres for the cultivation of wisdom – Oxford's twelfth-century charter describes it as 'a place of religion and learning' – universities became in the Middle Ages academies for the concentrated development of intellect and erudition. The core curriculum comprised first the subjects of the 'trivium' – grammar, rhetoric and logic – and then the more detailed, technical subjects of arithmetic, geometry, astronomy and music: the 'quadrivium'. The 'trivial' subjects were those deemed fundamental and of ubiquitous value in the accurate conduct of human affairs; the medieval skills, if you like, of lifelong learning – at least those of a gentleman and a scholar.

College as an intellectual rite of passage

Since the seventeenth century, however, the separation of disciplines from each other, and of academia from the practicalities of life, has proceeded apace. Students and lecturers came to know more and more about less and less, and the hegemony of the analytical and critical intellect became increasingly absolute. Universities zoomed in on 'knowledge' – timeless, certain, incorrigible knowledge – and the skills for its creation, manipulation and retention. Young men (and, slowly, women) who were suited by the accidents and privileges of birth, and then increasingly of their prior education, to sharpen their wits in this fashion were able to do so, provided they could pay.

Scholarly knowledge and analytical intelligence came to be seen not as just one kind of knowledge, and one way of knowing, but as the best. Imagination, intuition and practical expertise derived from experience were judged second-rate, and rewarded less. A university education, regardless of its practical value, opened doors to larger incomes and wider choices of lifestyle and career. A degree became a key that gave access to places of wealth and power that had previously been the preserve of the aristocracy. Having developed a certain kind of mind became a symbol of a person's standing in society. The rapid democratization of the universities, which gave access to higher education to those without privileges of birth, reinforced the underlying premise that clever minds deserve the best rewards. To this day the top positions in government administration and the media in the USA and UK, for example, are still dominated by Ivy League and Oxbridge alumni.

It is only a short step from the logic of access to the logic of entitlement. Not to be able to put BA or BSc after your name became seen, more and more widely, as a social stigma, so more and more young people were encouraged to enter universities with the expectation that they would emerge, successfully, with the necessary 'badge'. And because many of the traditional courses were both hard and arcane, the range of subjects on offer has become broader and the intellectual demands less rigorous. Despite protestations from those who are inside this culture, what many courses now offer is a kind of homogenized, pre-digested Academia Lite. Such courses no longer generally provide an effective apprenticeship in the hard craft of precise, analytical thinking for the minority of youth with a scholarly bent; nor a preparation for a specific vocation; nor a further stage in the development of general-purpose lifelong learning power.

As degrees in Sports Equipment Design and Barbecue Studies proliferate, and the proportion of 'first class' degrees continues to rise, so the value of the badge declines. Employers no longer trust degrees, any more than school examinations, to provide a true indication of an applicant's real-life skills of learning and communication. Despite the huge increase in the number of graduates leaving UK universities each year, a survey by the Association of Graduate Recruiters reveals that British employers are unhappy with applicants' abilities to speak and write clearly, to engage intelligently with real-life problems and to work in teams.

The unresilient student

The effect of this confused set of values and beliefs on students is, naturally, to confuse them. Levels of alcohol intake are high, as are the incidence of stress, anxiety, depression and eating disorders. And these seem to be related to an underlying lack of learning power; many students have a general 'inability to deal effectively with the demands of everyday life', and specifically, to 'manage their workload'.[1] Resilience, especially amongst the brightest students, is worryingly low. Mark Phippen, head of Cambridge University's Counselling Service, sees many clever young people with what he has come to call Imposter Syndrome: the constant anxiety that they are not as academically able as they are supposed to be, and will sooner or later be found out.

The lack of resilience, even of genuine courage and curiosity, of university students seems to be world-wide. As studentship becomes a universal initiation rite into adulthood, so concern about the quality of student learning and engagement mounts. Mark Edmundson, professor of English literature at the conservative, traditional University of Virginia, mused in the September 1997 issue of *Harper's* magazine on the decline of real curiosity and passionate engagement in his students. The predominant mode on campus these days is one of polite ennui and gentle scepticism, he says. Students do not challenge their teachers, for fear of upsetting them and thus not getting the grade they need. Rather they wait patiently to be entertained, ready to be roused by a witty remark, a risqué allusion or a juicy bit of post-modern debunking, but remaining essentially untouched – insulated from deeper questions or more personal doubts. Edmundson bemoans the rarity of a Joon Lee, a student who 'has decided to follow his interest and let them make him into a singular and rather eccentric man; in his charming way, he doesn't mind being at odds with most anyone'. It's not that Joon Lee is brighter than the others: 'in terms of intellectual ability they are all I could ask for'. It's that his robust, passionate, personal curiosity is stronger than his commitment to conformity and achievement.[2]

Perhaps, Edmundson speculates, the commitment to inquiry makes one look vulnerable, even absurd, in a culture that draws its role models from television – a 'cool' medium, as Marshall McLuhan put it, which rewards the controlled, the polished and the ironic, and is inhospitable to improvisation, experimentation and accidents of all kinds. The tyranny of the 'cool' prevents students inhabiting, with the requisite equanimity, the Ground Zero of learning, which is 'I don't know'. 'My students, alas, usually lack the confidence to acknowledge what would be their most precious asset for learning: their ignorance.'

Or perhaps a generation of timid, conformist students reflects a generation of parents who failed to understand that the development of learning power requires role models of robust learning, and just enough support to engage with things that were hard and confusing. Says Edmundson, 'It's my generation of parents who sheltered these students, kept them away from the hard knocks of everyday life, making them cautious and over-fragile; who demanded that their teachers, from grade school on, flattered them endlessly, so that the kids are shocked if their college professors don't reflexively suck up to them.'

And perhaps some professors perpetuate the dumbing down because their jobs depend upon good student feedback, and their university's finances depend upon good recruitment. Universities are fighting for customers in a fiercely competitive global market-place. Academic emissaries from Europe, the USA and Australia, all of them in pursuit of new pools of students and their fees, collide in hotel lounges in Kuala Lumpur and Hong Kong as they battle to sign degree deals with Asian colleges keen to gain the prestige (and thus the increased income) associated with a high-status partner.

If, in such a crowded commercial milieu, you dare to make your courses too challenging or to fail a few assignments, the next cohort of punters will go next door. The less students are challenged, made to try to think harder or write more clearly, the less they come to expect it – and to be able to tolerate it when it comes. And as self-esteem becomes more brittle, and resilience collapses, so teachers, out of a curious amalgam of caring and self-interest, back off.

Reflection: the return of Socratic learning

As with primary and secondary schools, there is plenty of opportunity for colleges of higher education to broaden their conception of teaching and learning, and to incorporate into their ways of working a concern with enhancing learning power. Many of the lessons of school can be carried through to this higher rung on the educational ladder. Here, let me offer a few examples that highlight the kinds of learning that might be particularly appropriate for the more mature learner.

Where the primary personal task of adolescence was to construct a workable identity, the slightly older student may be ready for some deconstruction: the work of calling into question that which has been taken for granted, and of becoming conscious of that which has been tacit. We know, from the work of Robert Kegan and others which we looked at in Chapter 11, that this is not an easy task. It requires new reserves of resilience, resourcefulness and reflectiveness. For many young people, being invited to use their studies as a mirror in which to inspect the personality they have con-cocted, and the values they have chosen, may be as welcome as having their stomach pumped and inspecting the contents. It is said that a Columbia University professor used to set the following questions at the end of his course: 'One: What book did you most dislike on this course? Two: What intellectual or character flaws in you does that dislike point to?'[3] Not all students, it is safe to assume, relished the challenge. But as universities open their doors to non-traditional clienteles, so they are discovering groups of students for whom such reflec-tion is more timely and more welcome. They are eager to put themselves in the learning frame, and to explore the known as well as to accumulate new knowledge and skill. For them, the boundaries between the domains of personal values, professional expertise and intellectual inquiry are weaker. They may be ready for Socratic education.

For Socrates, educated minds are able to 'live in a state of creative ignorance, of inner perplexity and the emotional unease such perplexity creates'.[4] The goal is to engage the learner at a personal as well as an intellectual level, and to bring her to the point where she 'knows that she does not know'. She is confronted with the doubtful nature of what she had presumed to be true. To do this, tutors use scholarly rigour and intellectual resources to irritate the learner and provoke a fruitful discombobulation – while affecting to have no position of their own. The Socratic method takes learners from unreflective certainty through floundering doubt to the admission of ignorance and on into passionate, open-minded curiosity. The teacher does not then reassure, resolve and inform. Her attitude, says Socrates, is at that point 'maieutic', like a midwife, helping the learner to give birth to their own new understanding.

Matthew Arnold, Professor of Poetry at Oxford in the nineteenth century, summed up the possibility of a living, continuing Socratic tradition in the closing pages of *Culture and Anarchy*:

> Socrates has drunk his hemlock and is dead; but in his own breast does not every man carry about with him a possible Socrates, in that power of a disinterested play of consciousness upon his stock notions and habits, of which this wise and admirable man gave all through his lifetime the great example, and which was the secret of his incomparable influence? And he who leads men to call forth and exercise in themselves this power, and who busily calls it forth and exercises it in himself, is at the present moment, perhaps, as Socrates was in his time, more in concert with the vital working of men's minds, and more effectually significant, than any House of Commons orator, or practical operator in politics.[5]

Intellectual craftsmanship

Not every university department can be expected to contain its own fully fledged Socrates. The intellectual skills and personal qualities required to bring people to a point of disillusionment, and to support them in seeing this as an opportunity rather than a disaster, are considerable and not quickly acquired. Nevertheless tutors can deal with students, structure courses and offer advice in ways which do foster the development of an inquiring mind.

One vital tool for questioning the known, which can be encouraged and coached, grows out of the kind of learning log or personal journal of inquiry which we saw five-year-olds capable of in Chapter 17. In it you can record the loose ends of thought and observation: those fragments of experience, ideas, quotations, fleeting images and snippets of dialogue which seem provocative, allusive or pregnant with meaning. Their routine collection in a way that allows them to be mulled over is invaluable, for they encourage the different compartments of the learning toolkit to interact in increasingly subtle ways. A detail of experience can, through reflection, spark a mixture of intuitive thinking, creative imagination and hard-nosed analysis.

In an essay on intellectual craftsmanship the great American sociologist C. Wright Mills described the function of such journals:

> In this file you, as an intellectual craftsman, will try to get together what you are doing intellectually and what you are experiencing as a person. Here you will not be afraid to use your experience and relate it directly to various work in progress . . . it also encourages you to capture 'fringe-thoughts': various ideas which may be by-products of everyday life, snatches of conversation overheard on the street or, for that matter, dreams. . . . Accomplished thinkers . . . treasure their smallest experiences [because] experience is so important as a source of original intellectual work. To be able to trust yet be sceptical of

your own experience, I have come to believe, is one mark of the mature workman.[6]

In the apt phrase of poet and university teacher Peter Abbs, 'the journal is the larder of reflexive intelligence', and university tutors are remiss if they do not encourage, and even model, the collecting and valuing of all sorts of pre-intellectual glimmerings and seeds. On his pioneering master's course in the performing arts at the University of Sussex, Abbs coaches his students in the assiduous and perpetual replenishing of this mental pantry. 'The quintessential aim of the journal is to catch the mind's activity in its emergent phase,' says Abbs.

The complement to this subtle process of inner germination and harvesting is the further development of hard thinking: the tools for sharp, critical scrutiny of what others have produced. Tutors model and coach the development of the requisite skills and dispositions, so that it becomes second nature to the student to adopt this critical perspective spontaneously, for herself. Does the argument hang together? What unarticulated, possibly unjustified, assumptions have been made? How has a key word slid from being used in one sense to another? Where has an assertion been used where an argument, or some evidence, was required? What solecisms are there? What non sequiturs? In the form of expression, what is felicitous and what superfluous?

One of the major ways in which tutors coach this development is through their reactions to students' work, both verbally, in the way they deal with students' questions or comments in seminars, and more formally, through the written feedback they provide as part of the assessment procedures. When tutors (or schoolteachers – the argument is the same) see such feedback only in summative terms – as a concluding judgement on a piece of work that is complete – rather than as formative – a contribution to a longer-term process of intellectual development – and see writing reports as a chore that has little bearing on learning, they encourage students to adopt the same attitude. Thus the formative opportunity is lost. To make use of such feedback, students have to construe it as a contribution to their own learning; an exemplification of the kinds of questions they could be asking themselves, in order to become better judges of their own work – a useful real-life ability if ever there was one.

At university, writing itself can develop into a powerful set of learning tools if tutors see it as such, and see it as part of their job to stimulate its development. Intellectual inquiry does not have just a single, polished, public voice: it has other styles that are more private, preliminary and exploratory. To develop an argument it may be useful to try writing it as a letter to a friend, or as a dialogue between characters holding differing views. Through such imaginative means unseen flaws in one's own position may stand revealed and unexpected syntheses may appear.

It may also be useful to dwell in an almost poetic fashion on the key words and terms around which the central argument revolves, so bringing to light their connotations. Small insights and widenings of perspective have recently occurred to me, for example, by realizing that the etymology of the word 'respect' is 'to look at again', or 'to see afresh'; while 'recreation', normally seen as 'mere play', means at a deeper level 'to create again; to re-make oneself'. The connections of ideas and the structure of an argument can be presented through diagrams and images as well as through connected prose. All these tools of exposition and exploration are of potential value to the practising lawyer or architect as well as to the dedicated academic. If the opportunity to hone and extend these learning tools is missed at university, through the blind necessity to transmit wodges of content and the canonical methods of manipulating it, then a degree becomes a rite of passage without much real-world value.

Self-evaluation

Many universities have now devised ways of cultivating students' ability to evaluate their own work, and have realized that this is an important ingredient of lifelong learning. In Australia David Boud, Professor of Adult Education at the University of Technology, Sydney, says: 'Whenever we learn we question ourselves. "How am I doing?", "Is this enough?",

"Is this right?", "How can I tell?", "Should I go further?" In the act of questioning is the act of judging ourselves and making decisions about the next step. This is self-assessment.' In general, in the learning society, it is more and more up to individuals to assess for themselves what they know, and what they *need* to know. To be able to monitor and check your own progress; to know when you have done good work; to diagnose your own learning strengths and needs; to develop professional judgement; to take stock of achievement: for all these reasons, the cultivation of the disposition and the ability to self-assess is invaluable.[7]

When tutors involve students in self-assessment, there is more at stake than merely being trusted to suggest a mark for your own work. It is not just a device to save tutors' time, like the little gizmos that add up the price of customers' own shopping to save time at the supermarket check-out. It is a shift of perspective and priority, in which students are invited to think about what 'good work' means both in their own terms and in those of the university criteria. What are the official criteria? How are they derived and applied? What weights are different criteria given? What of value is left out?

By opening a dialogue with students about the nature of quality, their ability to monitor and manage their own learning is increased. They develop a finer nose for what is elegant, satisfying, appropriate and effective – a sensibility which, again, the nurse, the lawyer, the copywriter and the bank manager all have need of. Of course there are many occasions on which a more expert tutor needs to correct the performance and guide the progress of her students. But each of these professions is as much about judgement as it is about knowledge, and someone who has always been told what is right and wrong lacks the experience to use judgement in unprecedented cases. They respond correctly in routine situations, and lack initiative in others. So the need to evaluate students has to be balanced by a concern with their evolving ability to evaluate their understanding for themselves.

Even within a relatively conventional view of higher education, the form of assessment has a profound impact on what students learn, how they learn, and what they consequently learn about learning. Where external assessment is the norm, the biggest influence on how students learn is the kind of assessment they anticipate. Tests of memory direct learners towards strategies of verbatim retention and away from the attempt to assimilate and interpret – after all, the sense you make of something might be different from the sense your lecturer intended you to make, and you will lose marks. Tests of comprehension and application drive learning strategies that are intended to deliver a deeper or more practical grasp of the subject-matter. Whilst lecturers may bemoan some students' lack of comprehension, the very methods of teaching and assessing that they use often encourage a superficial approach.[8]

The worry that students will be tempted to cheat, or at least to be generous in awarding themselves grades, is justified much more rarely than one might suppose. The old paradox applies: when people are given no responsibility, they tend to act irresponsibly; when they are treated as responsible, they tend to behave responsibly. Whilst tutors often have to reserve the right to moderate self-assigned marks, the discrepancy between their judgements of students' work, and the students' own assessment, is normally small. Students have a fair idea how they are doing, and will award themselves an honest mark if given the opportunity to do so.[9] Robert Edwards at the University of Glamorgan in Wales let students assess their own learning in a data-processing class. After being given a range of open-ended tasks which involved setting up and manipulating computer data files they designed their own competency standards and assessed themselves accordingly. The criteria and grades were then the subject of a discussion between student and tutor.

> In order to have her marks recorded in my register of marks, a student had to spend at least ten minutes discussing with me what she has actually done to deserve her marks. . . . When a student gave herself a high mark for what seemed to me to be a poor understanding of the ideas involved, I simply asked appropriate questions, ending with 'Do you really deserve the mark you have given yourself?' Every student seemed content to reduce

her mark herself. Equally frequently, students gave themselves below-average marks for very good understanding.
Here I tried to help the student compare her work with
that of others, and so to accept that she deserved a higher
mark. Despite the occasional need for me to intervene in
this way, more than three-quarters of the students' marks
needed no such discussion.[10]

Students' response to self-assessment varies. It can take a
little getting used to after years of accepting that it is the
teacher's responsibility to tell them how well they have done.
Some accuse tutors of shirking their legitimate responsibilities. Some find the responsibility onerous and prefer the
traditional position of passive, dependent recipient of a mark.
But by and large students appreciate the purpose and the value
of self-evaluation, despite its initial strangeness. A typical
student comment on the process was: 'Difficult to begin,
but once I got started I enjoyed it – it helped to clarify and
elaborate on my goals – which helped me to realize what I had
accomplished.' Another echoed: 'Rather difficult to do. One is
tempted to give what appears to be expected. To do it honestly
(which is really what is expected) is truly a reflective process.'
A third spoke for many as she reflected on the value of the
exercise: 'This is an essential skill for life. We are so often
assessed by our superiors and we assess the ones below us. This
self-assessment procedure is practical, revealing and makes us
conscious of our direction in study and work . . . the most
valuable thing I've learned in the course.'

Problem-based learning

To be a successful professional requires more than mastery of
specific skill and subject-matter; it demands the ability to apply
one's knowledge and know-how creatively and appropriately
in the face of a succession of unprecedented predicaments. The
way to encourage students to develop the requisite flexibility is
to build into their studies tolerable degrees of uncertainty
almost from the start. Information and instruction get converted into fluid expertise through their application to pro-

blems that are not well-defined and which allow some room to exercise responsibility. In many areas of professional training, such problem-based learning is becoming well-known.

Changes in medical education are now widespread. Pioneered at McMaster University in Hamilton, Ontario, in the 1960s, problem-based learning confronts groups of students with clinical predicaments which they tackle with the help of a mentor. Admissions to the McMaster programme are based on academic performance, but also on a simulated tutorial in which the applicant's ability to solve problems and work in a group are assessed. Starting from local experiments such as these, many problem-based professional degrees, in a wide variety of subjects, are now to be found around the world. They make a stark contrast to the modularized sausage-factories that many other courses have become.

Since 1986 Jan Lovie-Kitchin at Queensland University of Technology has been developing a very successful problem-based course in which final-year optometry students form 'communities of inquiry' not unlike those discussed in Chapter 17. To tackle the difficult issue of how to manage patients with very poor vision, she divides the students into teams of six or seven and gives them a series of cases to consider. Eileen, for example, is an elderly patient who suddenly became totally blind in her right eye three years ago, and has gradually been losing central vision in her left eye for the last two years. The team's first job is to identify all Eileen's potential problems and their implications: difficulties reading mail and recognizing friends in the street, for example. After a class discussion, each team assigns research jobs to pairs of students. This may involve library work, contacting clinical experts and discovering what social supports and rehabilitation services there are in the area. Summaries of their findings are collated by the tutor and distributed to the rest of the team before their next weekly meeting. Over several weeks this cycle of research and review results in a detailed assessment, treatment and rehabilitation plan for the patient, which is presented to the group as a whole by the team's spokesperson. Cases are chosen which afford a variety of different approaches and some delicate decisions and judgements, which are exposed and debated in the class discussion.[11]

Lovie-Kitchin collected students' reactions to the course through a questionnaire, and it is interesting to see how responses to this method of learning changed between 1986 and 1990. Perceptions of professional relevance and quality of learning increased from around 80 per cent to 100 per cent, and enjoyment from 65 per cent to 80 per cent. Overwhelmingly the students liked and appreciated the value of the experience. The rapid change in the culture of learning, however, is dramatically signalled by the proportion of students who balanced this appreciation with a feeling that problem-based learning was too demanding or too time-consuming. In 1986, when the method was radically at odds with normal practice, nearly 60 per cent of the students complained that it was too hard. By 1990, when the method had become a more familiar part of university teaching and learning culture, only 4 per cent found it too demanding and too costly in time.

William Macauley and Gian Pagnucci teach a first-year class in English composition at Indiana University of Pennsylvania, a large public college with an enrolment of predominantly working-class white and African-American students. Students start by reviewing a variety of professional publications including magazines, newsletters and web pages, picking out ones they like, and trying to identify what it is about the language and the presentation which made it appealing. They then write proposals for publications they would like to create which are circulated by e-mail, and the class forms teams to bring these visions into being. The finished publications are evaluated by the production team and presented to the class as a whole.[12]

In 1996 the products included a fashion guidebook, a children's geography book and a student cookbook. The quality of work was significantly higher than the tutors had come to expect from similar students taught more conventionally. Ninety per cent of the students said that the course was 'more' or 'much more' work than other courses of equal credit value; 85 per cent said that what they had learnt in the course was valuable – dealing with deadlines, frustrations and interpersonal conflicts, as well as writing, researching and designing; 85 per cent said they would recommend the course to a friend, though several students said that they were disconcerted, to begin with, by the amount of responsibility they were given. The title of Macauley and Pagnucci's report echoes the reaction of one such student: 'But this isn't how an English class is supposed to be'.

Perhaps the biggest change is reflected in the tutors' impression of the classroom climate.

> In the past, our classes were full of students who slouched in the back of the room, looked bored, and waited for us to perform our teaching. Sometimes they listened, sometimes they slept. We ran the class, and they did what we told them to do. We moved through classes like wading through mud, and the measure of success was usually endurance.
>
> After their redesign, our courses were full of students who raced around the room collecting printouts, checking information on the web, and seeking advice. They would not wait for us. They depended on each other, ran their teams, and told us what they needed. The class became a swirl of movement, sound and energy. . . . The students worked harder than we ever expected.

In some ways, new approaches to higher education are bringing back into adult learning methods and attitudes that are more familiar in a primary or even a playschool. Having become infatuated with disembedded, solitary, intellectual ways of learning, university lecturers are now rediscovering the value of direct immersion in experience, of the use of imagination and intuition, of collaboration, of engaging with problems that mimic the complexity and uncertainty of real life, and of building up students' ability and willingness to take back responsibility for their own learning.

Students, it would appear, are still alive to learning. The lethargy and recalcitrance of which Mark Edmundson complained so eloquently reflect not so much a lack of curiosity or initiative, but more, perhaps, an intuitive realization that traditional teaching methods, regardless of the explicit content, are not building the learning muscles that they know the real world requires. With a bit of imagination their latent learning enthusiasm can be rekindled, and universities can, perhaps, become places where people of all ages develop learning tools and attitudes that are of real value in the outside world.

NINETEEN

Learning Goes to Work: The Business World

Throughout life, in every aspect of it, people are learners. Lifelong learning embraces parenthood, separation and bereavement; coping with illness and misfortune, both one's own and others'; living in new cultures; learning new skills; practising hobbies and leisure activities; mastering new technology; developing a position with respect to current affairs. But the area of adult life which learning permeates more persistently than perhaps any other is work.

Uncertainty in the workplace

As we saw in Chapter 15, working life for the vast majority of people in the developed world is changing rapidly. Even for those still employed by conventional companies, uncertainty and insecurity are daily realities. It is not just that complex problems appear more frequently than in the past; the whole basis of workplace cultures is now more fluid, needing to be continually responsive to a global swirl of uncontrollable changes, threats and opportunities. It is only the very rare organization that can hope to prosper by hunkering down and continuing to do what it has always done in the way it has always done it. And, as we saw, an increasing proportion of the adult workforce no longer owes continuing allegiance to a single firm, while a declining proportion turns up, nine to five, day after day, at the same place to do the same job.

In the UK, a recent report by the Royal Society of Arts (RSA),

Redefining Work, says confidently that 'The world of work in twenty years' time . . . will be an uncertain world, and for many a very uncomfortable one. Managing uncertainty will be the name of the game.' The new competencies that will be required include 'how to learn new skills and knowledge' – *not* the 'new skills and knowledge' themselves, but the abilities to master what we cannot yet envisage – as well as 'how to take charge of your own learning', 'how to cope with change coming at you', 'how to manage risk and uncertainty', 'how to manage your own time' and 'how to make the best of your creative talents'. The report rightly notes that it will take some time – it estimates, optimistically, ten years – to get geared up to help equip young people with these abilities 'because we do not yet have some of the major tools, like the new pedagogy that will be necessary'. Refreshingly, the RSA admits that we do not yet know how to help people become better learners – an admission of ignorance, which is the sine qua non of learning.[1]

As we saw in Chapters 17 and 18, schools and universities do not reliably deliver these vital resources. The RSA report bluntly says:

> The incessant [world-wide] educational reforms of the 1980s and 1990s have simply bolted change on to a system which is essentially a nineteenth-century one, serving the social and cultural norms of that period. That will not do for the knowledge society. . . . The education system must develop in students . . . the personal skills that will be needed, at much higher levels, to cope successfully with a more complex world characterised by uncertainty. . . . There can be no question about the importance of literacy and numeracy [for example] . . . but they are only a start.

In the age of uncertainty, the development of individual learning power is clearly a top priority. But, additionally, corporate cultures have to change to permit the expression and development of learning power at both individual and organizational levels.

Organizational cultures and beliefs

Organizations are cultures, in the sense in which the term was used in Chapter 14. Through its structures, goals, management styles, lines of communication, jargon, shared histories, sub-cultures and responses to difficulty and uncertainty, each organization embodies and enacts a set of (largely unarticulated and unacknowledged) beliefs about the nature of knowing and learning. These beliefs reside in the minds of the members of the organization, and also in the practical details of 'the way we do things here'. The senior members of the organization may be so steeped in a traditional culture that their every comment, reaction and judgement serve both to embody that culture and to reinforce it. What they notice and reward, the personal traits that they value through the distribution of incentives and promotions, all perpetuate a general modus operandi, and especially the habits and attitudes that are to do with learning.

Newcomers absorb this culture partly through formal and informal tuition, but mainly through direct observation. Are people offered the opportunity to take manageable amounts of responsibility? And when people do show initiative, how is it received? Who talks to whom, formally and informally, and about what? What encouragement is there for people to bring their out-of-work lives and interests into the workplace? Do senior managers find ways to model and practise what they preach in the way of learning? Do they dare display uncertainty, and how is it perceived if they do? What kinds of pressure are there to display only certain kinds of emotion – frustration with newcomers, cynicism towards managers, an insincere charm towards customers? These tangible manifestations of the workplace culture generally have a much greater impact on people's presence than any amount of rhetoric and exhortation.

In a traditional workplace culture, for example, confusion and indecision, in the face of a complex predicament, may be interpreted as weakness. Above all the culture, through its senior members, approves the appearance of certainty and control. The manager who asks for more time to ponder a problem may get about as much sympathy as Oliver Twist when he asked for more food. Decisiveness, in the sense of being able to come up fast with superficially plausible analyses and solutions, becomes valued in its own right, regardless of the quality of the proposal. Mistakes may be harshly dealt with, however ingenious the thinking behind them or potentially interesting the results. If you didn't meet your target, you can wave that promotion goodbye. Performance-related pay keeps your eyes firmly fixed on a set of narrowly defined 'performance indicators', and closes down any deviant tendencies to think about what you are doing and question procedures (even if the company rhetoric is preaching openness, creativity and camaraderie). Such a culture, whatever its rhetoric, suppresses learning and genuine creativity.

In a learning culture, on the other hand, the different manifestations of learning are more welcome. As Peter Senge says in *The Fifth Discipline Fieldbook*: 'In a learning organization . . . we surrender the belief that a person must be 'in control' to be effective. We become willing to reveal our uncertainties, to be ignorant, to show incompetence – knowing that these are essential preconditions for learning because they set free our innate capacity for curiosity, wonder and experimentalism.' While another business guru, Tom Peters, says succinctly: 'If you're not confused, you're not thinking clearly.' To attempt to maintain the illusion of comprehension and control in the face of unprecedented complexity is self-defeating. Hard thinking becomes bad thinking when it has to be maintained, to the detriment of learning, as part of a rigid, macho business posture. Managers who think they are being strong in this sense are just being stupid.[2]

Of course mistakes can be costly, but some are more costly than others, and not allowing people to try things out, and sometimes get it wrong, can also be expensive. Of course there are deadlines that have to be met; but that does not mean that all decisions have to be taken at a gallop. Of course you need good information and hard, analytical thinking; but so too does the innovative, responsive company need to foster imagination and intuition. Finding time to entertain possibilities and play with ideas without immediately having to justify and explain: that too is cost-effective. Of course managers and leaders need to project an air of confidence and competence. The workforce needs to feel that there are people with vision and assurance at the corporate tiller. But the leaders of learning organizations need also to model the ability to be uncertain without being insecure; to respect and embrace what other people have to say without seeming to lack a mind of their own.

Resilience and the psychological contract

One key area in which traditional company beliefs and practices may need to be reviewed is that of the psychological contract between employer and employee: the tacit understanding about what each can fairly expect from the other that underpins any more explicit contractual agreement. A core element of the psychological contract has traditionally traded security for competence and loyalty: if employees do their jobs well and are loyal, the organization will offer in return some measure of job security. But this mutual expectation is, in many companies, an anachronism. Competent, dependable employees now get made redundant all the time, and competent, dependable employees leave to take new jobs or to downshift their lifestyles, choosing to move out of paid employment for a while.

Unless this tacit compact is explicitly rewritten, either employer or, more usually, employee feels aggrieved when the other side does not keep their side of the bargain. The result is recrimination and a damaging of trust, which may well weaken the morale not only of those directly affected but of the company as a whole. Other employees may, for example, feel the need to defend themselves against the resultant insecurity by withdrawing their goodwill in some way to protect themselves from being exploited, and/or by focusing more single-mindedly on their financial rewards. Thus an unrecognized ambivalence about what constitutes fair treatment – a 'gentleman's agreement' which each side expects the other to abide by, but feels free to violate when it suits *them* – can lead to a lowering of the corporate resilience of the company. As people become entrenched, or psychologically distance themselves, so they bring less of their flexibility, creativity and commitment to work with them. Just when change occurs and learning is needed most, the organization becomes brittle and recalcitrant.

The solution, according to organizational consultants Frost Rowley, is to renegotiate the psychological contract. Instead of offering security, the company offers employability: in return for employees' productivity and commitment to corporate goals and practices for as long as they are there, the company supports them in developing transferable skills that enhance their cognitive capital, making them more attractive to other employers. Frost Rowley suggests that companies 'offer individuals the tools, the open environment and the opportunities for assessing and developing their skills. In return, employees accept responsibility for and have loyalty to their own careers, and offer the organization an adaptable and responsive skill base, and commitment to the company's success.'[3] While employer and employee are both winning, in these terms, their association continues. When either ceases to do so, partings of the ways can in theory occur without recrimination. Provided the provisional basis of their association is clearly understood from the beginning, there should be no grounds in principle for feeling let down when separation occurs.

In 1991 Sun Microsystems employees were angry when they felt that the old psychological contract had been breached as a result of the notorious volatility of employment in the microelectronics industry. As business fell, those at risk of redundancy felt very ill-equipped to compete in the job market, and their insecurity was weakening the company. Sun decided to try to renegotiate the psychological contract, and to offer all employees a learning package that was designed to put them back in control of their working lives. Now individuals are regularly helped to assess their skills, interests and values, so that, with company support, they can continually invest in their own career development. The security of having a long-term job is replaced by the (relative) security of knowing that your growing portfolio of skills and attitudes makes you attractive to other employers in the same sector.

Helping people feel they can cope with uncertainty is vital

to business success in changing times. Attending to the emotional well-being of the workforce is no bleeding heart option; it is an essential facet of smart management. It is estimated that 90 per cent of failed attempts to bring about change in a company are due to an inadequate appreciation of people's insecurities, and of the real cost of their defensive reactions when those insecurities are not addressed. People's resilience, as we have seen, is a function of both the beliefs and habits that are the residues of their histories, and the current conditions in which they find themselves. In the long term, young people can be helped to develop greater resilience: that is, to stay open and engaged even in adverse conditions. But the nature of the organization in which people find themselves also affects how much uncertainty they can tolerate before closing up and becoming self-protective. Frost Rowley have identified six characteristics of the resilient organization.

First and foremost is the corporate *attitude towards change*. Resilient organizations recognize the need to change sooner than do more rigid ones. Change is more likely to be perceived as a challenge than as a threat, and the accompanying anxiety is consequently lower. The company also supports change and development in employees and has a more positive attitude towards lifelong learning.

Second is the quality of *communication*. In a resilient organization people know what is going on, at all levels of the company, whether they like it or not. Communication is direct and frank, and there are low levels of subversive rumour and gossip. Where there is a continuing attempt to make the implicit explicit, there is less chance of the psychological contract being misunderstood. Employees' comments on vision and strategy are welcome, and appraisal interviews are supportive and learning-orientated, rather than punitive.

Third, employees see themselves as being part of the organization – they feel they belong, and have some ownership of corporate goals – whilst retaining having their own unique contribution and identity. They are noticed and respected as *individuals* – very different from the traditional industrial model of the worker as a small replaceable cog in the corporate machine.

Fourth, the resilient organization has a clear but flexible *power structure*. As the organization responds to changing conditions, members remain clear about their changing roles and responsibilities, and the company is willing to provide the resources that such changing conditions demand.

Fifth, there is a strong *reality sense*: the company has an accurate image of itself, and of the pressures and possibilities in the world that surrounds it. Everyone knows what is going on in the market, and what the implications are both for the company as a whole and for the learning and development of its employees.

Sixth and finally, there is the quality of *relationships*, especially of trust. When hidden agendas and covert expectations are minimized, there is less opportunity for unacknowledged resentments to undermine the corporate spirit. When people do leave, whether voluntarily or not, there is a greater chance that their exits can be managed with dignity and without rancour. Frost Rowley suggest that attention to these factors, in a business world that is endemically uncertain, 'is not only desirable but is essential for organizational survival. The development of a resilient workforce may be the ultimate source of an organization's power in the market place.'

One current example of corporate double-speak, which purports to support learning whilst actually undermining it, concerns the over-used notion of 'empowerment'. There is much rhetoric about the value of 'empowering' employees, yet all the evidence is that it has little positive effect on company performance, and sometimes a negative one. 'Managers love empowerment in theory, but the command-and-control model is what they trust and know best,' says organizational development guru Chris Argyris. The truth is that they want employees who use their initiative and take responsibility, but within lower limits than those employees would like. Profit remains the bottom line, not personal development, and managers who do not make it clear what exactly they are offering and in return expecting, and who espouse empowerment too glibly, risk losing their credibility and creating a climate of cynicism.

On the other hand, employees may say that they want more responsibility and self-determination, yet shy away from the reality of being responsible – and therefore accountable. The passive position (as we saw with some school students) requires less effort and is less risky. When change programmes are implemented without taking into account these intricate dynamics, the organization can end up worse off than it was to begin with. Like Peter Senge, Argyris advocates starting from the ignorance position. We know many of the ways in which change programmes foul up and run aground, but 'change programs that could create high levels of internal commitment and empowerment in corporations do not yet exist . . . it is time to begin the research and experimentation that is required to find some viable answers'.[4]

Using multiple learning tools: imagination and stories

So the successful company pays attention to its own assumptions about learning; to the emotional well-being of its members; and to the development of individual and corporate resilience. It also encourages the use of all the different compartments of the learning toolkit. On its own, clear-cut analytical reasoning does not cut the mustard: you need the other learning modes as well.

At 3M, new ways of thinking have been introduced as a result of a blinding realization: the ineffectiveness of the bite-sized logic of the ubiquitous list of bullet points to create learning and change. Everywhere you go, visions, missions, aims and objectives are boiled down to a short list of key points. Under pressure, the complex and confusing must be reduced, it appears, to the short and clear, if it is to be got across. Unfortunately, this method of communication is driven more by the constraints of PowerPoint and the attention span of a busy executive than it is by the intention to make a genuine difference. Bullet points are frequently too generic: they offer snippets of good-sounding practice that could apply to virtually any enterprise, and are therefore too abstract to offer a practical handle on a specific, real-life messy situation. They are so cut and dried that they seem to offer little room for argument and interpretation. And they lose the all-important wholeness, the inter-relatedness, of the situation. Complex predicaments require forms of representation and ways of thinking that retain a necessary degree of complexity and specificity. In the real world, the relationships between things matter just as much as the things themselves. 'Daughter of' or 'part of' are sometimes more important than 'Jill Brown" or 'gasket'. What relationships can a list of bullet points naturally capture? Sequence in time: top is first and bottom is last. Priority: top is most important and bottom least so. And assembly: all these things go together somehow, unspecified. With so much information removed, it is little surprise that an elegant-looking list of bullet points offers all the long-term satisfaction of a nouvelle cuisine platter of four artfully arranged snow peas and a ribbon of undercooked tuna.

So bullets offer the illusion of comprehension and control but often without the reality. They invite the possibility of 'genially tricking ourselves into supposing we have planned when, in fact, we've only listed some good things to do'.[5] How to improve the bottom line? Easy!

- reduce production costs
- accelerate new product development
- increase market responsiveness

Yes . . . but *how*, exactly?

So it is no surprise, either, that companies are exploring different ways of representing their plans and predicaments using different learning media. One way is to use visualization to come up with a graphic image that encapsulates some of a company's complex reality, and also suggests possible avenues for change. This strategy has boosted the performance and shifted the culture at the biggest aluminium manufacturer in Europe: Karmoy in Norway. At a business seminar the general manager, Tormod Bjork, had been forcibly struck by the value of visualization. A powerful image of his company as a changing garden had prompted renewed energy and a clearer vision of where he wanted things to go.

But instead of keeping the process to himself, he decided that he would invite all 1700 employees to attend a similar

seminar, and use imagery to clarify their own aspirations for
the company. What kinds of garden did they envisage? Instead of starting, as normally happens, from a focus on
problems and problem-solving, first individuals and then
teams constructed their images of the future, and worked
backwards from that to create practical proposals. Using
poems, models, drawing and collages, the company as a whole
gradually clarified a number of key across-the-board priorities.
One of these, totally unanticipated, turned out to be health –
of individuals, the workplace, families and the local environment. Now, several years on, there are far fewer accidents and
illnesses, much less absenteeism, thriving sports and fitness
clubs for employees, healthier food in the canteens, and the
factory generates much less pollution.[6]

At 3M they are using stories to achieve the same end. As we
saw in Chapter 8, a story makes a complex, yet memorable,
whole – very different from the list of abstract bullets. It is
made up of tangible interactions, events, processes and relationships. So stories dramatize issues, making them concrete
and personal in a way that logical explanations don't. Like
sensory imagery, a good story engages emotions, and through
its characters and its plot it can depict different kinds of
predicament, and different ways in which they can be met
and resolved. Stories enable us to create hypothetical courses
of action, envisage their effects – on people as well as on more
hard-nosed performance indicators – and thus base decisions
on a more rounded feel for their likely consequences. One of
the functions of children's stories, it has been suggested, is to
stimulate this imaginative 'planning' process; and there is
every reason to suppose that it works for adults too.[7]

The most famous 3M story concerns one of their scientists
who, while singing in a choir, got irritated that his bookmarks
kept falling out of the hymn book and went on to create 'the
glue that doesn't stick': the magical basis for Post-it notes.
More recently, 3M created a story for their Global Fleet
Graphics Division (GFG), which makes the kinds of signs
and logos that adorn fleets of company vans and trucks.
Things were getting tougher for GFG: customers wanted
new products – graphics for bus windows which you can
see through; logos that are easy to replace or modify – and

hungry new rivals such as AmeriGraphics and GraphDesign were eating away at their market share. A technological leap was required: digital technology to create images electronically, refine them on screen and store them in a central repository, from where they could be transmitted instantaneously to production facilities located world-wide.

When GFG's employees were introduced to a story about how they could resolve the problem, they found it much easier to become convinced and enthused by the tale than they had by previous lists of good intentions, and were able to bring their own flair and commitment to bear to make sure that fantasy became reality. As 3M's Director of Planning, Gordon Shaw, sums it up: 'When people can locate themselves in the story, their sense of commitment and involvement is enhanced. By conveying a powerful impression of the *process* of winning, narrative plans can motivate and mobilize an entire organization.'

In the UK, Charlene Collison and Alexander Mackenzie of Oracy have been developing a variety of ways in which employees can create effective stories for themselves. At ICI, delegates from around the world convened to address the fact that the company's vision for information technology was floundering. There was a feeling of 'stuckness' and a lack of creativity about how IT could lead to new ways of working. Working with the delegates over several days, Oracy interwove more focused, technical discussions with sessions in which they learned to turn flights of fancy into mythical tales, which they then examined for metaphorical leads and pointers that could apply to the practical predicament. 'Imagine a character, human, animal or mythical,' they might suggest. 'Now imagine a challenge or an obstacle which this character meets. What is it? What sources of help can your character draw upon? How is it overcome? . . . Now develop these fantasies into a story, and tell it to a partner. . . . Now imagine that your character is ICI. If this were a metaphor for the present predicament, how would it work? What would you have to change?' And so on. At the end of the programme, the group had developed a much clearer and more dynamic vision of the potential of IT for the company and a set of strategies for pursuing its implementation.[8]

Stillness in busy-ness

Companies are coming to realize the value of softer, slower kinds of thinking and problem-solving. If learning to intersperse periods of intent, focused work with phases of more relaxed, playful thinking, and learning to follow your nose and trust your hunches, is of recognized value to Nobel Prize-winning scientists, then it ought to be of value to managers when they are faced with seemingly intractable problems. Certainly some seem to think so. Sir David Simon, Chairman of British Petroleum, has commented: 'You don't have to discuss things. You can sense it. The tingle is as important as the intellect.' The 'tingle'? Where does that come on the MBA syllabus?

Research shows that senior managers especially do make most of their decisions intuitively. John Hunt, Professor of Organizational Behaviour at the London Business School, explains that 'Identifying solutions to business problems rarely follows the rational processes so admired by planners and researchers. Often these solutions appear as bolts from the blue or at the end of a hazy and meandering cognitive process.'[9] However, when challenged, managers tend to concoct a veneer of logical justification to cover up what they have been taught to see as second-class thinking. And they may well be right to do so. 'Shareholders and institutional investors are particularly unimpressed by intuitive decisions and judgements,' say Randall White and his colleagues in their book *The Future of Leadership*. 'As a result, annual reports and the like have become works of incredible fiction. If a Chief Executive hits on a brilliant idea while in the bath, it is not something he will proclaim at the AGM.'[10] So the real task is not how to get people at work to use intuition, but how to develop it, value it, and learn to use it when the time is right: how are we going to create cultures that recognize and reward the other ways of learning?

Weston Agor is Director of the Global Intuition Network based at the University of Texas at El Paso. In the age of uncertainty, he argues, situations are often too complex, confusing and fast-changing for traditional management techniques to work as well as they used to. Faced with these circumstances, says Agor,

> you as a leader and manager will need to develop and use skills that may have been ignored or not fully developed in the past. Intuition is one of these skills. Intuition may be defined as the phenomenon of knowing something directly without the use of rational processes. It includes hunches, vague feelings, revelations, insights, sudden inspirations, flashes of awareness and dozens of other ways of expressing the mind's capacity to accomplish many things simultaneously without our being fully aware of the steps involved.
>
> Research shows that managers who use and develop their intuitive ability are better able to sense what is coming in the future and know how to position their organization to respond to these emerging trends. They become particularly adept at generating new ideas and at providing ingenious solutions to old problems. They learn to function more productively in rapid change and crisis settings.[11]

Agor has devised a questionnaire known as the AIM (the Agor Intuitive Management survey) that reveals a person's propensity to use intuition. It contains questions that ask about your attitude to daydreaming, to the need to be carefully organized, the kind of thinkers you admire, and whether you get upset if someone questions the premises or assumptions you have been making. He suggests there are a number of ways in which the AIM can improve business performance.

First, you could use it as one of the instruments used to select applicants for jobs. Typical psychometric tests measure how adept people are at hard thinking, and soft thinking only shows up as a negative. If you think slowly, and don't finish the test, that counts against you. The GMAT, the standard instrument for selecting people for graduate business schools in the United States, weeds out all those whose mental preference is not for solving abstract logical puzzles fast under pressure. The AIM can act as a counterweight to that tendency.

Second, AIM scores can be used to help assign people to appropriate jobs, and to make sure that teams have a good balance of different types of minds. Third, AIM scores can contribute usefully to vocational and professional development, directed towards creating an optimal match between the needs of the organization and the learning power of employees. As we have seen, people *can* learn to use their intuition more appropriately and effectively, and to become more sensitive to its subtle promptings. Just as someone who loses their sight in adulthood develops an increased responsiveness in their other senses, so can people – if they take the risk of toning down the incessant, noisy activity of hard thinking – become more attuned to fainter sources of valuable understanding.

There are many exercises which investigate and strengthen one's powers of intuition. One of the simplest is to sit quietly with a partner who is not well known to you, and take turns at intuitively 'reading' what the other person is like – their lifestyle, preferences, history, strengths and weaknesses and so on. Fortune-tellers and psychics have developed this ability to a fine art, drawing on small, almost subliminal clues from the other person that signal aspects of their character. In another exercise, you can share with a partner your experiences of using or ignoring intuition in your life, or especially at work. When did you heed it and go wrong? When did you ignore it and miss an opportunity? What was the difference between times when you heeded and those when you ignored? Between times when intuition 'worked' and those when it didn't? Subsequently, you might decide to keep an 'intuition journal', recording for yourself the different kinds of intuition you experience, when, and what the result of your reaction was.

Mindfulness

So far in this chapter I have illustrated the way in which the first two Rs, resilience and resourcefulness, affect how people learn at work. To conclude I want to say a few words about the third R, reflection, one form of which is mindfulness. Mindfulness, you recall, is the opposite of mindlessness – the state of mind in which you assume that things are running along familiar lines, whether they are or not, and will respond with the usual habits and routines, whether they work or not. When perceiving and behaving mindlessly, you simply don't notice very much. When being mindful, on the other hand, your awareness is bright, sharp and wide, so that departures from the routine are registered and stereotyped responses abandoned in favour of an inquiry into what will meet *this case, right now*.

William Kahn of the Management School at Boston University has identified several dimensions of mindfulness at work: what he calls 'presence'. Being fully present, says Kahn, means being 'all there', with all your resources of knowledge and know-how, your values and feelings, and your powers of reflection, engaged with the job at hand and available as ingredients of intelligent action. You are vigilant towards the task, sensitive to the other people around you, and in touch with your own values and feelings. When you are present, you are maximally intelligent and your learning power is at its greatest. When you drift off or withdraw, parts of your intelligence close down and you are more likely to be running on automatic pilot.[12]

To illustrate how presence affects learning, Kahn uses the example of a project manager with a firm of architects dealing mindfully with a small incident in her office. With a deadline fast approaching, one of Chryssoula's team seems to be struggling with what ought to be a fairly routine piece of drafting. As she walks over to talk to him, she notices that her hands are clenched and her face stern, and registers the build-up of frustration, both with the draughtsman and with the unreasonable deadline and the vice-president who set it up. She takes a couple of deep breaths and asks the man what the problem is. She listens carefully as he relates his struggles and frustration with what he considers to be an under-specified brief: he hasn't got all the information he needs. She asks further questions to clarify his perception of the situation, and cracks a joke that shows she acknowledges the apparent unreasonableness of the task he has been set (making him feel that his perspective has been understood, and enabling

him to relax). She then points out that while he is correct up
to a point, he does have relevant information which he has
overlooked, and offers a couple of suggestions about how he
might move forward. Throughout the conversation she is
herself relaxed, direct and concerned.

The first dimension of presence is *attentiveness*: Chryssoula
is aware of the deadline and sees that her draughtsman is
having problems. She notices her own frustration and anxiety, but does not react by shutting down her awareness. Notes
Kahn: 'Defences against anxiety absent people psychologically by closing them off from potentially threatening information and experiences; they reduce the extent to which
parts of their selves are fully there in the immediate situation.'
By noticing her physical tension, and correctly diagnosing her
own feelings, she is able to deal with them without projecting
and dumping them on the draughtsman. When judgements
are delivered as irritable criticism, the usual effect (as we all
know) is to make matters worse.

Self-awareness leads to a non-defensive and non-judgemen-
tal attitude, which makes available the second feature of
presence: *connection*. Not having to deal with any distress of
her own, Chryssoula can turn the bulk of her attention out-
wards, towards the draughtsman and the work that needs to
be done. She experiences some empathy with him, and is able
to be absorbed in the problem, bringing her full intelligence to
bear. The draughtsman, the deadline and the problem are all
experienced as 'my business', and she is engaged not in
control-and-command mode, but as a leader in a joint enterprise. The two of them are collaborators, co-learners, on a
shared task; when the blockage is resolved and the task
completed, they both win, so she automatically looks for a
win-win solution.

Thus her connection helps her maintain the third facet of
presence: *focus*. She is pleasantly, not aggressively, on task.
Within her role as manager, her job is to get the job done, and
this is her primary concern. She does not inadvertently lapse
into other roles such as that of counsellor or co-critic of the
organization, but draws as appropriate on different sides of
herself – her humour, her empathy, her technical knowledge,
her self-awareness, her ability to offer a balanced, rational

appraisal of the situation – to move the work forward. In other words, she shows *integration* of her different values, perspectives and resources: the fourth facet of presence. Though she is firmly in her role, she can draw on all her resources to support that role. She comes across as a real person. People say: 'You know where you stand with Chryssoula.'

Ellen Langer at Harvard has identified one particular quality of a manager like Chryssoula that encourages their staff to adopt a learning rather than a defensive or absent attitude. She calls it 'confident uncertainty': the ability to convey simultaneously a positive assurance that the job will get done – things will turn out fine – and a lack of clarity about what the best way will be to do it. The certainty of a group of managers was assessed by asking them questions like: 'How many of the decisions you make each day have absolute, correct answers?' Their general level of confidence in their ability to bring jobs to successful completion was also evaluated. The questionnaires were given to these managers' employees to discover the quality of their working relationships and the degree of presence which they encouraged. Those managers who were confident but relatively uncertain were evaluated by their workforces as more likely to allow independent judgement and a general freedom of action, and this in turn encouraged greater participation and connectedness. Says Langer: 'If managers make clear that they see certainty as foolhardy, it is easier to ask questions based on one's own uncertainty. . . . We are likely to think, "If he's not sure, I guess I don't have to be right 100 per cent of the time", and risk-taking becomes less risky.'[13]

The world of work exemplifies the central theme of this book: the urgent need to recognize and develop learning power in everyday life; and the confused and sometimes subversive attitudes that may get in the way of this happening. Individuals carry forward from their childhoods and schooldays outmoded assumptions that breed narrow approaches to learning, and beliefs about themselves which can turn practical uncertainty into personal insecurity and thus encourage a defensive rather than an inquiring mind-set. When these assumptions are echoed in the structures and habits of a workplace culture, and modelled and purveyed by senior managers, then individuals withdraw from learning and companies become rigid and myopic. When leaders develop the insight to inspect these belief systems, and the courage to share that reflective journey of corporate self-discovery with the workforce, remarkable shifts can take place and true 'learning organizations' become a real possibility.

TWENTY

The Future of Learning

As the world moves into the age of uncertainty, nations, communities and individuals need all the learning power they can get. Our institutions of business and education, even our styles of parenting, have to change so that the development and the expression of learning power become real possibilities. But this will not happen if they remain founded on a narrow conceptualization of learning: one which focuses on content over process, comprehension over competence, 'ability' over engagement, teaching over self-discovery. Many of the current attempts to create a learning society are hamstrung by a tacit acceptance of this outmoded viewpoint, however watered down or jazzed up it may be. The new science of learning tells us that everyone has the capacity to become a better learner, and that there are conditions under which learning power develops. It is offering us a richer way of thinking about learning, one which includes feeling and imagination, intuition and experience, external tools and the cultural milieu, as well as the effort to understand. If this picture can supplant the deeply entrenched habits of mind that underpin our conventional approaches to learning, the development of learning power, and the creation of a true learning society, might become realities. In this final chapter, let me summarize the lessons that the new science of the learning mind has taught us.

Learning is impossible without resilience: the ability to tolerate a degree of strangeness. Without the willingness to stay engaged with things that are not currently within our

sphere of confident comprehension and control, we tend to
revert prematurely into a defensive mode: a way of operating
that maintains our security but does not increase our mastery.
We have seen that the decision whether, when and how to
engage depends on a largely tacit cost-benefit analysis of the
situation that is influenced strongly by our subjective evaluations of the risks, rewards and available resources. These
evaluations derive from our beliefs and values, our personal
theories, which may be accurate or inaccurate. Inaccurate
beliefs can lead us to over- or underestimate apparent threats
and to misrepresent to ourselves what learning involves.

So when you find people declining an invitation to learn, it
is not because they are, in some crude sense, lazy or unmotivated: it is because, for them, at that moment, the odds stack
up differently from the way in which their parents or tutors or
managers would prefer. Defensiveness, seen from the inside, is
always rational. If the stick and the carrot don't do the trick, it
may be wiser to try to get a clearer sense of what the learner's
interior world looks like. Often you will find that somewhere,
somehow, the brakes have got jammed. Sensitivity to the
learners' own dynamics is always smart.

Some of these beliefs refer to the nature of knowledge and of
learning itself. For example, if we have picked up the ideas
that knowledge is (or ought to be) clear and unequivocal, or
that learning is (or ought to be) quick and smooth, we withdraw from learning when it gets hard and confusing, or when
we meet essential ambiguity. Some beliefs refer to hypothetical psychological qualities such as 'ability'. The idea that
achievement reflects a fixed personal reservoir of general-
purpose 'intelligence' is pernicious, leading people to interpret difficulty as a sign of stupidity, to feel ashamed, and
therefore to switch into self-protection by hiding, creating
diversions or not trying. Some beliefs determine how much
we generally see the world as potentially comprehensible and
controllable ('self-efficacy', we called it). High self-efficacy
creates persistence and resilience; low breeds a brittle and
impatient attitude. Some beliefs forge a connection between
self-worth on the one hand and success, clarity and emotional
control on the other, making failure, confusion and anxiety or
frustration induce a feeling of shame. All these beliefs can

affect anyone, but there are a host of others that specifically undermine or disable the learning of certain groups of people, or which apply particularly to certain types of material. For example, girls and boys have been revealed as developing different views of themselves as learners of mathematics.

We saw that these beliefs are rarely spelt out, but are transmitted implicitly and insidiously through the kinds of culture that are embodied in the settings that learners inhabit, such as family, school or workplace. Learning messages are carried by a variety of media. The habits and rituals of the culture enable certain kinds of learning and disable others. The apprentice Liberian tailors were being inducted into a very different learning culture from that of an American undergraduate. How the 'elders' comment on and evaluate learners' efforts teaches the learners how to think about themselves. For instance, the groups of parents and teachers in Brazil gave children very different messages about the relative value of self-discovery and 'correctness'. American parents passed on different beliefs about the causes of success in mathematics to their sons from those they passed on to their daughters. Business leaders' critical responses to workers' initiative will create a play-it-safe atmosphere. Elders may also model attitudes and values at variance with their rhetoric, for example by their reluctance to exhibit confident uncertainty in the face of their own learning challenges.

The implications of these conclusions for the kinds of learning cultures we create are self-evident. Parents, teachers and managers have to be vigilant, reflective and honest about the values and beliefs which inform the ways they speak, model and organize the settings over which they have control. Inadvertently create the wrong climate and the development and expression of learning power are blocked. Experience in childhood, at home and at school, is particularly important because these early belief systems, whether functional or dysfunctional, can be carried through into people's learning lives as adults. Though these attitudes are not set in stone, and though adult cultures can considerably influence people's willingness to learn, nevertheless their adult dispositions often contain strong though unconscious echoes of their earlier experience. For people to prosper in the age of uncertainty, setting them off on the right trajectory is crucial.

We have seen that cultures influence the development of resourcefulness – the range of learning tools and strategies that people develop and employ – as well as of resilience. The tendency to overemphasize conscious, deliberate ways of learning and knowing, for example, can lead to the other compartments of the learning toolkit being neglected, and failing to grow and develop. Especially dangerous here is the belief that these other learning tools are somehow primitive or childish, to be superseded by rigorous rationality wherever, and as soon as, possible. Throughout life, tomorrow's learners will be called upon to master a wider range of skills, to solve a broader range of problems, to craft satisfying personal responses to a deeper and more complex set of freedoms and responsibilities, than probably any other generation in the history of the world. To do that well, they will need to have all their learning modes available to them, and to develop them to the fullest extent. As lifelong learners they will need to be playing with a full deck of learning strategies and sensitivities.

Learning through direct, open-minded immersion in experience – the natural learning ability of the brain – remains the foundation of learning throughout life. We saw how adults can draw on this non-intellectual learning to gain mastery over complex domains (controlling a classroom, managing an industrial process); that this kind of learning is often faster and more efficient than trying to figure things out; that direct instruction and the effort to exert conscious mental control can actually impede the development of expertise; and that immersion can capture greater complexity than conscious comprehension. Too much understanding and explaining can divert attention from areas of experience that are not easy to put into words; can make expertise more vulnerable to stress (remember the golf putters who went to pieces under pressure, and the stammering, self-conscious second language learners); and can interfere with creative forms of problem-solving. The relationship between knowledge and know-how is much more delicate than our culture often admits. People can very easily become articulate incompetents, and conversely inarticulate virtuosi. Though an intellectual grasp may be more convenient to assess, it does not guarantee practical intelligence in real-life settings.

We do well to remember the basic amplifiers of this natural learning ability with which evolution has equipped us. First there is the ability to alter the focus of attention from the broad open-mindedness, which is the default mode of the mind, to the tighter, more selective scrutiny which actively searches for details and tests hypotheses. We saw the risk of getting stuck at either end of the spectrum, and the value of being able to vary the cone of attention to suit conditions, sometimes being contemplative and receptive, sometimes being focused and analytical. In particular there is a danger of over-focusing, again when under pressure, so that apparently incidental, but actually relevant, features of a problem are overlooked. We saw the value, throughout the lifespan, of exploration, observation, imitation, practising and especially playing. Even though the latter may result in a temporary regression, it may uncover analogies and connections that a more earnest attempt to get it right would preclude. Play enables the familiar scenarios and scripts of the brainscape to be distilled into a more flexible network of concepts and skills. Those who see play, whether in children or in adults, as a diversion from learning proper, or a lightweight version of it, simply don't understand its special function – it enables the human mind to enrich itself from within.

And play, when internalized, makes possible the development of imagination: 'going to the movies in your head', as Jack Nicklaus put it. The research, though, shows that not all imagining is effective in promoting learning. It is much better to visualize the process of achieving a goal than merely a successful outcome; and to visualize from the inside, so that feelings and physical responses are included as well as visual and auditory aspects of the scene. Such visualization aids the development of practical skill, and prepares you for sustained learning (like revising for an exam) or dealing with difficult or stressful predicaments. Sensory imagery provides an inner language for exploring different ways of responding to situations that involve complex perceptions and/or feelings: where the data is hard to put into words, and is best dealt with in terms of holistic patterns. And the cultivation of states of relaxed reverie maximize the vividness and the value of such explorations.

Language, both spoken and written, is first acquired through the brain's brilliant natural ability to register recurrent patterns, even small and subtle ones, in the world around us. Understanding how this happens enables us to cut through some of the ideology that has become attached to different methods for teaching reading, such as phonics and look-and-say; and to challenge the need to inflict formal tuition in reading and writing on children before many of them are ready. Literacy can be taught in a way that either protects and develops children's wider learning power (especially their resilience) or which neglects or even undermines it. Learnacy must not be sacrificed on the altar of literacy. We noted the familiar risk of getting stuck in a single reading style – for example one in which you say the words to yourself as you read – which is limiting, and the ease with which such bad habits can be modified to restore greater flexibility.

Not all the learning value of language lies in its logic, though. Although we saw that talking to yourself can get in the way of learning and executing practical skills, it can also help, principally by providing the voice of an internalized coach. Language can be linked with imagination through the reading and writing of stories: we learn through narrative as well as through conceptualization. We saw how stories are effective teaching devices that give access to the private, inner worlds of others; that create, like fantasies, possible worlds that can be explored; that enable children and adults to be shown how their culture (be it African tribe or multinational company) works and what it values; and that put human flesh on the conceptual bones of, for example, a new company policy, and thus make it easier for people to master and identify with. Again, though, the craft of story-telling itself has to be learnt (and may have to be relearnt, on first going to school for example, if a new culture values different types of stories, or tells them in a different way). Children also learn how to use story-telling and other forms of language, sometimes in conjunction with imagery, to aid their memories.

Language opens up the third learning compartment, the intellect, greatly expanding the range of information and ideas which we can learn, and learn with, and laying the foundation on which special-purpose learning strategies, such as those for understanding conceptually difficult written and spoken material, can be built. Language, and other symbolic systems such as mathematics, make possible rigorous, deliberate, analytical thinking, which is a powerful learning tool in domains that are well described by small numbers of clearly defined concepts interacting in lawful ways (for instance geometry, physics and logical brainteasers). It turns out that normal education does a poor job of developing a capacity for hard thinking that is spontaneously and appropriately deployed in the face of real-life problems. Even deliberate attempts to train thinking skills frequently have disappointing results: the skills tend not to come to mind when they are needed. To teach people to think successfully, they have to understand what is involved in hard thinking; what are the right kinds of problems; and how to think about their own learning, as well as coaching and practice in the skills themselves.

But hard thinking runs out of steam when the world becomes more complex, more shadowy or more unfamiliar. Its reliance on the categories of language, and on narrow-focus attention, makes it good at problem-solving and bad at creativity. In the solution of difficult, unprecedented, ill-defined problems hard thinking lays the ground and, when understanding dawns, takes an insight and checks and develops it; but in between comes the leisurely incubation of imagery and hunch, intuition and inkling. And learning power is developed by cultivating a familiarity with this less-controlled mental world, learning to trust and enjoy it, and developing some of the quiet qualities and sensitivities, such as patient attentiveness to subtle bodily processes ('focusing'), for mastering it. Purposeful striving must be suspended; even positive incentives can narrow the cone of attention too much.

Artistic, scientific and everyday creativity can be enhanced by learning the rhythms of effort and relaxation, hard and soft thinking: small pauses, hunch breaks, playtime and holidays. Damasio's research even suggests that intuition is the vital medium that glues together rational intelligence and practical action. There is also a rhythmic balance between solitary and sociable inquiry. We saw ways in which both too little and, more surprisingly, too much communication can jeopardize the discovery of optimal solutions. In business, education and elsewhere, cultures that continually pressurize people to deliver the goods, and in which leaders show disdain for the half-baked or indecisive, suppress creativity. The implications of this research for schools and companies are as plain as they are radical.

The third R of learning power is reflectiveness – the inclination to stand back from learning and take a strategic view, combined with the awareness and self-awareness to do so accurately and successfully. Open-mindedness allows one to see new possibilities in familiar settings, and again enhances the flexibility with which knowledge and know-how can be deployed. Mindlessness assumes that things are as they have always been; it looks for confirmation of preconceptions and misses the telling (or enlightening, or amusing) incongruity. Mindlessness is encouraged by a teaching style which transmits canonical bodies of knowledge or ways of thinking as if they were incontrovertible. Mindfulness and creativity are enhanced by substituting 'could be' for 'is'. Young children are well able to handle this degree of uncertainty; their world of pretend play is intrinsically a 'could be' world.

Reflection also enables you to see through your own assumptions, and various forms of mindfulness training are effective at developing such pragmatic self-awareness. For the same purpose reflective writing is a useful tool that can be acquired with the aid of some models of good practice and some sympathetic coaching. The failure to see that reflection is a family of learning tools that have themselves (as always) to be learnt has bedevilled the fashion in adult education and professional development for self-directed learning. Many students could benefit if time were taken to show them clearly how to do it and what the point is. It is mentally harder, and emotionally more demanding, than tutors and trainers often realize. All these skills contribute to a greater ability to manage and monitor one's own learning.

Learning power depends on developing certain dispositions, qualities and capabilities; but, as with all other knowledge and know-how, these are embedded within a shifting intuitive sense of when, where and for what purposes they are best employed. Skills that are learnt in one setting, for one purpose, with one kind of material content, are, through further experience, gradually disembedded from these original details, so that their sphere of relevance (their 'range of convenience', we called it) extends. Knowledge and know-how that are learnt intellectually have to be re-embedded through reflective practice in the functional networks of the brainscape before they can turn into fluent expertise. We reviewed a number of studies that showed how sensitive these pockets of expertise are to apparently trivial changes in content, context and even in physiology and mood. This research shows why 'dipstick' examinations are so unreliable. Regurgitation of knowledge under weird and pressurized conditions says little about people's practical intelligence.

The implications for teaching as well as assessment are profound. One has to teach for retrieval, under the anticipated real-life conditions; not just for acquisition and examination performance. School is not an absence of context, imparting general-purpose knowledge and know-how; it is a very particular, and rather arcane, context out of which learning – unless pains are taken to ensure otherwise – transfers rather badly. Explicitly pointing out the limits of applicability of new knowledge; embedding skills in a wide variety of different contents; using realistic simulations of anticipated use settings; and creating opportunities for playful discovery of boundary conditions: all these become vital aspects of teaching and training.

Another corollary of the learning toolkit approach emphasizes the importance of external tools and resources as well as internal ones. In fact, so widespread is such tool use that the practically intelligent system is, to all intents and purposes, person-plus. Tools include physical space (an office floor), materials (paper), hi- and low-tech instruments (computers, pencils), reference works (directories), symbol systems and languages (calculus, spreadsheets), and other people. Learning power involves the development of the skills and dispositions to look for and if necessary create such resources for oneself. A learning coach will help students develop expertise in using appropriate tools, and a general disposition to seek out the relevant affordances in any environment. In the person-plus world, it makes no sense to deprive people of the resources that are normally available to them and then assess their performance. In learning to use tools, whether technological or symbolic, the development of the learner's inner, mental resources is also channelled: 'mind' grows into the grooves that our tool use requires. We saw how insidiously information technology invites the development of certain learning styles and habits (literal, factual, fast), and neglects others (intuitive, poetic, leisurely). Unless engagement with tools is mindful, there is a risk of a kind of mindless dependency developing which cuts right across learning power.

At different ages, different facets of learning power come to the fore. Childhood is the time to establish a firm foundation of resilience and the basic resources of curiosity, play, imagination and the mastery of language. Schooldays should develop all the compartments of the learning toolkit: immersion in experience, imagination, intellect and intuition. College and university can develop more sophisticated form of intellectual skills, including flexibility and variety in ways of reading and writing, recording and integrating information and ideas, and the beginnings of reflection. During adulthood, reflection and self-awareness, and the ability to take a strategic and responsible overview of one's own learning path, can be further developed.

Parents and childhood educators need to establish a culture in which security and clarity of expectations are balanced with the encouragement of playfulness, inquisitiveness and self-reliance. Too much emphasis on correct performance ('being good' and 'being right') makes children fearful of mistakes and brittle in their engagement with learning challenges. Interpretations of success and failure in terms of 'ability' need to be replaced with encouragement for sustained engagement. Too much praise makes children dependent on adult judgements and reactions. Too much tuition and 'showing how' frustrate children's natural desire for mastery. Criticism and correction, where necessary, should be aimed at what children are doing, not at how they are being. 'Hothousing' children's development may accelerate their achievement, but it can easily undermine the foundations of learning power. Children need to be able to watch older brothers and sisters, parents and teachers being learners in their own right, modelling resilience and the willingness to try a variety of approaches to real uncertainties. Through their interactions with children as they go about their own learning, adults can offer tools that enable the child to reach out beyond his own current limitations, and to practise and test out for himself new learning strategies. This kind of in-the-moment reciprocity, revolving around the child's own activity, is more helpful than a carefully planned schedule of predetermined learning tasks.

Many schools focus too much on achievement, exercise only the intellectual compartment of the toolkit, and deprive children of sustained opportunities to grapple with real difficulties and challenges. Even in their own terms, schools are not very successful at establishing the bases of literacy, numeracy and rationality, and, at the same time, may unwittingly undermine resilience. Tinkering with the content of the curriculum, with the structures of school and with forms of school management do not seem to be achieving the necessary improvements. Practical examples from around the globe show that it is perfectly possible to cultivate young people's emotional literacy – their ability to handle the feelings and manage the stresses of learning – directly; to create opportunities for young people to develop their learning muscles and their learning stamina through working on real problems; to show how imagination, play and dramatic improvisation function as valuable real-life learning tools; to model how teachers themselves tackle genuine uncertainties; to develop the skills of collaborative inquiry and research; and to learn to think about their own learning, developing the ability to reflect upon and manage their own learning processes and projects.

In higher education there are ways of escaping from the homogenized rigmarole of attendance, retention and regurgitation which some undergraduate programmes have become. Even at this level and beyond, resilience and practical intelligence can still be weak. The development of knowledge bases and analytical skills in the context of subject disciplines and prospective professional careers is fine, but this should be

done alongside a concern with cultivating more widely ap-
plicable skills and habits of intellectual inquiry, and critical
reflection on prior models and assumptions. Cultivating the
ability to make honest and productive self-evaluations of both
learning progress and process, and to give and take construc-
tive feedback without feeling personally wounded, are important concerns. Even when such tuition initially makes
students uncomfortable or resistant, the vast majority, with
appropriate support and explanation, come to value the
resultant learning highly. Problem-based learning not only
cultivates greater flexibility and confidence in particular domains; it further develops skills of collaboration, inquiry and
research.

Finally, the changing nature of working life with its increasing uncertainties, complexities and responsibilities at all organizational levels, and for the self-employed, means that
resilience, resourcefulness and reflection are vital qualities
throughout adulthood. Ample opportunities are needed to
create workplace cultures that encourage the expression and
development of practical learning power throughout adult life.
All the skills of immersion, imagination, intellect and intuition
contribute to corporate success and individual job satisfaction.
Innovative companies are making use of stories and imagery to
produce richer, more engaging visions than can be created by
exhortations; and they are recognizing the value, and the
educability, of intuitive ways of learning and knowing. Managers need to lead by example, demonstrating confident uncertainty; and to ensure that any rhetoric about empowerment
or the learning organization is carried through into workplace
reality. Structural reorganization needs to be matched with a
concern with more nebulous, but also more important, aspects
of the culture such as communication and the distribution of
both formal and informal recognition and reward. On an
employer's part the psychological contract needs to replace
security, with genuine support for the enhancement of transferable employability and cognitive capital.

There is a substantial body of evidence to show that the
enhancement of learning power is an achievable goal, and
that a process started in childhood can profitably continue
throughout life. If it is true, as I believe it is, that tomorrow's

world will be one that places unprecedented demands on ordinary people to be good lifelong learners, then we have the beginnings of a vision of how we can prepare ourselves and our children to meet the challenge. Round the world thousands of experiments, large and small, are taking place which show that vision can be translated into practical reality. But this too is a learning adventure. Those who are concerned to build a global learning society have themselves to develop their own resilience, resourcefulness and reflection. It is a challenging and uncertain undertaking. But I know of no more important one.

Notes

Introduction

1. This example is based on the research of Jerome Kagan (1994), *Galen's Prophecy: Temperament in Human Nature*, New York: Westview Press.
2. This example reflects the findings of Carol Dweck (1984), 'The power of negative thinking', *Times Educational Supplement*, London, 21 September.
3. Research on 'soft thinking', on which this example is based, is reviewed in Guy Claxton, *Hare Brain, Tortoise Mind: Why Intelligence Increases When You Think Less*, London: Fourth Estate, 1997; Hopewell, NJ: Ecco Press, 1999.

Chapter 1

1. N. Caplan, M. H. Choy and J. K. Whitmore (1992), 'Indochinese refugee families and academic achievement', *Scientific American*, vol. 266 (February), pp. 18–24.
2. J. B. Biggs (1996), 'Western misconceptions of the Confucius-heritage learning culture', in D. A. Watkins and J. B. Biggs (eds), *The Chinese Learner: Cultural, Psychological and Contextual Influences*, Comparative Education Research Centre, University of Hong Kong.
3. Robert Sternberg, Barbara Conway, Jerry Ketron and Morty Bernstein (1981), 'People's conceptions of intelligence', *Journal of Personality and Social Psychology*, vol. 41, pp. 37–55.
4. We must keep in mind here a distinction between 'espoused' and 'embodied' beliefs – between what people say they believe, and what they act as if they believed. Many teachers now espouse a view of science, for example, as a human creation, a network of conjectures, rather than a body of immutable 'facts' hewn from nature by the

painstaking application of a systematic method. Yet in their actual classroom behaviour and commentary, they may give no sense that this is so (apart, perhaps, from the occasional informal discussion with an older class). See C. Feldman and J. Wertsch (1976), 'Context dependent properties of teachers' speech', *Youth and Society*, vol. 8, pp. 227–58.

5. Ellen Langer, Michael Hatem, Jennifer Joss and Marilyn Howell (1989), 'Conditional teaching and mindful learning: the role of uncertainty in education', *Creativity Research Journal*, vol. 2, pp. 139–50.

6. Michael Howe (1984), *A Teachers' Guide to the Psychology of Learning*, Oxford: Blackwell.

7. F. Salili (1996), 'Accepting personal responsibility for learning', in Watkins and Biggs, op. cit. I am grateful to Siti Reduan of the University of Bristol Graduate School of Education for permission to draw on her research into Asian cultures of learning.

8. Patricia Broadfoot and Marilyn Osborn (1993), *Perceptions of Teaching: Primary School Teachers in England and France*, London: Cassell; Marilyn Osborn (1996), 'Being a pupil in England and France: findings from a comparative study', paper presented to the 17th Comparative Education Society in Europe Conference, Athens, October.

9. IQ is defined as the ratio of the age that is typical of the score a person achieves on a standardized test, to their actual age, multiplied by a hundred (i.e. mental age ÷ chronological age × 100). Thus performance that is typical of a person's actual age receives an IQ score of around 100; performance that is characteristic of younger people gets a score of below 100; performance normally associated with older people gains an IQ of greater than 100.

10. This research is fully reviewed by Stephen Ceci (1996), *On Intelligence*, Cambridge, Mass: Harvard University Press.

11. Robert J. Sternberg (1997), 'The concept of intelligence and its role in lifelong learning and success', *American Psychologist*, vol. 52, pp. 1030–7.

12. Richard Herrnstein and Charles Murray (1994), *The Bell Curve: Intelligence and Class Structure in American Life*, New York: Free Press. The flaws in Herrnstein and Murray's reasoning are well summarized by David Perkins (1995), *Outsmarting IQ: The Emerging Science of Learnable Intelligence*, New York: Free Press.

13. Sternberg, op. cit.

14. Ulric Neisser et al. (1996), 'Intelligence: knowns and unknowns', *American Psychologist*, vol. 51, pp. 77–101.

15. Michael Howe (1988), 'Intelligence as an explanation', *British Journal of Psychology*, vol. 79, pp. 349–60.

16. Sternberg, Conway, Ketron and Bernstein, op. cit.; and Hannu Raty and Leila Snellman (1992), 'Does sex make any difference? Common sense conceptions of intelligence', *Social Behavior and Personality*, vol. 20, pp. 23–34.

17. Marlene Schommer (1990), 'Effects of beliefs about the nature of knowledge on comprehension', *Journal of Educational Psychology*, vol. 82, pp. 498–504; and (1993), 'Epistemological development and

academic performance among secondary students', *Journal of Educational Psychology*, vol. 85, pp. 406–11.

18. Dweck, op. cit.
19. Edward de Bono (1982), *De Bono's Thinking Course*, London: BBC Publications.
20. Robert Bernstein, quoted in Roy Rowan (1986), *The Intuitive Manager*, Boston: Little, Brown.

Chapter 2

1. Keith Oatley (1992), *Best Laid Schemes: Towards a Psychology of Emotion*, Cambridge: Cambridge University Press.
2. Daniel Goleman (1996), *Emotional Intelligence*, London: Bloomsbury.
3. James Pye (1989), *Invisible Children: Who Are the Real Losers at School?*, Oxford: Oxford University Press.
4. See, for example, Hans Selye (1976), *The Stress of Life*, New York: McGraw-Hill.
5. John Holt (1965), *How Children Fail*, London: Pitman.
6. Isobel Menzies Lyth (1989), 'Social systems as a defence against anxiety', in *Containing Anxiety in Institutions: Selected Essays*, London: Free Association Books.
7. This literature is reviewed in Ted Thompson (1993), 'Characteristics of self-worth protection in achievement behaviour', *British Journal of Educational Psychology*, vol. 63, pp. 469–88.
8. Quoted in R. Beery (1975), 'Fear of failure in the student experience', *Personnel and Guidance Journal*, vol. 54, pp. 191–203; quoted in Thompson, op. cit.
9. Thompson, op. cit.
10. Martin V. Covington (1985), 'Strategic thinking and the fear of failure', in J. W. Segal, S. F. Chipman and R. Glaser (eds), *Thinking and Learning Skills, Vol. 1: Relating Instruction to Research*, Hillsdale, NJ: Erlbaum.
11. For a review of research on 'tactical inattention' see Daniel Goleman (1998), *Vital Lies, Simple Truths: The Psychology of Self-Deception*, London: Bloomsbury.
12. Note in this context a rather enjoyable transatlantic slanging match. 'Americans do not enjoy the process of thinking. When they do concentrate, it is in order to escape all thought' – Jean-Paul Sartre; versus 'Most Englishmen would die sooner than think, and many do' – Dorothy L. Sayers.
13. For a summary of some of this research see Thomas Gilovich (1993), *How We Know What Isn't So: The Fallibility of Human Reason in Everyday Life*, New York: Free Press.
14. Hilaire Belloc (1999), *Complete Verse*, London: Cape.
15. Robert Levenson (1995), 'Can we control our emotions, and how does such control change an emotional episode?', in Richard Davidson and Paul Ekman (eds), *Fundamental Questions about Emotions*, Oxford: Oxford University Press.

16. Bruce McEwen and Eliot Stellar (1993), 'Stress and the individual: mechanisms leading to disease', *Archives of Internal Medicine*, vol. 153, 27 September.
17. Kenneth Gergen (1991), *The Saturated Self: Dilemmas of Identity in Contemporary Life*, New York: Basic Books.
18. See Michael W. Eysenck (1997), *Anxiety and Cognition: A Unified Theory*, Hove, UK: Psychology Press.
19. See, for example, A. Mathews and C. MacLeod (1994), 'Cognitive approaches to emotion and emotional disorders', *Annual Review of Psychology*, vol. 45, pp. 25–50.
20. Nicholas Xenos (1989), *Scarcity and Modernity*, London: Routledge.
21. Dorothy Holland and Debra Skinner (1987), 'Prestige and intimacy', in D. Holland and N. Quinn (eds), *Cultural Models in Language and Thought*, Cambridge: Cambridge University Press. Also discussed in Roy D'Andrade (1994), *An Introduction to Cognitive Anthropology*, Cambridge: Cambridge University Press.
22. Michael Lewis (1992), *Shame: The Exposed Self*, New York: Free Press.
23. For further discussion and justification of these beliefs see my *Live and Learn* (Buckingham, UK: Open University Press, 1987), Chapter 6, and *Being a Teacher* (London: Cassell, 1989), Chapter 3.
24. J. L. Collins (1982), 'Self-efficacy and ability in achievement behavior', paper presented at the annual meeting of the American Educational Research Association, New York; cited in Albert Bandura (1989), 'Perceived self-efficacy in the exercise of personal agency', *The Psychologist*, vol. 2, pp. 411–24.
25. A. Bandura and R. E. Wood (1989), 'Effect of perceived controllability and performance standards on self-regulation of complex decision-making', *Journal of Personality and Social Psychology*, vol. 56, pp. 805–14.
26. N. E. Betz and G. Hackett (1986), 'Applications of self-efficacy theory to understanding career choice behavior', *Journal of Social and Clinical Psychology*, vol. 4, pp. 279–89; cited in Bandura, op. cit.
27. John Holt (1989), *Learning All the Time*, Reading, Mass: Addison Wesley.
28. Mihaly and Isabella Csikszentmihalyi (1992), *Optimal Experience: Psychological Studies of Flow in Consciousness*, Cambridge: Cambridge University Press.
29. Quoted in Goleman (1996), op. cit.
30. Jeanne Nakamura (1988), 'Optimal experience and the uses of talent', in Csikszentmihalyi, op. cit.
31. Goleman (1996), op. cit.

Chapter 3

1. S. C. Kak (1996), 'The three languages of the brain: quantum, reorganizational and associative', in K. H. Pribram and J. King (eds), *Learning as Self-Organization*, Mahwah, NJ: Erlbaum.
2. Paul Rozin (1976), 'The evolution of intelligence and access to the

cognitive unconscious', in J. M. Sprague and A. N. Epstein (eds), *Progress in Psychobiology and Physiological Psychology, Vol. 6*, New York: Academic Press.

3. American TV documentary *Extraordinary Dogs*, shown on New Zealand TV One channel, 15 February 1998.
4. R. F. Caron, A. J. Caron and R. S. Myers (1982), 'Abstraction of invariant facial expressions in infancy', *Child Development*, vol. 53, pp. 1008–15.
5. Arlene Walker-Andrews (1986), 'Intermodal perception of expressive behaviors: relation of eye and voice', *Developmental Psychology*, vol. 22, pp. 373–7.
6. Howard Gardner (1991), *The Unschooled Mind: How Children Think and How Schools Should Teach*, New York: Basic Books.
7. Gardner, op. cit., p. 10.
8. This account is adapted from a passage originally published in my book *Live and Learn*, op. cit.
9. Dianne Berry and Donald Broadbent (1988), 'Interactive tasks and the implicit–explicit distinction', *British Journal of Psychology*, vol. 79, pp. 251–72.
10. P. Lewicki, T. Hill and M. Cyzyewska (1992), 'Nonconscious acquisition of information', *American Psychologist*, vol. 47, pp. 796–801.
11. Arthur Reber (1993), *Implicit Learning and Tacit Knowledge: An Essay on the Cognitive Unconscious*, Oxford: Oxford University Press.
12. See Peter John (1996), 'Understanding the apprenticeship of observation in initial teacher education', in Guy Claxton, Terry Atkinson, Marilyn Osborn and Mike Wallace (eds), *Liberating the Learner*, Routledge: London. See also Dan Lortie (1975), *Schoolteacher: A Sociological Study*, University of Chicago Press.
13. How to represent the different facets of brain function in a model that enables one to think accurately but intuitively about how it works is a perennial problem. The convention in the 'artificial neural network' literature is to allow the three spatial dimensions to represent three of the many dimensions of the 'feature space', and then to show connectedness in terms of surfaces and trajectories within the 'volume' thus created (see, for example, Paul Churchland (1995), *The Engine of Reason, The Seat of the Soul*, Cambridge, Mass: MIT Press). I follow David Marr ((1970), 'A theory for cerebral neo-cortex', *Proceedings of the Royal Society*, Series B, vol. 176, pp. 161–234), and others in preferring the convention of a two-dimensional feature space, with concepts being mapped as 'probabilistic mountains' in that space – except that I turn Marr's landscape upside down and represent tight-knit assemblies of cells as basins rather than as hills. This enables us to conceive of activation as running downwards along the deepest valleys, and gravitating towards the bottom of conceptual dips and dells. The two flat dimensions of the metaphorical terrain represent the features of the perceptual world that any animal, humans included, inhabits. These parameters will be different, depending on the world itself and on the nature and the range of the sensory systems with which that animal has been evolutionarily endowed. The third vertical dimension indicates the strength of functional bonding between features.

14. Gary Cottrell (1991), 'Extracting features from faces using compression networks; face, identity, emotion and gender recognition using holons', in D. Touretzky, J. Elkman, T. Sejnowski and G. Hinton (eds), *Connectionist Models: Proceedings of the 1990 Summer School*, San Mateo, CA: Morgan Kaufmann. My description is based on the account of Cottrell's work in Churchland, op. cit.

Chapter 4

1. David LaBerge (1995), *Attentional Processing: The Brain's Art of Mindfulness*, Cambridge, Mass: Harvard University Press.
2. See Guy Claxton (1994), *Noises from the Darkroom: The Science and Mystery of the Mind*, London: HarperCollins; Claxton (1997), op. cit; and Norman Dixon (1971), *Subliminal Perception: The Nature of a Controversy*, New York: McGraw-Hill. There is good evidence now for subliminal influences of all kinds, and no doubt that we can register and be influenced by events unconsciously. The only disappointing news is that sleep learning is a dream. The idea that people can learn foreign vocabulary in their sleep, for example, by putting a tape recorder under the pillow has been put to rigorous tests, but learning only takes place while people are awake. If you wire people up an electroencephalograph (EEG) machine, which monitors their brain activity and tells you what stage of sleep they are in, and turn the tape recorder off whenever they approach the waking threshold, no learning happens. See A. Greenwald, E. Spangenberg, A. Pratkanis and J. Eskenazi (1991), 'Double-blind tests of subliminal self-help audiotapes', *Psychological Science*, vol. 2, pp. 119–22.
3. See David Gelernter (1994), *The Muse in the Machine: Computers and Creative Thought*, London: Fourth Estate.
4. Some animals have developed the strategy of 'self-startling'. The birds, squirrels and rabbits in my garden, for example, do not allow themselves to get absorbed for very long in eating or grooming while they are out in the open. If they did, they would be all the more vulnerable to predators. So every few seconds they indulge in a general-purpose alert to check for real or potential threats. They are not just distractible; they are recurrently self-distracting. Their life may depend on it. When people who inhabit worlds that are (objectively) safe start to deploy the distractible and hyper-vigilant attention patterns of the rabbit, in a way that prevents them functioning effectively, they are said to suffer from generalized anxiety disorder. See Eysenck, op. cit.
5. E. Schenk (1960), *Mozart and His Times*, ed. and trans. from German by R. and C. Winston, London: Secker and Warburg; quoted in Michael J. A. Howe (1998), *Principles of Abilities and Human Learning*, Hove, UK: Psychology Press. The other examples are also taken from Howe.
6. J. M. Haviland and M. Lelwica (1987), 'The induced effect response: ten week old infants' responses to three emotional expressions', *Developmental Psychology*, vol. 23, pp. 97–104.

7. These studies are reviewed in Paul Harris (1989), *Children and Emotion: The Development of Psychological Understanding*, Oxford: Blackwell.

8. K. Anders Ericsson and Neil Charness (1994), 'Expert performance: its structure and acquisition', *American Psychologist*, vol. 49, pp. 725–47.

9. David Premack (1988), ' "Does the chimpanzee have a theory of mind?" revisited', in R. Byrne and A. Whiten (eds), *Machiavellian Intelligence*, Oxford: Clarendon Press. C. Ristau (1991), 'Injury-feigning and other anti-predator behaviours by plovers: intentional behaviour?', in *Cognitive Ethology: The Minds of Other Animals*, Hillsdale, NJ: Erlbaum.

10. Andy Clark and Annette Karmiloff-Smith (1993), 'The cognizer's innards: a psychological and philosophical perspective on the development of thought', *Mind and Language*, vol. 8, pp. 487–519. The discussion that follows is based on this seminal paper.

11. Beate Hermelin and Neil O'Connor (1991), 'Intelligence and musical improvisation', *Psychological Medicine*, 'in press', cited by Annette Karmiloff-Smith (1990), 'Constraints on representational change: evidence from children's drawing', *Cognition*, vol. 34, pp. 57–83.

Chapter 5

1. Jack Nicklaus (1976), *Play Better Golf*, New York: King Features.

2. Goleman (1996), op. cit.

3. G. E. Schwartz, S. L. Brown and G. L. Ahern (1980), 'Facial muscle patterning and subjective experience during affective imagery', *Psychophysiology*, vol. 17, pp. 75–82.

4. Bruce Cuthbert, Scott Vrana and Margaret Bradley (1991), 'Imagery: function and physiology', *Advances in Psychophysiology*, vol. 4, pp. 1–42.

5. D. L. Feltz and D. M. Landers (1983), 'The effects of mental practice on motor skill learning and performance', *Journal of Sports Psychology*, vol. 5, pp. 25–57.

6. A fourth group, instructed to visualize throwing the darts while standing in front of the board making their natural throwing action, was no different from the 'pure imagination' group. Dwight Mendoza and Harvey Wichman (1978), ' "Inner" darts: effects of mental practice on performance in dart throwing', *Perceptual and Motor Skills*, vol. 47, pp. 1195–9.

7. B. D. Hale (1994), 'Imagery perspectives and learning in sports performance', in A. A. Sheikh and E. R. Korn (eds), *Imagery in Sports and Physical Performance*, Amityville, NY: Baywood.

8. R. L. Woolfolk, M. W. Parrish and S. M. Murphy (1985), 'The effect of positive and negative imagery on motor skill performance', *Cognitive Therapy and Research*, vol. 9, pp. 335–41.

9. Dave Smith, Dave Collins, Paul Holmes and Katherine Layland (1998), 'The effect of mental practice on strength performance and EMG activity', *Research Quarterly for Exercise and Sport*, in press.

10. Much of my discussion in this section is based on Shelley Taylor, Lien Pham, Inna Rivkin and David Armor (1998), 'Harnessing the imagination: mental simulation, self-regulation and coping', *American Psychologist*, vol. 53, pp. 429–39.

11. In line with these findings, I have been told of a research study which looked at children's performance on school tasks. A baseline was established for a group of average students, who were then asked to undertake an equivalent task but to imagine doing it 'as if they were a very bright student'. Their performance improved dramatically! Unfortunately I have not been able to track this study down. It is reminiscent of a well-conducted piece of research by Ellen Langer of Harvard, in which she showed that people's visual acuity increased when they were actively imagining themselves to be fighter pilots (see Ellen Langer (1991), *Mindfulness: Choice and Control in Daily Life*, London: Harvill). Imagination is able to increase our learning potential not just by allowing us to explore new possibilities, but by freeing us from habitual constraints on the way we think, learn and even perceive. There are several lines of research which suggest that habit, rather than basic, immutable character, is responsible for much of who we think we are.

12. Norman Vincent Peale (1982), *Positive Imaging: The Powerful Way to Change Your Life*, New York: Fawcett Crest.

13. P. Lang, B. G. Melamed and J. Hart (1970), 'A psychophysiological analysis of fear modification using an automated desensitization procedure', *Journal of Abnormal Psychology*, vol. 76, pp. 220–34.

14. D. N. Levin, E. W. Cook and P. J. Lang (1982), 'Fear imagery and fear behaviour: psychophysiological analysis of clients receiving treatment for anxiety disorders', *Psychophysiology*, vol. 19, pp. 571–2.

15. Yuan Tseh Lee (1996), 'The importance of imagery in understanding chemistry', in Warren Beasley (ed), *Chemistry: Expanding the Boundaries*, Proceedings of the 14th International Conference on Chemical Education, Brisbane, July.

16. Steven Lynn and Judith Rhue (1986), 'The fantasy-prone person: hypnosis, imagination and creativity', *Journal of Personality and Social Psychology*, vol. 51, pp. 404–8.

17. Peter McKellar (1957), *Imagination and Thinking: A Psychological Analysis*, London: Cohen and West.

Chapter 6

1. K. Nelson, G. Carskaddon and J. D. Bonvillian (1973), 'Syntax acquisition: impact of experimental variation in adult verbal interaction with the child', *Child Development*, vol. 44, pp. 497–504.

2. Holt (1989), op. cit.

3. Peter Bryant and Lynette Bradley (1985), *Children's Reading Problems: Psychology and Education*, Oxford: Blackwell. Several of the references in this section are summarized in Howe (1998), op. cit.

4. A. Ninio and J. S. Bruner (1978), 'The achievement and antecedents of labelling', *Journal of Child Language*, vol. 5, pp. 1–15.
5. Quotations taken from Howe, op. cit., p. 33.
6. John Morton (1966, 1998), 'A two-hour rapid reading course', *Nature*, vol. 211, pp. 323–4.
7. Graham Gibbs, Trevor Habeshaw and Sue Habeshaw (1987), *53 Interesting Ways of Helping Your Students to Study*, Bristol, UK: Technical and Educational Services.
8. These illustrations are drawn from study skills books such as Robert Carman (1984), *Study Skills: A Student's Guide to Survival*, New York: Wiley; Mike and Glenda Smith (1990), *A Study Skills Handbook*, Oxford: Oxford University Press.
9. John Nisbet and Janet Shucksmith (1986), *Learning Strategies*, London: Routledge.
10. Claire Weinstein and Vicki Underwood (1985), 'Learning strategies: the how of learning', in Segal, Chipman and Glaser (eds), op.cit.
11. More detail on comprehension strategies is given in Chapter 8, and by, for example, Ann Brown, Annemarie Palincsar and Bonnie Armbruster (1984), 'Instructing comprehension-fostering activities in interactive learning situations', in H. Mandl, N. Stein and T. Trabasso (eds), *Learning and Comprehension of Text*, Hillsdale, NJ: Erlbaum.
12. Mills, op. cit.
13. Mills, op. cit.
14. Trace-It was developed by P. Kollberg at the Royal Institute of Technology in Sweden. See M. Nilsson and P. Kollberg (1994), *Trace-it 2.0 Users' Manual*, Department of Numerical Analysis and Computing Science, Royal Institute of Technology, Stockholm, Sweden.
15. Colette Daiute and John Kruidenier (1985), 'A self-questioning strategy to increase young writers' revising processes', *Applied Psycholinguistics*, vol. 6, pp. 307–18.

Chapter 7

1. This description of hard thinking is a condensed version of a lengthier treatment in Chapter 1 of my book *Hare Brain, Tortoise Mind: Why Intelligence Increases When You Think Less* (op. cit.), from which some of the material about the shortcomings of hard thinking (I called it 'd-mode' in the earlier book) in this and Chapter 8 is drawn.
2. Jonathan Schooler, Stellan Ohlsson and Kevin Brooks (1993), 'Thought beyond words: when language overshadows insight', *Journal of Experimental Psychology: General*, vol. 122, pp. 166–83. The solution to the problem, incidentally, is, left to right, the jack (knave) of hearts, the king of diamonds and the queen of spades.
3. Peter Wason and Philip Johnson-Laird (1972), *The Psychology of Reasoning: Structure and Content*, London: Batsford.

4. Wason and Johnson-Laird, op. cit. Holt (1989), op. cit.
5. W. S. Messer and R. A. Griggs (1989), 'Student belief and involvement in the paranormal and performance in introductory psychology', *Teaching in Psychology*, vol. 16, pp. 187–91.
6. Diane Halpern (1998), 'Teaching critical thinking for transfer across domains', *American Psychologist*, vol. 53, pp. 449–55.
7. Sir Peter Medawar (1967), *The Art of the Soluble*, London: Methuen.
8. For evidence, see Gilovich, op. cit.
9. David Perkins (1985), 'Post-primary education has little impact on informal reasoning', *Journal of Educational Psychology*, vol. 77, pp. 562–71.
10. Keith Stanovich (1994), 'Dysrationalia as an intuition pump', *Educational Researcher*, vol. 23, pp. 11–22.
11. Perkins (1985), op. cit.
12. Ray Nickerson (1988), 'On improving thinking through instruction', *Review of Research in Education*, vol. 15, pp. 3–57.
13. For reviews of the evaluation of 'teaching thinking' programmes, see John Nisbet and Peter Davies (1990), 'The curriculum redefined: learning to think, thinking to learn', *Research Papers in Education*, vol. 5, pp. 49–72; Ray Nickerson, David Perkins and Edward Smith (eds) (1985), *The Teaching of Thinking*, Hillsdale, NJ: Erlbaum.
14. Edward de Bono, quoted in B. Z. Presseisen (1988), 'At-risk students and thinking perspectives from research', National Education Association: Washington, DC, and Research for Better Schools: Philadelphia (quoted in Nisbet and Davies, op. cit.)
15. E. Hunter-Grundin (1985), *Teaching Thinking*, London: SCDC Schools Council.
16. J. Edwards and R. B. Baldauf (1983), 'Teaching thinking in secondary science', in W. Maxwell (ed.), *Thinking: The Expanding Frontier*, Philadelphia: Franklin Institute Press.
17. M. A. de Sanchez and M. Astorga (1983), 'Proyecto aprendar a pensar: estudio de efectos sobre una muestra de estudieantes venezolanos', Caracas, Venezuela: Ministerio de Educacion; quoted in Nickerson et al. (1985), op. cit.
18. David Perkins and Tina Grotzer (1997), 'Teaching intelligence', *American Psychologist*, vol. 52, pp. 1125–33.
19. Nickerson et al. (1985), op. cit., p. 58.

Chapter 8

1. Stephen Krashen (1987), *Principles and Practice in Second Language Learning*, New York: Prentice-Hall International.
2. J. M. Barrie (1967; first published 1904), *Peter Pan*, Harmondsworth: Puffin; quoted in Jerome Bruner (1996), *The Culture of Education*, Cambridge, Mass: Harvard University Press.
3. Mary van der Riet (1998), 'Socialization through story-telling', paper delivered to the fourth Congress of the International Society for

Cultural Research and Activity Theory, Aarhus, Denmark, June. Van der Riet's Xhosa children's bedtime stories, the *intsomi*, were collected in Mdeni Village, Amatole Basin, Middledrift District, South Africa, in 1996–7. Her informants were mainly mothers and grandmothers. See also H. Scheub (1975), *The Xhosa Ntsomi*, Clarendon Press: Oxford.

4. Gordon Wells (1998), 'Knowledge: transmission or co-construction?', unpublished paper, Ontario Institute for Studies in Education, University of Toronto, Canada.

5. Shirley Brice Heath (1983), *Ways with Words: Language, Life and Work in Communities and Classrooms*, New York: Cambridge University Press.

6. Howard Gardner and Ellen Winner (1979), 'The development of metaphoric competence: implications for humanistic disciplines', in S. Sacks (ed.), *On Metaphor*, Chicago: University of Chicago Press.

7. Lois Holzman (1997), *Schools for Growth: Radical Alternatives to Current Educational Models*, Mahwah, NJ: Erlbaum.

8. Michael Gazzaniga (1990), *Mind Matters: How Mind and Brain Interact to Create our Conscious Lives*, Boston: Houghton Mifflin.

9. Mary Midgley (1992), *Science as Salvation: A Modern Myth and Its Meaning*, London: Routledge.

10. J. Turnure, N. Buium and M. Thurlow (1976), 'The effectiveness of interrogatives for promoting verbal elaboration productivity in children', *Child Development*, vol. 11, pp. 780–7.

11. G. H. Bower and M. C. Clark (1969), 'Narrative stories as mediators of serial learning', *Psychonomic Science*, vol. 14, pp. 181–2.

12. Gaby Wood, 'A dark and stormy knight', *Guardian*, London, 5 December 1998.

13. R. N. Haber and M. H. Erdelyi (1967), 'Emergence and recovery of initially unavailable perceptual material', *Journal of Verbal Learning and Verbal Behavior*, vol. 26, pp. 618–28.

Chapter 9

1. Donald Schon (1983), *The Reflective Practitioner: How Professionals Think in Action*, New York: Basic Books.

2. Arthur Koestler (1999), *The Act of Creation*, London: Vintage.

3. Albert Einstein (1996), quoted in Jacques Hadamard, *The Mathematician's Mind: The Psychology of Invention in the Mathematical Field*, Princeton, NJ: Princeton University Press.

4. Quoted in Koestler, op. cit.

5. Frances Vaughan (1988), *Awakening Intuition*, New York: Anchor Books.

6. K. S. Bowers, G. Regehr, C. Balthazard and K. Parker (1990), 'Intuition in the context of discovery', *Cognitive Psychology*, vol. 22, pp. 72–110; K. S. Bowers, P. Farvolden and L. Mermigis (1995), 'Intuitive antecedents of insight', in S. M. Smith, T. B. Ward and R. A. Finke (eds), *The Creative Cognition Approach*, Cambridge, Mass: Bradford/MIT Press.

7. Mark C. Price (1999), 'Now you see it, now you don't': preventing consciousness with visual masking', in P. G. Grossenbacher (ed.), *Finding Consciousness in the Brain: A Neurocognitive Approach*, Amsterdam: John Benjamin.

8. Herbert Spencer, quoted in Brewster Ghiselin (1952), *The Creative Process*, Berkeley, CA: University of California Press.

9. Arthur Combs and Charles Taylor (1952), 'The effect of perception of mild degrees of psychological stress on performance', *Journal of Abnormal and Social Psychology*, vol. 47, pp. 420–4.

10. Carl Vesti (1971), 'Effect of monetary rewards on an insight learning task', *Psychonomic Science*, vol. 23, pp. 181–3.

11. J. A. Easterbrook (1959), 'The effect of emotion on cue utilization and the organization of behaviour', *Psychological Review*, vol. 66, pp. 183–201.

12. H. P. Bahrick, P. M. Fitts and R. E. Rankin (1952), 'Effect of incentives upon reaction to peripheral stimuli', *Journal of Experimental Psychology*, vol. 44, pp. 400–6.

13. Milton Rokeach (1950), 'The effect of perception time upon the rigidity and concreteness of thinking', *Journal of Experimental Psychology*, vol. 40, pp. 206–16.

14. Sigmund Freud (1912/1958), 'Recommendations to physicians practising psychanalysis', in J. Strachey (ed. and trans.), *The Standard Edition of the Complete Psychological Works of Sigmund Freud*, Vol. 12, London: Hogarth Press.

15. Marcel Kinsbourne (1993), 'Integrated cortical field theory of consciousness', in *CIBA Symposium 174, Experimental and Theoretical Studies of Consciousness*, Chichester: Wiley.

16. Colin Martindale (1995), 'Creativity and connectionism', in Smith, Ward and Finke, op. cit.

17. A. R. Luria (1987), *The Mind of a Mnemonist*, Cambridge, Mass: Harvard University Press.

18. Rokeach, op. cit.

19. Sidney Parnes (1961), 'Effects of extended effort in creative problem solving', *Journal of Educational Psychology*, vol. 52, pp. 117–22.

20. George Spencer Brown (1969), *Laws of Form*, London: Allen and Unwin.

21. J. W. Getzels and M. Csikszentmihalyi (1975), 'From problem-solving to problem finding', in I. A. Taylor and J. W. Getzels (eds), *Perspectives in Creativity*, Chicago: Aldine.

22. Diana Hinds, 'Nothing is such fun as boredom', *The Independent*, London, 23 July 1998.

23. Rokeach, op. cit.

24. Eugene Gendlin (1981), *Focusing*, New York: Bantam; and (1996) *Focusing-Oriented Psychotherapy*, New York: Guilford Press.

25. Jonathan Schooler and Joseph Melcher (1995), 'The ineffability of insight', in Smith, Ward and Finke, op. cit.

26. See Gendlin (1981 and 1996), op. cit.

27. Siegfried and Theresa Engelmann (1981), *Give Your Child a Superior Mind*, New York: Cornerstone Library; quoted in Nell Noddings and

Paul Shore (1984), *Awakening the Inner Eye: Intuition in Education*, New York: Teachers' College Press.

Chapter 10

1. Mihaly Csikszentmihalyi and Keith Sawyer (1995), 'Creative insight: the social dimension of a solitary moment', in R. J. Sternberg and J. E. Davidson (eds), *The Nature of Insight*, Cambridge, Mass: Bradford/MIT Press.
2. Kevin Dunbar (1995), 'How scientists really reason: scientific reasoning in real-world laboratories', in Sternberg and Davidson, op. cit.
3. Colleen Seifert, David Meyer, Natalie Davidson, Andrea Patalano and Ilan Yaniv (1995), 'Demystification of cognitive insight: opportunistic assimilation and the prepared-mind perspective', in Sternberg and Davidson, op. cit.
4. Edwin Hutchins (1994), *Cognition in the Wild*, Cambridge, Mass: MIT Press.
5. E. B. Dennehy, P. Bulow, F. Y. Wong, S. M. Smith and J. B. Aronoff (1991), 'A test of cognitive fixation in brainstorming groups', unpublished manuscript, cited in Smith, Ward and Finke, op. cit; M. Diehl and W. Strobe (1986), 'Productivity loss in brainstorming: toward the solution of a riddle', *Journal of Personality and Social Psychology*, vol. 53, pp. 497–509.
6. Csikszentmihalyi and Sawyer, op. cit.
7. Not all problems are necessarily or obviously one form or the other. Part of the challenge of learning is that you often do not know in advance what the best approach is going to be. And indeed some problems are amenable to more than one approach. For example: if a knock-out tennis tournament starts in the first round with 128 players, and reduces them by half until the final, what is the total number of matches played? The analytical route, which will deliver the answer eventually, involves working out the number of matches per round and adding them together. The insight route involves the realization that, as each match must produce one loser, and there has to be a total of 127 losers to leave just one champion, there must be 127 matches.
8. Steven Smith (1995), 'Getting into and out of mental ruts: a theory of fixation, incubation and insight', in Sternberg and Davidson, op. cit.
9. Ed Vulliamy, 'The prophet of profit', *Observer*, London, 8 March 1998.
10. These studies are reviewed in Jonathan Schooler and Joseph Melcher (1995), 'The ineffability of insight', in Smith, Ward and Finke, op. cit.; and Jonathan Schooler and Stephen Fiore (1997), 'Consciousness and the limits of language: you can't always say what you think, or think what you say', in J. D. Cohen and J. W. Schooler (eds), *Scientific Approaches to Consciousness*, Mahwah, NJ: Erlbaum.
11. Ian Stewart (1987), 'Are mathematicians logical?', *Nature*, vol. 325, pp. 386–7; quoted in Ceci, op. cit.
12. Sylvia Scribner (1984), 'Studying working intelligence', in B. Rogoff

and J. Lave (eds), *Everyday Cognition: Its Development in Social Context*, Cambridge, Mass: Harvard University Press.

13. D. Dorner, H. Kreuzig, F. Reither and T. Staudel (1983), *Lohhausen: Vom Umgang mit Umbestimmtheit und Komplexität*, Bern: Huber; described in Ceci, op. cit.

14. Antoine Bechara, Hanna Damasio, Daniel Tranel and Antonio Damasio (1997), 'Deciding advantageously before knowing the advantageous strategy', *Science*, vol. 275, pp. 1293–5.

15. Timothy Gallwey (1974), *The Inner Game of Tennis*, London: Cape.

16. R. S. W. Masters (1992), 'Knowledge, knerves and know-how: the role of explicit versus implicit knowledge in the breakdown of a complex motor skill under pressure', *British Journal of Psychology*, vol. 83, pp. 343–58. See also Steven Berglas and Roy Baumeister (1993), *Your Own Worst Enemy: Understanding the Paradox of Self-defeating Behaviour*, New York: HarperCollins.

17. Berry and Broadbent, op. cit.

18. Louis Sass (1993), *Madness and Modernity: Insanity in the Light of Modern Art, Literature and Thought*, New York: Basic Books; and (1995), *The Paradoxes of Delusion: Wittgenstein, Schreber, and the Schizophrenic Mind*, New York: Cornell University Press. See also the excellent review of these two books by Iain McGilchrist, 'It's not so much thinking out what to do, it's the doing of it that sticks me', *London Review of Books*, 2 November 1995.

19. McGilchrist, op. cit.

20. Gregory Bateson (1979), *Mind and Nature: A Necessary Unity*, London: Wildwood House.

Chapter 11

1. Theodore Levitt (1960), 'Marketing myopia', *Harvard Business Review*, vol. 38, pp. 45–56.

2. E. Langer, L. Perlmutter, B. Chanowitz and R. Rubin (1988), 'Two new applications of mindlessness theory: alcoholism and aging', *Journal of Aging Studies*, vol. 2, pp 289–99.

3. Langer, Hatem, Joss and Howell, op. cit.

4. Langer, *Mindfulness*, op. cit.

5. Jacob Getzels and Peter Jackson (1961), 'Family environment and cognitive style: a study of the sources of highly intelligent and highly creative adolescents', *American Sociological Review*, vol. 26, pp. 351–9.

6. See Carlo Ginzburg (1990), *Myths, Emblems, Clues*, London: Hutchinson Radius.

7. A. R. Luria (1979), *The Making of Mind: A Personal Account of Soviet Psychology*, Cambridge, Mass: Harvard University Press.

8. Jacques Maritain (1953), *Creative Intuition in Art and Poetry*, London: Harvill.

9. George Whalley (1989), 'Teaching poetry', in Peter Abbs (ed.), *The Symbolic Order*, London: Falmer Press.

10. Ted Hughes (1967), *Poetry in the Making*, London: Faber.
11. For a description of mindfulness or *vipassana* training, see Joseph Goldstein and Jack Kornfield (1987), *Seeking the Heart of Wisdom: The Path of Insight Meditation*, Boston: Shambhala.
12. Daniel Brown and Jack Engler (1986), 'The stages of mindfulness meditation: a validation study', in K. Wilber, J. Engler and D. P. Brown (eds), *Transformations of Consciousness: Conventional and Contemplative Perspectives on Development*, Boston: Shambhala.
13. Daniel P. Brown (1977), 'A model for the levels of concentrative meditation', *International Journal of Clinical and Experimental Hypnosis*, vol. 25, pp. 236–73.
14. Terry Lesh (1970), 'Zen meditation and the development of empathy in counsellors', *Journal of Humanistic Psychology*, vol. 10, pp. 39–74.
15. John P. Miller (1994), *The Contemplative Practitioner: Meditation in Education and the Professions*, Westport, Connecticut: Bergin and Garvey.
16. Gerald Grow (1991), 'Teaching learners to be self-directed', *Adult Education Quarterly*, vol. 41, pp. 125–49. See also such texts as Stephen Brookfield (1987), *Developing Critical Thinkers*, San Francisco: Jossey-Bass; Jack Mezirow (1991), *Transformative Dimensions of Adult Learning*, San Francisco: Jossey-Bass; Malcolm Knowles (1990), *The Adult Learner: A Neglected Species*, Houston: Gulf; Philip Candy (1991), *Self-Direction for Lifelong Learning: A Comprehensive Guide to Theory and Practice*, San Francisco: Jossey-Bass.
17. Robert Kegan (1992), *In Over Our Heads: The Mental Demands of Modern Life*, Cambridge, Mass: Harvard University Press.
18. This description of Perry's work is based on the account given in Kegan, op. cit.
19. Kathy Hall and Julia Myers (1999), ' "That's just the way I am": metacognition, personal intelligence and reading', *Reading*, vol. 32, in press; Kathy Hall, Helen Bowman and Julia Myers (1999), 'Metacognition, reading and nine-year-olds in Ireland and England', *Educational Research*, vol. 41, in press; Kathy Hall and Julia Myers (1999), 'Promoting metacognition in reading lessons', *Education 3–13*, vol. 27, in press.
20. Alfred North Whitehead (1950), *The Aims of Education*, London: Benn.

Chapter 12

1. E. L. Thorndike (1924), 'The measurement of intelligence: present status', *Psychological Review*, vol. 31, pp. 219–52; quoted in Ceci, op. cit.
2. Margaret Donaldson (1978), *Children's Minds*, London: Fontana.
3. This effect was demonstrated by Maggie Mills of Bedford College (as it then was, now Royal Holloway), London University, in a Thames Television series of psychology programmes called *All in the Mind*. See John Nicholson and Martin Lucas (1984), *All in the Mind*, London: Methuen.

4. S. Strauss and R. Stavy (1983), 'Educational-developmental psychology and curriculum development: the case of heat and temperature', in H. Helm and J. D. Novak (eds), *Proceedings of the International Seminar on Misconceptions in Science and Mathematics*, Ithaca, NY: Cornell University Press.

5. Kurt Reusser (1986), 'Problem-solving beyond the logic of things', manuscript quoted in Alan Schoenfeld (1991), 'On mathematics as sense-making: an informal attack on the unfortunate divorce of formal and informal mathematics', in James Voss, David Perkins and Judith Segal (eds), *Informal Reasoning and Education*, Hillsdale, NJ: Erlbaum.

6. Stephen Ceci and Urie Bronfenbrenner (1985), 'Don't forget to take the cupcakes out of the oven: strategic time-monitoring, prospective memory and context', *Child Development*, vol. 56, pp. 175–90.

7. Geoff Lowe (1980), 'State dependent recall decrements with moderate doses of alcohol', *Current Psychological Research*, vol. 1, pp. 3–8.

8. Gordon Bower (1981), 'Mood and memory', *American Psychologist*, vol. 36, pp. 129–48.

9. George Kelly (1963), *A Theory of Personality*, New York: Norton.

10. Halpern, op. cit.

11. Mike Wallace (1996), 'When is experiential learning not experiential learning?', in G. L. Claxton, T. Atkinson, M. Osborn and M. Wallace (eds) op. cit.

12. John Clement (1991), 'Non-formal reasoning in physics: the use of analogies and extreme cases', in Voss, Perkins and Segal, op. cit.

13. Gavriel Salomon and Tamar Globerson (1987), 'Rocky roads to transfer', Second Annual Report to the Spencer Foundation, Tel-Aviv University, Israel, October.

Chapter 13

Many of the examples of 'distributed cognition' in this chapter are borrowed from Andy Clark's brilliant book *Being There: Putting Brain, Body and World Together Again*, Cambridge, Mass: Bradford/MIT Press. The discussion throughout the chapter is much influenced by this seminal work.

1. Clark op. cit.

2. This account is based on the discussion by James Wertsch (1995), 'The need for action in sociocultural research', in James Wertsch, Pablo del Rio and Amelia Alvarez (eds), *Sociocultural Studies of Mind*, Cambridge: Cambridge University Press.

3. D. H. Clements and D. F. Gullo (1984), 'Effects of computer programming on young children's cognitions', *Journal of Educational Psychology*, vol. 76, pp. 1051–8.

4. Gavriel Salomon (1997), 'Of mind and media', *Phi Delta Kappa*, January, pp. 375–80. The arguments and examples in this section are

largely drawn from this paper and from a talk by Salomon entitled 'Novel constructionist learning environments and novel technologies: some issues to be concerned with' given to the EARLI conference, Athens, August 1997.

5. Salomon, op. cit., p. 380.
6. Quotations from Gavriel Salomon (ed.) (1993), *Distributed Cognitions: Psychological and Educational Considerations*, Cambridge: Cambridge University Press.
7. David Perkins (1993), 'Person-plus: a distributed view of thinking and learning', in Salomon (ed.), op. cit.

Chapter 14

1. This discussion is my attempt to summarize the family of approaches to learning that has developed from the work of Russian psychologist and educator Lev Vygotsky. These perspectives go by a variety of names: sociocultural theory, cultural psychology, activity theory and CHAT – 'cultural-historical activity theory' – are some of the most common. See, for example, L. S. Vygotsky (1978), *Mind in Society: The Development of Higher Mental Processes*, Cambridge, Mass: Harvard University Press; J. S. Bruner (1996), *The Culture of Education*, Cambridge, Mass: Harvard University Press; J. V. Wertsch (1991), *Voices of the Mind: A Sociocultural Approach to Mediated Action*, Cambridge, Mass: Harvard University Press.
2. This is a slightly elaborated version of an example used in R. G. Tharp and R. Gallimore (1988), *Rousing Minds to Life: Teaching, Learning and Schooling in Social Context*, Cambridge: Cambridge University Press.
3. Laura Berk (1994), 'Why children talk to themselves', *Scientific American*, vol. 271, pp. 78–83.
4. Jean Lave and Etienne Wenger (1991), *Situated Learning: Legitimate Peripheral Participation*, Cambridge: Cambridge University Press.
5. See Robert Silman (1972), 'Teaching the medical student to become a doctor', in T. Pateman (ed.), *CounterCourse: A Handbook for Course Criticism*, Harmondsworth: Penguin.
6. Pamela Frome and Jacquelynne Eccles (1998), 'Parents' influence on children's achievement-related perceptions', *Journal of Personality and Social Psychology*, vol. 74, pp. 435–52.
7. Holland and Skinner, op. cit.
8. Hutchins (1994), op. cit.
9. I have drawn here on interpretations of Hutchins' work by Clark, op. cit; and Roy D'Andrade op. cit.
10. Edwin Hutchins (1991), 'The social organization of distributed cognition', in L. B. Resnick, J. M. Levine and S. D. Teasley (eds), *Perspectives on Socially Shared Cognition*, Washington, DC: American Psychological Association; and Hutchins (1994), op. cit.
11. Richard Boland, Ramkrishnan Tenkasi and Dov Te'eni (1997), 'Design-

ing information technology to support distributed cognition', in J. R. Meindl, C. Stubbart and J. F. Porac (eds), *Cognition Within and Between Organizations*, London: Sage.

Chapter 15

1. Disgust is prototypically an emotion that relates to food. It signals the awareness that one might be about to ingest, or has already ingested, something noxious. By extension, cultures teach us to exhibit similar reactions, and experience similar feelings, when our minds have been, or are in danger of being, invaded by perceptions or ideas that are anathema to our worldview. See Paul Rozin and April Fallon (1987), 'A perspective on disgust', *Psychological Review*, vol. 94, pp. 23–41.
2. Kegan (1994), op. cit.
3. Clare Garner, 'North-East's Jewel Quickly Loses Its Shine', *The Independent*, London, 1 August 1998.
4. Robert B. Reich (1991), *The Work of Nations: Preparing Ourselves for 21st Century Capitalism*, London: Simon and Schuster.
5. Duane Elgin (1993), *Voluntary Simplicity*, New York: William Morrow.
6. See, for example, Charles Handy (1984), *The Future of Work*, Oxford: Blackwell.
7. Gergen (1991), op. cit.
8. For a general account of how identity has become shrunken and internalized in Western cultures, see Edward E. Sampson (1993), *Celebrating the Other*, Hemel Hempstead, UK: Harvester/Wheatsheaf.
9. Midgley, op. cit., p. 60.
10. Lovelock's ozone research is described by Midgley, op. cit.
11. Harry Collins (1985), *Changing Order: Replication and Induction in Scientific Practice*, Sage: London.
12. Even by the year 1600, according to Lancelot Law Whyte ((1979), *The Unconscious before Freud*, London: Julian Freedman), 'the person thinking for himself ceased to be a social freak inhibited by his difference from others, and began to claim the opportunity to realise himself . . .'. And as the seventeenth century unfolds, 'we can recognise the germ of a new experience and a new way of living which in our own time has become a social commonplace: the existentialist complaint that there is no tradition which makes life bearable. . . . From then onward every sensitive and vital young person had to make his own choice.'

By the eighteenth century, the inclination and the ability to think for oneself was becoming firmly accepted as the goal of development, and the essential characteristic of maturity. Immanuel Kant, in his little 'Essay on Enlightenment', says: 'Enlightenment is the leaving behind by man of his self-caused minority. Minority is the impossibility of using one's own reason without the guidance of another. That minority is *self-caused* when it is due not to the lack of reasoning power but to the lack of decision and courage to make use of it without the guidance of another. . . . It is so easy for me not to be of age. If I have a book that understands for me, a pastor who has a conscience for me, a physician who decides my diet, and so forth, I need not trouble myself. I need not think, if I will only pay. Others will readily undertake the irksome work for me. . . . "Have the courage to make use of your *own* reason!' is thus the motto of the Enlightenment" (Immanuel Kant, 'Essay on Enlightenment', quoted in Midgley, op. cit; and Henri Ellenberger (1970), *The Discovery of the Unconscious*, New York: Basic Books).

Chapter 16

1. Kagan, op cit.
2. Patricia Smiley and Carol Dweck (1994), 'Individual differences in achievement goals among young children', *Child Development*, vol. 65, pp. 1723–43.
3. Margaret Carr (1998), *Technological Practice in Early Childhood as a Dispositional Milieu*, D.Phil. thesis, University of Waikato, New Zealand.
4. Carol Dweck (1991), 'Self-theories and goals: their role in motivation, personality and development', in R. A. Dienstbier (ed.), *Nebraska Symposium on Motivation 1990*, Lincoln, Nebraska: University of Nebraska Press.
5. See Harris, op. cit.
6. Craig T. Ramey and Sharon Landesman Ramey (1998), 'Early intervention and early experience', *American Psychologist*, vol. 53, pp. 109–20.
7. L. J. Schweinhart and D. P. Weikart (1993), 'A summary of significant benefits: the High/Scope Perry preschool study through age 27', Ypsilanti, Michigan: High/Scope; quoted in Kathy Sylva (1994), 'School influences on children's development', *Journal of Child Psychology and Psychiatry*, vol. 34, pp. 135–70. See also Kathy Sylva (1994), 'The impact of early learning on children's later development', in Sir Christopher Ball (ed.), *Start Right: The Importance of Early Learning*, London: Royal Society of Arts.
8. A. G. Broberg, H. Wessels, M. E. Lamb and C-P. Leung (1997), 'Effects of daycare on the development of cognitive abilities in 8-year-olds: a longitudinal study', *Developmental Psychology*, vol. 33, pp. 62–9.
9. Mihaly and Izabella Csikszentmihalyi (1993), 'Family influences on the development of giftedness', in G. R. Bock and K. Ackrill (eds), *CIBA Foundation Symposium 178: The Origins and Development of High Ability*, Chichester, UK: Wiley.
10. In M. Csikszentmihalyi, K. Rathunde and S. Whalen (1993), *Talented Teenagers: The Roots of Success and Failure*, New York: Cambridge University Press.
11. See Daniel Stern (1977), *The First Relationship: Infant and Mother*, Cambridge, Mass: Harvard University Press; and Colwyn Trevarthen (1979), 'Instincts for human understanding and for cultural coopera-

tion: their development in infancy', in M. von Cranach, K. Foppa, W. Lepenies and D. Ploog (eds), *Human Ethology: Claims and Limits of a New Discipline*, Cambridge: Cambridge University Press.

12. Howe (1998), op. cit.
13. Unpublished research cited in Frome and Eccles, op. cit.
14. Carr, op. cit.
15. Anne Smith (1996), *The Quality of Childcare Centres for Infants in New Zealand*, New Zealand Association for Research in Education: Palmerston North; (1997) 'Defining and choosing quality: messages from research', paper to conference on Quality Contexts for Children's Development, Invercargill, New Zealand, March.
16. H. H. Ratner and L. J. Stettner (1991), 'Thinking and feeling: putting Humpty Dumpty together again', *Merrill-Palmer Quarterly*, vol. 37, pp. 1–26.
17. This point is made by Frome and Eccles, op. cit.
18. This research by Doreen Arcus is described in Kagan, op. cit.
19. Holt (1989), op. cit.
20. Teresa Amabile (1983), *The Social Psychology of Creativity*, Springer-Verlag: New York; M. R. Lepper, D. Green and R. E. Nisbett (1973), 'Undermining children's intrinsic interest with extrinsic reward: a test of the overjustification hypothesis', *Journal of Personality and Social Psychology*, vol. 9, pp. 260–5; cited in Howe (1998), op. cit.
21. Holt (1989), op. cit.
22. This interaction is taken from D. Wood, L. McMahon and Y. Cranstoun (1980), *Working with Under Fives*, Oxford: Blackwell.
23. This commentary draws on the analysis of Margaret Carr, op. cit.
24. James V. Wertsch, Norris Minick and Flavio Arns (1984), 'The creation of context in joint problem-solving', in Barbara Rogoff and Jean Lave (eds), *Everyday Cognition: Its Development in Social Context*, Cambridge, Mass: Harvard University Press.
25. Carole Ames and Jennifer Archer (1987), 'Mothers' beliefs about the role of ability and effort in school learning', *Journal of Educational Psychology*, vol. 79, pp. 409–14.
26. See Harris (1989), op. cit.

Chapter 17

1. Bill Clinton (1998), 'Education is the global priority', speech to the Education World Congress, Washington Hilton; reported in *The Independent*, London, 6 August 1998.
2. UK figures: Sir Christopher Ball (1995), 'Towards a global core curriculum', Presidential Address to the Third Oxford Conference on Globalization and Learning, New College, Oxford, September. US figures: US Department of Education (1999), *America's Children 1998*.
3. T. P. Carpenter, M. M. Lindquist, W. Matthews and E. A. Silver (1983), 'Results of the third NAEP mathematics assessment: secondary school', *Mathematics Teacher*, vol. 76, pp. 652–9.

4. 'Alarm as literacy skills fall', *Observer*, London, 24 August 1997.
5. *Speaking Up, Speaking Out! The 2020 Vision Programme Research Report*, London: The Industrial Society, October 1997.
6. See 'The Family Strikes Back', a video introduction to home-schooling, Nottingham: Educational Heretics Videos.
7. David Hargreaves (1998), 'A road to the learning society', *School Leadership and Management*, vol. 17, pp. 9–21.
8. 'Singapore tries trendy teaching', *Sunday Times*, London, 8 June 1997.
9. 'Lowest common denominator', *Harper's Magazine*, November 1997.
10. As reported by Nick Cohen in *Observer*, London, 11 January 1998.
11. This felicitous phrase is borrowed from the title of the inaugural lecture of Professor David Boud of the University of Technology, Sydney, Australia.
12. Holt (1965), op. cit.
13. This work is described in more detail in Karen Stone and Harold Dillehunt (1978), *Self Science: The Subject Is Me*, Santa Monica: Goodyear Publishing Co.
14. Schoenfeld, op. cit.
15. Mike Forret (1998), *Learning Electronics: An Accessible Introduction*, D. Phil. thesis, University of Waikato, New Zealand.
16. Holzman, op. cit.
17. Marcy Singer Gabella (1995), 'Unlearning certainty: toward a culture of student inquiry', *Theory into Practice*, vol. 34, pp. 236–42.
18. Ann L. Brown (1997), 'Transforming schools into communities of thinking and learning about serious matters', *American Psychologist*, vol. 52, pp 399–413. The article is her acceptance speech for the American Psychological Association's prestigious Distinguished Scientific Award for the Application of Psychology, 1996.
19. This account of PEEL draws on personal conversations with Ian Mitchell, and on the following publications: Ian Mitchell (1992), 'Student learning and student change', paper presented to a conference on History and Philosophy of Science Education, Kingston, Ontario; Richard White and Ian Mitchell (1994), 'Metacognition and the quality of learning', *Studies in Science Education*, vol. 23, pp. 21–37; John Baird and Jeff Northfield (eds) (1995), *Learning from the PEEL Experience*, 2nd edition, Clayton, Victoria, Australia: Monash University Press.
20. Hilary Dyer (1995), 'Learning logs as ethnographies of Year 1 and 2 children learning at school', paper presented to the CEDAR conference Ethnographies of Teachers and Students at Work, Warwick, UK, September.
21. Hall, op. cit.
22. K. Matheny and C. Edwards (1974), 'Academic improvement through an experimental classroom management system', *Journal of School Psychology*, vol. 12, pp. 222–32; M. Wang and B. Styles (1976), 'An investigation of children's concepts of self-responsibility for their school learning', *American Educational Research Journal*, vol. 13, pp. 159–79; R. de Charms (1976), *Enhancing Motivation: Change in the Classroom*, New York: Halsted. All cited in Howe (1998), op. cit.

Chapter 18

1. Robin Humphrey, Peter McCarthy and Frank Popham (1998), a research project on student stress at Newcastle University published in *Higher Education Quarterly* and summarised in 'Student stress . . . no, really' and 'A helping hand', *Guardian*, London, 21 April.
2. Mark Edmundson (1997), 'On the uses of a liberal education', *Harper's Magazine*, September, pp. 39–49.
3. Quoted in Edmundson, op. cit.
4. Quoted from Peter Abbs (1994), *The Educational Imperative: A Defence of Socratic and Aesthetic Learning*, London: Falmer Press. My discussion of Socratic learning draws heavily on Abbs's account.
5. Matthew Arnold (1869), *Culture and Anarchy*, quoted in Abbs, op. cit.
6. C. Wright Mills (1959), *The Sociological Imagination*, Oxford: Oxford University Press.
7. David Boud (1995), *Enhancing Learning Through Self Assessment*, London: Kogan Page.
8. F. Marton, D. Hounsell and N. Entwistle (1984), *The Experience of Learning*, Edinburgh: Scottish Academic Press.
9. See the case studies in Boud, op. cit. Much of the material in this section is drawn from this source.
10. Robert Edwards (1989), 'An experiment in student self-assessment', *British Journal of Technological Education*, vol. 20, pp. 5–10. Quoted in Boud, op. cit.
11. Jan Lovie-Kitchin (1991), 'Problem-based learning in optometry', in D. Boud and G. Feletti (eds), *The Challenge of Problem-based Learning*, London: Kogan Page.
12. William Macauley and Gian Pagnucci (1997), 'But this isn't how an English class is supposed to be . . .', in R. Hudson, S. Maslin-Prothero and L. Oates (eds), *Flexible Learning in Action: Case Studies in Higher Education*, London: Kogan Page.

Chapter 19

1. Valerie Bayliss (1998), *Redefining Work: An RSA Initiative*, London: The Royal Society for the Encouragement of Arts, Manufacturing and Commerce.
2. Peter Senge (1994), *The Fifth Discipline Fieldbook*, London: Nicholas Brealey.
3. Max Frost, Steve Rowley and Patricia Hind (1996), 'The resilience audit and the psychological contract', unpublished paper, Frost Rowley: London. The argument in this section draws on their analysis.
4. Chris Argyris (1998), 'Empowerment: the Emperor's new clothes', *Harvard Business Review*, May–June.

5. Gordon Shaw, Robert Brown and Philip Bromiley (1998), 'Strategic stories: how 3M is rewriting business planning', *Harvard Business Review*, May–June.
6. The story of Karmoy is depicted in the Open University 'Creative Management' course video, B882.
7. William Calvin, in *Scientific American*, October 1994; quoted in Shaw et al., op. cit.
8. Charlene Collison and Alexander Mackenzie (1988), 'The power of story in organizations', *Internal Communication Focus*, April; and personal communication with Charlene Collison, August 1998.
9. John W. Hunt (1998), 'Hunch says intuition is here to stay', *Financial Times*, London, 26 August.
10. Randall P. White, Phil Hodgson and Stuart Crainer (1996), *The Future of Leadership*, London: Pitman; quoted by Des Dearlove, 'No substitute for bright ideas', *Times*, London, 3 July 1997.
11. Weston H. Agor (1992), 'Intuition in decision making', *The Global Intuition Network*, El Paso, Texas. See also Weston Agor (1989), *Intuition in Organizations: Leading and Managing Productively*, Newbury Park, CA: Sage.
12. William Kahn (1992), 'To be fully there: psychological presence at work', *Human Relations*, vol. 45, pp. 321–49.
13. E. Langer and D. Heffernan (1988), 'Mindful managing: confident but uncertain managers', unpublished paper, Harvard University; quoted in Langer, *Mindfulness*, op. cit.

Index